VANESSA BELL

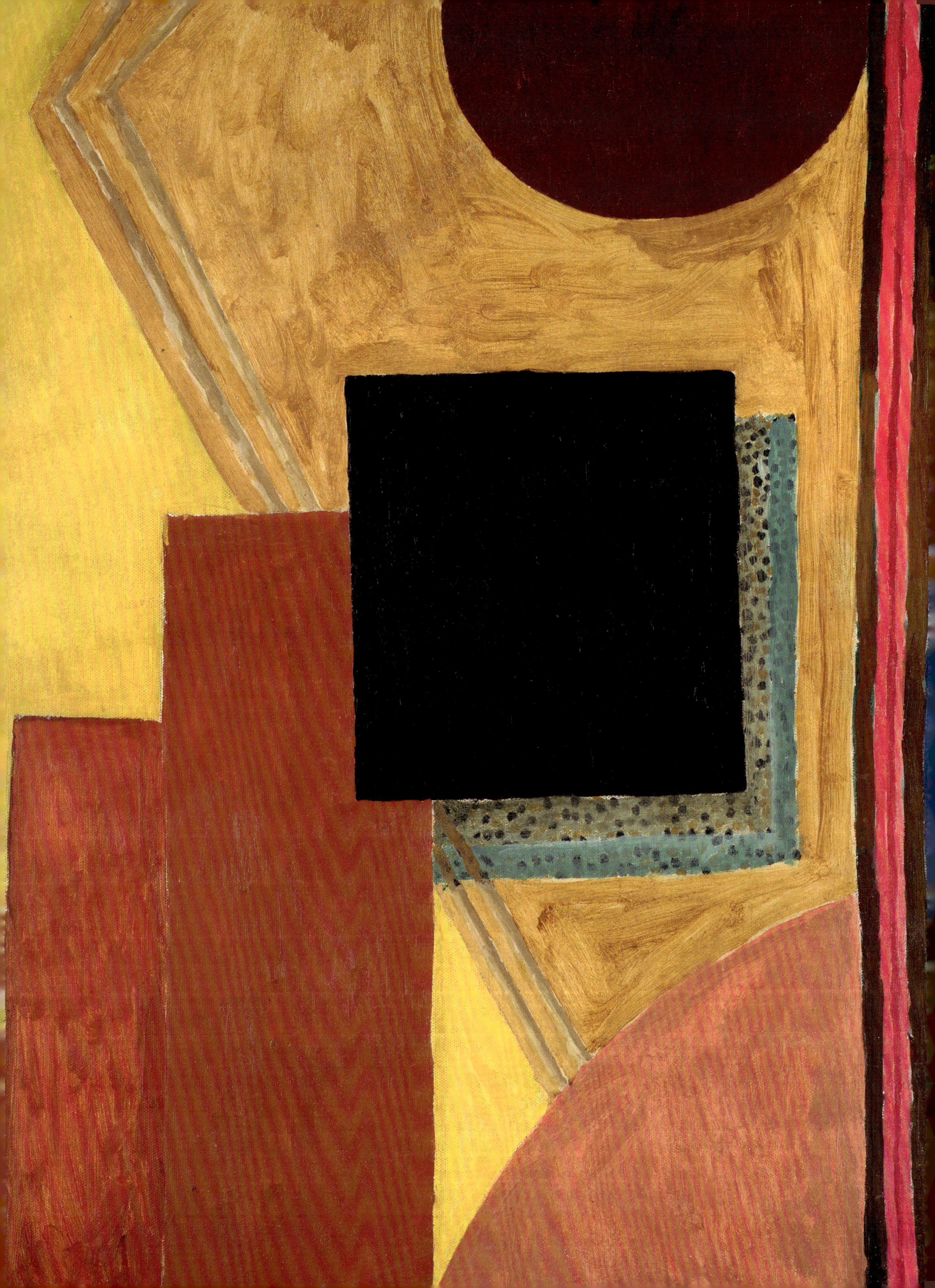

VANESSA BELL

A WORLD OF FORM AND COLOUR

Edited by
Fay Blanchard &
Anthony Spira

CHARLOTTE
CHANGQIAN

MK Gallery

PWP

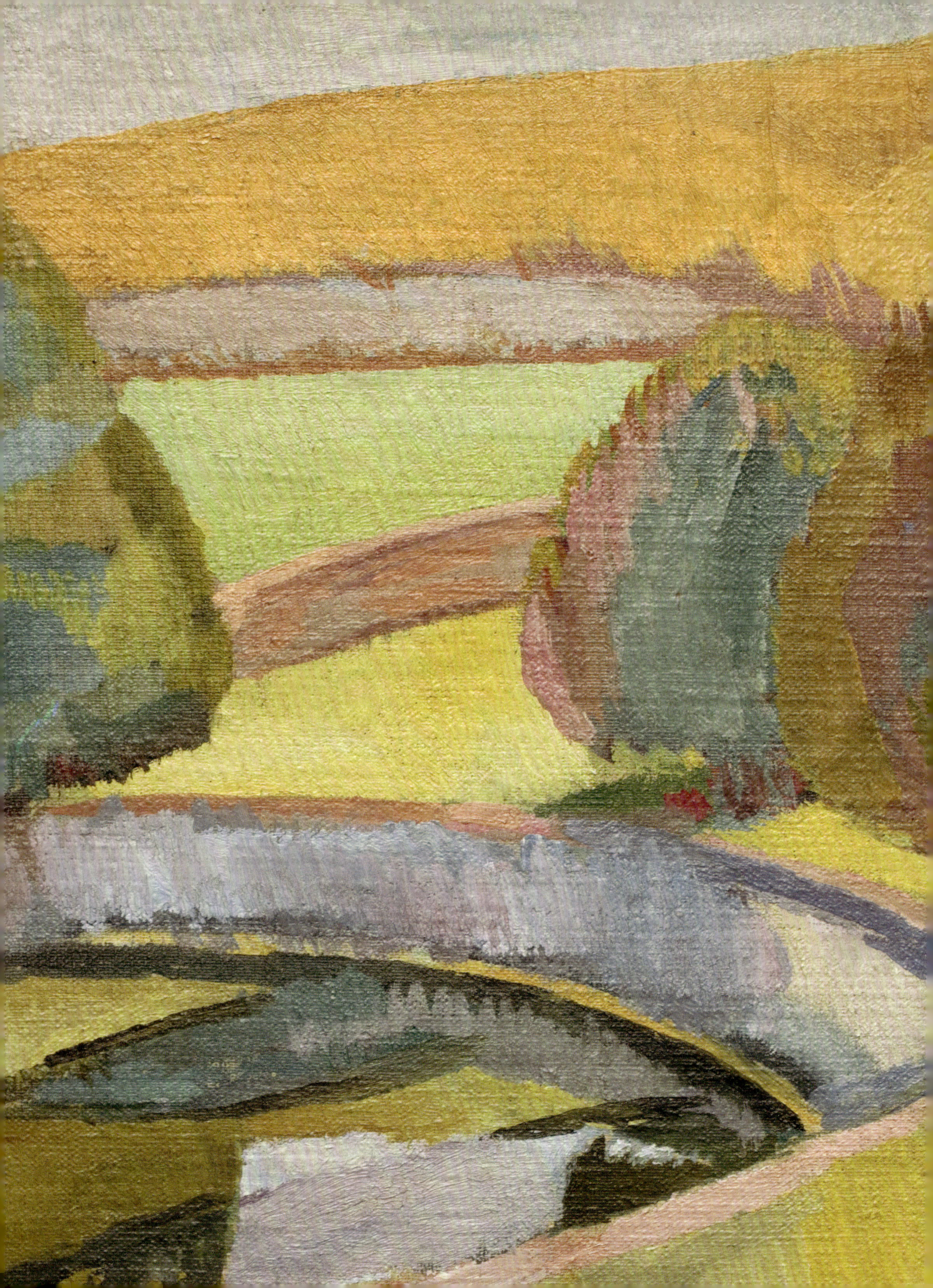

CONTENTS

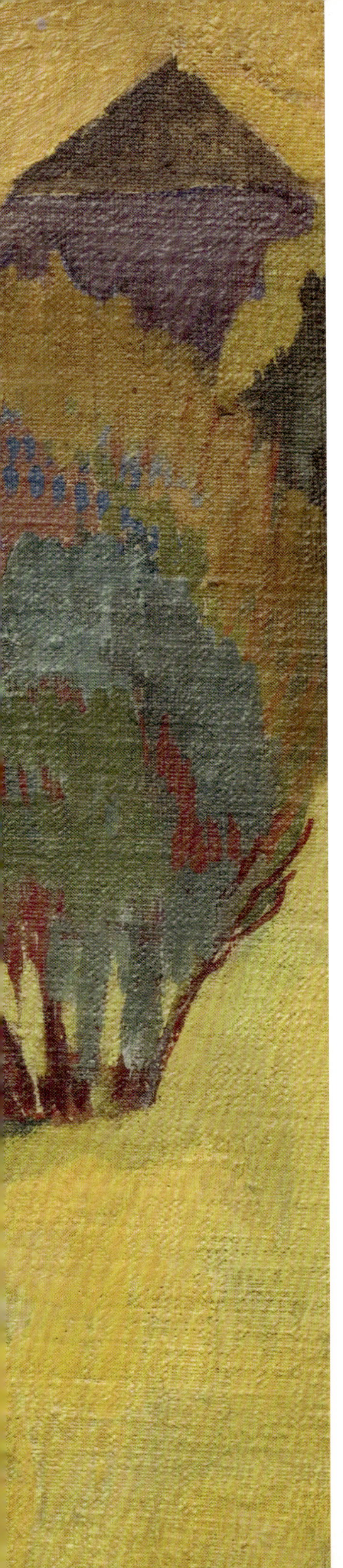

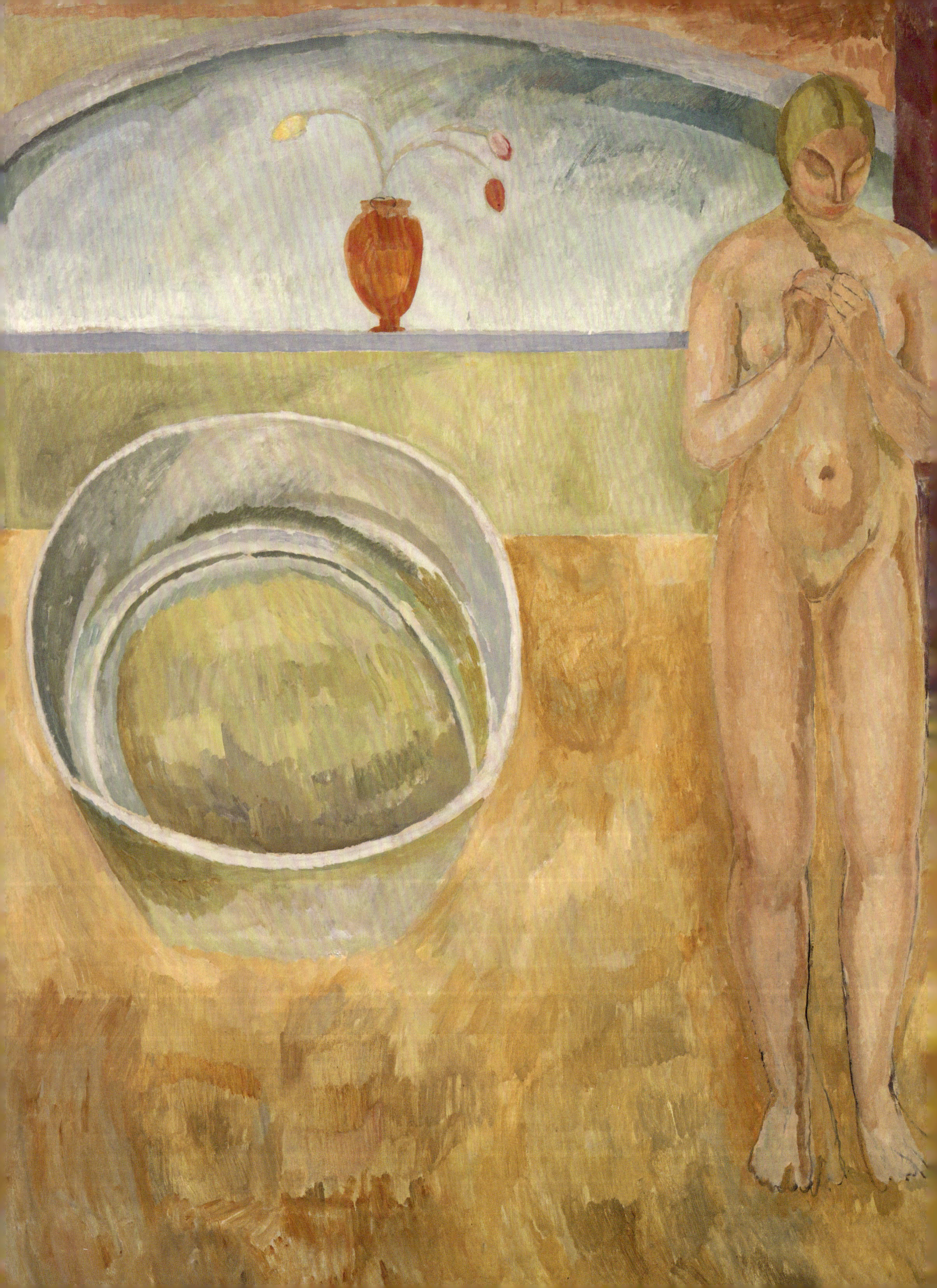

INTRODUCTION

It is indeed so exciting and so absorbing, this painters' world of form and colour...

This publication and the exhibition it accompanies present the largest overview to date of the pioneering modernist painter Vanessa Bell. Here we look at the artist's wider approach to creativity, encompassing design, furniture, ceramics and drawings, as well as paintings. Her general approach to art as an everyday practice found its ultimate expression in her home at Charleston, in East Sussex. It was here, as well as in Bloomsbury, London, that Bell and the circle of brilliant people with whom she surrounded herself captured the imagination and attracted widespread acclaim.

Born in 1879 to a wealthy literary family, Bell (née Stephen) was immediately immersed in a cultural environment that included members of the Pre-Raphaelite Brotherhood and other art-world grandees. Bell studied art in South Kensington and at the Royal Academy Schools, but felt excluded from the art world, namely the New English Art Club (an alternative to the Royal Academy), for being 'that terrible low creature, a female painter'.[1]

Travels on the Continent introduced Bell to both the Italian masters (Jacopo Tintoretto was 'an absolute revelation'[2]) and the French avant-garde (meeting Auguste Rodin and others in Paris), all of whom had a profound and lasting impact on her practice. During this period she also met her future husband, the critic Clive Bell, whose art theory of 'significant form' – that art should provoke 'aesthetic emotion' – was to become very influential on British art.

The Tub, 1917.

In 1904 Bell moved into unfashionable Bloomsbury with her
siblings, hosting social evenings, overturning Victorian attitudes and
'the Ethics of Empire', and seeking out 'experiments and reforms'.[3]
She set up the 'Friday Club', an active discussion group where female
and male artists (including her future life partner and collaborator
Duncan Grant) were regarded as equals, and planned exhibitions together. Her sister Virginia (soon to be Woolf) observed that 'Old Nessa
… is said to have a genius for organisation.'[4] In 1905 Bell exhibited her
first work, at the New Gallery, London, which was also her first commission, a portrait of Eleanor, Lady Robert Cecil (p. 33), who was to
become an important figure in the women's suffrage movement.

After various exhibitions and travels to Italy, as well as
regular visits to Studland Bay in Dorset, Bell exhibited
Iceland Poppies (p. 35) at the New English Art Club in
1909. This painting's restrained palette and reductive
composition signal the direction her painting was to
take in the coming years. Soon after, she met the artist
and critic Roger Fry, whose exhibition *Manet and the
Post-Impressionists* (which included Cézanne, Van Gogh,
Gauguin, Matisse, Picasso and others) marked a turning
point in British art and had a profound effect on Bell. She
recalled: 'That autumn of 1910 is to me a time when everything seemed springing to new life – a time when all was a
sizzle of excitement, new relationships, new ideas, different
and intense emotions all seemed crowding into one's life.'[5]

Bell's own artistic experiments were further stimulated
by the dramatic colours and fabrics in the stage sets and
costumes of Sergei Diaghilev's *Ballets Russes*. In 1913 she co-founded,
with Roger Fry and Duncan Grant, the Omega Workshops. In a rejection of nineteenth-century and Edwardian aesthetics and ideals, the
Workshops provided a sociable, collaborative enterprise that embraced
early modernism, breaking down the barriers between fine and applied
arts to focus on the design of stained glass, furniture, ceramics and textiles. In advance of opening, Bell wrote to Fry: 'it seems one can never
get away from this fatal prettiness. Can't we paint stuffs etc which won't
be gay and pretty?'[6] Simultaneously, in her individual painting practice,
Bell embarked on a radical abstract phase, which corresponded with
the formal freedoms afforded to her by the designs produced for Omega,
including rugs and textiles. By moving away from representation, Bell
was exploring what Fry described as 'visual music'.[7]

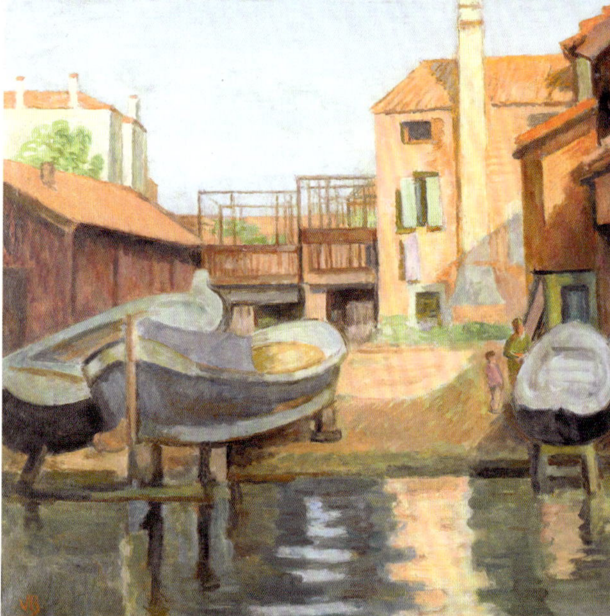

Venetian Boatyard, undated.

In 1914 the writer Gertrude Stein introduced Bell to Pablo Picasso
and Henri Matisse in Paris. Around this time she produced a portrait
of her friend Mary 'Molly' MacCarthy, made entirely from painted
and cut paper (p. 75), among the earliest and most important British
experiments in collage, as well as abstraction. Her forays into pure
abstraction were nonetheless short-lived, although she pursued her
interest in bold colours, simplified forms and flattened perspectives in
paintings such as *A Conversation* (1913–16, p. 63). She wrote to Leonard
Woolf: 'The reason I think that artists paint life and not patterns is
that certain qualities of life, what I call movement, mass, weight have
aesthetic value. But where I would quarrel with Clive … is when he says
one gets the same emotion from flat patterns that one does get from
pictures. I say one doesn't, because of the reason I have just given – that
movement etc. give me important aesthetic emotions.'[8]

Bell continued her involvement with the Omega Workshops until it
closed in 1919, but later described the impact of the First World War
as follows: 'The excitement and the joy had gone. The hostility of the
general public was real now.'[9] She eventually moved to Charleston,
which she retained for the rest of her life, with her children and
companions, but continued to travel, often with Duncan Grant and
friends, including the economist John Maynard Keynes, and regularly
exhibited and sold work in London and Paris.

Over the next few years Bell continued to collaborate with Grant
in the spirit of the Omega Workshops on the decoration of private
houses. Between 1929 and 1931 they decorated the author Lady
Dorothy Wellesley's house in Sussex. Six large painted panels were
surrounded by bold, striking designs of curtains, carpets and octagonal mirrors. In 1931 Bell produced a painting of Alfriston church
near Charleston, made up of loose dabs of colour, to advertise the
English countryside for Shell-Mex (p. 124). She also produced decor
and costumes for a Sadler's Wells
production of *Pomona* in 1933, and
developed her work with ceramics.
Significantly, she produced the
Famous Women Dinner Service
(pp. 129–35) in collaboration with
Duncan Grant. Commissioned
by the art historian Kenneth
Clark, this collection included 50
hand-decorated plates celebrating

Tea Things, 1919.

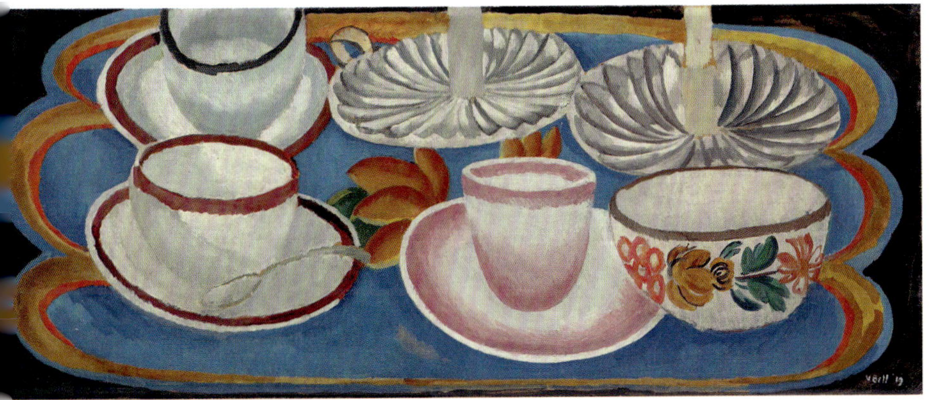

famous women from across history, from the Queen of Sheba and
Elizabeth I to Charlotte Brontë and Greta Garbo.

Throughout the Second World War Bell lived at Charleston, which
became a focal point for her circle of friends and a testament to her
vision and creativity. She transformed the house into a collaborative
'total work of art' with collected objects and decorations made with
Grant, which became the subject of many of her paintings. Much of her
early work was destroyed by an incendiary bomb at her London studio.
In the early 1940s she was commissioned, with Grant and her son
Quentin Bell, to decorate the interior of Berwick Church in Sussex and
continued to produce designs for several book covers for Virginia Woolf,
including *Between the Acts* and *The Death of the Moth* (pp. 149–51).
Two late self-portraits conclude this survey of Bell's career, both tightly
framed, presenting the artist as a solitary figure in a large straw hat.
The earlier painting, *c.*1952 (p. 171), shows the artist defiantly at work,
paintbrushes firmly in hand, her features receding into the vigorous
brushstrokes and all-over patterns of the composition. The later work,
from 1958 (p. 169), is a portrait of unflinching introspection, with the
artist melancholy and frail. Nevertheless, her quiet, intense focus is
conveyed through an interplay of light, colour and form that permeated and distinguished her lifelong practice. Bell's life and work were
characterized by her insistence on doing things on her own terms: 'I
am absolutely indifferent to anything the world may say about me, my
husband or my children.... If you cannot accept me as I seem to you to
be, then you must give me up, for I have no intention of confessing my
sins or defending my virtues.'[10]

For this publication, we are hugely grateful to all the writers, the
art historians and artists who have provided significant new insights
into the work of Vanessa Bell. Rebecca Birrell's essay analyses Bell's
work in abstraction and places her practice in the social context of
female artists of the time. It also discusses the interplay of Bell's
still-life painting with the 'living canvas' of Charleston and her wider
representation of women. Paulina Olowska reflects on Bell as an
inspiration, paving the way 'for self-expression and the construction of
female artistic identity'. Hayley Tompkins recalls visiting Charleston,
its impact on her own work and the permission it gave 'to get lost
and found again in painting things'. Judy Chicago discusses Bell and
Grant's *Famous Women Dinner Service* in relation to her own *The
Dinner Party* (1974) and 'numerous attempts by women to counter
the centuries-old ideas about women's inferiority'. Finally, The Singh

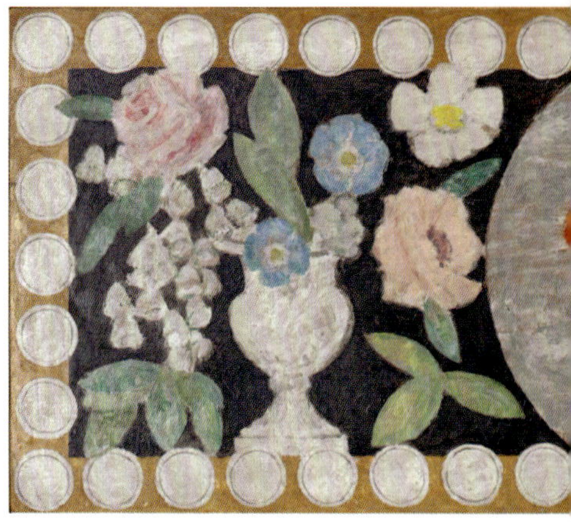

*Decorative Panel with Flowers and
Goldfish*, undated.

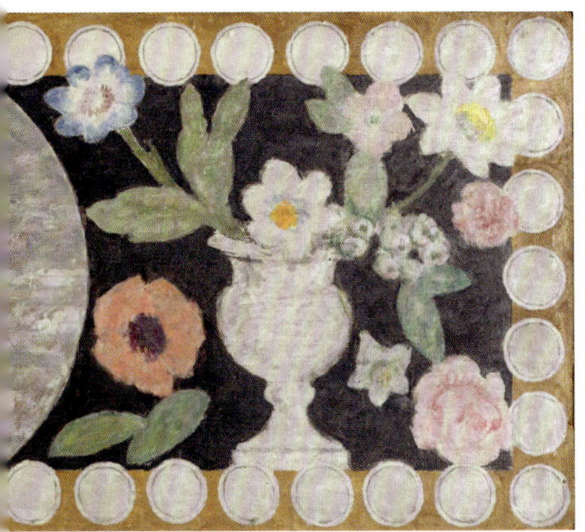

Twins call attention to the inspiration Western post-impressionist artists, such as Bell, took from non-European traditional art forms.

We are especially grateful to Lara Wardle and the team at the Jerwood Foundation for providing essential financial support that enabled these new perspectives and the production of this publication. Our thanks also go to Clare Martelli and Natasha Collin at Philip Wilson Publishers and to Lucy Morton for designing this catalogue.

As ever, this project has depended on the generosity, commitment and faith of many people. We are hugely grateful to the Estate of Vanessa Bell for permission to reproduce her incredible work in this catalogue. We are of course indebted to all the lenders to the exhibition, the many private and public collections who have kindly parted temporarily with their work, as well as the assistance of auction houses and private galleries for introducing us to the present owners of various works; all are listed at the end of this book.

We are extremely grateful to Matthew and Robert Travers and Piano Nobile for their assistance throughout the development of this project. Their enthusiasm, knowledge and networks have been invaluable in bringing together such an important and extensive body of work. We are also indebted to Matthew Travers for chairing the Vanessa Bell Circle of Friends, whose support has been indispensable in helping to bring large new audiences to Bell's work.

At MK Gallery, the whole team have pulled together, as always, to deliver this project, not least the technical staff who so expertly installed the show. Particular thanks go to Madeleine Jordan, Exhibitions Coordinator, for all her incredible work on this publication and exhibition. The project would not have happened without MK Gallery's Head of Exhibitions, Fay Blanchard. We are extremely grateful for her enthusiasm, insight and tenacity, which have shaped this beautiful and important project.

This exhibition brings together more works by Vanessa Bell than any other before it. Charleston would like to thank MK Gallery and its team for a partnership which celebrates this extraordinary artist. Thanks to all involved in this incredible project from across Charleston's teams, including our curatorial department and exhibitions, retail and communications teams, in making the exhibition a success at MK Gallery and at Charleston, Lewes. It feels like a homecoming.

ANTHONY SPIRA, DIRECTOR, MK GALLERY
NATHANIEL HEPBURN, DIRECTOR, CHARLESTON

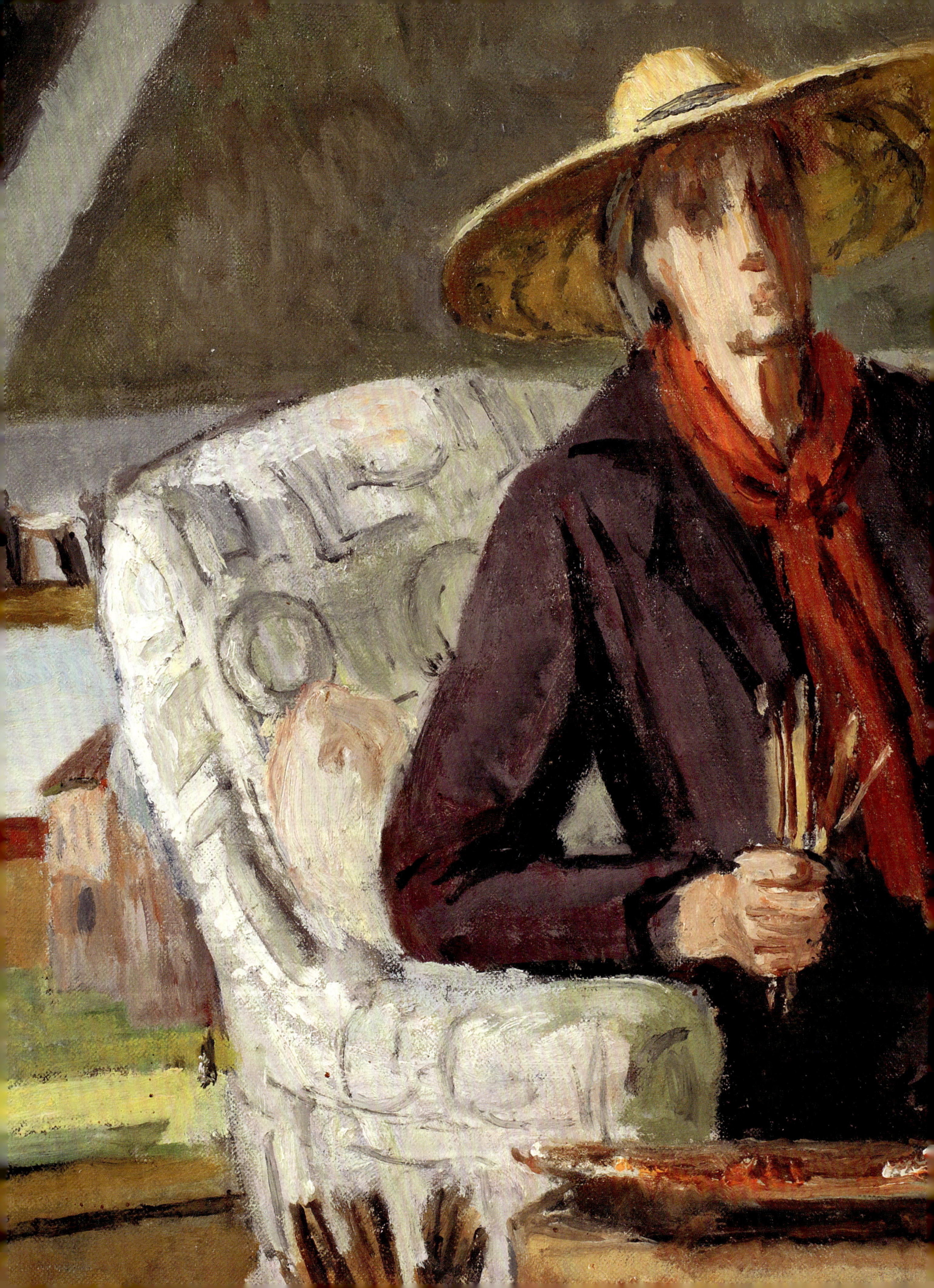

CHRONOLOGY

1879 Vanessa Stephen was born on 30 May, the oldest child of Sir Leslie Stephen and his second wife Julia Duckworth (niece of the photographer Julia Margaret Cameron). Living at 22 Hyde Park Gate, Kensington, London, this primarily literary family were also visited by prominent artists including Edward Burne-Jones, G.F. Watts and William Rothenstein.[1] She was raised as agnostic and educated primarily by her mother; her father's view was that 'women ought to be as well educated as men'.[2]

1880 Birth of brother, Julian Thoby Stephen.

1882 Birth of sister, Adeline Virginia Stephen (later Virginia Woolf).

1882 Begins annual family holidays, until 1894, to Talland House, St Ives.

1883 Birth of youngest sibling, Adrian Leslie Stephen.

1894 Begins studying drawing with Ebenezer Cooke, follower of influential critic John Ruskin.[3]

1896 Studies with Sir Arthur Cope RA at his school in South Kensington.[4] 'When I got into the grubby, shabby, dirty world of art students at South Kensington I wanted nothing else in the way of society. They were separate entirely from my home life and so a great relief. They knew no more about my private life than I about theirs and in their company one could forget oneself and think of nothing but shapes and colours and the absorbing difficulties of oil paint.'[5]

1897 Following the deaths of her mother and half-sister, Vanessa assumes caring responsibilities for her elderly father and the domestic duties of an upper-middle-class Victorian woman: 'For two years this meant more than ever a life of seclusion from our generation.'[6]

1899 Thoby Stephen studies at Trinity College, University of Cambridge, meeting Leonard Woolf, Saxon Sydney-Turner, Clive Bell and Lytton Strachey.

1901 Begins to attend the Royal Academy Schools, taught by James McBey and John Singer Sargent, who 'generally tells me that my things are too grey. The one thing he is down upon is when he thinks anyone is trying for an effect regardless of truth.'[7]

1902 Charles Furse exhibits portrait of Vanessa Stephen at New English Art Club, whose members 'seemed somehow to have the secret of the art universe within their grasp, a secret one was not worthy to learn, especially if one was that terrible low creature, a female painter'.[8]

April: Visits Rome and Florence with her siblings and half-brother George Duckworth.

September: Meets Clive Bell, close friend of her brother Thoby.

1903 Reads *The French Impressionists* by Camille Mauclair (1903), the first book in English on the group.

1904 February: Death of father, Sir Leslie Stephen.

April–May: Visits Venice – where Tintoretto is 'an absolute revelation'[9] – as well as Florence and Paris, where she visits Rodin's studio.[10]

October: The four Stephen siblings move out of Kensington into 'unfashionable' Bloomsbury at 46 Gordon Square. 'It seemed as if in every way we were making a new beginning ... it was exhilarating to have left the house in which had been so much gloom and depression, to have come to these white walls, large windows opening on to trees and lawns, to have one's own rooms, be master of one's own time, have all the things in fact which come as a matter of course to many of the young today but so seldom then, to young women.'[11]

Autumn: Briefly attends the Slade, where she is taught by Henry Tonks, 'a most depressing master, I made no friends there and soon left'.[12] Attends lecture on French Impressionism by Frank Rutter at the Grafton Gallery.

1905 February: Thoby Stephen hosts weekly Thursday 'at homes' for friends from Cambridge University, including Leonard Woolf, Lytton Strachey, Saxon Sydney-Turner and Clive Bell, to which his sisters also came. 'We were full of experiments and reforms. We were going to do without table napkins ... we were going to paint; to write; to have coffee after dinner instead of tea at nine o'clock. Everything was going to be new, everything was going to be different. Everything was on trial.'[13]

Summer: Founds and runs the 'Friday Club' for artists to discuss their work, listen to lectures and organize exhibitions. Members included non-artists such as Virginia Stephen and Saxon Sydney-Turner as well as Vanessa Stephen's artist friends: Mary Creighton, Sylvia Milman, Gwen Darwin (later Gwen Raverat) and Duncan Grant. It would later include Mark Gertler, Ka Cox, Winifred Gill, Edward Wadsworth and Percy Wyndham Lewis. The Club 'enabled her to establish an autonomous artistic identity on her own terms, and to exhibit on an equal footing with male artists as well as other women'.[14] Exhibitions included famous French artists such as Pierre-Auguste Renoir, Camille Pissarro, Honoré Daumier and Pierre Puvis de Chavannes, which helped attract visitors and align member artists to the European avant-garde. The Friday Club's existence was 'a testimony to Vanessa's organisational prowess. It was she who, through the exercise of diplomacy, united disparate artists, arranged for talks to be given and kept a healthily argumentative society under control. "Old Nessa goes ahead, and slashes about her," Virginia observed.'[15]

Receives her first commission, *Portrait of Lady Robert Cecil*, which is also the first work she exhibits, at the New Gallery.

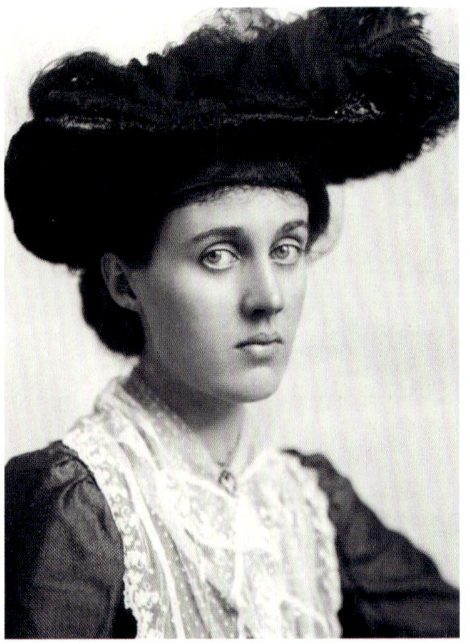

Vanessa Bell, *c.*1910.

August: Clive Bell proposes to Vanessa Stephen – she turns him down: 'I should be quite happy living with anyone whom I didn't dislike if I could paint and lead the kind of life I like – yet for some mysterious reason one has to refuse to do what someone else very much wants to. It seems absurd. But absurd or not I could no more marry him than I could fly – so there's an end of it.'[16]

1906 January: First meeting with Duncan Grant, at Friday Club.

July: Clive Bell proposes again and is rejected a second time: 'For you see if marriage were only a question of being very good friends and of caring for things in the same way, I could say yes at once. I like you better than I like anyone else (other man I suppose I ought to say!) outside our family, and I am sure that our friendship means quite as much to me as it can to you. But I suppose that something more is wanted which now I don't feel.'[17]

September–October: Travels to Greece, where she falls ill and on her return reaches out to Clive: 'I am quite sure that a visit from you would do me a lot of good … but I must wait.'[18]

20 November: Thoby Stephen also falls ill; he dies of typhoid fever.

22 November: Clive Bell again proposes to Vanessa and is accepted.

1907 7 February: Clive Bell and Vanessa Stephen (aged 28) marry at St Pancras Registry Office.

April: Honeymoons in Wales and then Paris. Siblings Virginia and Adrian meet them in Paris, where they dine with Duncan Grant, who writes: 'What a quartet! I seem to like them all so, so much.'[19] Adrian and Virginia Stephen move out of 46 Gordon Square, leaving it to the newlyweds, moving to 29 Fitzroy Square, a few streets away.

Bell begins to exhibit her work, including at the New English Art Club (NEAC) and Allied Artists' Association.

1908 4 February: Birth of the Bells' first son, Julian. Julian's birth puts pressure on her marriage to Clive, who became close to Virginia, writing to her: 'I see nothing of Nessa. I do not even sleep with her; the baby takes up all her time.'[20]

June–August: Exhibits at Friday Club Exhibition, Baillie Gallery, London, and Allied Artists' Association, Albert Hall, London.

September: Travels with Clive and Virginia to Italy, visiting Siena and Perugia and then Paris.

1909 April–May: Travels to Florence with Clive and particularly admires Botticelli's *Primavera* (c.1480, Uffizi, Florence).[21]

Summer: Exhibits *Iceland Poppies* at the New English Art Club. Receives encouragement from Walter Sickert, who writes to her 'Continuez!'[22]

Makes regular visits to Studland Bay, Dorset, until 1911.

1910 January: After a chance meeting at Cambridge train station, the painter and critic Roger Fry joins the Bells' circle, attending Thursday 'at homes' and lecturing at the Friday Club.

March–June: Exhibits at NEAC Summer Exhibition and the Friday Club exhibition at Alpine Club Gallery.

19 August: Birth of the Bells' second son, Quentin.

November–January 1911: First Post-Impressionist exhibition, *Manet and the Post-Impressionists*, organized by Fry, attracts over 25,000 visitors at

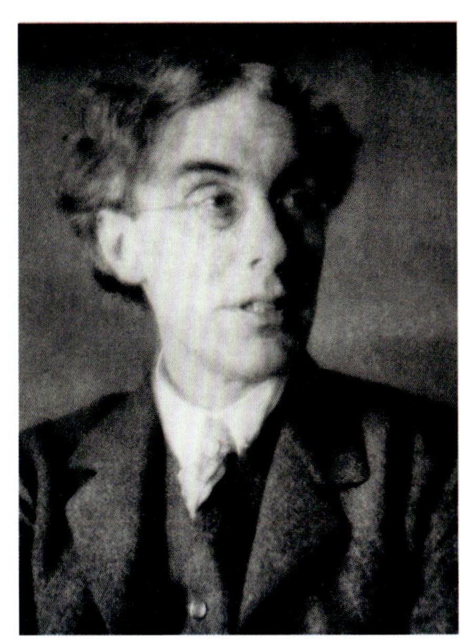
Roger Fry, 1913.

the Grafton Galleries, showing Paul Cézanne, Vincent Van Gogh, Paul
Gauguin, Henri Matisse, Pablo Picasso and others. Bell recalled: 'London
knew little of Paris, incredibly little it seems now and English painters
were on the whole still under the Victorian cloud, either conscientiously
painting effects of light, or trying to be poets or neo-pre-Raphaelites...
It is impossible I think that any other single exhibition can ever have had
so much effect as did that on the rising generation ... here was a sudden
pointing to a possible path, a sudden liberation and encouragement to
feel for oneself which were absolutely overwhelming... But it was as
if at last one might say things one had always felt instead of trying to
say things that other people told one to feel. Freedom was given one
to be oneself and that to the young is the most exciting thing that can
happen.'[23] Virginia Stephen summarized its effect: 'on or about December
1910 human character changed'.[24]

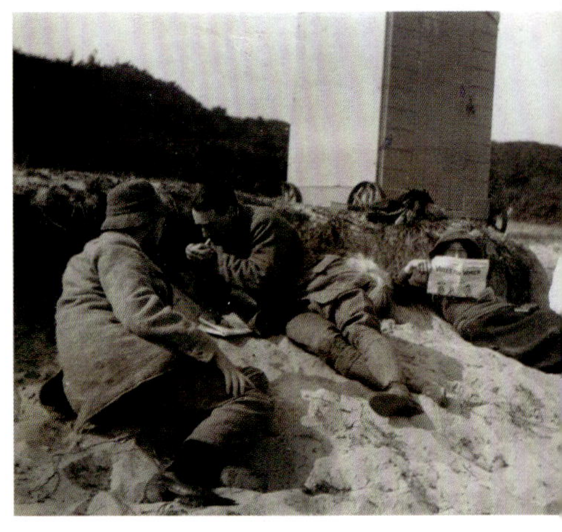

Left to right: Clive Bell, Desmond
MacCarthy, Marjorie Strachey and
Molly MacCarthy (reading *Votes for
Women* paper), 1910, photograph by
Vanessa Bell.

1911 February: Further Friday Club exhibition (again in 1912). Stays at Little
Talland House, Firle, Sussex, rented by Virginia Stephen.

April: The Bells travel to Turkey with Roger Fry and mathematician Harry
Norton. At Bursa Vanessa Bell has a miscarriage and falls seriously ill.
Fry cares for her and they begin an affair lasting until around 1913, when
Vanessa fell in love with the predominately homosexual Duncan Grant.

Summer: Stays at Millmead Cottage, Guildford, recovering from illness.

October: Visits Paris with Clive and Fry; they buy Picasso's still life *Pots et
Citron* (1907).

1912 February: Stays at Asheham House, Sussex, rented by Virginia Stephen.

May: Visits Italy with Clive and Fry; paints Siena and Pisa.

July: Has six paintings included in *Exposition de Quelques Indépendants
Anglais* at Galerie Barbazanges, Paris.

August: Sells *The Spanish Model* (1912, Leicester Museums and Galleries)
to the Contemporary Art Society for 5 guineas. Virginia Stephen marries
Leonard Woolf.

October: *Second Post-Impressionist Exhibition* opens at Grafton Galleries
and attracts over 50,000 visitors. Includes work by Matisse, André
Derain, Picasso and Georges Braque, as well as English and Russian
work. Bell designs poster with Grant, Fry and Frederick Etchells, and four
of her paintings are included.[25] Reviews of the show are scathing. P.G.
Konody writes: 'Mrs Bell's *Asheham* belongs to the inlaid linoleum type of
Post-Impressionist landscape; whilst in her *Nosegay* she is so bent upon
searching for non-existent angles that the flowers look as if they had
been badly cut out of paper.'[26]

1913 January: Leaves the Friday Club and, together with Fry and Grant, co-
founds the Grafton Group. Exhibits with Lewis, Etchells, Grant and Fry at
the Alpine Club Gallery. Artists were exhibited anonymously, 'liberating
women in the Group from sexist commentary and anticipating the
practice of the Omega Workshop'.[27]

May: Visits Italy with Clive Bell, Fry and Grant, particularly admiring Piero
della Francesca.[28]

8 July: Opening of the Omega Workshops at 33 Fitzroy Square, London:
Vanessa Bell, Fry and Grant are shareholding co-directors.

August: Goes to summer camp at Brandon, Norfolk, with Fry, Grant and
John Maynard Keynes.

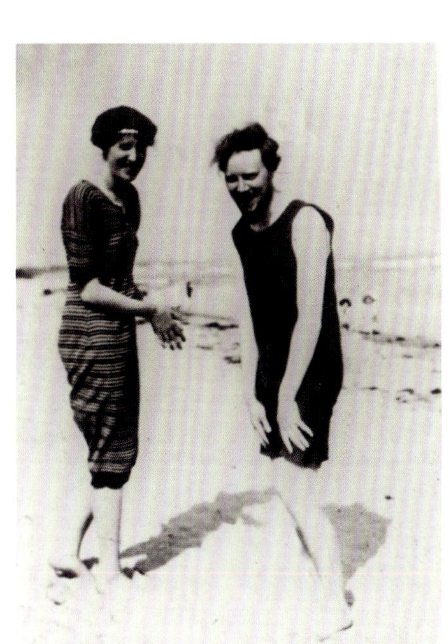

Virginia Woolf with Clive Bell,
Studland Beach, 1910s.

1914 Collaborates with Grant on wall paintings at Fry's house in Guildford.

January: Five paintings and a screen are exhibited in a Grafton Group show at Alpine Club Gallery, alongside work by Max Weber and Wassily Kandinsky. The critic for *American Art News* notes: 'She manages to convey a greater sense of emotion' than the other exhibited artists.[29]

The Bells visit Paris, where Gertrude Stein introduces them to Picasso. Vanessa writes afterwards to Grant that 'he is probably one of the greatest geniuses who has ever lived. His gifts seem to me simply amazing.' They also visit Matisse.[30]

May–June: Five paintings exhibited in *Twentieth Century Art* at Whitechapel Gallery.

July: Start of the First World War. Later Bell writes: 'It must now be almost incredible how unaware we were of the disaster so soon to come. I do not know how much the politicians then foresaw, but I think that we in Bloomsbury had only the haziest ideas as to what was going on in the rest of Europe. How could we be interested in such matters when first getting to know well the great artists of the immediate past and those following them, when beauty was springing up under one's feet so vividly.'[31]

August–September: Stays at Asheham House, Sussex.

1915 Works for anti-conscription organizations. Grant writes: 'It is very unusual to see Bloomsbury at work in an office… Bob Trevi, Vanessa, I and Norton sit in a row doing innumerable jobs from morning to night and sticking on stamps when all else fails.'[32]

Bell writes to Fry that Grant, David 'Bunny' Garnett and Lytton Strachey 'are all agreed that they would rather go to prison than be forced to become soldiers and horrible though that would be it will be better than the other'.[33]

Spring: Stays at friends Mary and St John Hutchison's house in West Wittering, Sussex, with Grant and his then lover David Garnett.

June: Exhibition of cloaks, coats, dresses, waistcoats and parasols designed for the Omega Workshops.[34]

August: Stays at The Grange, Bosham: 'The garden is on the road, so all that goes on in it must be irreproachably respectable – no posing naked as at Asheham.'[35]

1916 January: Military Service Act imposed conscription on all single men aged between 18 and 41, unless exempted. Bell writes: 'how damnable it is that people with ideas utterly different from ones own should have so much power over ones life.'[36]

Solo exhibition of paintings at the Omega Workshops.

March: Stays at Wissett Lodge, Suffolk. Grant and Garnett work in fruit farming, as conscientious objectors seeking exemption from conscription.

June: After several appeals and tribunals Grant and Garnett given exemption from combatant service to undertake farm work for the rest of the war. Bell notes that 'Bloomsbury was not destroyed as probably many other circles were destroyed by the departure of all its young men to the wars. Perhaps one reason for much of the later abuse was that many were Conscientious Objectors… So for a time Bloomsbury still existed even if crushed and bored by the outer world. The excitement and the joy had gone. The hostility of the general public was real now, no longer a ridiculous and even stimulating joke.'[37]

October: Rents Charleston House, Firle, Sussex, a house she would retain for the rest of her life. Maynard Keynes takes on the lease of 46 Gordon Square. 'Facing legal persecution and popular prejudice, Bell moved her children and companions to a farmhouse, where the men worked six days a week as manual labourers on food rations so insufficient that Grant grew thin and rheumatic.'[38]

Clive Bell's pamphlet *Peace at Once* (1915) is burnt by order of the Lord Mayor of London.

1917 May: Sends five paintings for Fry's exhibition of 'copies' at the Omega Workshops, which is a failure with the critics and public.[39]

September–October: *The New Movement in Art* exhibition in Birmingham and Heal's furniture shop on Tottenham Court Road includes eight works by Bell.

Bell and Grant agree to decorate Mary and St John Hutchinson's River House, Hammersmith, for £12, undercutting the Omega Workshops by £8 and infuriating Fry. He writes begging them to refuse the commission: 'as directors and original members of the Omega ... it would avoid a thing that gives me great and I daresay unreasonable pain; it dots the I's so very much of you and D's secession from the Omega in the eyes of the world; and, after all, I have done a good deal in the past to give both you and D. your present position.'[40]

1918 August: Six pictures in *Englische Moderne Malerei* exhibition at the Kunsthaus Zürich.

September: October: Bell and Grant commissioned by Maynard Keynes to decorate 46 Gordon Square.

November: Woodcuts for *Kew Gardens* by Virginia Woolf, published by Hogarth Press in 1919.

December: Birth of daughter, Angelica – fathered by Duncan Grant and raised by Clive Bell. Vanessa Bell writes to Grant: 'They think it [copulation] should be kept for one person and that it is monstrous and fatal ever to copulate from kindness or for any reason but lust, love or intense curiosity – I said it was sometimes difficult to know where to draw the line.'[41]

1919 March: Takes a flat at 36 Regent Square as her London base for a year. Uses Charleston as a holiday home until returning permanently in 1939.

May–June: Derain visits London and moves into Bell's Regent Square flat for a month.

September: Omega Workshops closes after becoming too expensive to run; everything is sold off cheaply over the summer. Bell later asserts that Bloomsbury died with the war: 'Nothing happens twice and Bloomsbury had had its day. It dissolved in the newer world and the younger generation now known as the Twenties.'[42]

November: Exhibits with the London Group (and again almost annually until her death).

1920 May: Visits Italy with Maynard Keynes and Grant, seeing Picasso in Paris on the way back: 'He showed us quantities of his latest works and things he is actually at work on, nearly all more or less abstract designs though I suppose usually suggested by nature. Some were amazingly beautiful.

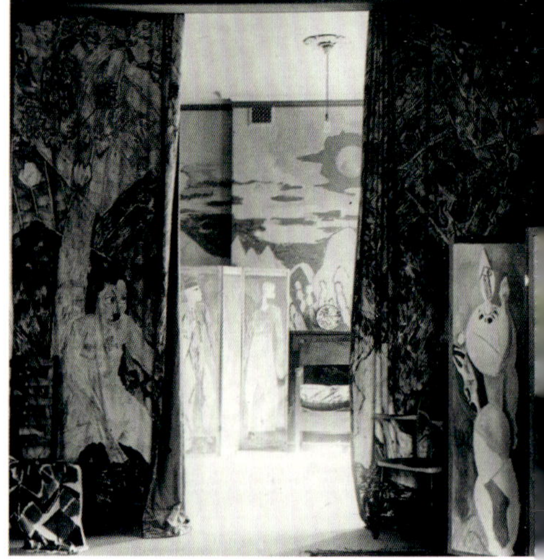

Omega Workshops, 1913.

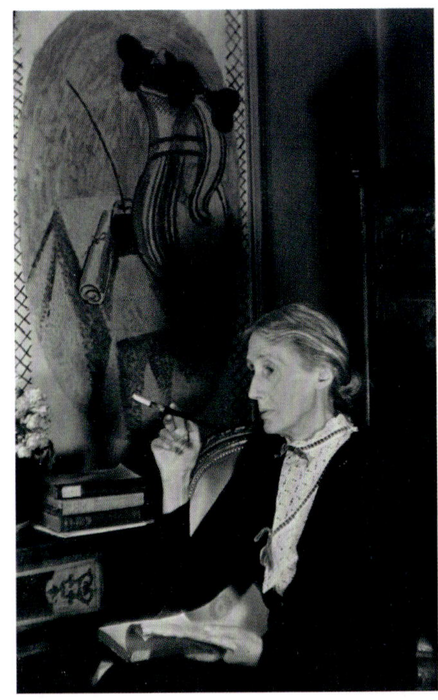

I think all gave one very definite sensations and he was interested to find out whether they were the ones he wanted to produce.'[43] They also dine with Derain, Braque and Erik Satie. Moves to 50 Gordan Square as London base until 1923.

Spring: Exhibits in group show at Galerie Vildrac, Paris.

November: Exhibits at the Independent Gallery, London (and again in 1921).

With Grant decorates Maynard Keynes's rooms at Webb's Court, King's College, Cambridge.

Start of the Memoir Club, designed to preserve the friendships of 'Old Bloomsbury', which had become dispersed after the war. Over several years Bell contributed five known papers.[44]

1921 May: Visits Paris, meeting Derain, Picasso, Satie and Braque.

October–January 1922: In St-Tropez with Grant.

Decorative commission for Adrian and Karin Stephen's rooms at 50 Gordon Square.

1922 February: In Paris for a month with Grant.

June: Solo exhibition at the Independent Gallery. Writes to Clive Bell the day after opening: 'I am astonished that I have already sold seven pictures and drawings – so at any rate I shan't be out of pocket over it.'[45] Reviewed by Fry: 'The first quality of Vanessa Bell's painting is its extreme honesty... One feels before her works that every touch is the outcome of her complete absorption in the general theme... The attention is held at once by the peculiar charm and purity of her colour and by the harmony of her designs. In these she always shows an admirable sense of proportion... She shows, indeed, a keen sense of the underlying architectural framework... But after all it is as a colourist that Vanessa Bell stands out so markedly among contemporary artists. Indeed, I can not think of any living English artist that is her equal in that respect.'[46]

1923 October–November: London Group Exhibition. R.R. Tatlock states in the *Burlington Magazine* that Vanessa is 'the most important woman painter in Europe'.[47]

Moves back to 46 Gordon Square.

1924 Decorations with Grant for Leonard and Virginia Woolf's Tavistock Square flat.

May–June: In Paris, has several meetings with Picasso, Derain, Segonzac and others.

1925 Bell and Grant take rooms at 37 Gordon Square.

Decorative commissions for L.A. Harrison's country home Moon Hall, Surrey, and Raymond Mortimer's flat, 6 Gordon Place, London, for which they were paid £45.[48]

Visits Spain and Paris with Fry and Grant.

October: Contributes to *Modern Designs in Needlework* at Independent Gallery.

1926 February: Fry writes in an article for *Vogue:* 'Her great distinction lies in her reticence and her frankness. Complete frankness of statement, but with never a hint at how she arrived at her conviction. It is with her a point of honour to leave it at that, never to explain herself, never to underline a word, never to exercise persuasion.'[49]

Virginia Woolf at 52 Tavistock Square, London c. 1939, with wall decoration by Vanessa Bell and Duncan Grant.

May–June: First exhibition of the 'London Artists' Association' (LAA) in London and then Berlin, New York and Pittsburgh. The Association was set up in 1925 by Samuel Courtauld and Maynard Keynes at the instigation of Fry, in order to assist young artists by giving them a regular income in the event that they fail to sell pictures.

May–June: Visits Italy with Grant. Exhibits at the Venice Biennale, and again in 1928, 1930 and 1934.

October: Decorative commissions, with Grant, for fireplaces for Margaret Bulley and Clive Bell's flat at 50 Gordon Square.

1927 January–May: Takes the Villa Corsica in Cassis, France.

May: One-person exhibition at 163 New Bond Street, showroom of the LAA.

August: Decorative commissions for Mary Hutchinson at 3 Albert Gate, Regent's Park, and at Ethel Sands and Nan Hudson's house Château d'Auppegard near Dieppe. Bell writes to Fry: 'Please send us a glimpse of ordinary rough and tumble, dirty everyday existence. I am beginning to collapse from rarefaction here... The extraordinary thing is that it's not only the house but also the garden that's in such spotless order... No wonder they hardly ever paint.'[50]

1928 January–May: First visit to La Bergère in Cassis, paying a £600 advance for repairs for a ten-year lease on the house.[51] Meetings with Picasso, Segonzac and Jean Marchand in Paris.

November: Exhibits in *Modern English Pictures* at Marie Sterner Galleries, New York.

1929 January–February: Visits Germany, Austria and Prague with Grant.

Decorative commissions for Lady Dorothy Wellesley at Penns in the Rocks, Sussex.

Gives up 37 Gordon Square. Takes 8 Fitzroy Street as her London studio, shared with Grant.

Commissioned by Shell-Mex to produce colour lithographs to advertise the English countryside.

1930 February–March: Exhibition at the Cooling Galleries, London, with catalogue introduction by Virginia Woolf. Bell writes: 'I have sold 12 pictures so far, amounting to £330 guineas, far more than I've ever done before, of course.'[52] The *Daily Telegraph* surmised: 'One of the very few important women painters of the present day. Her pictures all have a strongly personal flavour and she isn't afraid to be feminine, both in her delicacy of treatment, and, to a great extent, in her choice of subjects.'[53]

December: Wins third prize and £25 in a competition promoted by *Architectural Review* for 'Lord Benbow's Apartment' in which entrants were asked to design a modern yet discreet apartment for a wealthy sporting widower.

Wyndham Lewis publishes *The Apes of God*, dismissing Bloomsbury from the avant-garde: 'I think you can disregard them ... the bloom is gone.'[54]

1931 Resigns from the LAA and sells through Agnew & Sons and Reid & Lefevre, who offer a guaranteed salary offset against sales. Meets Phyllis Keynes and begins collaborating with her on decorating pottery.

September: Article by *Daily Telegraph* society columnist Marianne Mayfayre states: 'In the two farmhouses nestling in the folds of the

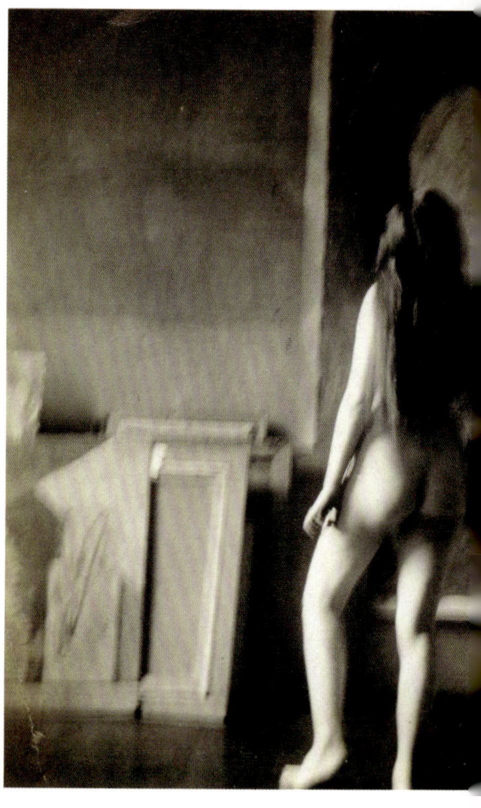

Marjorie Strachey or Molly MacCarthy posing nude in Vanessa Bell's studio *c.* 1914, with painting of two nude bathers behind (see p. 60).

Downs nearby live respectively Mrs Maynard Keynes and Mrs Duncan Grant.'[55] Vanessa writes to Clive light-heartedly suggesting suing, but only a retraction was issued: 'Vanessa Bell, the famous woman painter, is, of course, Mrs Clive Bell, and I regret that by a slip of the pen she should have been incorrectly described.'[56]

December: Exhibits a range of fabrics for textile designer Allan Walton.

1932 Designs sets for *High Yellow* by the Camargo Ballet.

June–July: Exhibition of *Recent Paintings by Duncan Grant, Vanessa Bell and Keith Baynes* at Agnew & Sons, London.

December: Decorative scheme for a music room installed at Lefevre Gallery.

Commissioned by Kenneth Clark to create a dinner service, resulting in *The Famous Women Dinner Service*.

1933 January: Decor and costumes for Sadler's Wells production of *Pomona*.

Autumn: Exhibits at the Carnegie International, Pittsburgh (and annually 1936–39).

Creates illustrations for Virginia Woolf's *Flush: A Biography* (Hogarth Press).

1934 March: Solo exhibition at Lefevre Gallery bringing in £500 of sales: 'It is of course horrifying to see all one's own works laid out like corpses and makes one feel exposed naked to the world.'[57] The *Daily Mirror* writes that she 'stands at the forefront of the English women artists of today'.[58] Décor for Ethel Smyth's ballet *Fête Galante*.

September: Death of Roger Fry.

October: Shows ceramics in *Modern Art for the Table* exhibition at Harrods and further ceramic commissions produced by A.J. Wilkinson & Co. under Clarice Cliff's *Bizarre* range. Bell and Grant's ceramics are singled out as 'ravishing in colour and sensitive in drawing... If a tea cup or a soup plate could be said to sing, these services could be called musical.'[59]

1935 Executes decorations for RMS *Queen Mary*. Bell's initial design is rejected, but another accepted. She receives £350 in total commission.

April–July: Visits Rome with Grant and family.

August: Julian Bell takes teaching post in China.

Artists' International Association exhibition *Artists Against Fascism and War*. Vanessa Bell, Virginia Woolf, Grant and Quentin Bell are active members of the Association, whose mission was for 'peace, democracy, and cultural development', and cautioned that artists' freedom is 'menaced by the threat of war and fascism'.[60]

1936 Spanish Civil War begins. Produces posters for the Artists' International Association to raise money to send medical help to Spain.[61] Vanessa writes to Julian hoping to persuade him not to volunteer: 'I do think nearly all war is madness. It's destruction and not creation, and it's mad to destroy the best things and people in the world... But I think you and other young people, who are the only hope of the world for the next 40 or 50 years, can do much more to help by not going out of your way to be shot.'[62] However, Julian returns from China and goes to Spain as an ambulance driver.

1937 January–July: Work included in *British Contemporary Art*, Rosenberg &

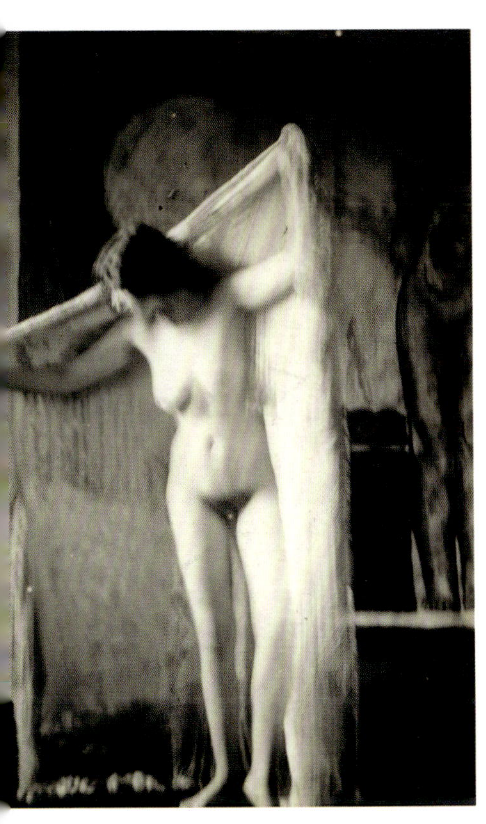

Helft, London; and *Contemporary British Artists*, Agnew & Sons, London. Solo exhibition at Lefevre Gallery.

May: Visits Paris with Grant and sees Picasso working on *Guernica*.

June: Signs, together with Grant, Virginia Woolf and others, a letter published in the *Daily Herald* urging people to attend a meeting at the Royal Albert Hall in support of Basque refugee children: 'It is our liberty not merely the liberty of one country that is being attacked and defended.'[63]

July: Death of Julian Bell (aged 29) in the Spanish Civil War. 'His death was a symbol of the growing horror of the decade and for Vanessa of the end of all real happiness. For some months after the arrival of the telegram telling of Julian's death she was confined to bed at Charleston.'[64]

Tells Angelica that Duncan Grant is her real father.

1938   Decorative commissions for Ethel Sands in Chelsea Square, London.

July: Teaches at the Euston Road School, connecting with the next generation of British artists: Graham Bell, William Coldstream, Victor Pasmore and Claude Rogers.

Autumn: After a final visit, gives up her house in France, La Bergère.

1939   Lives from 1939 to 1945 at Charleston.

Elected member of the Society of Mural Painters.

1940   September: Bell and Grant's London studios at 8 Fitzroy Street are destroyed by an incendiary bomb; much of her early work is destroyed.

Commissioned to produce two large panels for interior of Berwick Church, Sussex.

1941   March: Virginia Woolf drowns herself. Angelica Garnett recalls: 'At Charleston I found a fragile but not overwhelmed Vanessa: it must have been an event she had expected for most of her life, and now it had happened it had lost its power to shatter. Virginia's death merely confirmed the general pessimism and sense of futility which surrounded us.'[65]

June–July: Exhibition at the Leicester Galleries.

1942   Angelica Bell marries David 'Bunny' Garnett. Vanessa wrote to David at the time: 'I realise that it is entirely for you and Angelica to decide what you will do. I do not want to intend to say anything more about my feelings concerning it either now or at any time - you need not fear it.'[66]

1943   October: Completion of murals at Berwick Church, Sussex, in collaboration with Grant and Quentin Bell.

1944   Decorative commission, with Grant, for the Children's Restaurant, Devonshire Hill School, Tottenham, on the story of Cinderella.

Develops breast cancer and has a mastectomy at Hove hospital: 'Vanessa must have suffered enormously from an experience for which in those days there was no psychological preparation and no support to be found from sharing it with others... It was Vanessa's misfortune that at that time cancerous illnesses were regarded almost as though they were family scandals, to be brushed under the carpet.'[67]

1945   With Grant publishes lithographs in *Eight Lithographs* series, printed in an edition of 100 by Frances Byng-Stamper and Caroline Lucas, Miller's, Lewes.

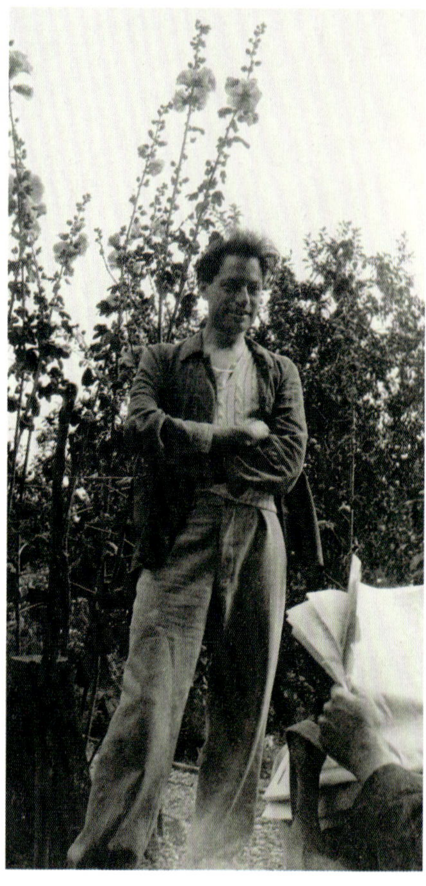

Duncan Grant at Charleston, Sussex, 1930.

1946 21 April: Death of Maynard Keynes.

Summer: Grant meets Paul Roche, with whom he would have a lasting relationship, particularly after Bell's death.

September: Visits Dieppe with Grant and Edward Le Bas.

1948 Autumn: Visits Venice and Lucca, Italy, with Grant and Le Bas.

1949 Joins committee of the Edwin Austin Abbey Memorial Trust Fund for Mural Painting (until 1959).

September: Visits Lucca.

1950 April: Exhibits with the Society of Mural Painters. First exhibition, Arts Council of Great Britain.

1951 Contributes *The Garden Room* to Arts Council's Festival of Britain exhibition *Sixty Paintings for '51*.

1952 June: Visits Perugia, Italy.

Lives at 26a Canonbury Square, Islington.

1953 August–September: Exhibition by past members of LAA, Ferens Art Gallery, Hull.

Sits on the jury for the Prix de Rome awards for young artists.

1954 Elected member of, and exhibits at, the Royal West of England Academy, Bristol.

1955 Spring: Visits Asolo, Italy, with Grant, Le Bas and Eardley Knollys.

Summer: Moves into Sydney-Turner's former flat 28 Percy Street, London, with Grant.

1956 February: Solo exhibition at the Adams Gallery, London.

1957 Contributes to a BBC radio broadcast on Virginia Woolf.

October: Visits Venice, Lucca and Cortona.

1958 Designs her final book jacket for Virginia Woolf's *Granite and Rainbow* (Hogarth Press).

1959 Visits Menton. Contracts bronchial pleurisy.

1960 Travels to Roquebrune-Cap-Martin with Grant and Grace Higgens; final visit to Paris.

1961 7 April: Dies at Charleston aged 82; is buried in Firle village churchyard.

October: Memorial exhibition at the Adams Gallery, London, with foreword by Segonzac: 'Never in her work does one meet with ... affected prettiness ..., nor yet with the facile but seductively picturesque: all is purity, frankness and perfect simplicity both in what is expressed and the means of expression. This accent of sincerity and truth has nothing to do with dull realism; it is stamped with a grand, natural distinction without a trace of affectation.'[68]

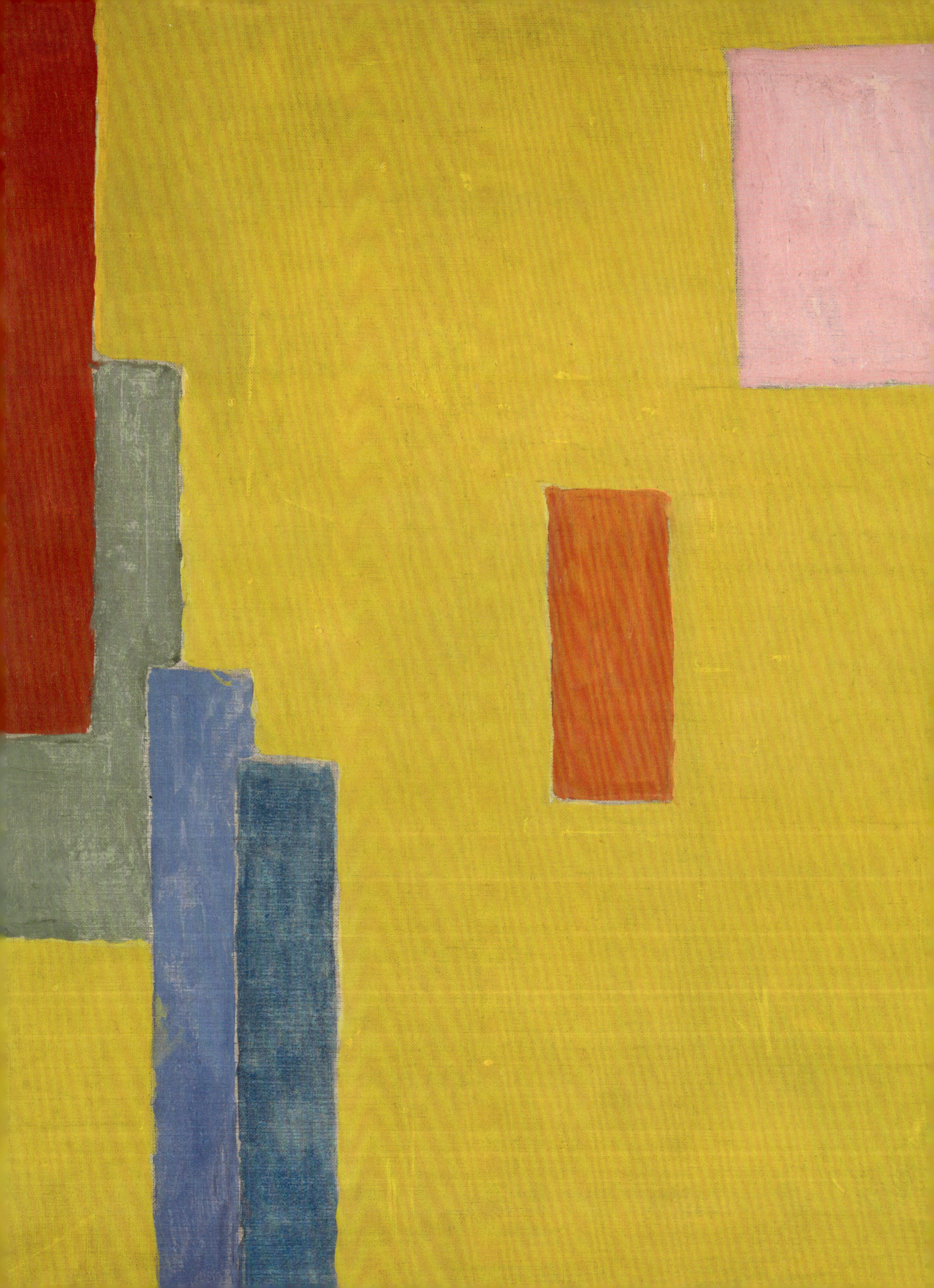

AN EMOTION, A PUZZLE

Rebecca Birrell

On a medium-sized canvas, yellow, blue, green and red oblongs descend from one side of the composition like a staircase. Beside them an orange tab floats. In the upper corner is a pale pink square reminiscent of a postage stamp. The scene might be a domestic space seen from an aerial perspective, its furniture abbreviated to blocks, or a sandy beach dotted with colourful towels and windbreaks. Though it is tempting to give meaning to these colours and shapes, their power is derived from their non-representational qualities, and their sense of possibility. With the austerity and drama of devotional art, and an attention to form typical of European modernism after 1910, the painting resists interpretation and remains enigmatic, absorbing. 'They give us an emotion, They offer a puzzle', Virginia Woolf wrote about the work of her sister Vanessa Bell. Decades later, Bell glossed this work, *Abstract Painting* (1914, p. 70), with an additional note, as though anxious this particular mystery was too opaque: 'Test for Chrome Yellow'. Woolf's description of Bell, its analysis evoking a simultaneous poignancy and remoteness, represents one possible reading of the artist's work. Another would trace Bell's prescient abstract impulses in 1914 through inventive uses of still life and portraiture to demonstrate the ambitions of an artist continually dismantling not only the formal constraints of her practice, but also its gendered expectations.

When Bell painted what she later clarified as an experiment in colour, she was familiar enough with the European avant-garde to understand the rebellious, at times political, nature of abstraction. Yet her adoption of its strategies might have had as much to do with private experiences as any desire to affiliate herself with modernist aesthetics. Recovering from measles in Italy in 1912, Bell was prescribed bed rest. To entertain her, the critic Roger Fry brought Bell a stack of coloured papers, scissors and a board, with which she could make a paper mosaic (see p. 40). Bell developed ideas about spatial relationships, about the interaction of certain shades and shapes, in a format that resembled a canvas but that had even greater flexibility than paint, inviting more daring arrangements. As Christopher Reed and Claudia Tobin note, Bell was also inadvertently practising the principles of abstraction through her work at the Omega Workshops, the design studio Bell established with Fry and the artist Duncan Grant in 1913, which produced painted furniture, ceramics and fabrics in bright, bold patterns. Structural affinities between these designs, which were mapped out on gridded paper, and Bell's works of abstraction reveal the porousness between her different projects, mediums and modes of thinking. Bell's 1914 painting was one of the earliest works of abstract art in Britain, but it seems she was unaware of its significance. Unvarnished, and without an inscription to indicate its orientation, *Abstract Painting* was not prepared in the conventional way for exhibition or sale. The fact that Bell was not accustomed to regarding work with such an obviously experimental intent as serious was partly a product of the age in which she was raised, and the many limitations felt by women artists in her position.

Woolf reflected on the changing circumstances for women of their generation in the foreword to her sister's spring 1930 exhibition. The foreword connects the restrictions on women artists surrounding the nude (considered 'until sixty years ago … corruptive of her innocency and destructive of her domesticity') to the fate of the archetypical Victorian aunt. Every modern woman, Woolf writes, has a spinster in their family tree who was forbidden to marry because a nineteenth-century patriarch couldn't bear to think of her looking at a naked man. Though this scenario is partly satirical, she uses it to link sexual and emotional freedoms to artistic ones. Woolf then draws the plight of the woman artist and the long-dead spinster even closer together. She imagines this figure as harbouring secret artistic ambitions, producing still life powerfully redolent of her suppressed will and autonomy.

> There drop out of the cupboard with her bones half a dozen flower pieces done under the shade of a white umbrella in a Surrey garden when Queen Victoria was on the throne.

The association of women's artistic output with irrelevance and embarrassing amateurism has changed, it's implied, by virtue of the occasion of this essay: a solo exhibition of Bell's work. Woolf's caustic tableau of frustrated female creativity contrasts a time when painting could only be a hobby for middle-class women fighting boredom to the freedoms of the interwar years, when a woman like Bell could exhibit in a gallery on Bond Street. The reasons for this transformation of women artists' ambitions were multifarious. Female literacy rose from around 50 per cent in 1840 to over 95 per cent by the 1920s, driven by social and political reforms, public libraries and the availability of paperback books. Women attended schools and universities, and entered the workforce for the first time, accepting positions in schools, hospitals, offices and shops. In 1928, ten years after the Representation of the People Act widened suffrage to include some women, laws were passed granting equal voting rights for all men and women. The fight for female suffrage did more than give women a concrete stake in how the country was run; it also offered them a new political vocabulary with which to voice dissatisfaction with their lives and their ambitions for the future. The loss of a generation of men in combat during the First World War created a surplus of unmarried women. Unlike Woolf's spinster, who endures a colourless life in service to scornful family members, these women could choose to live alone or to cohabit with other women. These same women made their own money and had no dependants, so were free to spend their disposable income on magazines, trips to the cinema, concerts, fashion and sports. Those women who did marry benefited from the rise of artificial contraception and increased openness in public on issues of reproductive health, meaning family sizes (and their unequal maternal responsibilities) fell by a third between the 1860s and the late 1920s. Even changes to women's fashion towards more androgynous styles – short sporty dresses and cropped hairstyles – radically altered perceptions of femininity and sexuality.

Bell's enjoyment of these freedoms was enhanced by the privileges afforded to her by her class and wealth. Her parents belonged to an established English cultural elite. Leslie Stephen was a historian who served as the first editor of the *Dictionary of National Biography*. Julia Prinsep Stephen was the niece of the photographer Julia Margaret Cameron, and grew up visiting Little Holland House, a salon-style meeting place for Victorian artists and writers. Though her family undoubtedly offered Bell great advantages culturally, accounts of her upbringing stress the emotional toll of growing up in an environment where tragedies were stoically borne and gender roles were occasionally questioned (women's education was gently encouraged) rather than overthrown altogether. After her mother's untimely death, the 16-year-old Bell became the de facto head of the household, struggling to balance the demands of her 'melancholy, deaf, rather helpless' father (her description) with her emerging ambitions as an artist. Nearly a decade later, when her father died, Bell moved with her sister to Bloomsbury, a change of address that allowed the sisters to push against the strictures of male authority and social convention that had all but smothered them at Hyde Park Gate. Their redecoration of the house reflected the sisters' belief that the overcrowded, stuffy and sepulchral Victorian interior shaped its inhabitants' inability to talk directly about important topics, chief amongst them sex. These acts of domestic rebellion no doubt had an effect on Bell's art too. In contrast to the careful, conventionally figurative Edwardian works of her early career, as well as the more psychologically charged scenes roughly contemporary to it (such as *Studland Beach* of 1912), *Abstract Painting* (1914) bristles with the pleasures of paring back and clearing space, as though Bell was replicating on canvas the freedoms she had found in transforming her home's interiors.

Bell's life as an artist was further bolstered by marriage to Clive Bell in 1907, the son of an industrialist who had made his fortune from coal mines. She had a full social calendar of concerts and parties, time spent in the studio, the city's galleries and restaurants or in her own rooms with lovers, friends and other artists. It was a lot to balance, and to do so Bell relied on female servants to buy and cook her food, to care for her children and clean her house. These women sometimes appear in Bell's paintings, but their domestic labour — in freeing Bell to concentrate on her art – underlies all her work. Bell enjoyed rights only dimly imaginable to her female relatives of previous generations, but her class status meant she had greater autonomy than many other women living in England at that time. Why, then, did Woolf declare Bell's ability to exhibit her work on Bond Street in a solo show in 1930 'unusual'?

Despite advances in certain areas of women's lives, many of the limitations of existing under a patriarchal society remained. Bell's experiences as an artist reflected these partial freedoms. Women were entering art schools in greater numbers, winning prizes, exhibiting work in major institutions and selling it amongst their

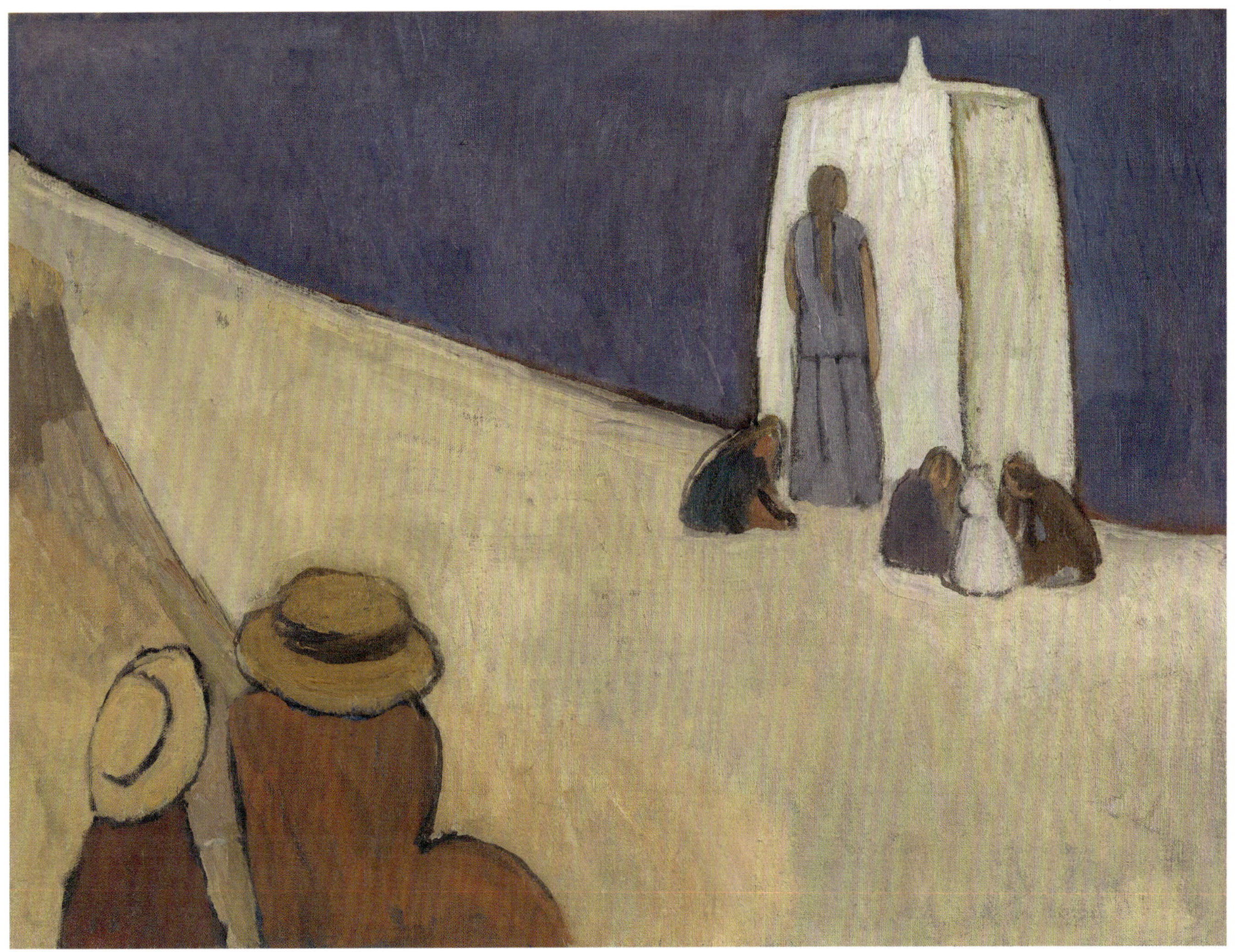

male counterparts in the metropolises' commercial galleries. They were modelling for and mentoring each other, networking at parties, in cafes, and in each other's studios, critiquing and celebrating one another's work. Yet the rewards of this were not always forthcoming or consistent. Many still shared the verdict of Charles Tansley in Woolf's 1927 novel *To the Lighthouse* that 'women can't write, women can't paint'. Tansley's comment is directed at the novel's burgeoning woman artist Lily Briscoe, generally regarded as loosely based on Bell. Briscoe internalizes Tansley's remarks, and concludes that the abstract portrait she spends much of the novel agonizing over is doomed to obscurity. 'It would be hung in the servant's bedroom,' she tells herself, 'it would be rolled up and stuffed under the sofa.' Not so different, ultimately, to the fate of the amateur spinster painter in Woolf's foreword.

Studland Beach, 1912.

Nevertheless, even early in her career Bell was confidently in conversation with her forebears, situating herself within an art-historical tradition. *Iceland Poppies* (1908–09, p. 35) reflects the restrained, graceful style of John Singer Sargent (who taught her at the Royal Academy Schools) and James Abbott McNeill Whistler. Yet there is a subtle suggestion of drama in Bell's still life that sees her surpassing these influences. The muted colour palette creates an icy, charged atmosphere that is intensified by symbolically loaded objects: a ceramic apothecary jar, a glass vial, a bowl and a single red poppy laid before these instruments of healing like an offering. The result is evocative without being narrowly allegorical, a reading Woolf expresses in several different ways in essays on Bell. 'Morality doesn't enter,' Woolf writes, 'psychology is held at bay.' Or, put simply, 'no stories are told'.

After seeing the European avant-garde at Roger Fry's exhibition *Manet and the Post-Impressionists* at London's Grafton Galleries in 1910, Bell's style shifted. Typical of this new aesthetic was the austere, rigorously simplified composition of *Studland Beach* (1912). A group of women and children are engaged in recognizable seaside activities, scrabbling in the sand and approaching a bathing hut to change, but they also resemble ancient rock forms arranged to face the sea, as though for some higher ritualistic purpose. They convey silence and tension, a hard surface beneath which intense feeling hums. But, as Woolf insists, it is emotion without the conventional scaffolding of a story. Instead, there is a sense of suspended time, of mounting intensity: the sea can be heard crashing in the distance, the cooling air is felt as it moves over the women's flesh.

Still life from this period features jagged, luridly coloured flowers in subtly distorted domestic spaces. Bell's still life paintings are gentle subversions of a tradition that had shifted from theological dramas about mortality and morality to secularized exemplars of middle-class taste. Form is Bell's focus in still life, but there is a sense too that everyday experience, witnessed by the domestic matter of the genre, is accorded a fresh significance. Partly this was because of the permeable boundaries between Bell's studio and her home, an innovation in the genre's history. Still life was conventionally arranged in studio settings which drew on the home's appearance – giving the impression of a real interior – while removing all its memories and emotion, and arguably its association with femininity. Bell's still life painting showed the domesticity of its subject's natural surroundings, and that context became as much the focus of the painting as the fruit or ceramics. By making the setting of her still life more recognizably homely, Bell aligned the genre with a world of female experience that the history of representation had previously devalued. Bell's attraction to still life reflected the special status of the home within her practice, especially after 1916 when she moved to the Charleston Farmhouse in Sussex. This home would become a living canvas for Bell and for her friend and collaborator Grant, an ongoing prompt to acts of spontaneous creative expression. Bright colours and whimsical decorative motifs covered every surface of the house, and over the years were subject to changes that reflected Bell's evolving ideas and living arrangements. Charleston became a haven for Bell's artist and writer friends, many of whom were queer, its spirit of openness encouraged by the camp eclecticism of the home's interior decor with its aesthetics of pleasure, desire and play. The Victorian home's layout, in which men, women and children were segregated in formally decorated and furnished rooms, was part of a system of social norms that reinforced the importance of marriage and the traditional family unit. Charleston's carefree, bohemian interiors reimagined domestic space as a safe space in which queer experience might flourish.

Portraits from Bell's early career, as with her still lifes, are characterized by an exaggerated colour palette and are similarly set against patterned backdrops that recall Bell's decorative designs for Omega. Bell's interest in abstraction shaped these settings, but more unconventionally it permeated the depiction of her subject's faces, which are frequently blurred. These faceless yet characterful heads might also be understood as reflections on interiority, as though Bell was withholding detail in acknowledgement of the sitter's essential unknowability, the selves that were in constant flux even over the course of a single afternoon of modelling. Later, in the 1920s, Bell's interest in abstraction faded, and she did not so much return to the figurative representation of her youth as embrace a relaxed, sumptuous figuration dedicated to domestic life in Sussex and London. The Omega Workshops closed in 1919, removing one of the main avenues of Bell's abstract thinking, but she was not alone in her shift in style. The First World War left many artists in Bell's position unwilling to pursue fragmentary or experimental approaches to art, which were perceived as replicating something of the conflict's chaotic and destructive drives. Fantasies of regeneration and order were realized through a return to classical or realist modes: just as Picasso disavowed Cubism,

Bell turned her back on abstraction. The calm characteristic of
Bell's late paintings insist upon a
hard-won normalcy of the interwar years. After her son Julian's
devastating death in the Spanish
Civil War in 1937, and the beginning of the Second World War,
Bell retreated further into the
comforts of this style.

Throughout Bell's career,
and regardless of which stylistic
evolution she was immersed
within, she displayed a keen
interest in representing intimacy,
in particular between women.
'Nobody moves and yet the room
is full of intimate relationships', Woolf wrote of Bell's
work in 1934. *A Conversation*
(1913–16, p.63) depicts three
women huddled together, their
expressions conveying deep
discussion. Two listen gravely,
and a third leans forward in a
gesture of revelation. Framed by
grey curtains suggestive of the
home as much as the stage, and
watched over by fleshly, colourful tulips that appear to lean forward
as though eavesdropping, Bell proposes an unprecedented drama
and importance to women talking. The solid bulk of the women in *A
Conversation*, their bodies curved over like punctuation marks, suggests a greater interest in their intelligence and inner worlds than in
the beauty standards dictated by conventional femininity. This would
become another hallmark of Bell's portraiture of women. *Mrs St
John Hutchinson* (1915), a portrait of Bell's husband's mistress Mary,
shows her in a lime green cloak that gives her the febrile presence of
a large tropical bird. In the society in which Bell was raised, femininity demanded delicacy and frailness. As though in response to such
a narrow idea of female beauty and behaviour, Bell presents Mary

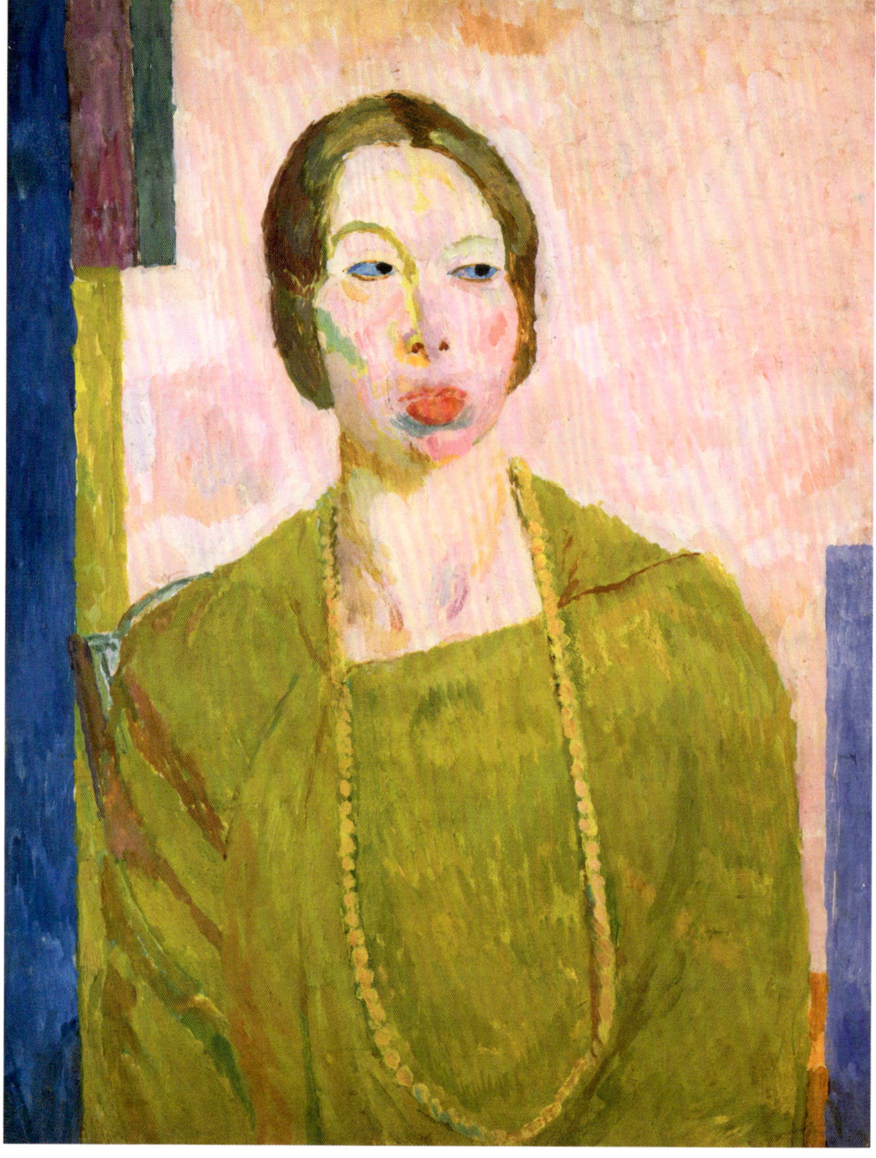

Mrs St John Hutchinson, 1915.

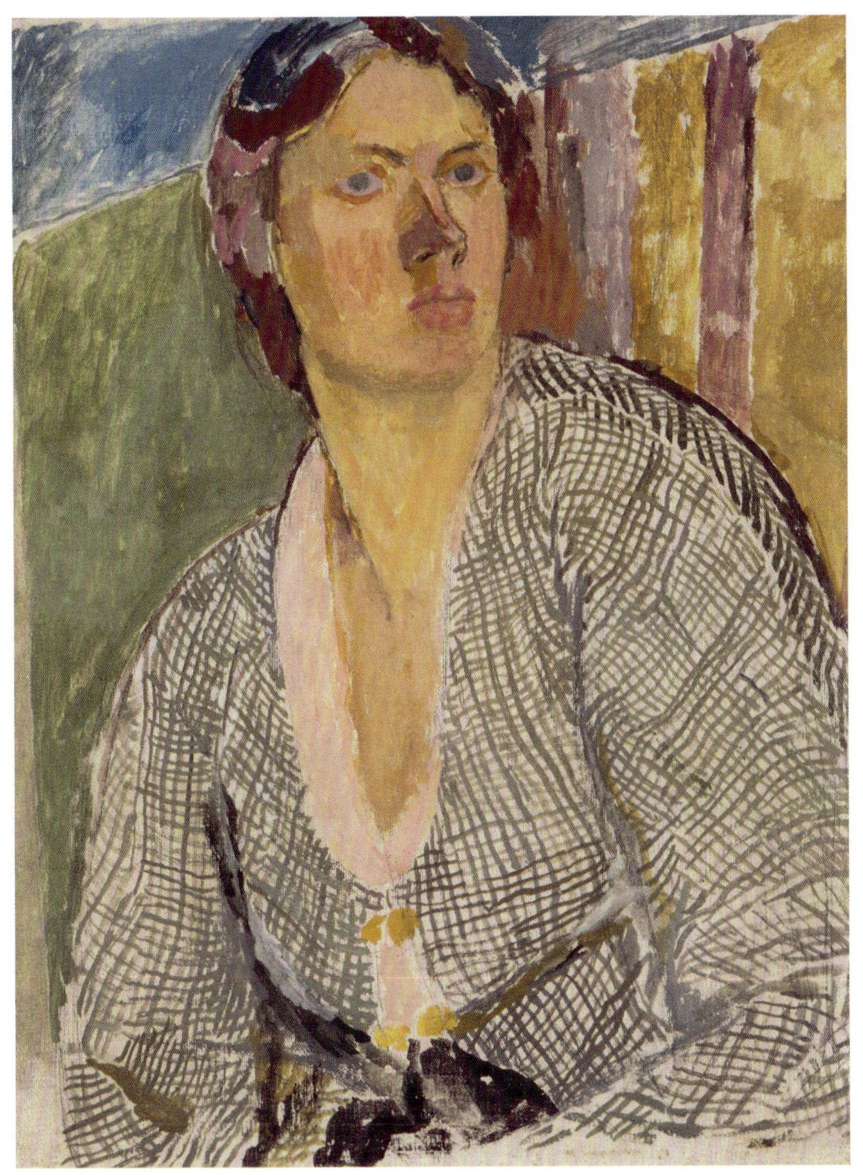

Self-Portrait, 1915.

as confident and self-possessed, her sour expression suggesting a broader refusal to be agreeable, a lack of interest in its possible appeal to men. The same treatment is given to Dr Marie Moralt in Bell's 1919 portrait of the physician (p. 99). In a large brown overcoat that increases the dimensions of her body, and with a black hat covering her hair, Moralt is a commanding and distinctly unfeminine figure. Instead of the narrowly defined grace and elegance that was traditionally the female portrait's focus, Bell explores the authority wielded by a woman in a male-dominated profession. In thick, expressive brushstrokes, and through their exaggerated size, attention is drawn to Moralt's hands, the intelligence and dexterity of which were vital to her practice of medicine. This tribute to Moralt was shaped by the same impulse that had Bell erase the faces of women in portraits that saw them resting, sewing or reading. The most vital part of these female selves is not their appearance, Bell implies, but in their capacity for thought and creativity. Bell's commitment in these portraits to alternative criteria of value for women extended into portrayals of herself. Her 1915 self-portrait shows her gazing powerfully into the distance. On the right side of her frame Bell adds more flesh to her shoulder, expanding the dimensions of her body without concealing evidence of this adjustment. The pattern on the additional section of Bell's arm is darker and runs in a different direction, and the line where her arm previously ended is still visible. Bell leaves in this awkward trace of her own working practice to emphasize the importance of process and experiment within the very substance of her identity, not just as a value applicable to the realm of art and ideas.

Motherhood was another subject Bell sought to reinvent. Her representations of mothering subvert both the Madonna-and-child imagery found in centuries of religious art and the sentimental, secular reinterpretations of the motif in French Impressionist painting. The dream-like *Nursery Tea* (1912, p. 56) shows Bell moving beyond idealistic clichés of maternity. Bell depicts nursemaids engaged in the childcare that enabled her own creative practice. In the strained body language of the women and the fraught expressions of their wards, all rendered in a pastel colour palette evocative of tenderness and innocence, Bell suggests inharmonious compromises. Focusing on the emotional bonds of motherhood stated the naturalness of this role for women, its apex of their emotional lives. *Nursery Tea* was part of a small body of work by women artists that revealed the labour involved in simply sustaining a child's life, acts that might be performed by anyone willing or financially obligated to do so. Though the nursemaids' faces are stripped of all identifying details, as blankly interchangeable as the domestic objects that surround them, they are not radically different to how Bell depicts women artists and writers, who are similarly featureless. Not only does Bell make the often unseen work of the nursemaids visible; she also inserts them into a network of valued, respected women who sustained her artistic life.

Femininity, domesticity, creativity and intimacy: these are only some of the ideas sparked by Bell's art, the diversity of which challenged even her sister's powers of summation. 'She is interested in children', Woolf writes. Immediately sensing the narrowness of this description, she continues 'one has to add, but she is equally interested in rocks.'

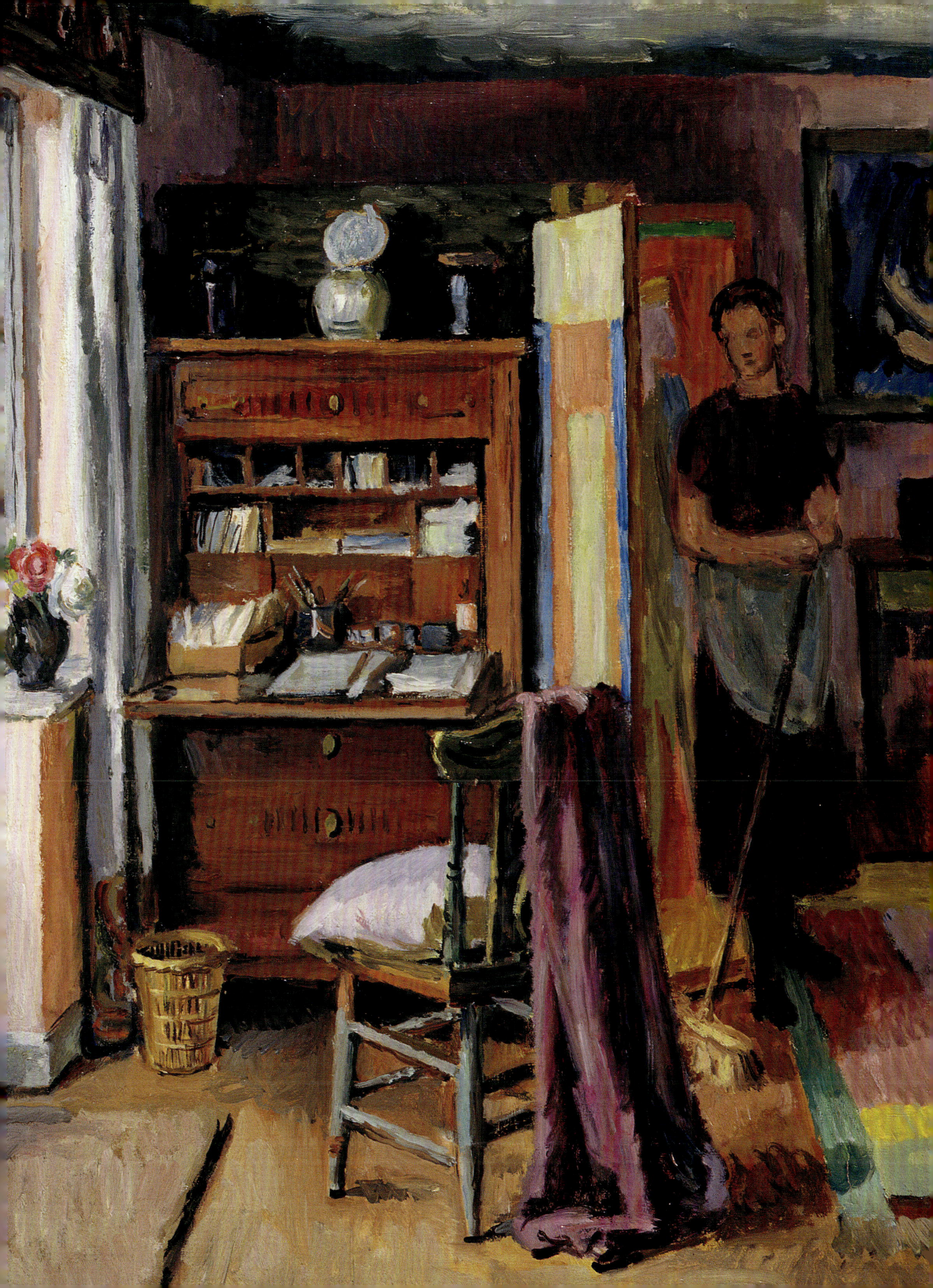

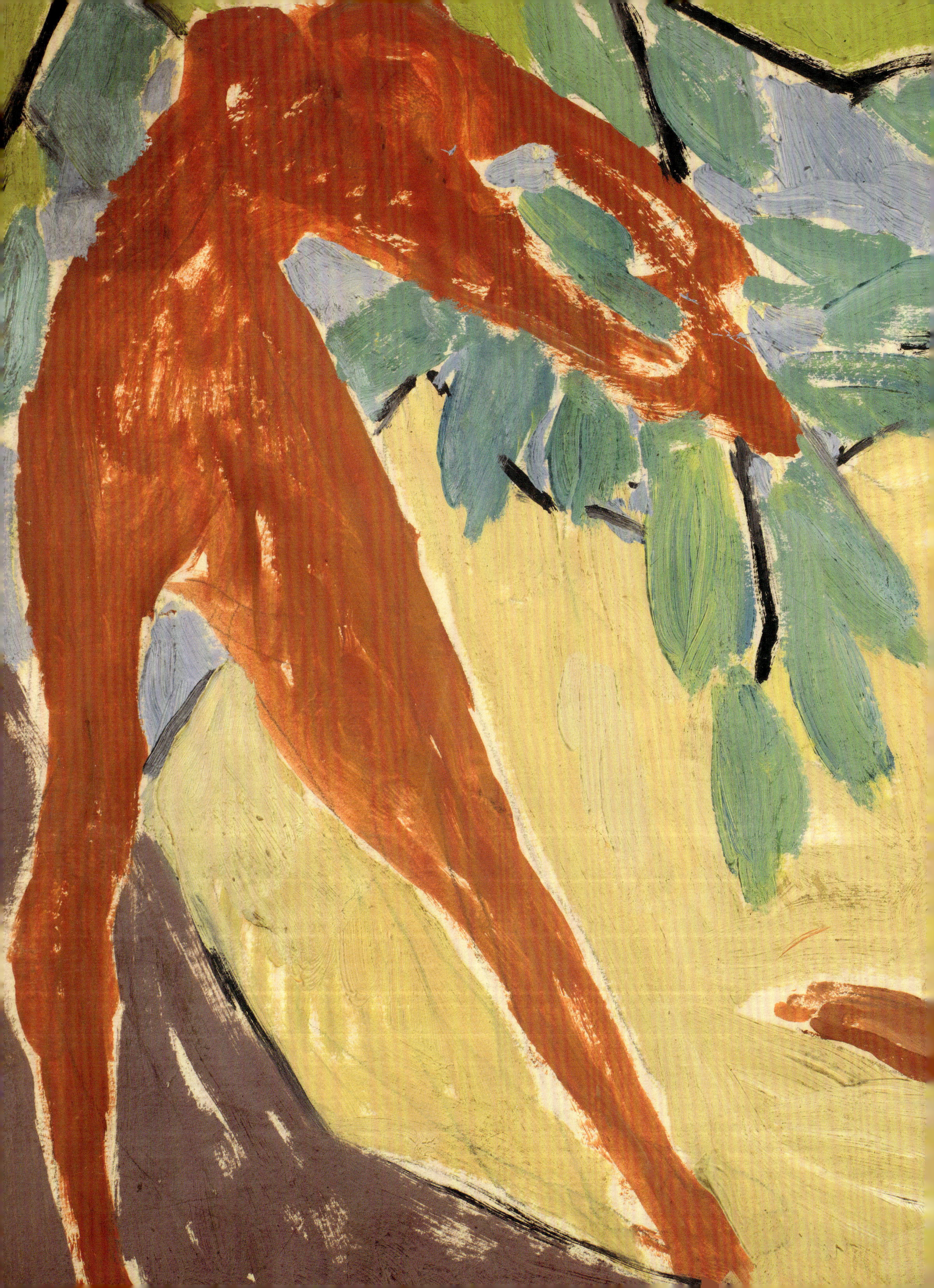

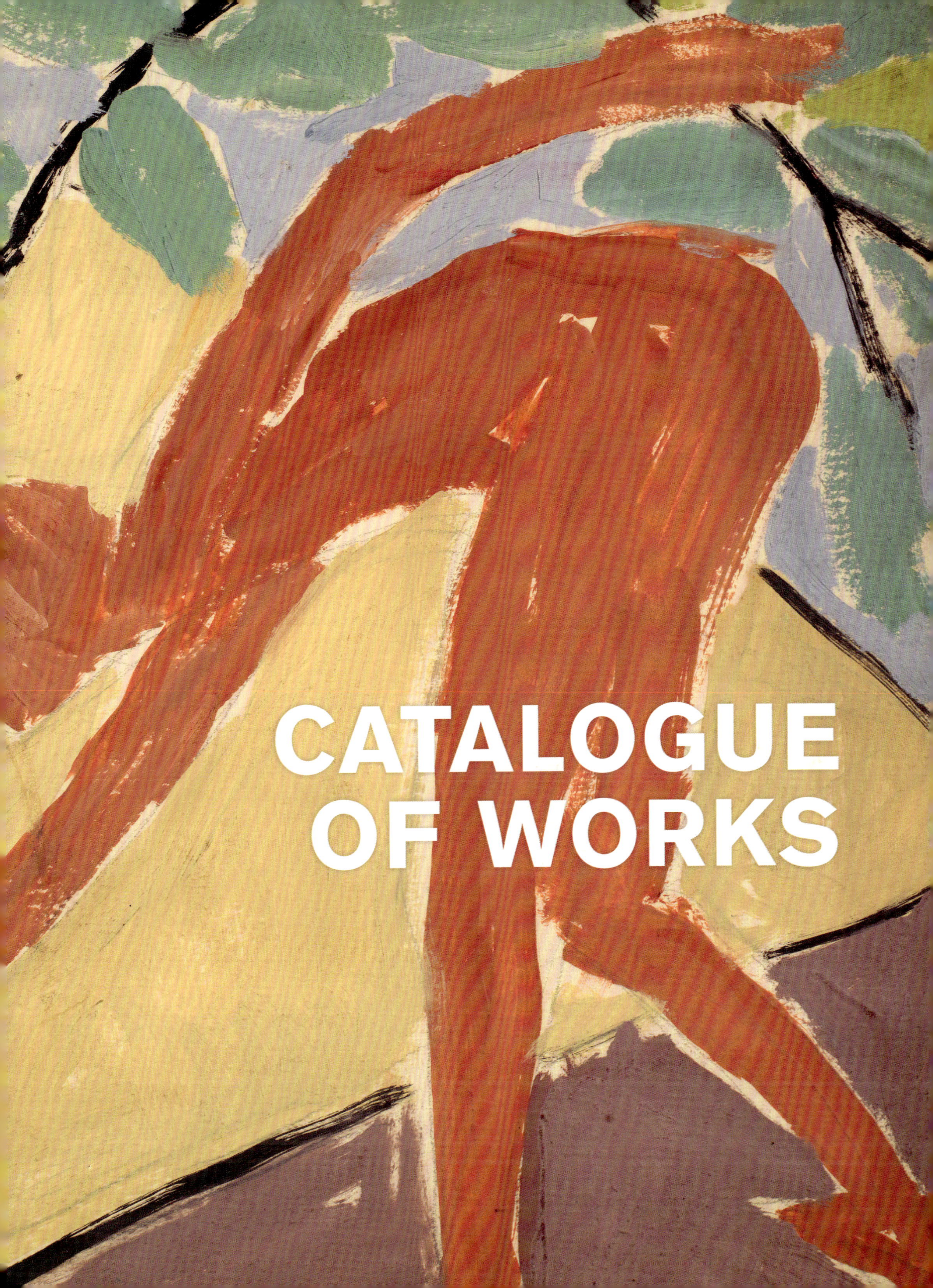
CATALOGUE
OF WORKS

Cornish Cottages

*c.*1900 | oil on board | 22.5 × 17.5 cm

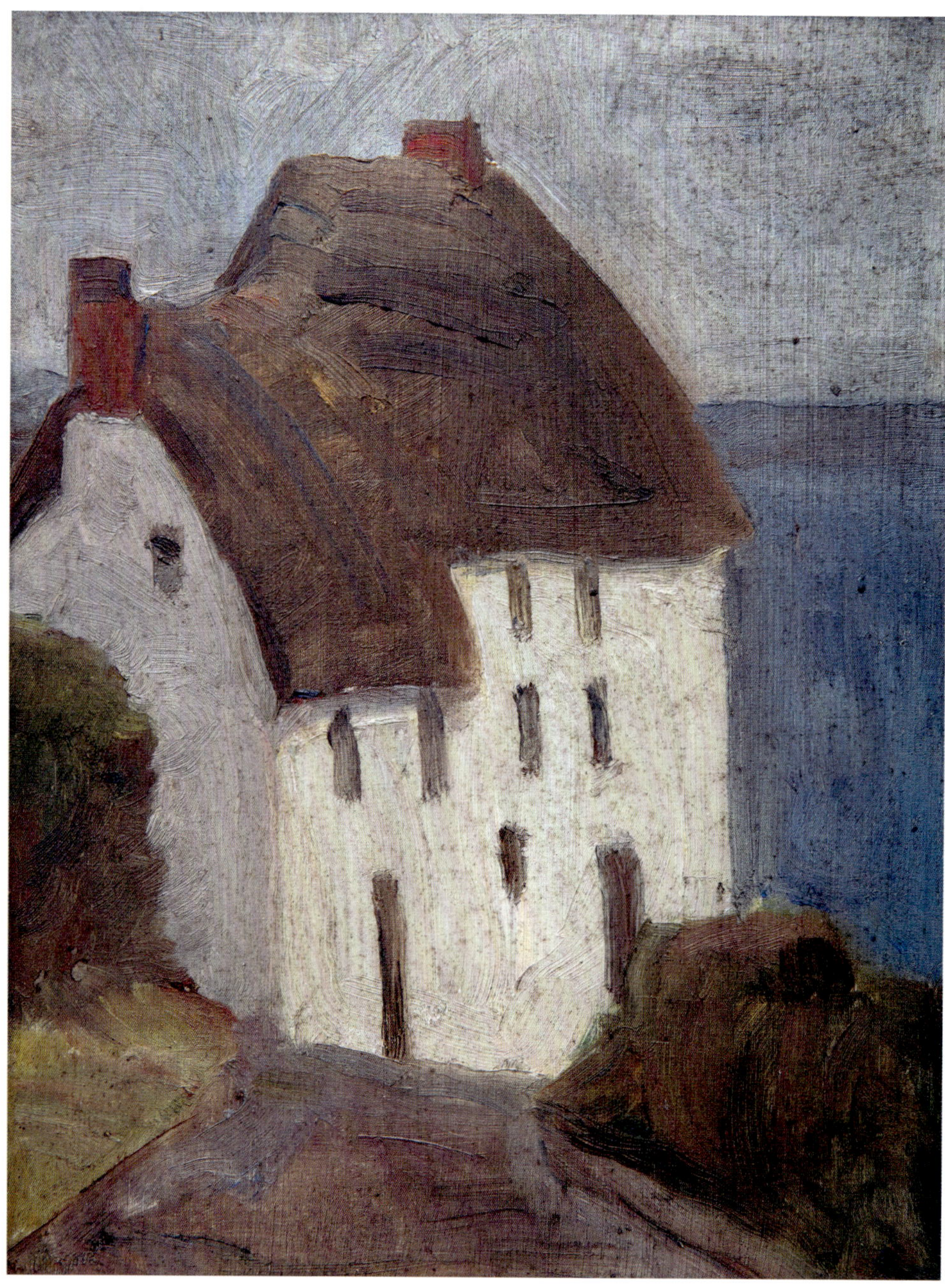

From 1882 to 1894 the Stephen family took annual holidays at Talland House, St Ives, Cornwall. This painting shows The Mariners cottage, Church Cove, The Lizard. Since around 1894, after her father Sir Leslie Stephen had noticed her drawing ability, Bell had been taking drawing classes with Ebenezer Cooke, a student of John Ruskin.

Portrait of Sir Leslie Stephen

1902–3 | oil on canvas | 67 × 60 cm

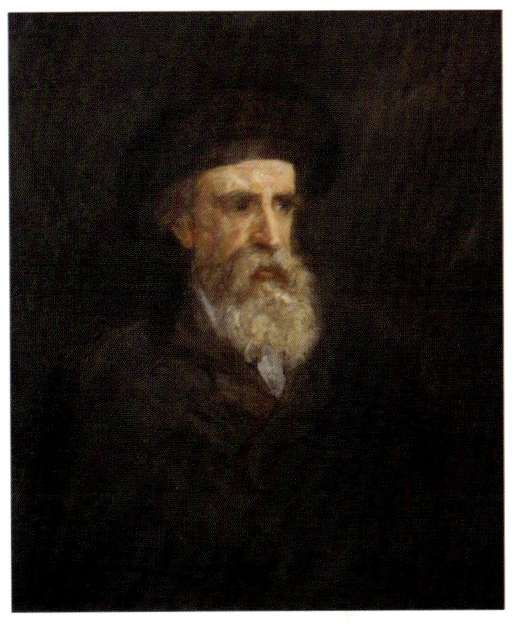

This is Bell's earliest known portrait. It depicts her father Sir Leslie Stephen (1832–1904) towards the end of his life, following the death of her mother, when Vanessa was running the Stephen household. Sir Leslie was an author, critic, historian, biographer, mountaineer and an early humanist activist. He wrote *The History of English Thought in the Eighteenth Century* (1876) and was editor of the *Dictionary of National Biography* 1885–91. Bell took lessons with Sir Arthur Cope R.A. before entering the Royal Academy Schools in 1901, where she was taught by James MacBey and John Singer Sargent. Her principal biographer, Frances Spalding, notes of her early work: 'These are obviously student essays in Old Master styles. Though she received special praise for her work soon after entering the Schools she took no prizes while there, nor did any of her friends – Mary Creighton, Sylvia Milman and Margery Snowden – with whom she was cloistered in the life-class, for until 1903 these classes remained segregated.'[1]

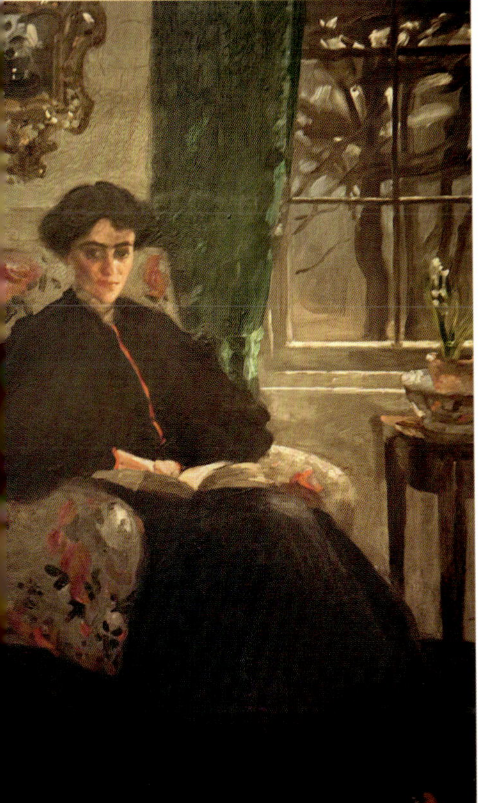

Portrait of Lady Robert Cecil

1905 | oil on canvas | 76.5 × 51 cm

This was Bell's first portrait commission and the first work she exhibited, at the New Gallery, London, in 1905. Lady Robert 'Nelly' Cecil (née Eleanor Lambton, 1896–1956) was a friend, early supporter of the Stephen sisters' professional endeavours and a prominent member of the suffrage movement.[2] Bell wrote of 'Nelly' affectionately that she was 'really artistic and has very good taste'.[3] A photograph shows Bell undertaking the commission from life. The canvas shown in the photograph faithfully reproduces the scene in front of the artist, including a framed picture above Nelly's head. However, in the final painting this has been replaced with an ornate mirror – perhaps referring to Jan van Eyck's *Arnolfini Portrait* (1434, National Gallery). As writer Rebecca Birrell describes, Lady Cecil appears here as 'a serene feminine archetype hemmed in by the necessities of the drawing room … polished and artificial, weighed down and defined through these gendered, upper-middle-class effects.'[4]

Saxon Sydney-Turner at the Piano

*c.*1908 | oil on canvas | 18.4 × 24 cm

Saxon Sydney-Turner (1880–1962) attended Trinity College, Cambridge, with Bell's brother Thoby Stephen. He was elected an Apostle (an elite intellectual society) in 1902, the same year as writers Lytton Strachey and Leonard Woolf, Bell's future brother-in-law. On 16 February 1905 Sydney-Turner became the first visitor to Thoby Stephen's Thursday evening gatherings at 46 Gordon Square. He spent his career in the civil service but also wrote poetry and a short story, 'Eidolon' (1905), which 'explores the fluidity of gender performance in a way that anticipates by twenty-five years the sex change in Woolf's *Orlando*'.[5] Reminiscent of the work of Bell's tutor John Singer Sargent, this painting was exhibited at a Friday Club exhibition in 1908 at the Baillie Gallery, London, alongside works by Pierre-Auguste Renoir and Paul-Émile Pissarro.

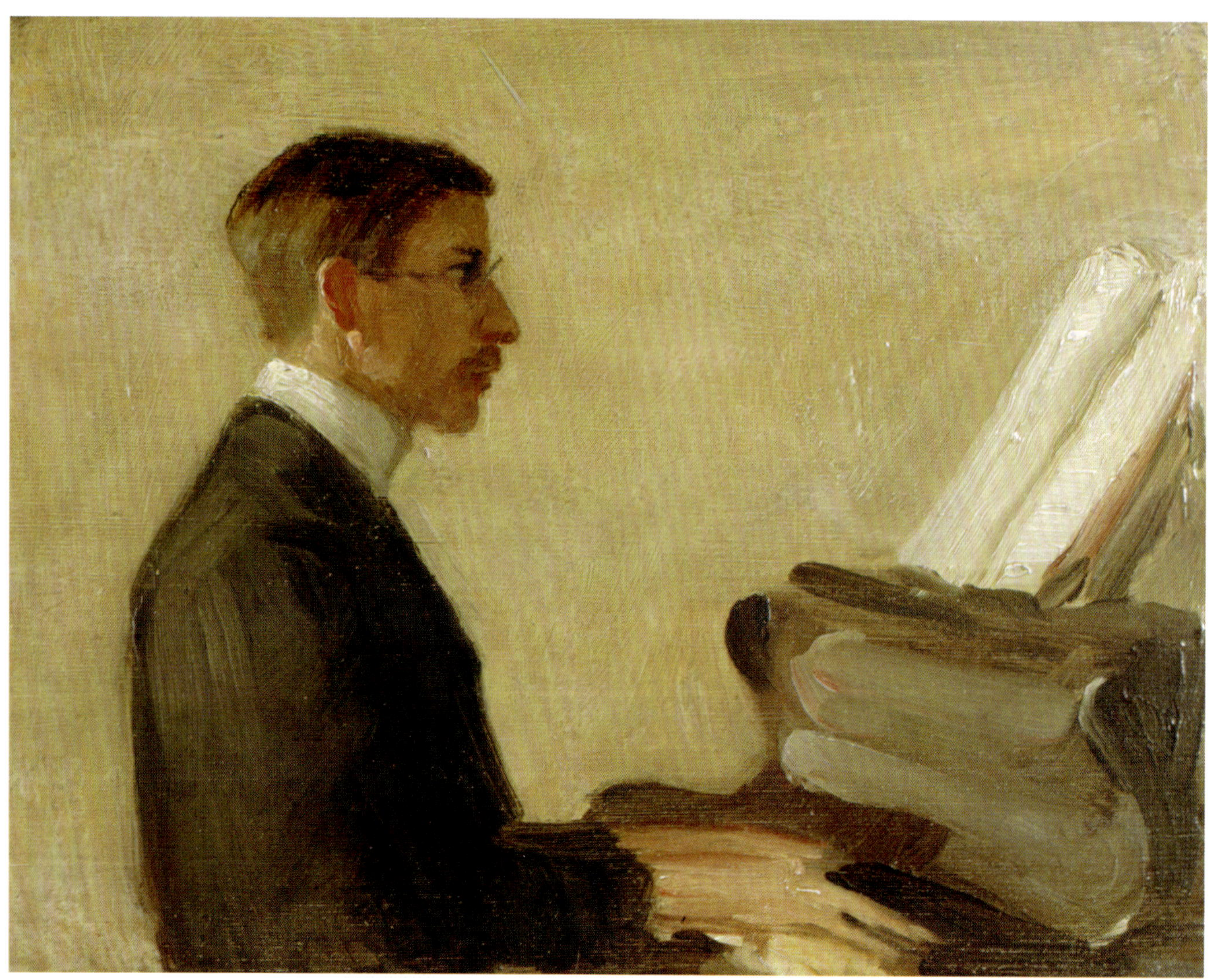

Iceland Poppies

1908-09 | oil on canvas | 54 × 45 cm

This carefully composed painting shows an eighteenth-century French pharmacist's jar, a small alabaster bowl, a green glass poison bottle and three Iceland poppies, poppies often being associated with their narcotic properties and sleep. In a list of Bell's paintings made *c.*1945 it is called *Poppies and Poison*.[6] Morpheus, the Greek god associated with sleep and dreams, appears on a bedhead at Charleston painted by Duncan Grant for Bell in 1916–17, while the foot of the bed shows two large red poppies. Also in 1916 Bell designed a bedhead for her friend the writer Mary Hutchinson, which featured a nude with poppies (p. 88). In its tonal range, *Iceland Poppies* appears to be influenced by James Abbott McNeill Whistler, whose work Bell had seen. It also evokes the work of William Nicholson, who was painting still life around the same time.[7]

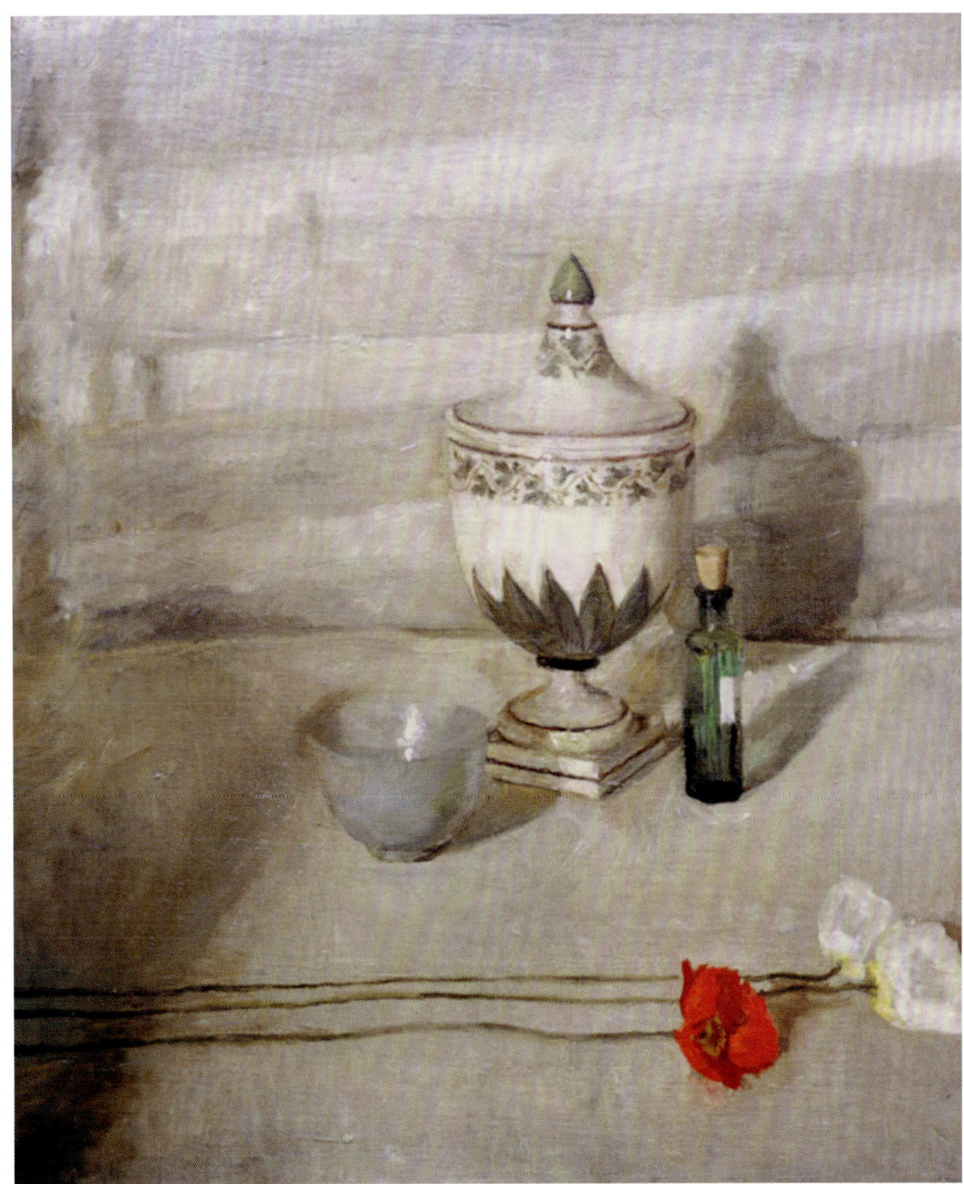

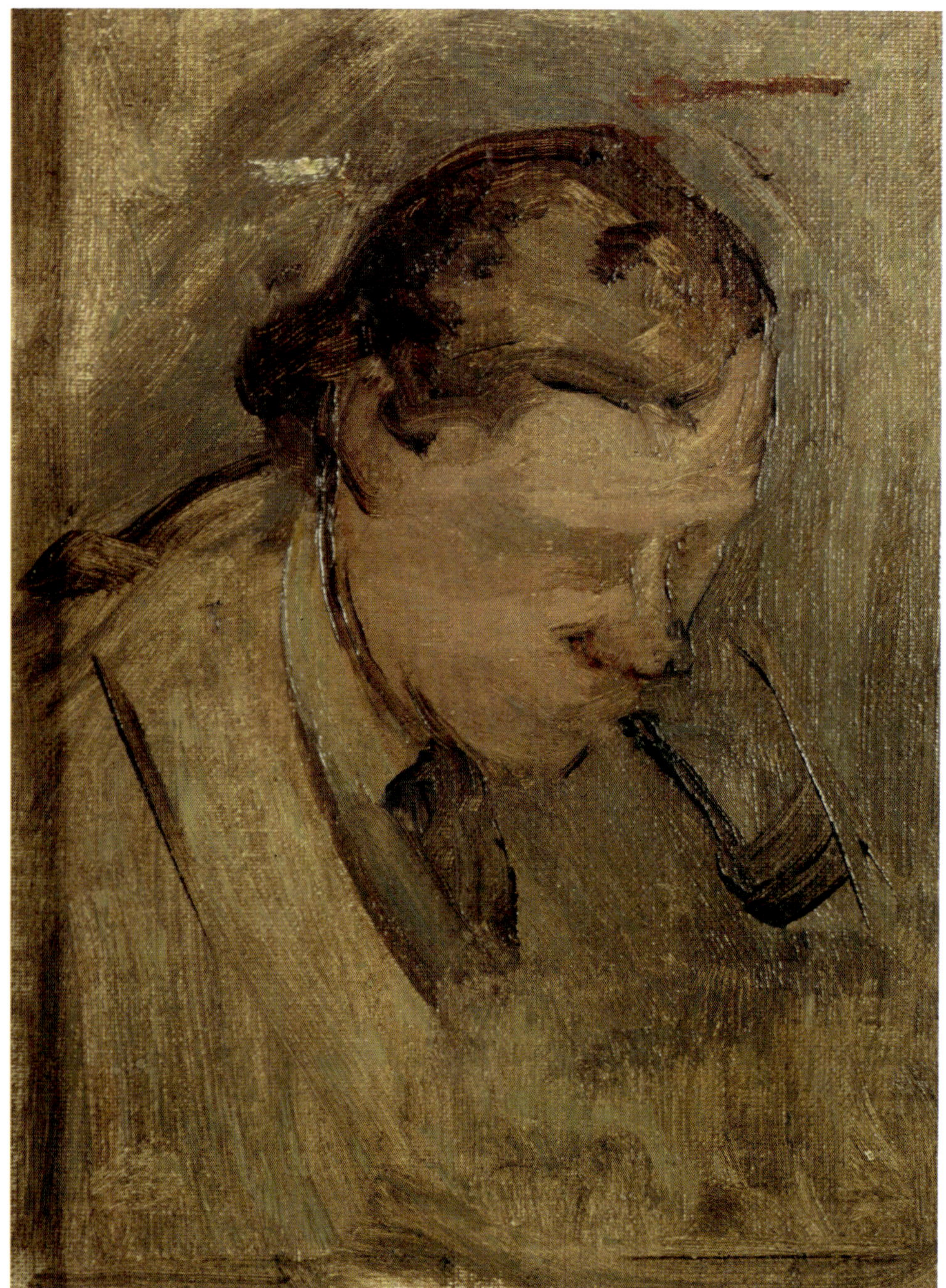

Clive Bell

*c.*1909 | oil on board | 23.5 × 18 cm

Clive Bell (1881–1964), an art critic associated with formalism, developed a theory known as significant form: 'The important thing about a picture is not how it is painted, but whether it provokes aesthetic emotion.'[8] He studied history at Trinity College, Cambridge, where he met Thoby Stephen and through him Vanessa in 1902. Vanessa and Clive married in 1907. Clive was born into a wealthy family which made their money from coal; they owned a large Victorian Gothic mansion, Cleeve House, in Seend, Wiltshire. Vanessa wrote of her frustration there: 'I am almost become a communist. Really the respectable rich with their dogs and their clothes and their cars all rolling in while they eat and play tennis and become soldiers are enough to make me want to revolt.'[9] Although they both had multiple affairs during their marriage, their letters reveal life-long affection, with Vanessa writing as 'Dolphin' in 1910: 'Dolphin does want you back very badly…. I am longing for news of you … your poor little bedfellow is so lonely of a morning … Dolphin rubs your orange whiskers with her snout and offers her tail to be stroked.'[10] Clive, 18 years later, wrote: 'In any new plans that may be forming I do beseech you not to leave me out entirely. I far prefer your society and Duncan's and "the Charleston atmosphere" to any other, and – strange as it may seem – in London and Paris I often feel terribly lonely.'[11]

Drawings of the artist's son Julian

Vanessa and Clive Bell's first child, Julian, was born on 4 February 1908. Before his birth Bell wrote to her sister Virginia: 'I am honestly terrified sometimes of the responsibility of having children. I'm not sure it doesn't mean hanging the most terrific millstone around one's neck…. I can look at it calmly now but when I have them I shall probably be so unreasonably fond of them that it won't strike me in that light.'[12] After Julian arrived, she produced huge numbers of drawings, photographs and several paintings of him, which are among the most closely observed of her works. Her letters also reveal her admiration: 'Julian's eyelashes are the loveliest colour you ever saw – like the down on a butterfly's wing. They are dark but shine with iridescent gold when you look at them from above with the light in them.'[13] Later in life, she also wrote: 'Oh Julian, I can never express what happiness you've given me in my life…. Just having children seemed such incredible delight.'[14]

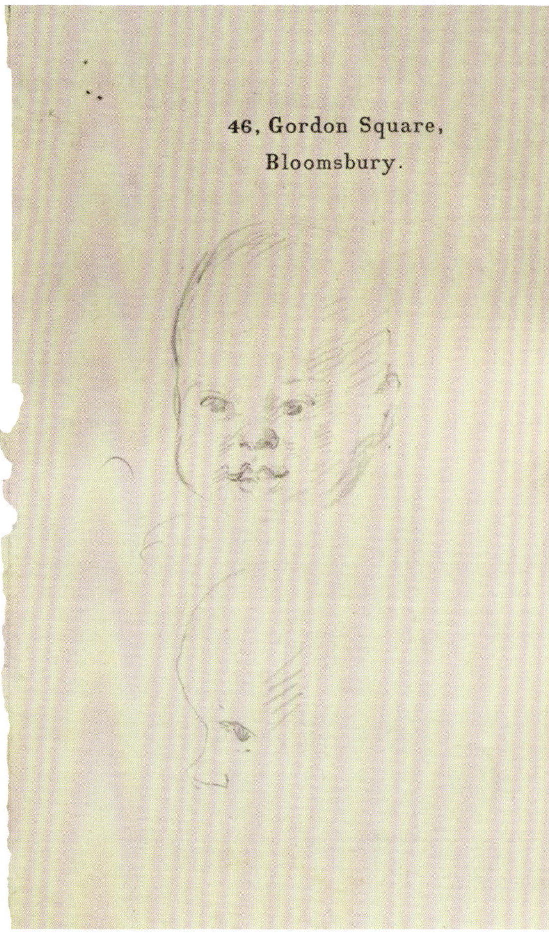

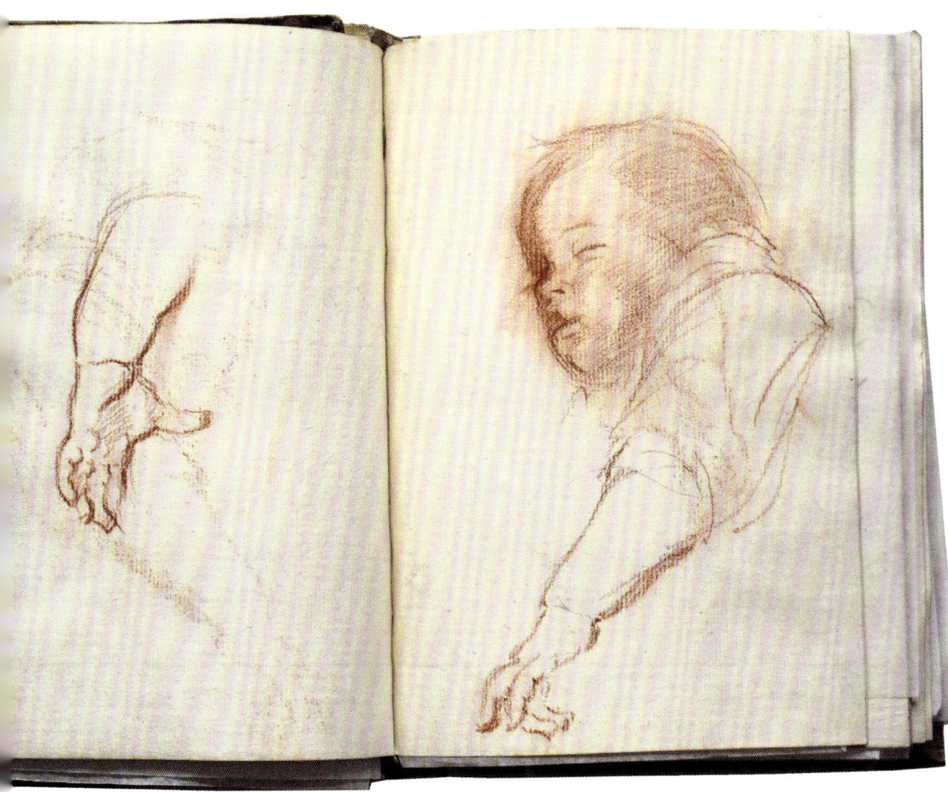

Baby portrait studies

The Bells' second son Quentin was born on 19 August 1910. These quick pencil studies show Bell recording her infant's appearance, here on a piece of '46 Gordon Square' headed paper. Quentin Bell (1910–1996) became a lecturer in Art History at the universities of Durham, Leeds, Oxford, Hull and Sussex. He also worked as an artist, principally in ceramics.

Cypresses in Turkey

1911 | oil on board | 35 × 25 cm

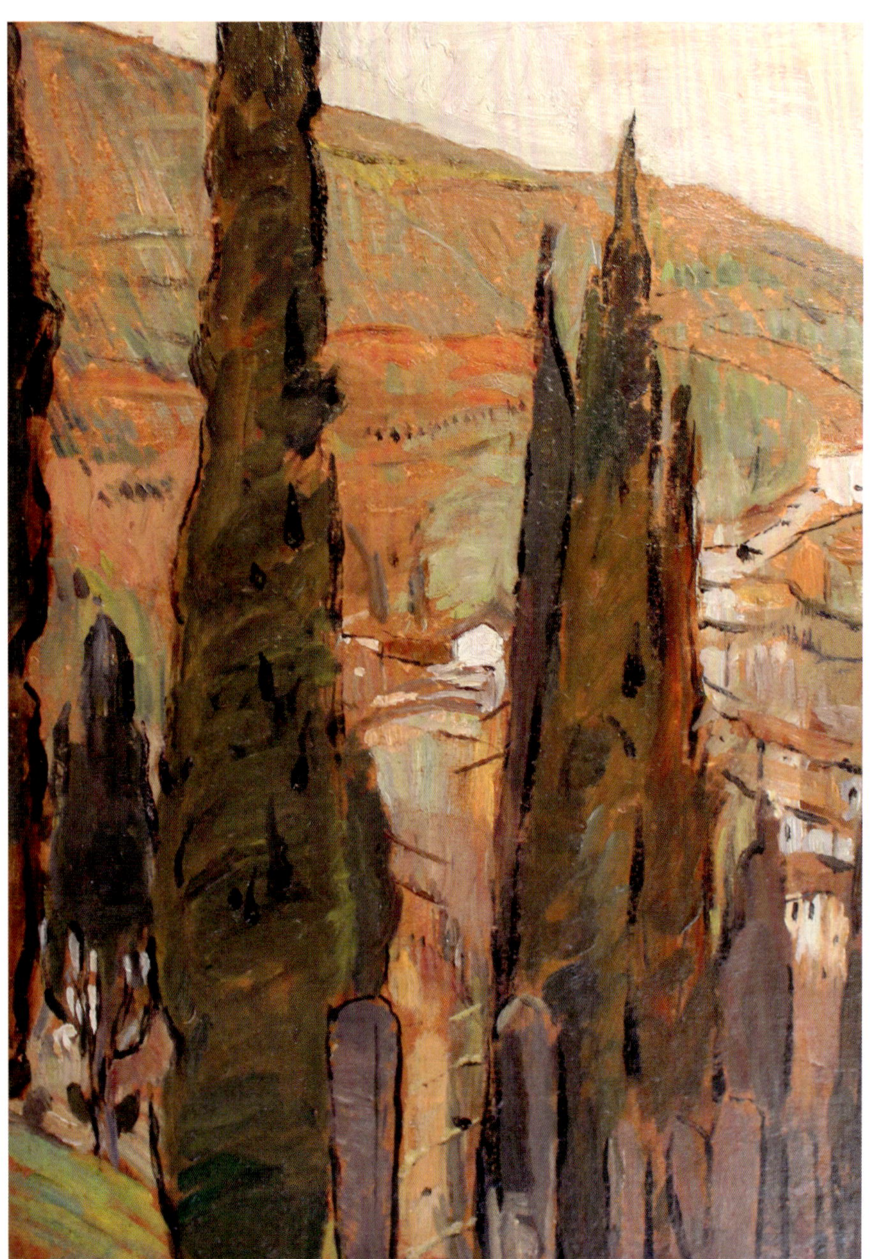

In April 1911 Clive and Vanessa Bell, together with art critic Roger Fry and mathematician Harry Norton, travelled to Turkey. However, at Bursa, after a few days painting in the hills with Fry, Bell suffered a miscarriage, bringing on a physical and mental break-down. Fry nursed and comforted her until she was able to return home, and this period of closeness led to an affair, lasting approximately until 1913, and long-term friendship. A very similar view of Cypress trees painted by Fry also exists.

Virginia Woolf in Fancy Dress

1911–12 | oil on canvas | 35.6 × 30.5 cm

Fancy dress, together with performing, was an important part of the social life of the Bloomsbury Group. Bell recalls the Post-Impressionist Ball: 'It was sometime during that winter [1911] that a fancy dress dance was held at Crosby Hall which a group of us attended dressed more or less like figures from Gauguin.... We got stuffs I had lately found at Burnetts' ... with which we draped ourselves ... and had very little on beneath the draperies and when we arrived in a body at Crosby Hall the dancers stopped and applauded us. However, our success was not universal for Mrs Whitehead was horrified at our indecency.'[15] In 1911 Virginia moved into shared housing at 38 Brunswick Square, with her brother Adrian Stephen, Duncan Grant, Maynard Keynes, and Leonard Woolf, whom she would marry in 1912.

Later, at a 1936 party at Charleston, Bell also recalls Duncan Grant dressing as a Spanish dancer: 'I have never seen something quite so indecent. He has made himself a figure in cardboard of a nude female, which is none too securely attached by tapes to his own figure, and then he wears a simpering mask, a black wig and a Spanish comb and mantilla, which partly conceals and reveals the obscene figure, while a Spanish air is played on the gramophone and Duncan flirts gracefully with a fan.'[16]

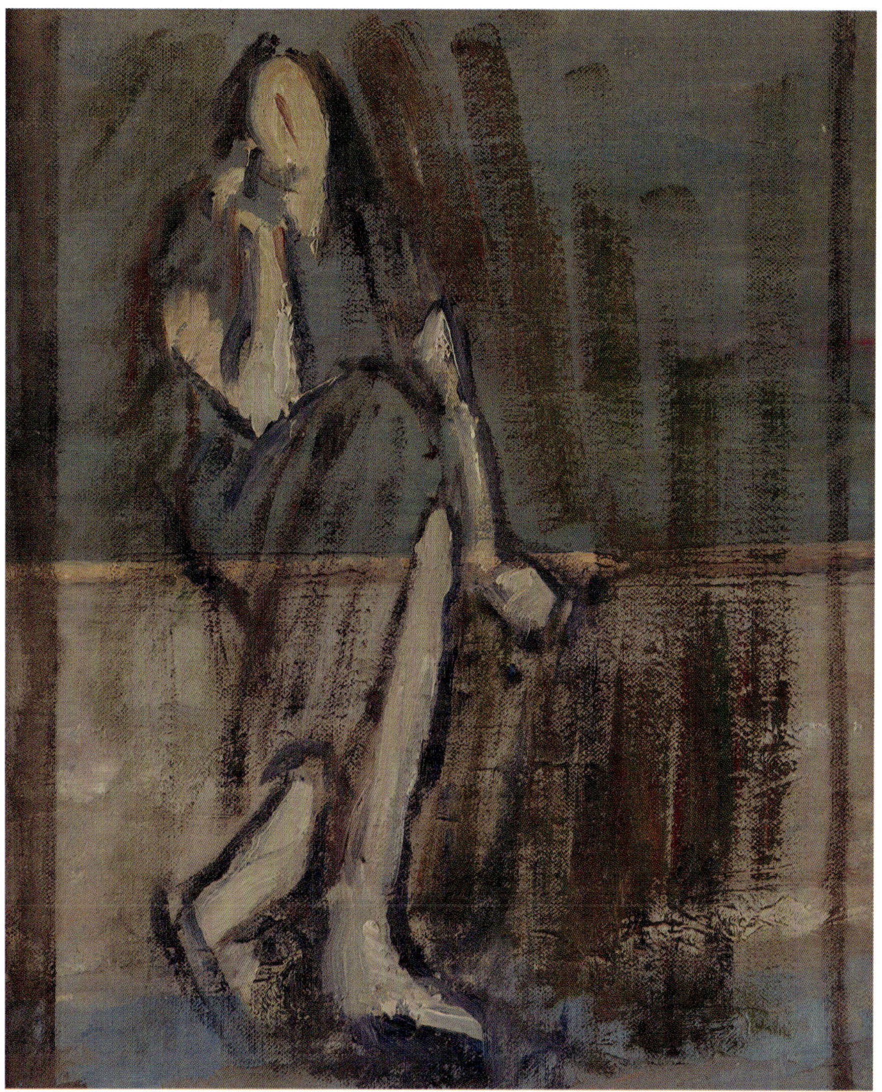

Paper mosaic of two women and a child

*c.*1912 | coloured paper, pencil, small squares of coloured papers, glue and cardboard | 37 × 54.5 cm

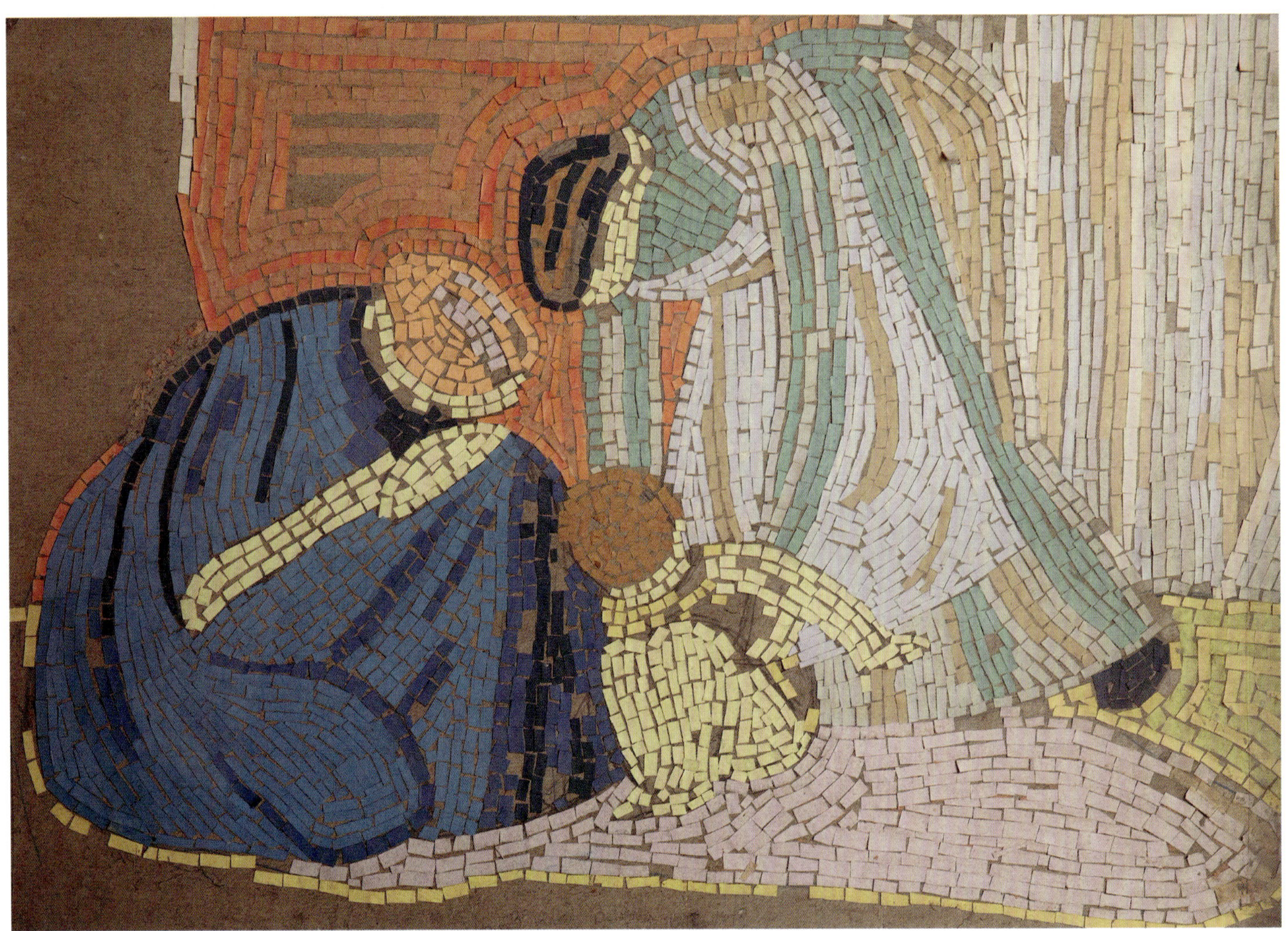

In the spring of 1912 the Bells, together with Roger Fry, went to Milan, where Vanessa became ill with measles. Again, Fry nursed her and brought her some coloured papers, which she cut into small squares and stuck on board, making paper mosaics. This collage is a rare surviving example of this technique, used to depict two stooped women tending to a child.

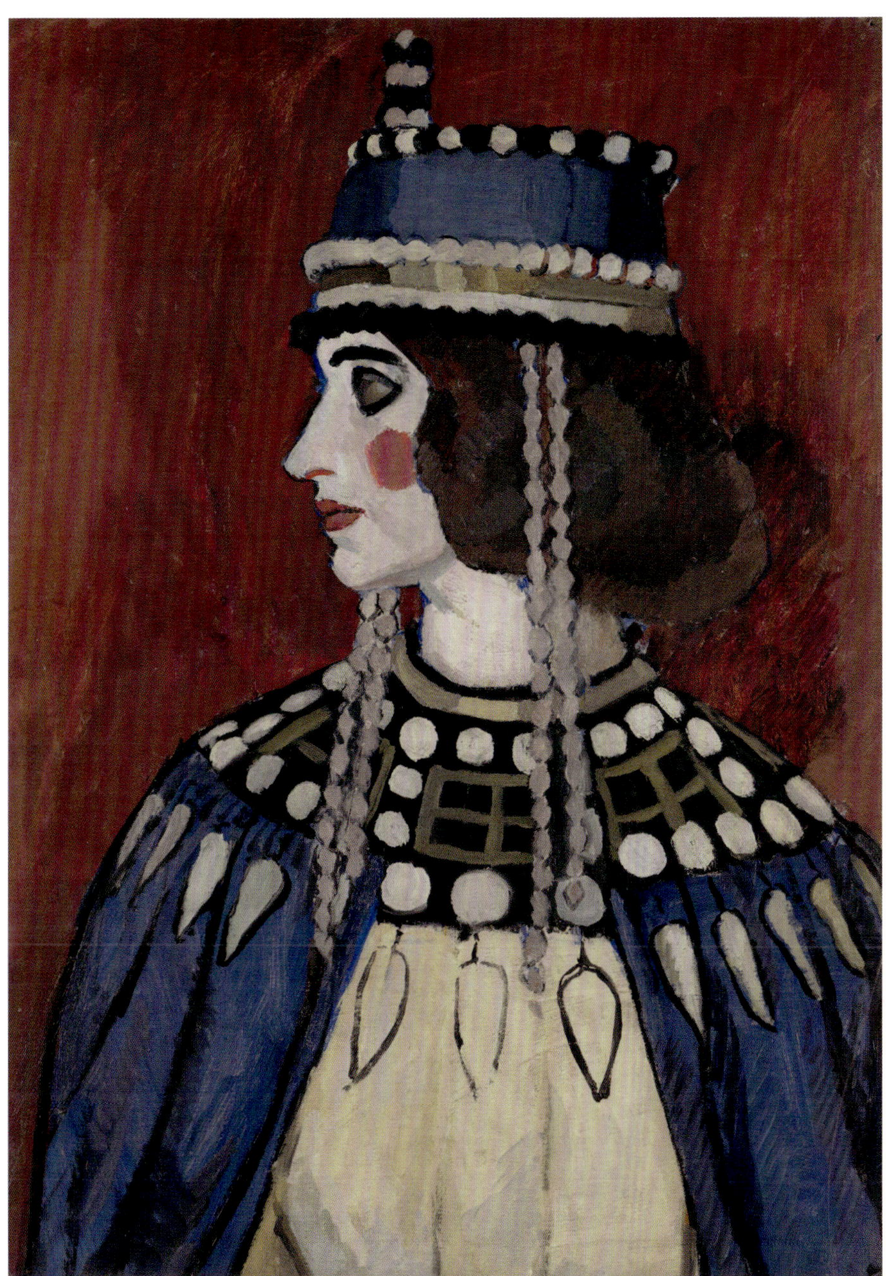

Byzantine Lady

1912 | oil on composite board |
72 × 51.5 cm

This painting shows a Spanish
model hired by Duncan Grant,
whom both artists painted. The
heavily made-up model is painted
in a style which Bell had just
started using, moving away from
the almost pointillist technique fa-
voured by Grant, to work in larger
patches of colour. In early 1912
Bell and Grant visited the sixth-
century mosaics at the Basilica of
San Vitale in Ravenna, in which
the Byzantine Empress Theodora
(r. 527–548) is a central figure.
The costume of *Byzantine Lady*
strongly references the mosaic,
which was also reproduced in Clive
Bell's book *Art* in 1914. Empress
Theodora appears again in Bell
and Grant's *Famous Women
Dinner Service* (1932–34, p. 129).

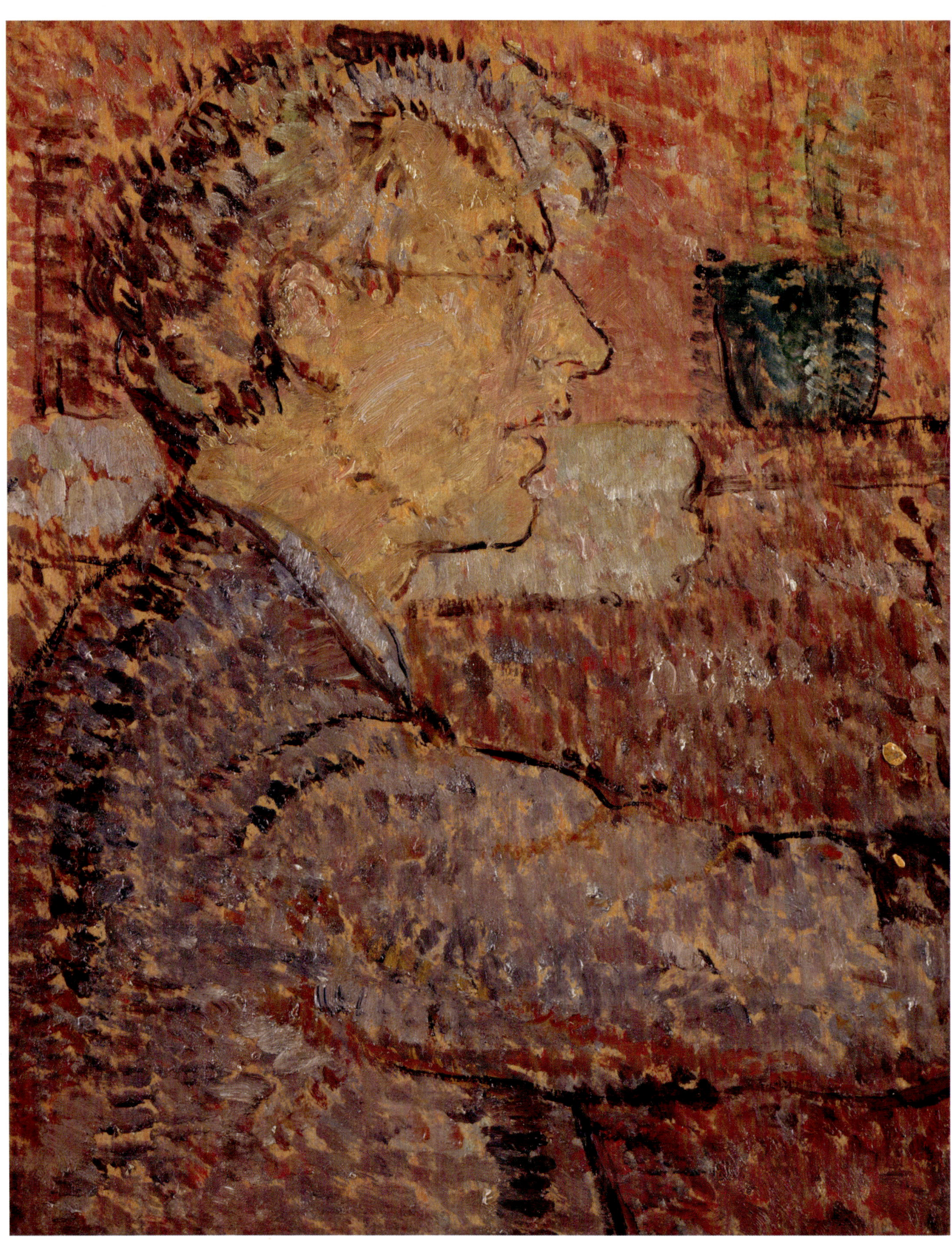

Roger Fry

1912 | oil on panel | 29.3 × 23.6 cm

Roger Fry (1866–1934) was a painter and critic. Initially an Old Masters scholar, he became an advocate of recent developments in French painting, which he named Post-Impressionism. He was the first to raise public awareness of modern art in Britain and was an early champion of abstraction and artists who 'Do not seek to imitate form, but to create form; not to imitate life, but to find an equivalent to life.'[17] Fry was a long-term friend and collaborator with Bell. This portrait was painted during a holiday on the Isle of Wight, in 1912, when they were also romantically involved. In this painting, Bell adopted a pseudo-pointilliste technique, using dabs of unmixed paint. Bell wrote to Clive: 'I did a sketch of Roger yesterday in Duncan's leopard manner with odd results but very like and today Roger is doing one of me. I've persuaded him to try the leopard technique too and he isn't at all happy in it but is spotting away industriously in the hopes of getting at something in the end.'[18] This is a rare work by Bell in this manner, and relates to other experimental pieces she produced around this time in paper mosaic (c. 1912, p. 40) and later works in which she applied larger patches of colour.

Virginia Woolf

c.1912 | oil on panel | 41 × 31 cm

Virginia Woolf (née Stephen, 1882–1941), considered one of the most important twentieth-century modernist authors, was a pioneer of the use of stream of consciousness as a narrative device. Her best-known works include the novels *Mrs Dalloway* (1925), *To the Lighthouse* (1927) and *Orlando* (1928). She is also known for her essays, such as *A Room of One's Own* (1929).

This is likely the first in a series of four portraits of Virginia by Bell made around 1912, and the only one in which Woolf's facial features are detailed.[19] In this example, the forms are outlined with a dark colour reminiscent of paintings such as Henri Matisse's *Girl with Green Eyes* (1908, San Francisco Museum of Modern Art), which Bell would have seen in Roger Fry's exhibition *Manet and the Post-Impressionists* at London's Grafton Galleries in 1910. The portrait seems to have been completed quickly, with the arms and hands appearing unfinished. It was made at a pivotal point in the two sisters' careers, with Woolf completing her first novel, *The Voyage Out* (1915), and Bell launching her career as a professional artist. Woolf wrote to her sister: 'Nobody except Leonard matters to me as you matter.... I always feel I'm writing more for you than for anybody.'[20]

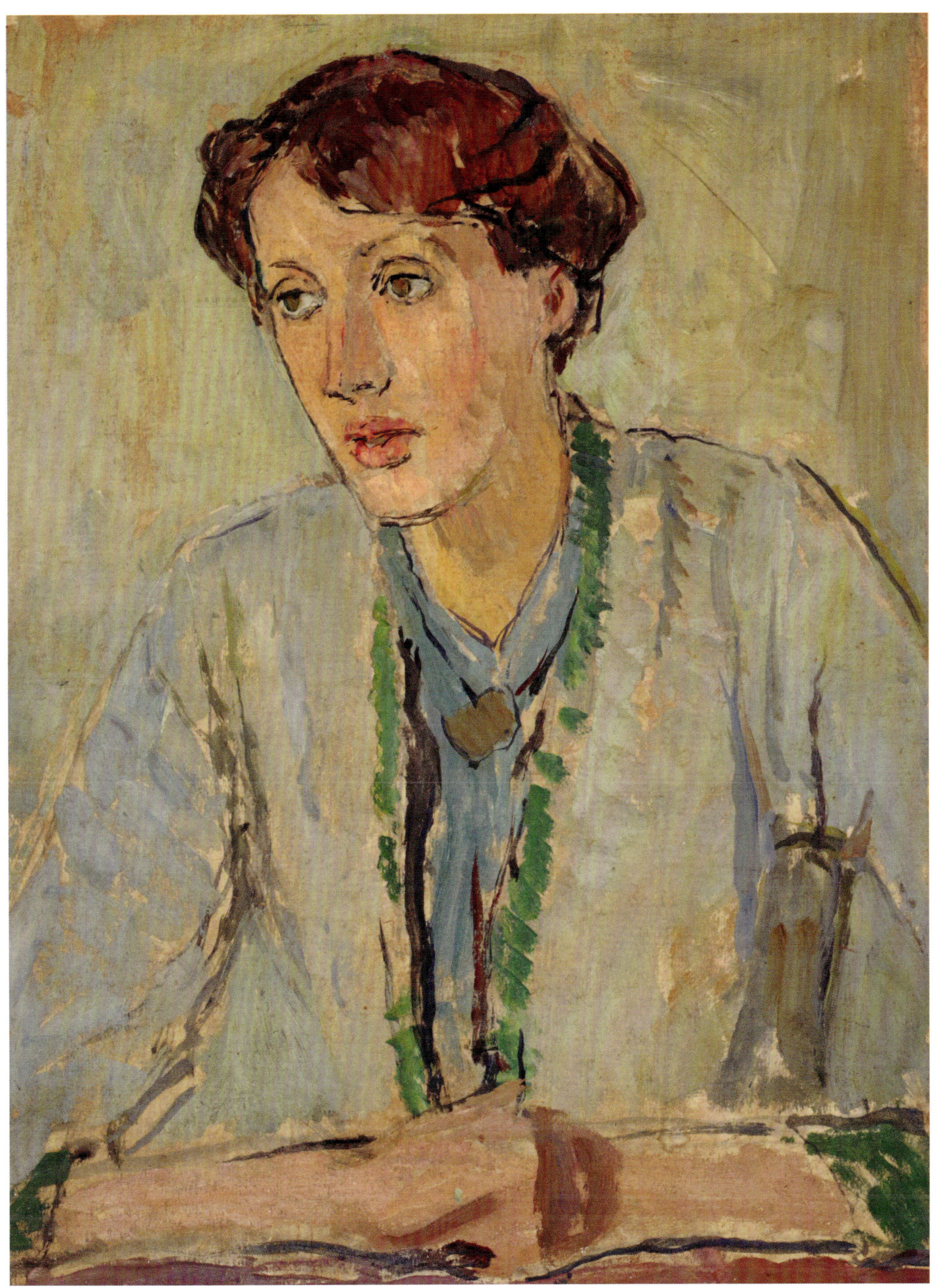

A MODERNIST APPROACH **PAULINA OLOWSKA**

When I was 28 I had my first solo show in a public gallery, entitled
she knew she had to reject the idea of a house as a metaphor, at the
Kunstverein Braunschweig, Villa Salve Hospes, in Germany. By
then I intuitively knew that I wanted to fill the villa with women
ghosts. The main room, adorned with Venetian mirrors and
an old parquet floor and overlooking the gorgeous park, in
springtime seemed to beckon like an invitation to a ball.
Virginia, Vanessa, Charlotte and Nina attended; they danced
until midnight. Afterwards, I awoke next to large panel
paintings on wheels representing Woolf, Bell, Perriand and
Hamnett.

This installation, envisioned as a modern *salon des femmes*,
featured portraits of my favourite women artists, painted
on-site during quiet evenings alone in the villa. By replicating
these selected portraits I aimed to emphasize the importance
of these figures – their forward thinking and independence,
which paved the way for self-expression and the construction
of female artistic identity. Despite their subtlety and
decadence, they managed to confound the authorities of
conventional taste-makers. Critics often considered their
work 'too genteel' to be highly avant-garde, as it was more a
continuation of traditional portraiture and applied art rather
than a break into new styles. Dressed in remarkably outlandish
avant-garde costumes, they positioned themselves as both
subjects and objects of a modernist network, challenging and
enriching the narrative of modernism.

The inspiration partly stemmed from my enchantment with
the Bloomsbury circle and Vanessa Bell. I marvelled at the idea
of a collective that integrated various forms of art, co-owned and
shared, which resonated with the ethos I admired in Bell's move to
Bloomsbury in 1904 with Virginia and their brothers, where they
mingled with the future members of the Bloomsbury Group and

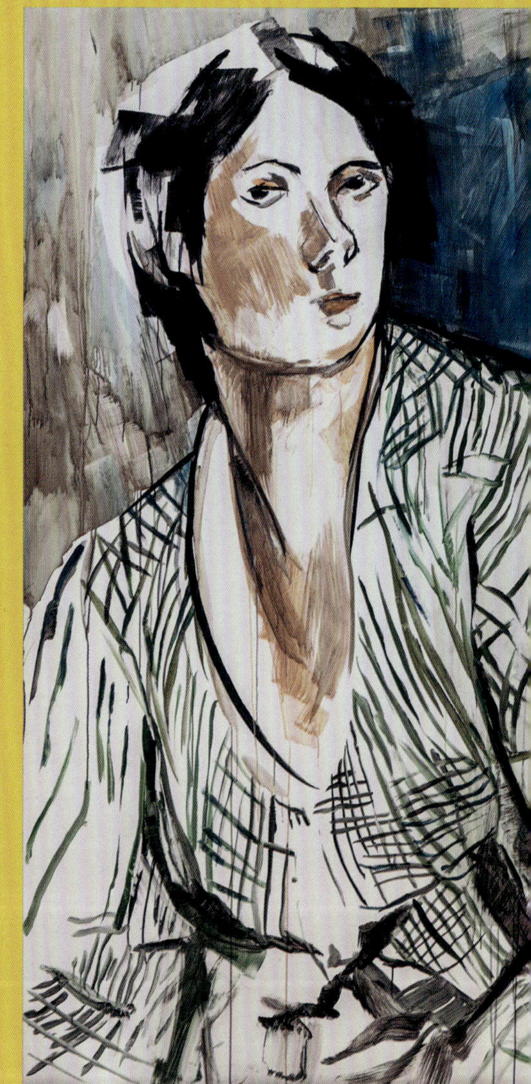

Paulina Olowska, *Vanessa*, 2004.

participated in the Omega Workshops.

My interest in the integration of all arts and the idea of sharing, co-owning works was apparent in the ceramic works of Roger Fry and Bell. This philosophy of living art was further exemplified by the Nova Popularna Salon/Bar project in Warsaw, which I co-created in 2004. We designed an entire setting to host guests, from chairs to bar paintings and whisky, embodying a creatively vibrant environment.

In *Woman Artists and Writers: Modernist (Im)positionings* (1994), Bridget Elliott and Jo-Ann Wallace provided profound insights into how the mode of dressing and expressing themes during the 1920s and 1930s could revolutionize and lead to a modernist approach in art. I was fascinated by how, through a classical approach to painting, these artists expressed more than those who sought to renew painting methods like Impressionism or Cubism. They achieved this through subject matter and colour saturation, and also by their choice of subjects. I am captivated by portraits, such as the one of her sister Virginia (p. 45); the compression and expression of the face are mesmerizing, including the *Portrait of Molly MacCarthy* (p. 52).

But I am also intrigued by the way Bell related to her figures, like in *Seated Female Nude* (c. 1915, private collection), where it is more about the nude woman's relationship to the sunflower, or having the models do knitted hand-work like *Woman in a Red Hat* (1915, p. 80). And a study of a woman where white panels serve as a background but evoke futuristic space motifs, *Study of a Woman* (c. 1917, p. 92). *Girl Drawing* (1932, p. 137) is also pre-feminist and wonderful, where a girl in a yellow scarf with flowers is deeply engaged in painting. Bell's paintings radiate *élan vital,* a sensitivity and openness to observe friendships and what painting should truly be about – capturing the momentum.

Paulina Olowska is a Polish painter and photographer who also works in performance, video and social action.

Walls of Siena

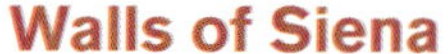

1917 | oil on canvas | 46 × 32 cm

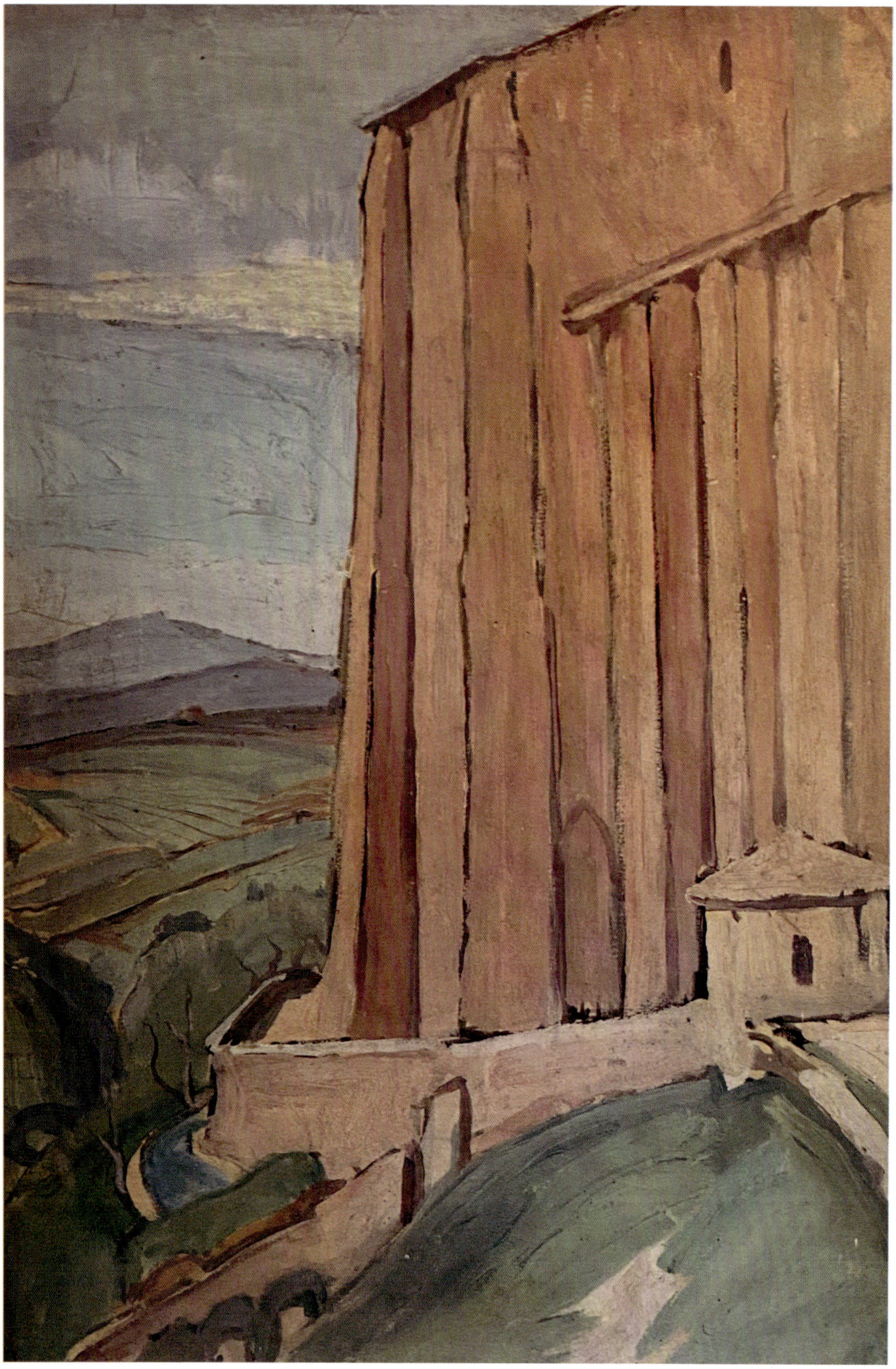

In spring 1912 the Bells and Roger Fry visited Italy. That summer, Vanessa developed the technique of freely outlining forms with a dark line, also seen in the work of Paul Gauguin and the Nabis. At this time, Bell's landscapes, strongly influenced by Paul Cézanne, focus on large blocks of colour and flattened planes with views often framed by windows, doorways and bridges. Bell enjoyed visiting Italy throughout her life: 'At almost every corner one comes on some colour or proportion which gives one extraordinary pleasure.'[21] Siena, she recorded, was 'most exquisite though very austere'.[22]

Fry later wrote to Bell: 'Do you remember Pisa and our excursion to S. Piero a Grado where you painted a haystack and I a Romanesque church (symbolic I suspect)?'[23]

Haystacks in Italy

1912 | oil on board | 34.6 × 24.4 cm

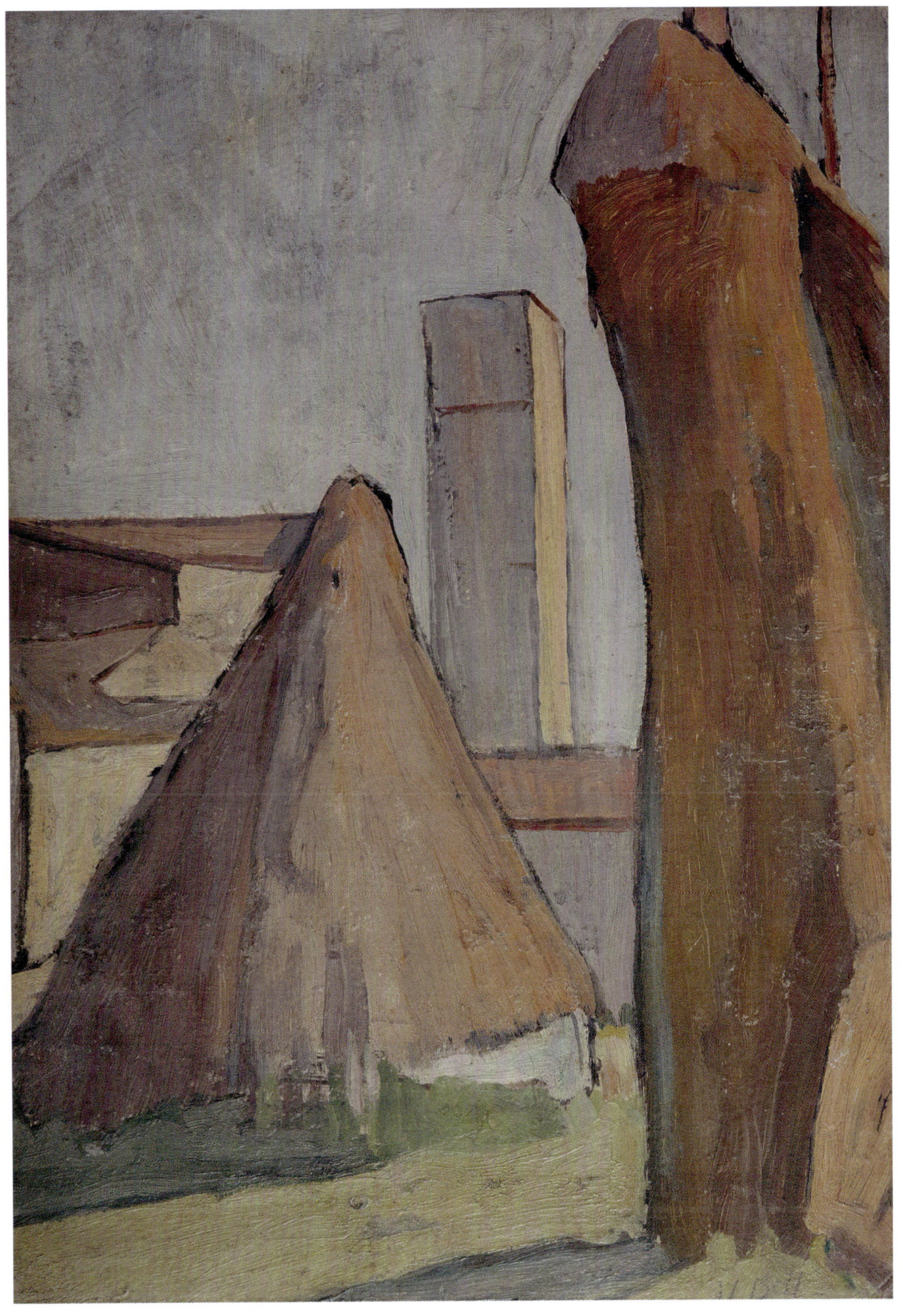

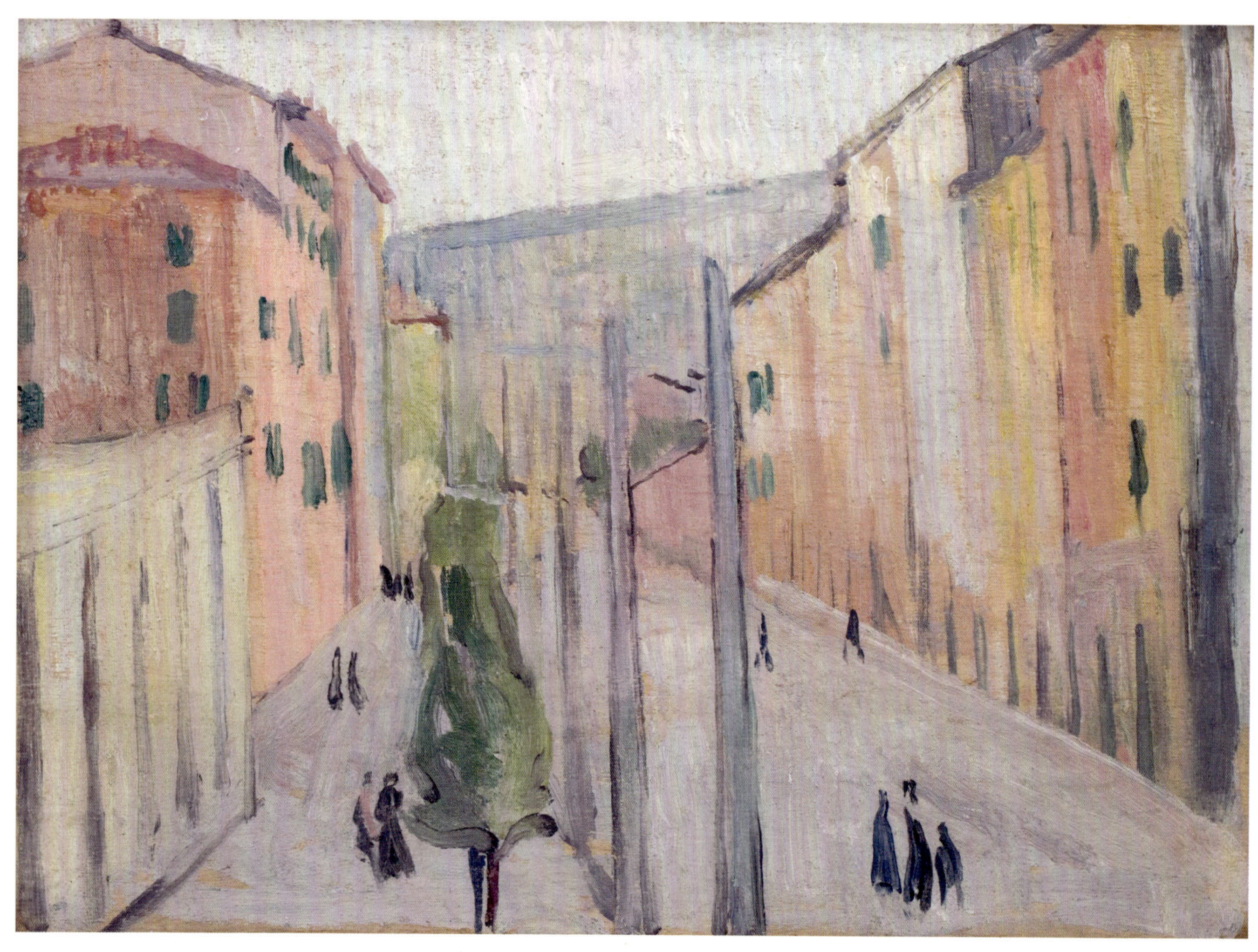

Street Scene in Tuscany

1912 | oil on panel | 25.4 × 35.9 cm

Still-life of Dahlias, Chrysanthemums and Begonias

1912 | oil on canvas | 73 × 51.7 × 2.4 cm

This dynamic painting shows Bell's interest in European Post-Impressionist styles during her most experimental period. Its explosive use of black amid bright colours and a cubist background creates power and movement which is almost unique in Bell's still lifes. Here, she uses free-flowing black lines to outline her forms, in a technique Roger Fry termed her 'slithery handwriting'.[24]

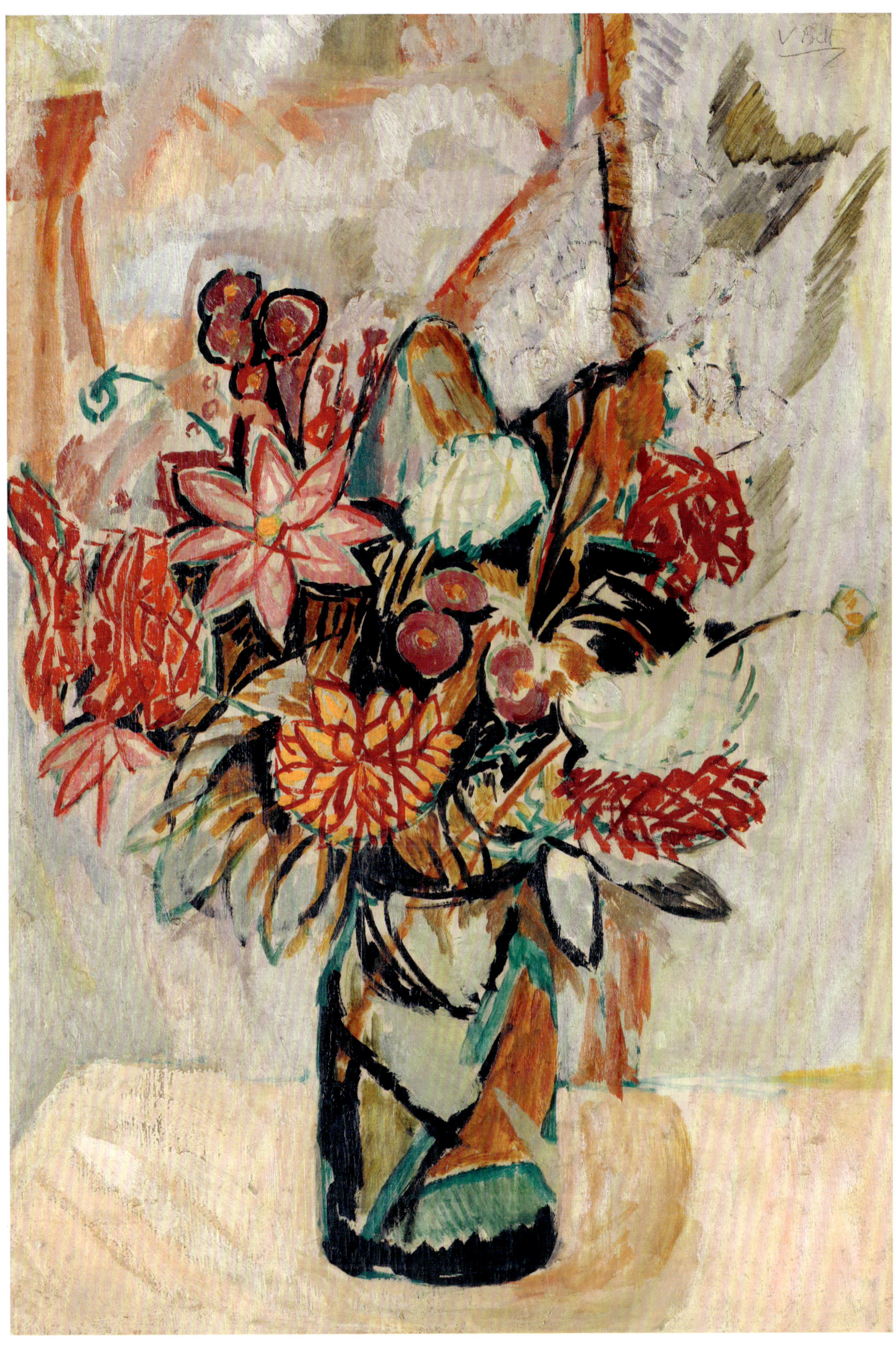

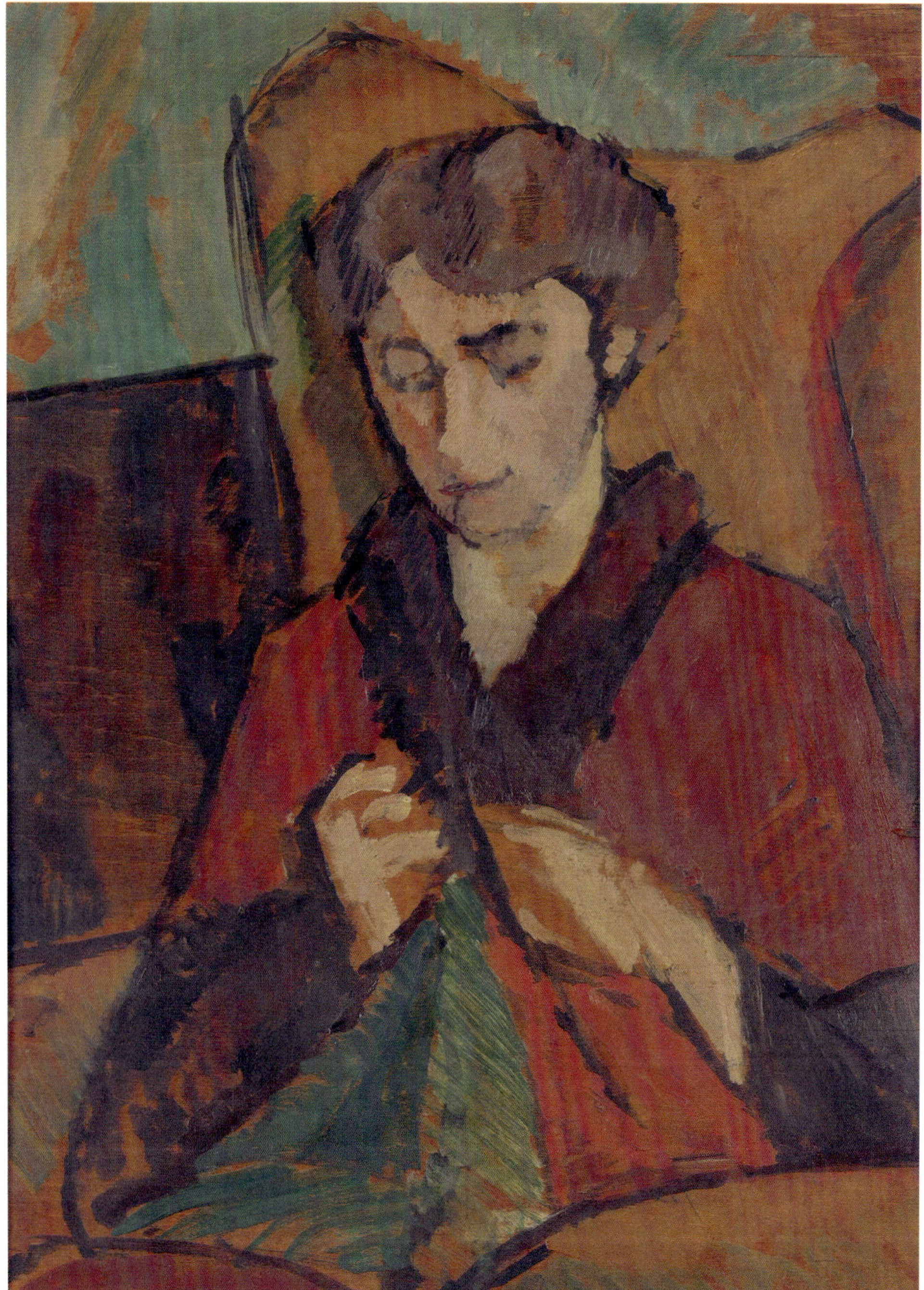

Portrait of Molly MacCarthy

1912 | oil on panel | 58.4 × 43.2 cm

Author Molly MacCarthy (née Mary Warre-Cornish, 1882–1953) and Bell were lifelong friends. Bell made several portraits of her, painted her at least three times at Asheham House in 1912 and photographed her naked in 1914 at 46 Gordon Square (see pp. 14–15). MacCarthy instigated the Memoir Club in 1920, at which its members, all early Bloomsbury Group figures, read short autobiographical papers. Her best-known book is *A Nineteenth-Century Childhood* (1924). In this portrait the sitter is shown concentrating on her sewing. The same orange armchair appears in numerous portraits of the period, including two of Virginia Woolf (both 1912, National Portrait Gallery and Smith College Museum of Art) and *Conversation Piece* (1912, p. 55).

Portrait of Henri Doucet

1912 | oil on panel laid to board |
41.8 × 34.5 cm

The French painter Henri Doucet
(1883–1915) met Roger Fry in Paris
in 1911 and was invited to his home
near Guildford, where he met
Bell and Duncan Grant.[25] Five of
Doucet's paintings were included
in the *Second Post-Impressionist
Exhibition* (1912), and in 1913
Doucet contributed decorations,
pottery and painted textiles to the
Omega Workshops.[26] The year 1912
was extremely important in Bell's
career, in which she embraced
Post-Impressionism and undertook
several experiments in style and
technique. Asheham House in
the Sussex Downs was rented and
became an outpost for the Bloomsbury Group and many visiting
artists. It was during his stay at
Asheham that Bell painted Doucet
several times, sometimes also with
Duncan Grant. This painting is an
example of her technique of laying
down large patches of colour,
outlined in black, with an abstract
background.

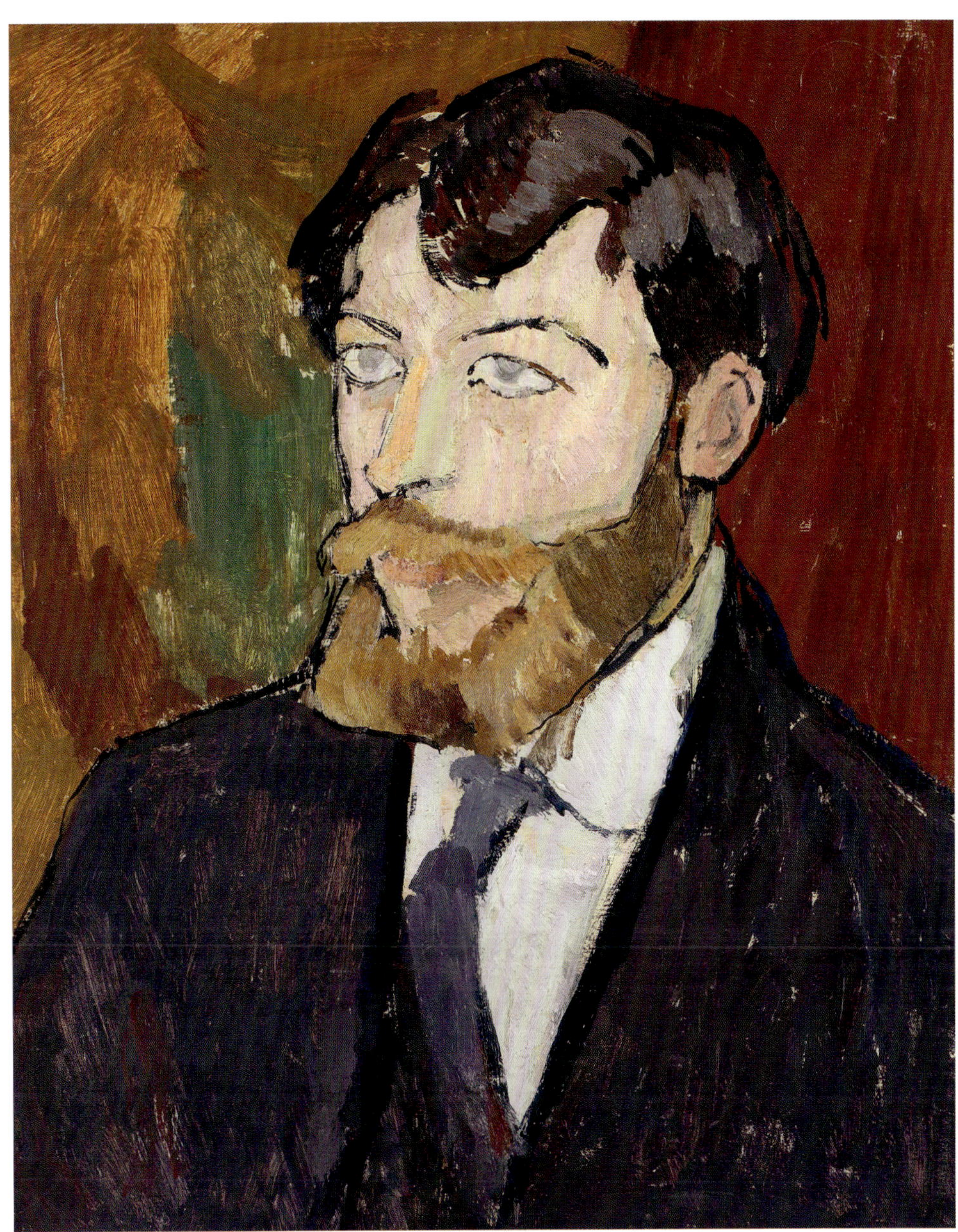

1912 | oil on wood | 51.1 × 53 cm

Frederick Etchells (1886–1973) was an artist and architect who contributed to the Omega Workshops before breaking away from the group with Wyndham Lewis. Etchells is best known for his English translation of Le Corbusier's *Vers une architecture* (*Towards a New Architecture*, 1927). His sister Jessie Etchells (1892–1933) was also an artist and showed at the *Second Post-Impressionist Exhibition* (1912) and with the London Group in 1914.

Bell made this painting when the Etchells visited Asheham in 1912. Jessie is seated on the floor with Frederick standing at an easel, outlined against an open French window. In this painting, for the first time, Bell abstracts her subject and omits all details, including facial features. The garden, seen through the open window, and the easels are reduced to flat bands of colour. The repeated red on Jessie's stocking and the curtain (which Bell made) and the green of the garden and the mat serve to flatten the space. The French doors were originally shown closed: the overpainted central vertical is visible immediately to the left of Frederick Etchells's figure.

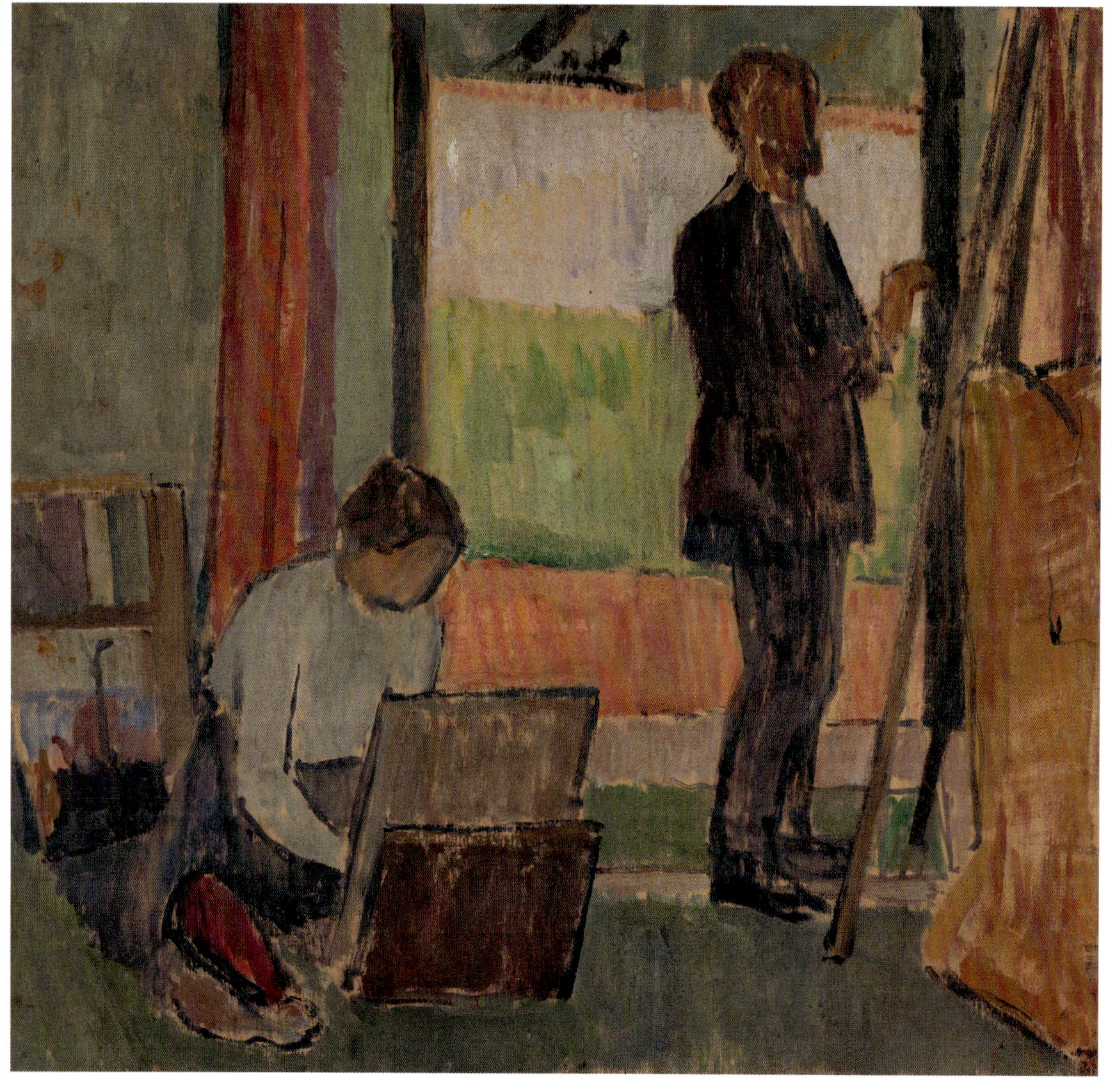

Conversation Piece

1912 | oil on board | 58.5 × 76.5 cm

Conversation Piece was painted either at Asheham House, near Lewes, or Little Talland House in Firle, a rural holiday home rented by Leonard and Virginia Woolf from 1911. [27] Three figures are shown chatting around a fireplace. Despite having featureless faces, they have been identified as: Clive Bell (on the right with blue socks); Leonard Woolf in the centre; and on the left Bell's brother Adrian Stephen, leaning forward as if in animated discussion. A fourth empty chair suggests that another participant has recently left (possibly the artist herself). During this period at Asheham Bell made several portraits with blank faces, including *Virginia Woolf* (1912, National Portrait Gallery) and *Frederick and Jessie Etchells Painting* (1912, p. 54). *Conversation Piece* forms part of this important group in which the artist erases details of faces and clothing to focus on form, gesture and Post-Impressionist colour, provided here by the orange, red and mauve of the chairs.

The years immediately preceding 1914 were revolutionary for the Bloomsbury Group, and conversation was the way in which ideas were worked out. As Leonard Woolf recalled, it was 'The springtime of a conscious revolt against the social, political, religious, moral, intellectual and artistic institutions, beliefs, and standards of our fathers and grandfathers.'[28]

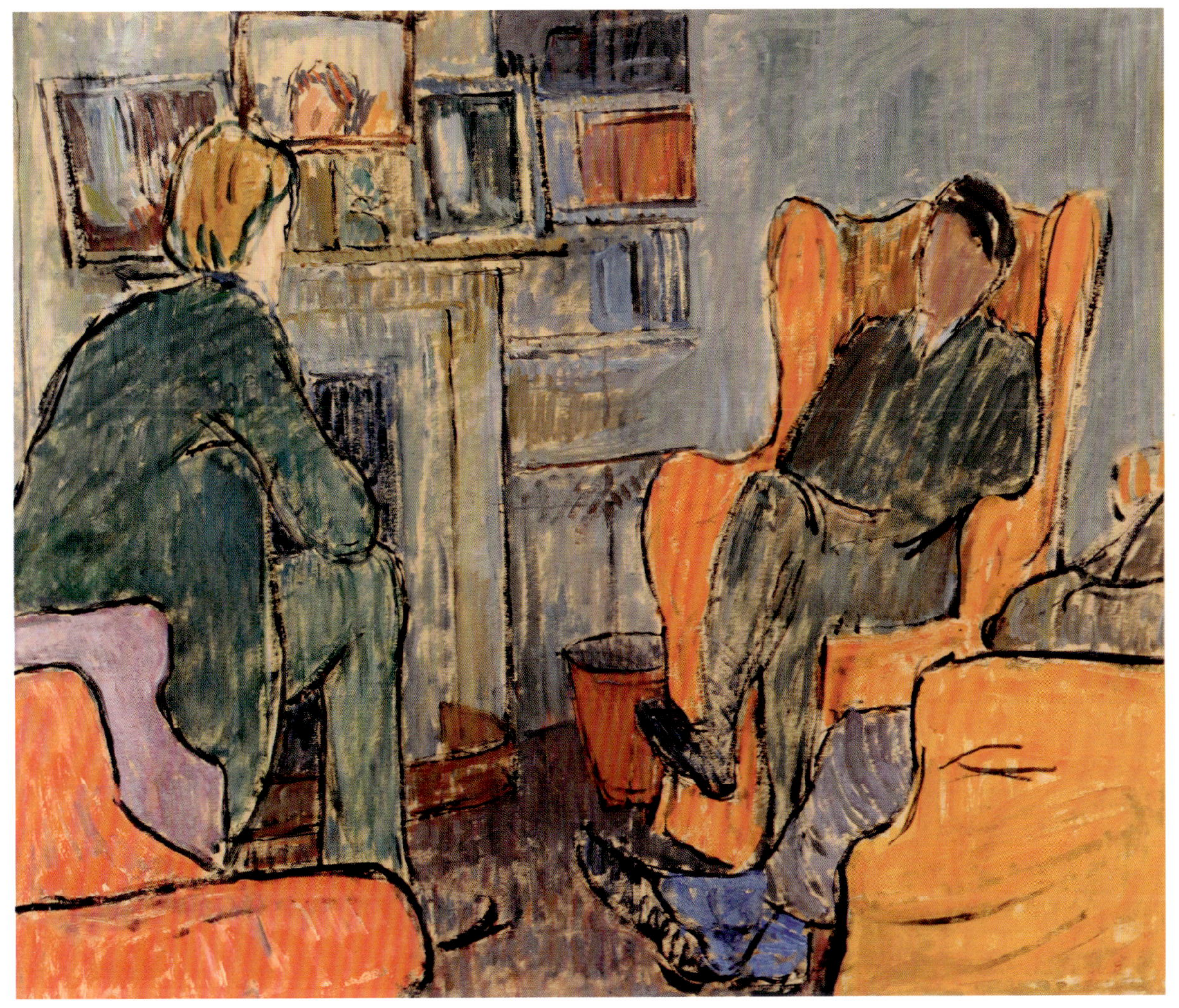

Nursery Tea

c.1912 | oil on canvas | 76.2 × 105.4 cm

Nursery Tea was the largest painting Bell had made and represented a new way of working. She wrote to Roger Fry in June 1912: 'I have been painting my nursery scene, which is rather comic, but I am just in an exciting stage as I flatter myself that I'm painting in an entirely new way.... I am trying to paint as if I were mosaicing, not by painting in spots, but by considering the picture as patches, each of which has to be filled by one definite space of colour, as one has to do with mosaic or woolwork, not allowing myself to brush the patches into each other'.[29] The painting shows two nursemaids with the artist's two young sons: Julian and Quentin, on the left, described by Bell in formalist terms: 'Quentin is the one spot of satisfactory colour with his orange hair in a bright pink dress.'[30]

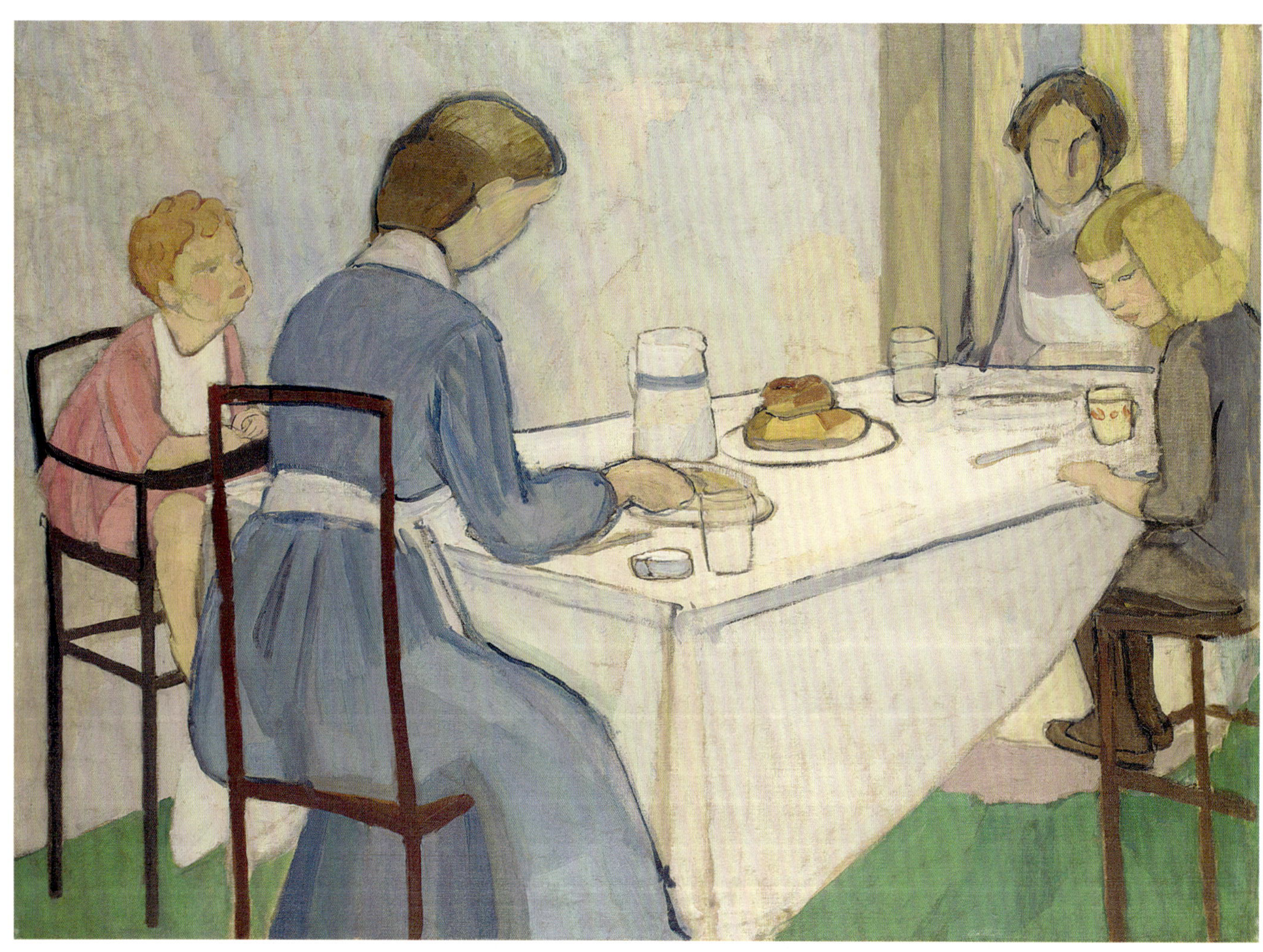

Landscape with Buildings

c.1912 | oil on plywood | 59 × 79 cm

In 1911 Clive Bell bought Pablo Picasso's painting *Pots et Citron* (1907) on a trip to Paris. He paid £4 for it and became one of the first people in Britain to own a Picasso. Vanessa wrote to Virginia Woolf that 'It's "cubist" and very beautiful colour.'[31] In *Landscape with Buildings*, probably painted the year after, echoes of *Pots et Citron* can be seen in the sharp triangle in the foreground, as well as the play of colour across the blue and grey roofs on the left and brown on the right. *Landscape with Buildings* was cut in half horizontally and used to make two shelves for a cupboard in Bell's bedroom.[32] The two halves were reunited and restored by the Charleston Trust. Clive Bell had to sell the *Pots et Citron* in 1957; in its place a copy made by Quentin Bell now hangs at Charleston.[33]

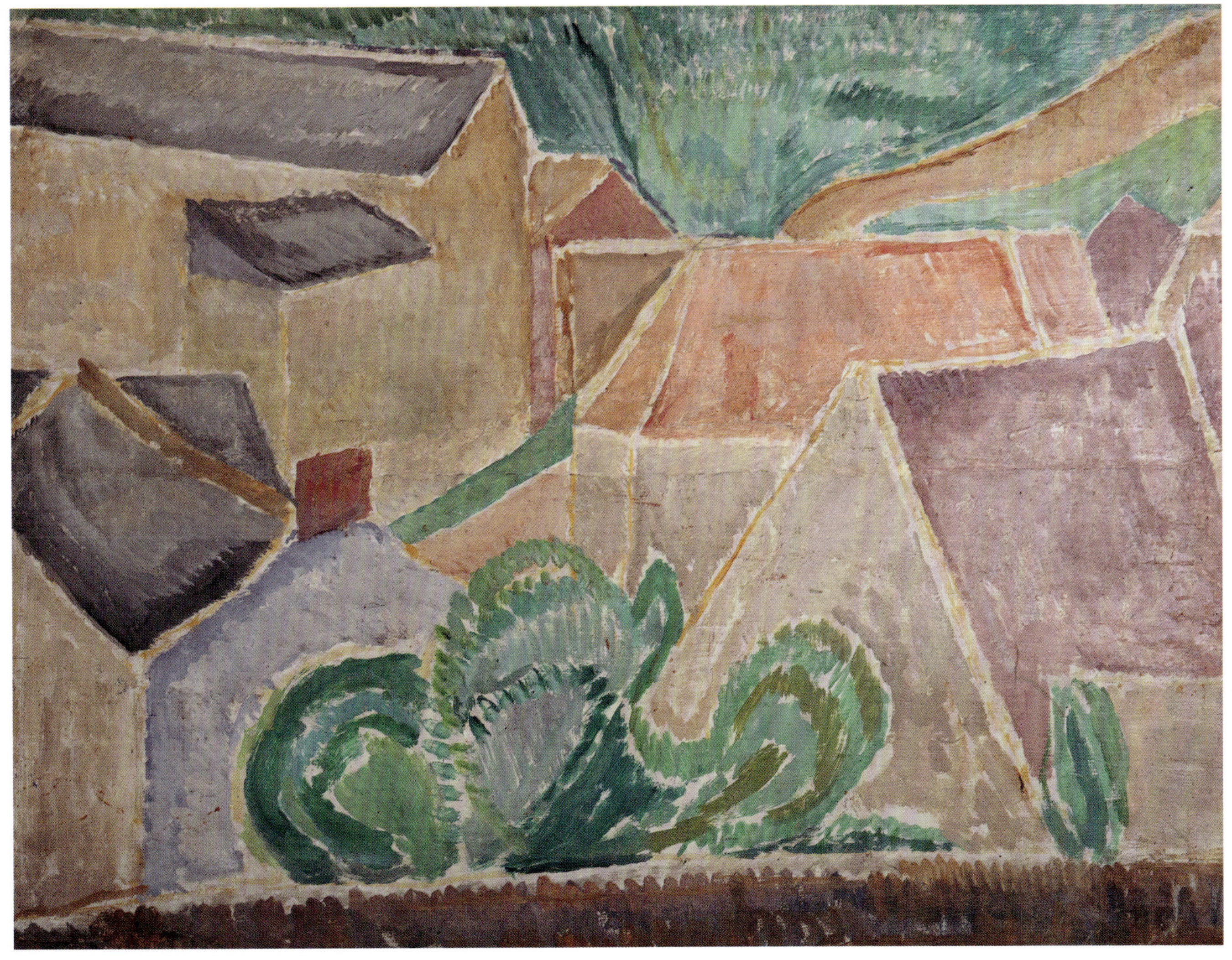

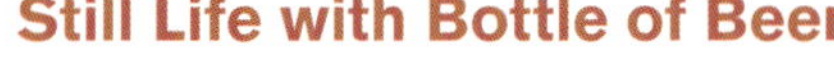

Still Life with Bottle of Beer

1913 | oil on board | 48.3 × 33 cm

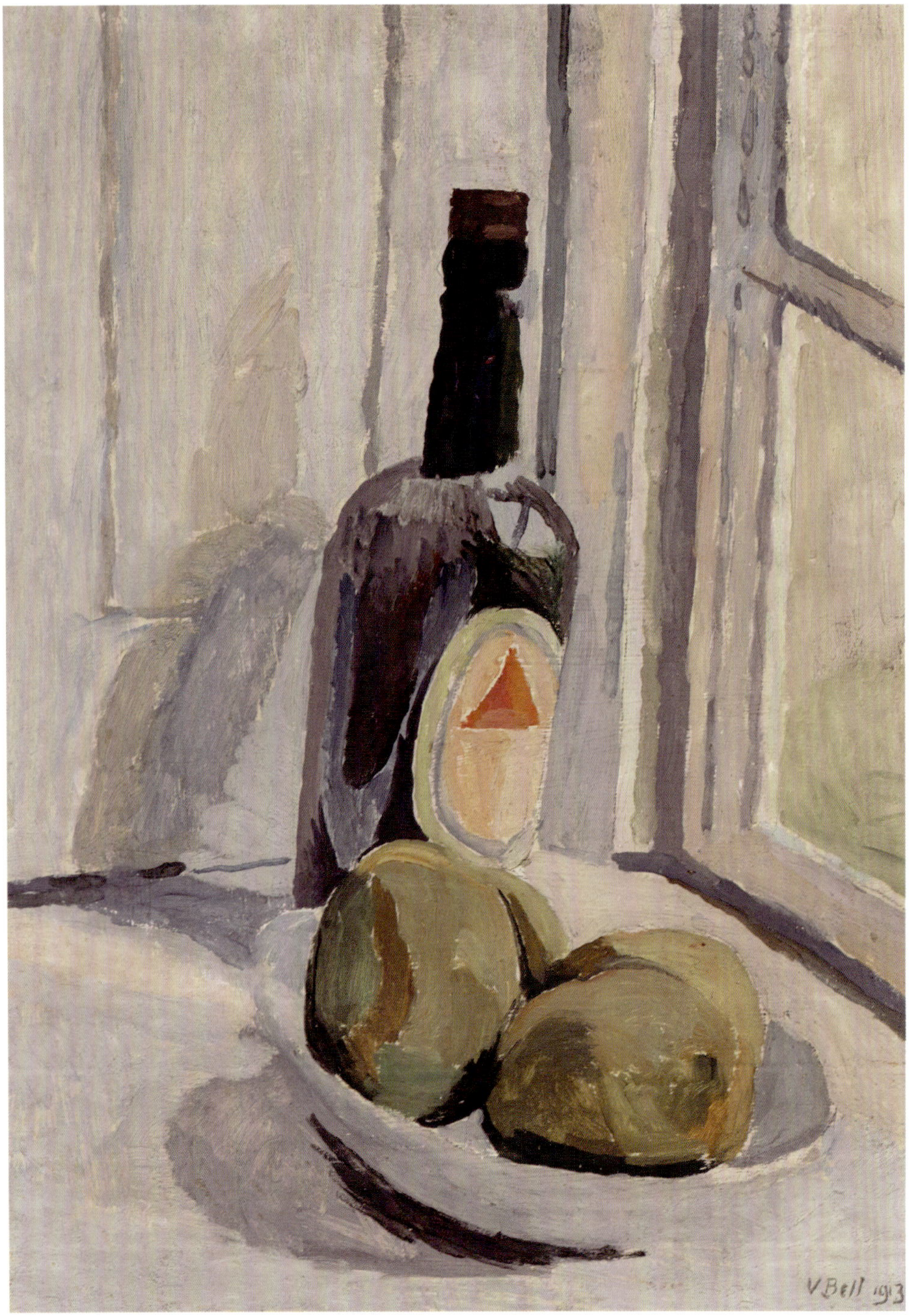

Still Life with Bottle of Beer is similar in its modulated greys to the earlier *Iceland Poppies* (1908–09, p. 35). Here, the red poppy is replaced with the red triangle of the Bass beer label. The bottle is tilted in a way reminiscent of Cézanne, and this is balanced by the strong vertical of the window frame, which Bell often includes in her still lifes. *Still Life with Bottle of Beer* can also be seen as a precursor to *Still Life (Triple Alliance)* (1914, p. 73).

Lytton Strachey

Lytton Strachey (1880–1932) was a writer and critic, another of Thoby Stephen's friends from Cambridge University and Duncan Grant's cousin. Best known for his book *Eminent Victorians* (1918), he established a new form of biography in which psychological insight and sympathy are combined with irreverence and wit.

This portrait shows Strachey reading in a chair. He was also painted by Roger Fry and Grant at the same time. Strachey is shown 'in his Augustus John phase' with a red beard and long hair, and depicted in Fauvist high keyed colour.[34] As art historian Ronald Pickvance wrote in the foreword to Bell's memorial exhibition (1964), it 'points to the road she was then to take.... There are no hesitations, no half-measures; she now combines her simplified schemata of shapes with a new effusion of colour, arbitrary and expressive.'[35]

Bell and Strachey were lifelong friends and she later wrote of him: 'Everyone knows his qualities as a writer, his wit and brilliance. But only those just getting to know him in those days when complete freedom of mind and expression were almost unknown, at least among men and women together, can understand what an exciting world of explorations of thought and feeling he seemed to reveal. His great honesty of mind and remorseless poking fun at any sham forced others to be honest too and showed a world in which one need no longer be afraid of saying what one thought.'[36] John Maynard Keynes later recorded: 'Lytton seems to carry on a good deal with his females, he has let Vanessa see his most indecent poems – she is filled with delight, has them by heart, and has made typewritten copies for Virginia and others.'[37]

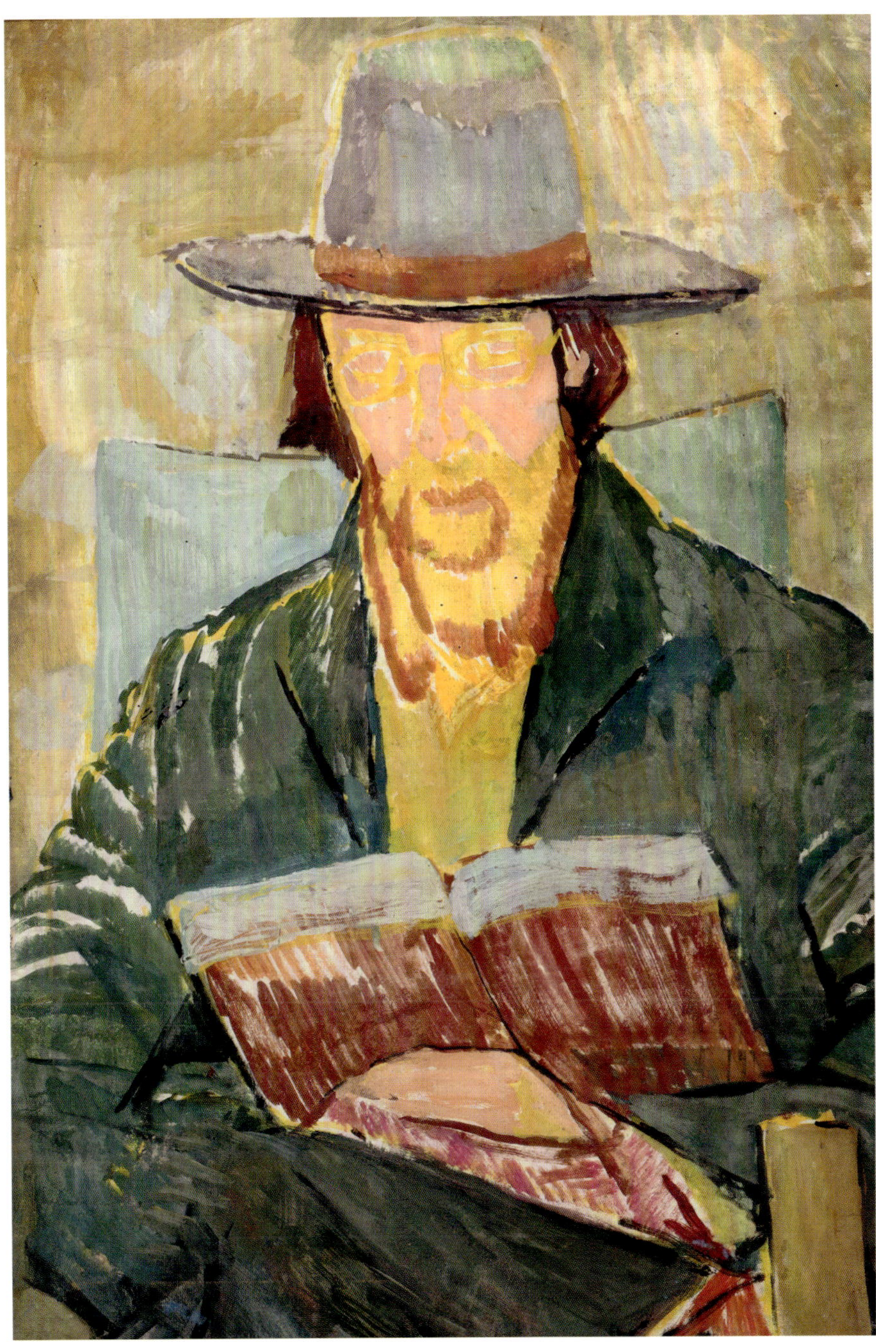

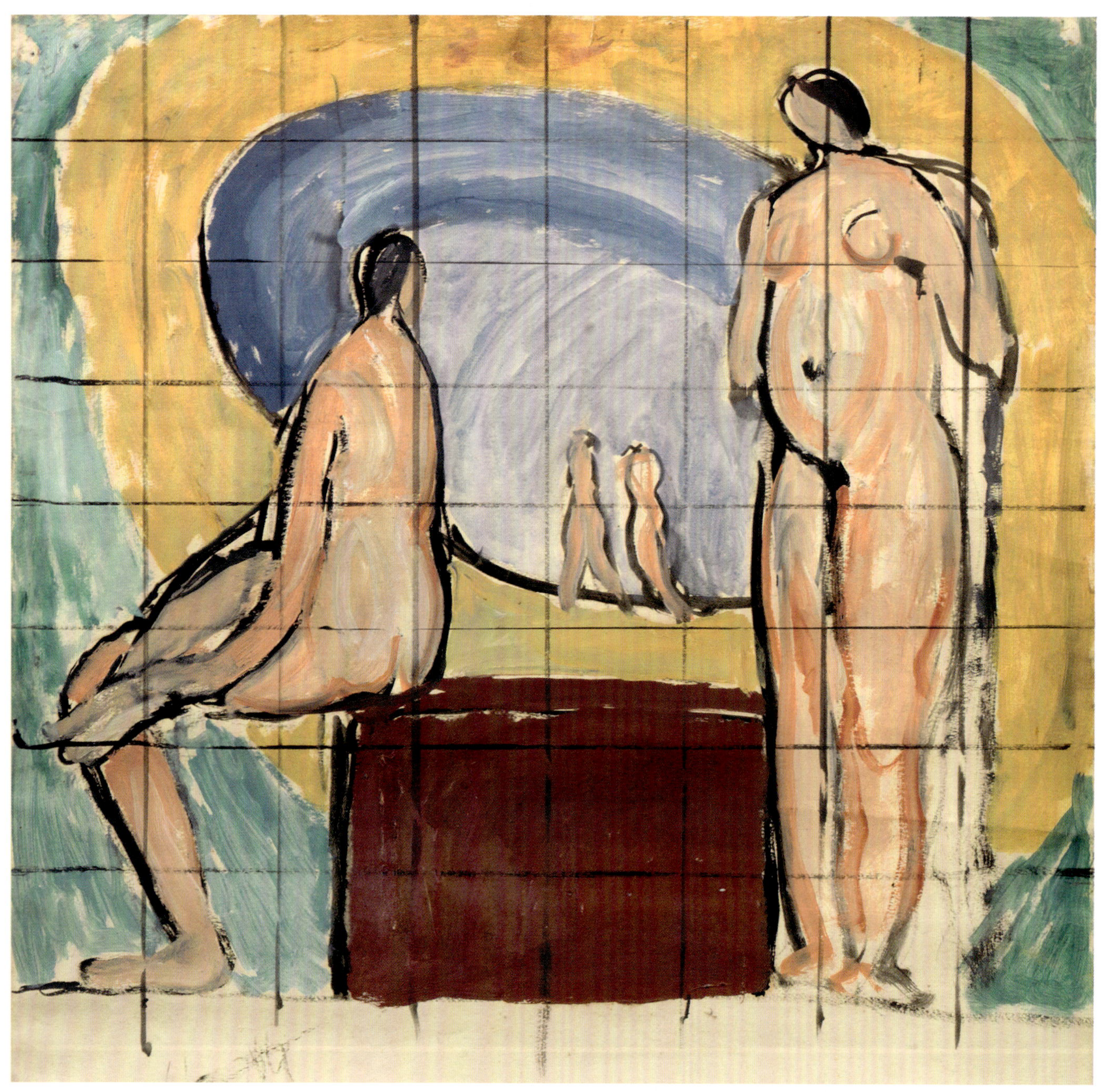

Design for fireplace mural

1912 | oil on paper | 76.3 × 55.8 cm

Two designs for fireplace murals exist by Bell from this period.[38] Both have large female nudes as their main features. These monumental female figures, in Bell's most simplified Post-Impressionist style, are found throughout her work in this period (see pp. vi and 62). In this design one figure sits casually on the mantelpiece. A very large painting corresponding to this design appears in the background of photographs taken by Bell of Marjorie Strachey, Molly MacCarthy and Bell herself, posing nude in her studio at 46 Gordon Square (see pp. 14–15).

Design for a folding screen: Adam and Eve

1913–14 | graphite, bodycolour and oil paint on wove paper | 35.7 × 50.9 cm

The Omega Workshops, established by Roger Fry in 1913 with Duncan Grant and Vanessa Bell as co-directors, sold furniture, fabrics and household accessories designed and made by artists. Designs rejected Edwardian taste, with bright colour and expressive design. They were anti-refinement and anti-expense, aiming to blur the distinction between fine and decorative arts. Objects were shown anonymously and sold unsigned.

The pose of the figure on the right of the screen strongly corresponds to a nude photograph of Bell's friend, the writer Molly MacCarthy, taken by Bell in her studio at 46 Gordon Square, with one arm twisted upwards and the other reaching down towards the floor. The design for this folding screen also appears to have been inspired by Matisse's first version of *The Dance* (1909, Museum of Modern Art, New York; exhibited at the *Second Post-Impressionist Exhibition*, 1912). Equally influential were the Ballets Russes, who first performed in London in 1911. Their 'artists and dancers shared a set of values, prioritising sexual heterodoxy, personal freedom and love of fantastic costume', which chimed with the Bloomsbury Group.[39] Art historian Christopher Reed has discussed Bell's recasting of the Adam and Eve narrative as an 'ambition to have Eden without the Expulsion…. On the left the female braces herself with legs wide apart as she pulls down a branch, as if to shake from it the fruit the male eagerly bends to retrieve. These energetic nudes dance their way through a narrative that promises to end, not with shame and banishment, but in the enveloping warmth of the yellow light they reach into.'[40]

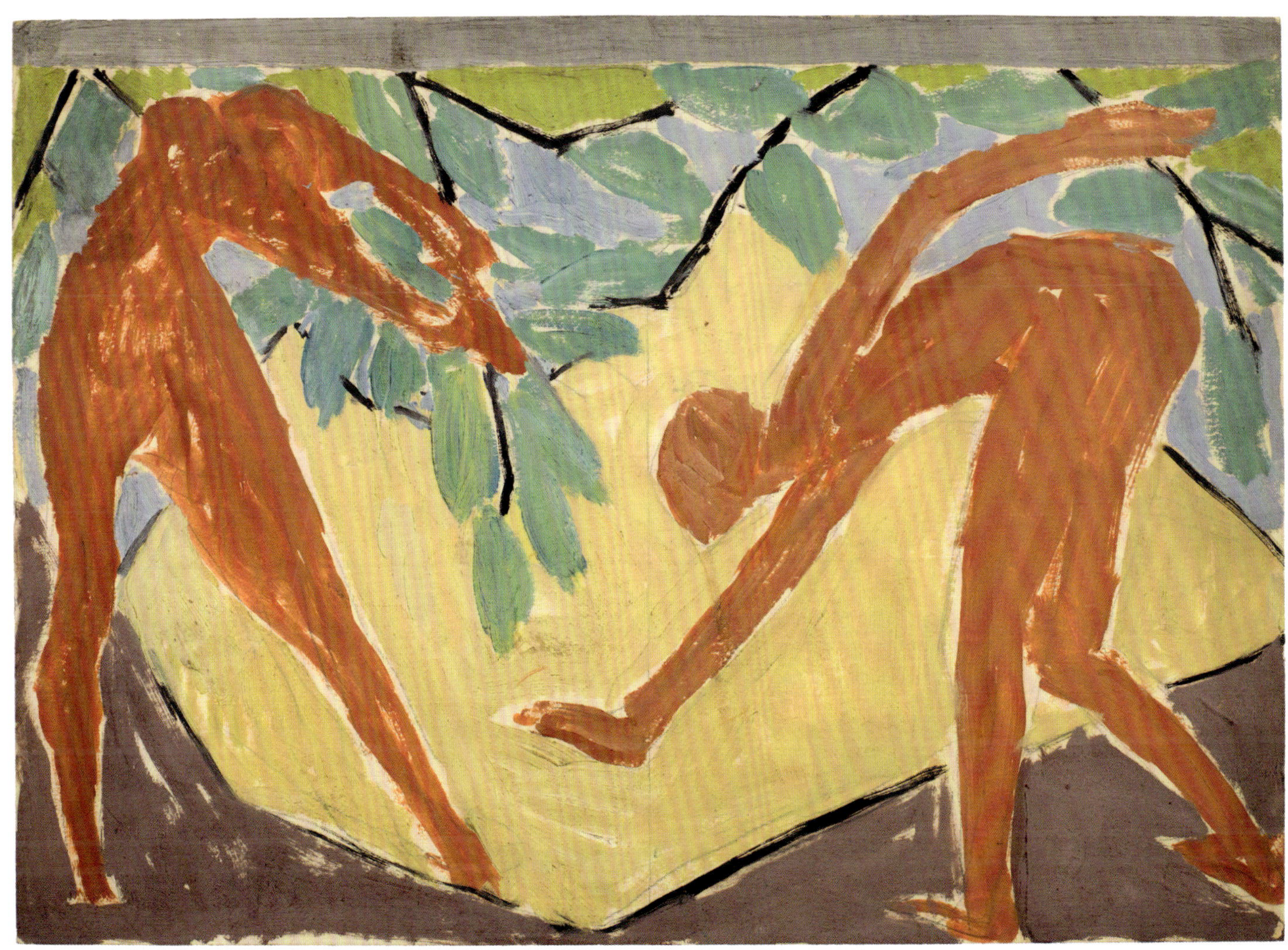

A Conversation

1913-16 | oil on canvas | 86.6 × 81 cm

A Conversation shows three women leaning into conspiratorial conversation. They are placed in front of a window looking out to a garden of colourful flowers. It is not clear whether two of the women are wearing hats or whether their heads line up with plants in the garden beyond. This levels them with the outside, flattening the composition. In the same year that Bell began this work, she wrote to her sister Virginia Woolf about seeing 'one of the best pictures in the world' by Piero della Francesca, in Urbino.[41] It is likely she refers to *Flagellation* (1459–60, Galleria Nazionale delle Marche, Urbino, Italy), which features three figures in conversation. Another important potential inspiration is Matisse's *The Conversation* (1908–12, State Hermitage Museum, Saint Petersburg, Russia), which was shown in the *Second Post-Impressionist Exhibition* (1912). It shows a man and a woman talking in front of a window looking onto a garden with patches of flowers.[42] Frances Spalding notes that it appears Bell reworked the women's dresses, likely making them darker to increase the contrast with the bright flowers.[43]

Virginia Woolf wrote to her sister after seeing the painting (then exhibited as *Three Women*): 'I think you are a most remarkable painter. But I maintain you are into the bargain, a satirist, a conveyor of impressions about human life: a short story writer of great wit and able to bring off a situation in a way that rouses my envy. I wonder if I could write the *Three Women* in prose.'[44] Later Woolf reflected on the absence of representation of female conversation: 'I tried to remember any case in the course of my reading where two women are represented as friends.... Almost without exception they are shown in their relation to men. It was strange to think that all the great women of fiction were, until Jane Austen's day, not only seen by the other sex, but seen only in relation to the other sex. And how small a part of a woman's life is that.'[45] As author Lauren Elkin notes, in *A Conversation* 'We strain to hear what they're saying, but it's only between them.'[46]

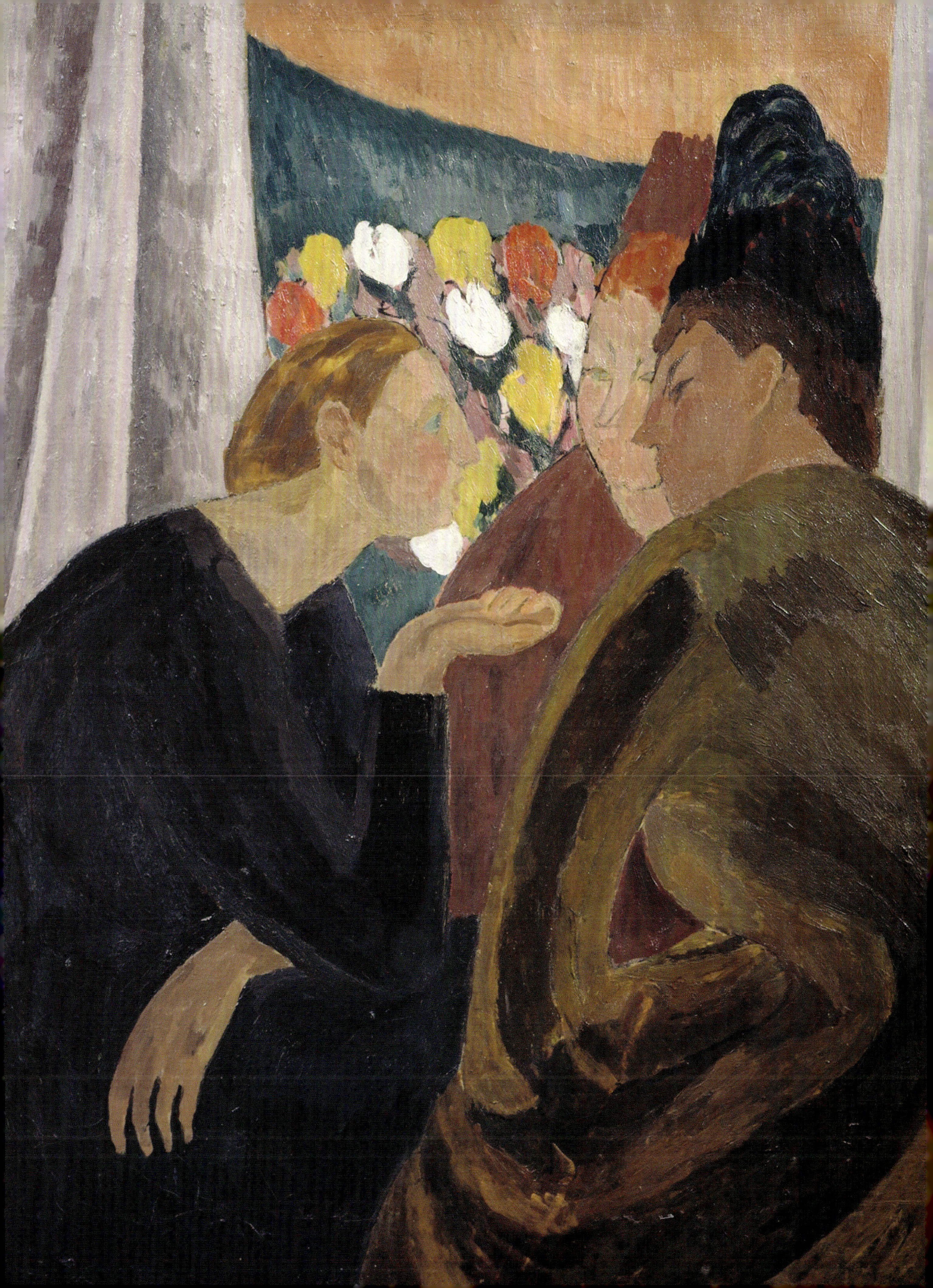

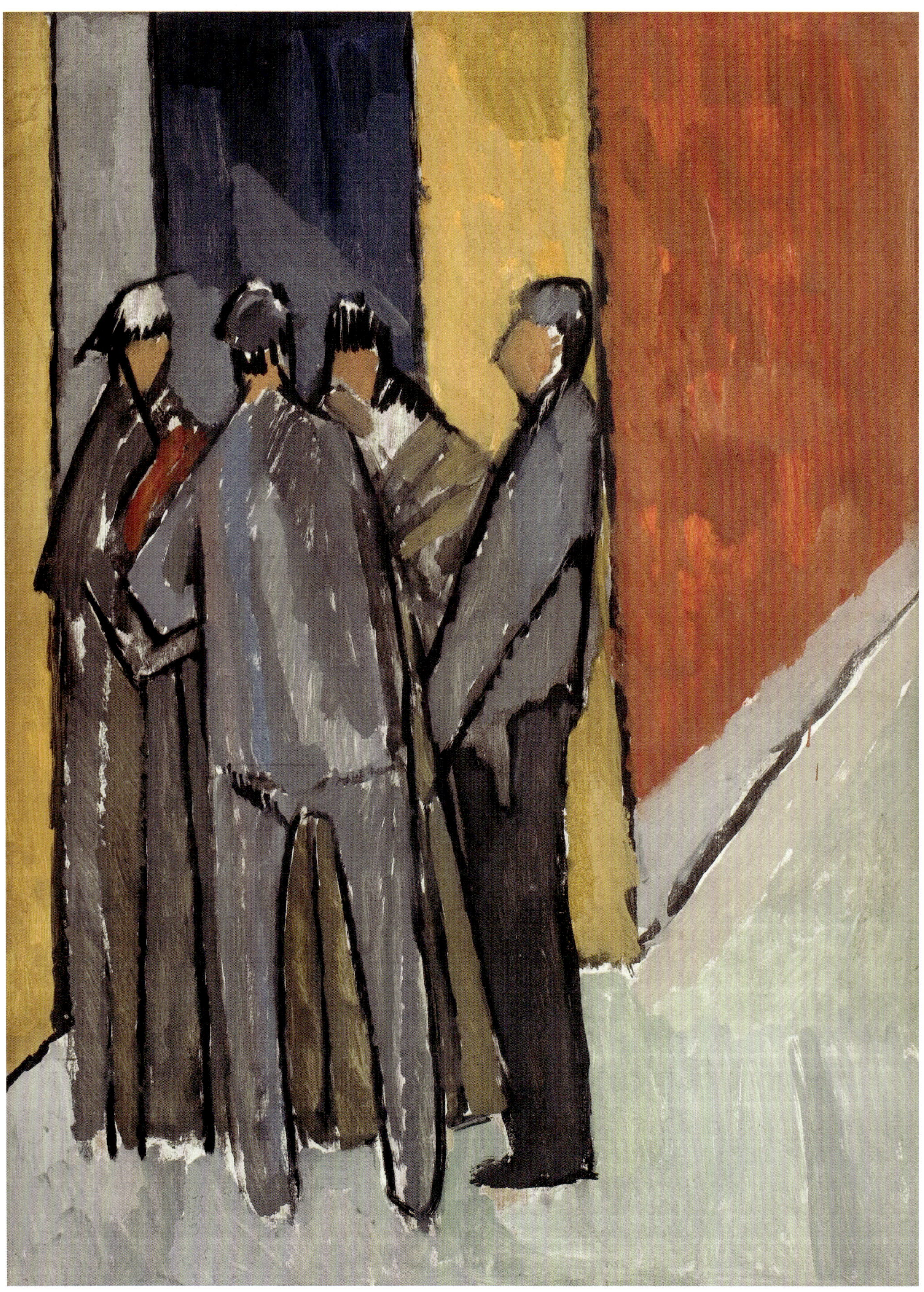

Street Corner Conversation

c.1913 | oil on board | 69 × 52 cm

Street Corner Conversation is one of a number of paintings from this period in which Bell depicts closely grouped figures, including *A Conversation* (1913–16, p. 63) and *Conversation Piece* (1912, p. 55). However, *Street Corner Conversation* is a radical departure in style, with a restricted palette, sharp diagonals and stark bands of colour. Bell's use of grey-greens, blue, ochre and Indian red with accents of black is also characteristic of the period, for example in *Tents and Figures* (1913, Victoria and Albert Museum). Together, these two works are clear precedents for Bell's abstract designs for the Omega Workshops, including *Omega rug design* (1913–14, p. 69) and, shortly after, her experiments in pure abstraction.

Rug design

1913–14 | graphite and bodycolour on wove paper | 47.9 × 56.5 cm

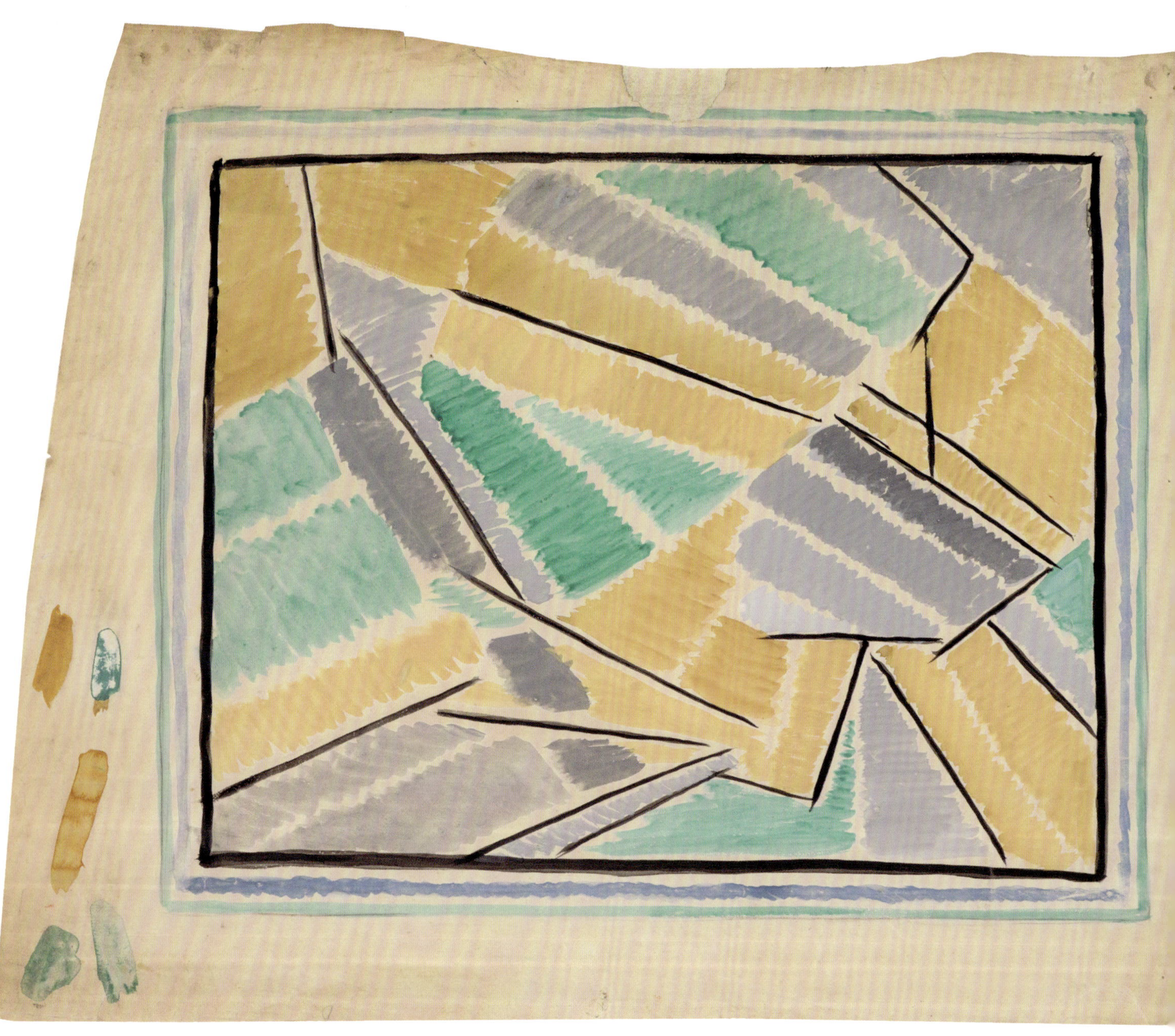

 VANESSA BELL

Rug design

1913–15 | graphite and bodycolour over a grid of pen and black ink lines, on wove paper | 42.5 × 57.3 cm

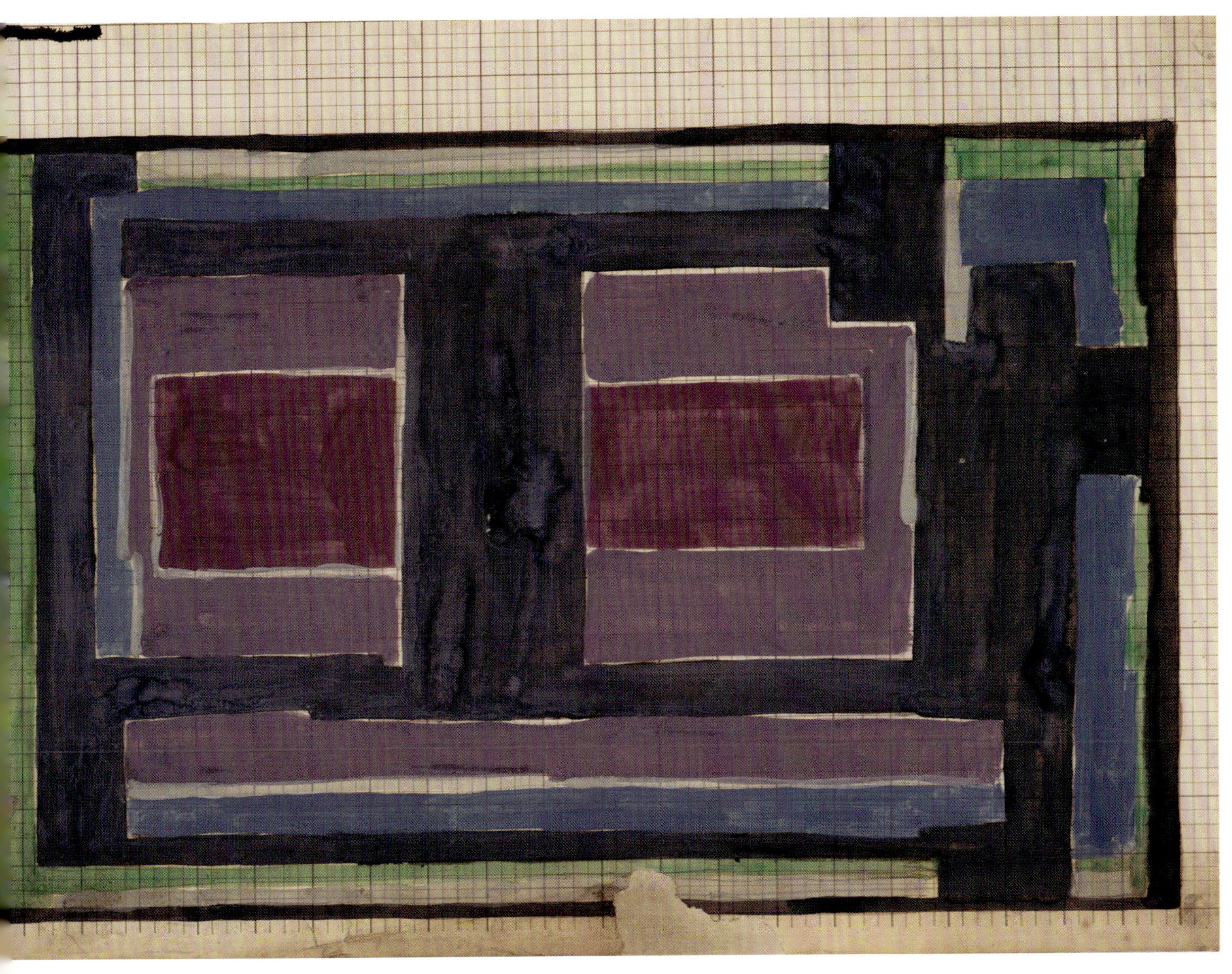

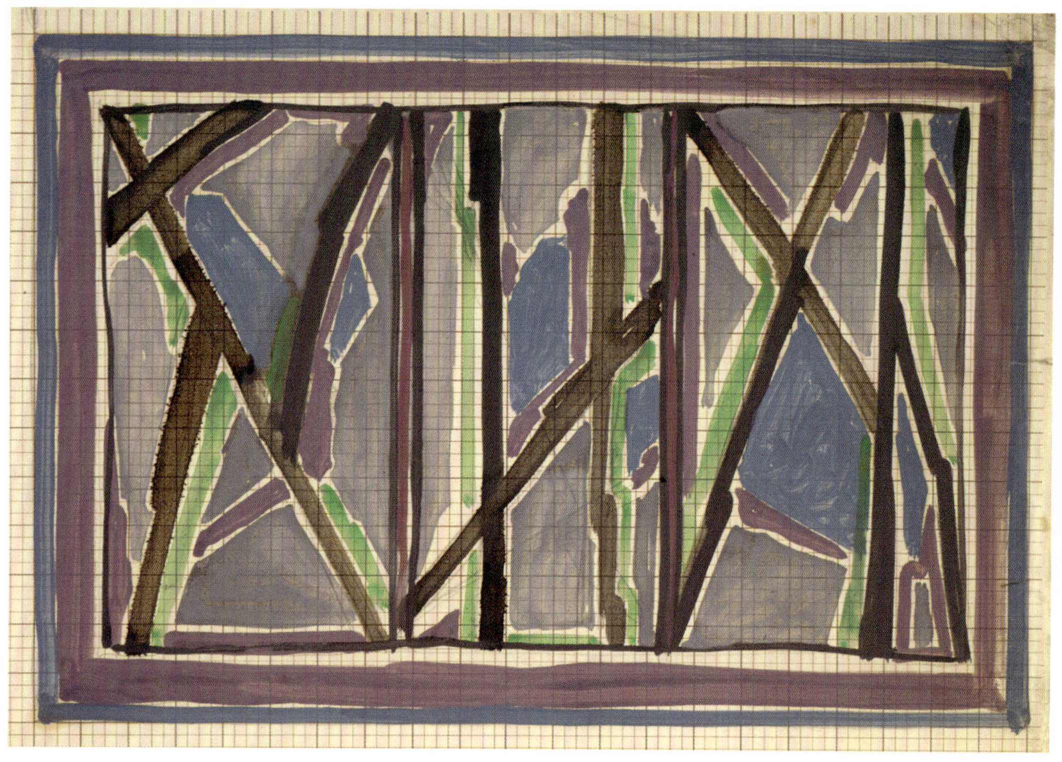

Preliminary design for Lady Hamilton rug

1914 | graphite and bodycolour on a grid of pen and black ink lines, on wove paper |
40.3 × 62.8 cm

These rug designs were made while Bell was working closely with Duncan Grant, so it is often not certain which artist produced the design. The first design illustrated here shows the influence of Cézanne, whose work Bell had seen in both Paris and London. Sir Ian and Lady Hamilton were early supporters of the Omega Workshops. In 1914 Lady Hamilton commissioned the Omega artists to decorate and furnish several rooms in her new London home, 1 Hyde Park Gardens. For this scheme Bell painted friezes, inlaid furniture, created mosaics and stained glass, and designed a special rug for the entrance hall. The final design is shown here, as well as a more densely packed preliminary design. The inspiration came from her screen *Tents and Figures* (1913, Victoria and Albert Museum), which emerged from the painting *Summer Camp* (1913, private collection). The abstract textile designs made by Bloomsbury artists for the Omega Workshops opened up the possibility of non-representational painting, leading Bell to experiment with pure abstraction in her paintings.

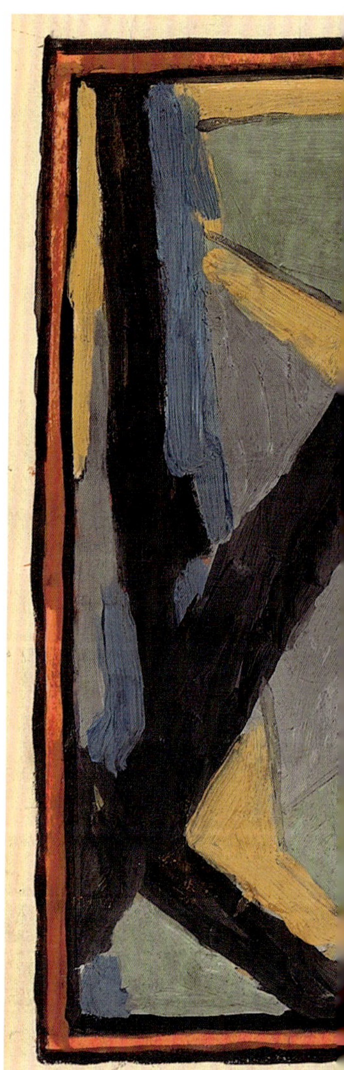

Omega rug design for Sir Ian and Lady Hamilton

1913–14 | oil on paper | 30.5 × 60.3 cm

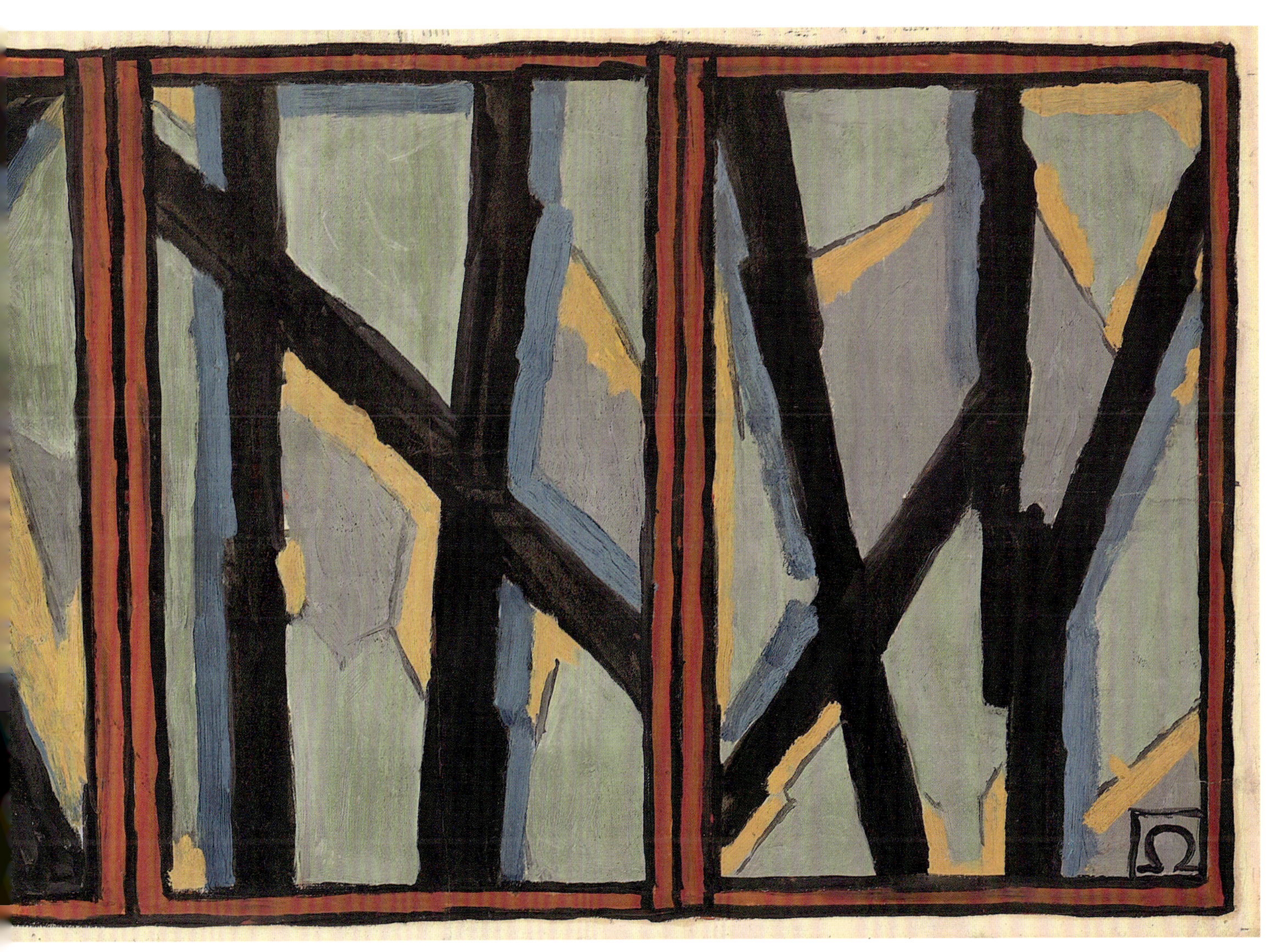

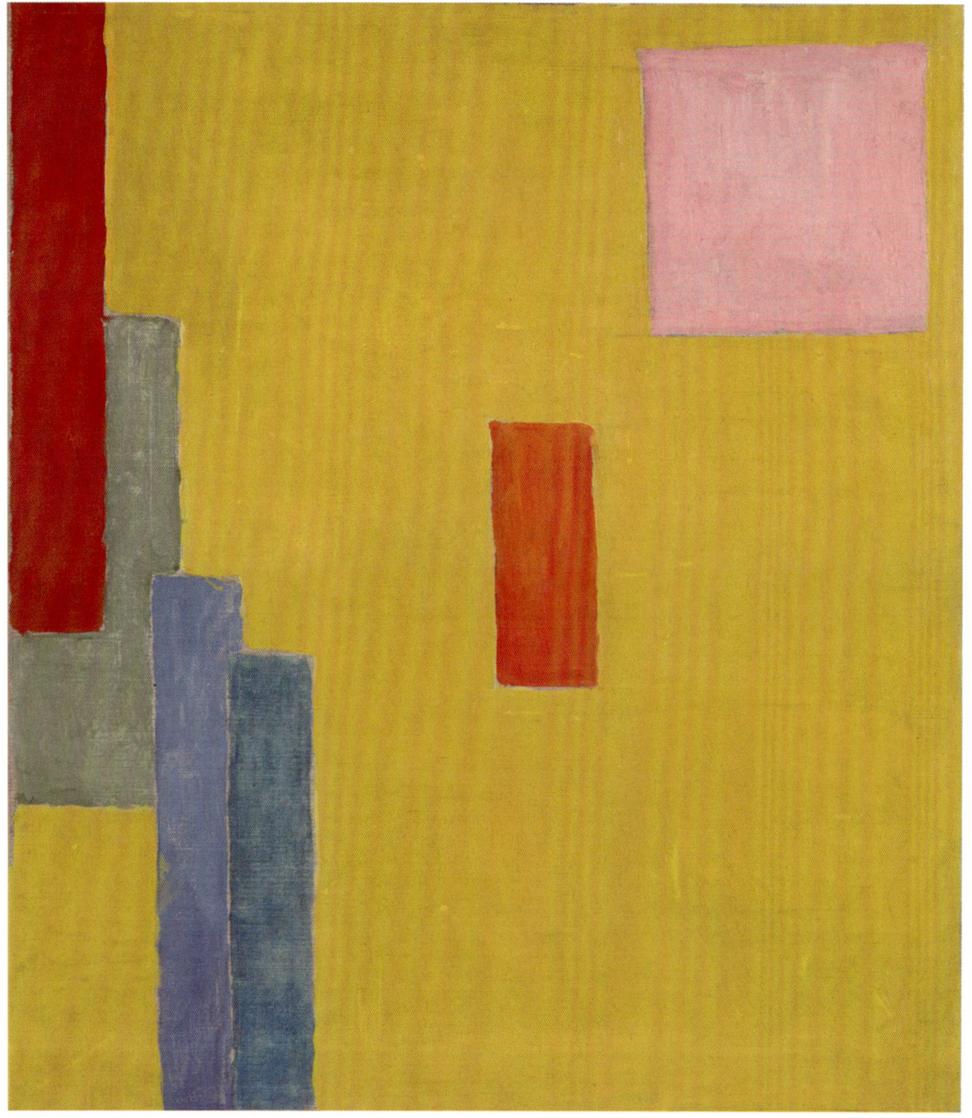

c.1914 | oil on canvas | 44.1 × 38.7 cm

Around 1914–15, Bell produced a handful of abstract collages and paintings, the next logical step after her applied art designs for the Omega Workshops. Perhaps the Omega technique of marking up a design on squared paper is translated here in Bell's angular, geometric compositions. The abstract paintings were also produced in collaboration, with Bell, Roger Fry and Duncan Grant working alongside each other, as they worked together at the Omega.[47] When asked later in life, Grant could not remember which of them had made the first move towards pure abstraction.[48] Bell had already been incorporating abstract elements into her paintings, for example the flat blocks of colour in the background of *Frederick and Jessie Etchells Painting* (1912, p. 54), which also includes the strong vertical of the curtain found in her abstractions and later work. Here, Bell ensured that no patch of colour could meet another: 'the hair's-breadth of bare white canvas that rims the shapes' and the thin paint revealing the weave of the flat canvas surface.[49]

Abstract Painting carries no inscription to indicate the correct orientation. The current orientation has been suggested by analysing the direction of the brush strokes.[50] In her inventory of

1951 Bell added to the title '(Test for Chrome Yellow)'. Chrome yellow pigment was available from the start of the nineteenth century, and became 'the colour of the hour … associated with all that was bizarre and queer in art and life, with all that was outrageously modern', the critic Holbrook Jackson wrote in 1913.[51]

It has been suggested that Bell's foray into pure abstraction may have come from seeing works by European artists František Kupka (shown at the *Salon d'Automne*, Paris, in 1912) or Wassily Kandinsky (shown at the Allied Artists' Salon in London in 1913) as well as recent pieces by British figures such as David Bomberg.[52] Bell worked in abstraction only for a very short period and they were private experiments, not exhibited or sold during her lifetime. Perhaps this was because her work in abstraction 'firmly marks her allegiance to a *European* avant-garde' towards which there was an immediate backlash in England during the First World War.[53]

The existence of Bell's work in pure abstraction still earn her 'a position at the forefront of non-objective art'[54] and her experiments in this area continued to influence the architecture and colour dynamics of her later work.

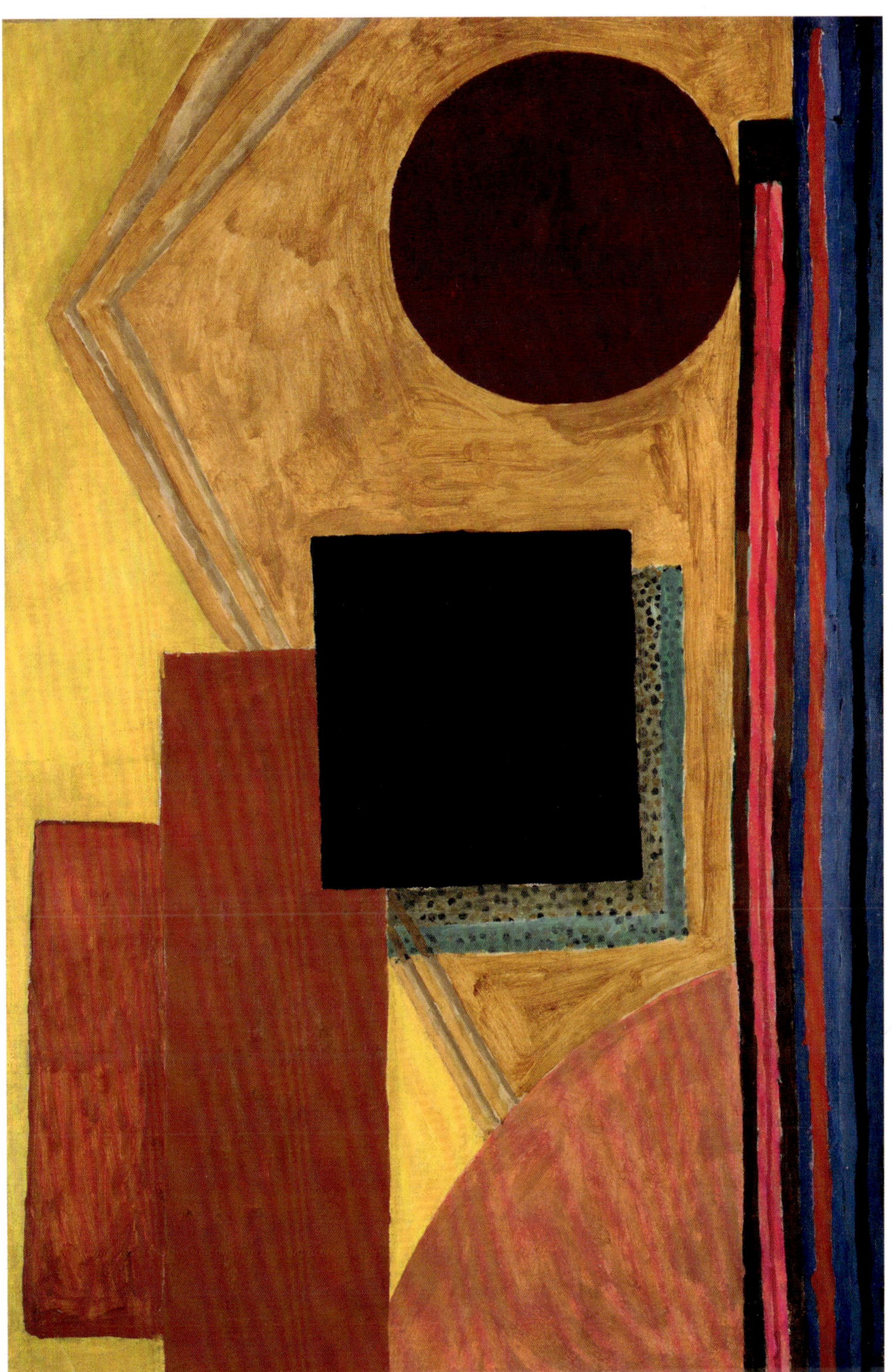

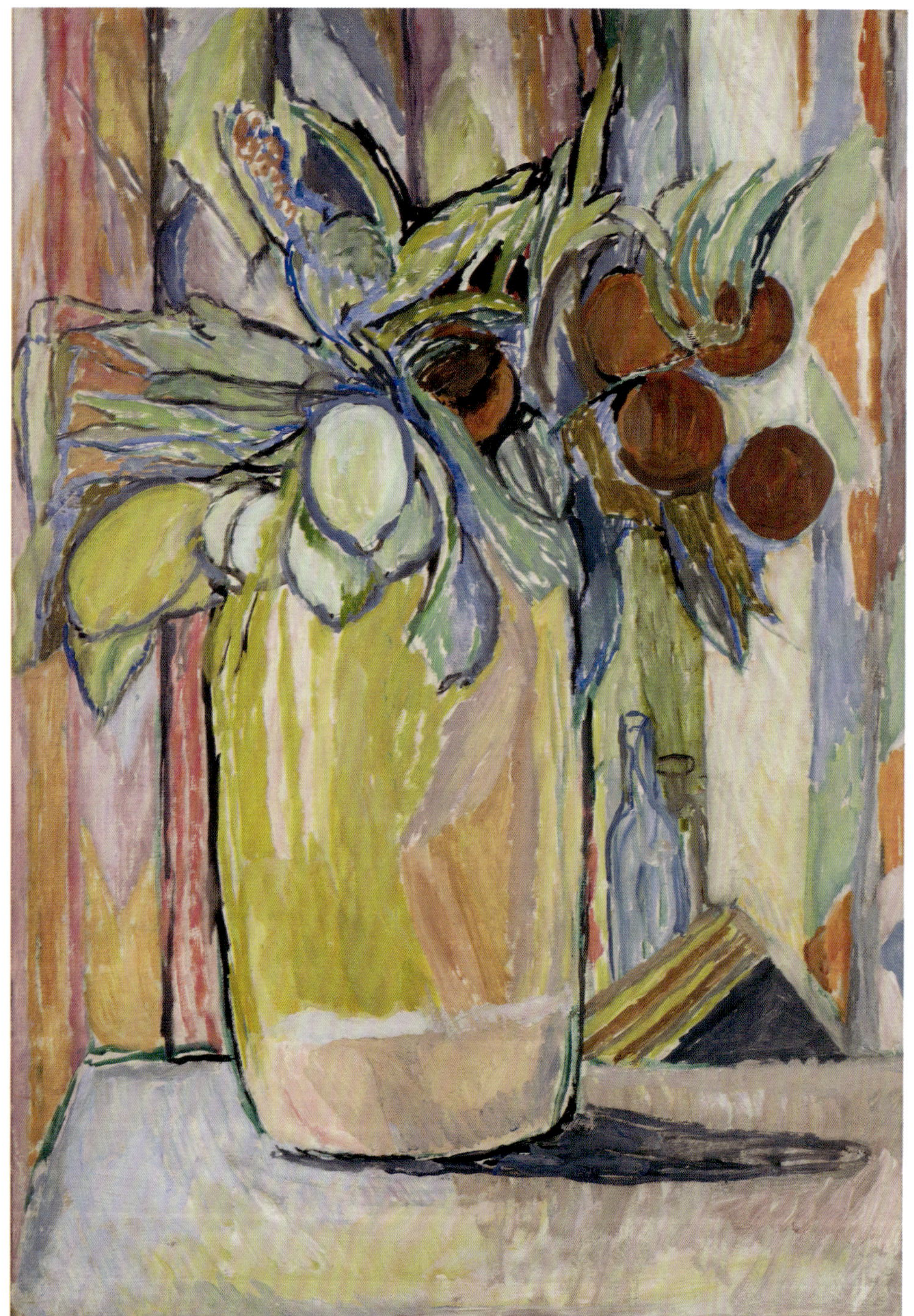

Oranges and Lemons

1914 | oil on cardboard | 73 × 51.5 cm

In January 1914 Duncan Grant visited Tunis and sent Bell some oranges and lemons. She immediately wrote to Grant: 'Your basket of oranges and lemons came this morning. They were so lovely that against all modern theories I suppose I stuck some into my yellow Italian pot and at once began to paint them. I mean one isn't supposed nowadays to paint what one thinks is beautiful. But the colour was so exciting that I couldn't [resist] it…. It was very clever of you I think to send them on stalks.'[55] Playfully dismissing the theoretical discussions of Roger Fry and Clive Bell, she 'colludes with Grant in expressing her ultimate fealty to visual intelligence above all else'.[56] The 'exciting' colour is also not naturalistic: the oranges are brown and most of the lemons are pale blue-green. The vase has been tilted and some of the shapes outlined in a black, which may have been influenced by Cézanne.[57] Bell's own design for an Omega textile *Maud* forms the background.

Still Life (Triple Alliance)

1914 | collage with newspaper, oil and pastel on canvas | 60.3 × 81.9 cm

The title *Still Life (Triple Alliance)* suggests both the 'Triple Entente' between Britain, France and Russia against Germany in 1914 and the objects depicted on the tabletop: a soda syphon, a wine bottle and an oil lamp. The collage combines current affairs – maps of conflict sites (Aix-la-Chapelle, the Meuse Valley) and newspaper clippings referring to the war – with personal details – 'a self-addressed blank cheque (the right hand bottle), train timetables (the lamp base) and commercial advertisements (the tabletop)'.[58] Art historian Grace Brockington compares this collage to Picasso's *Bottle of Suze* (1912, Mildred Lane Kemper Art Museum, St Louis), which Bell may have seen at his studio.[59] *Bottle of Suze* is collaged from clippings 'detailing the 1912–13 Balkan War, left-wing pacifist demonstrations and satirical fiction'.[60]

The collage was exhibited in Birmingham in 1917.[61] Whether or not this represents Bell's 'only overtly political work', reflecting the pacifist attitudes of the Bloomsbury Group, it is a rare example of her technical experimentations with collage following Bell's period of working in pure abstraction.[62]

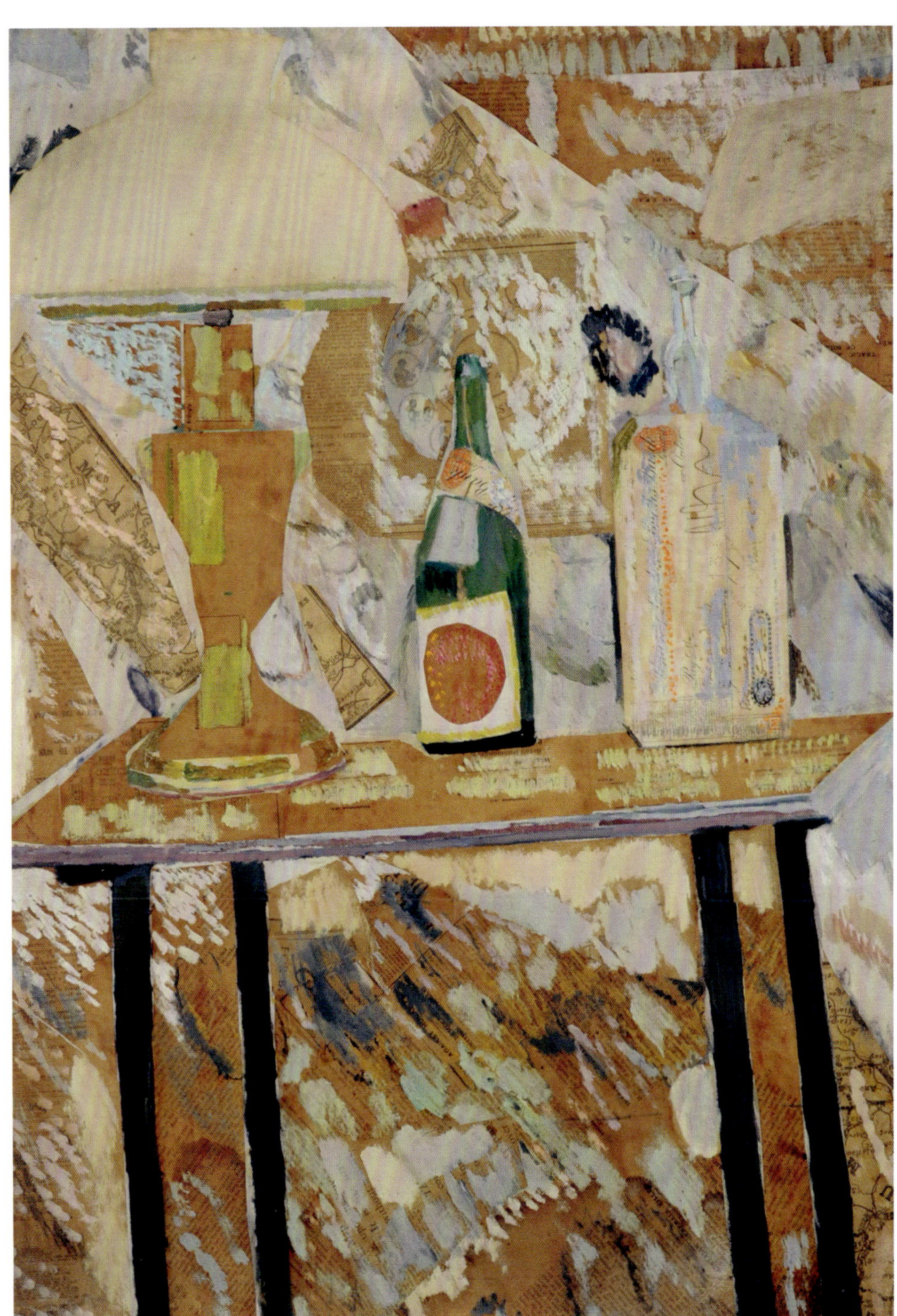

Portrait of Molly MacCarthy

1914-15 | gouache, oil and collage on board | 92 × 35.9 cm

This collaged portrait has a similar pose to the 1912 portrait of Molly MacCarthy (p. 52), but the dress and setting are different and the technique is a radical departure. In January 1914 Bell visited Pablo Picasso in Paris and was astonished by the artist's constructions and collages, which perhaps inspired this work. She wrote to Duncan Grant: 'The whole studio seemed to be bristling with Picassos. All the bits of wood and frames had become like his pictures.… They are amazing arrangements of coloured papers and bits of wood which somehow do give me great satisfaction.'[63] This portrait and *Still Life (Triple Alliance)* (1914, p. 73) are rare examples of Bell working in collage, as she didn't continue this strand of her practice.

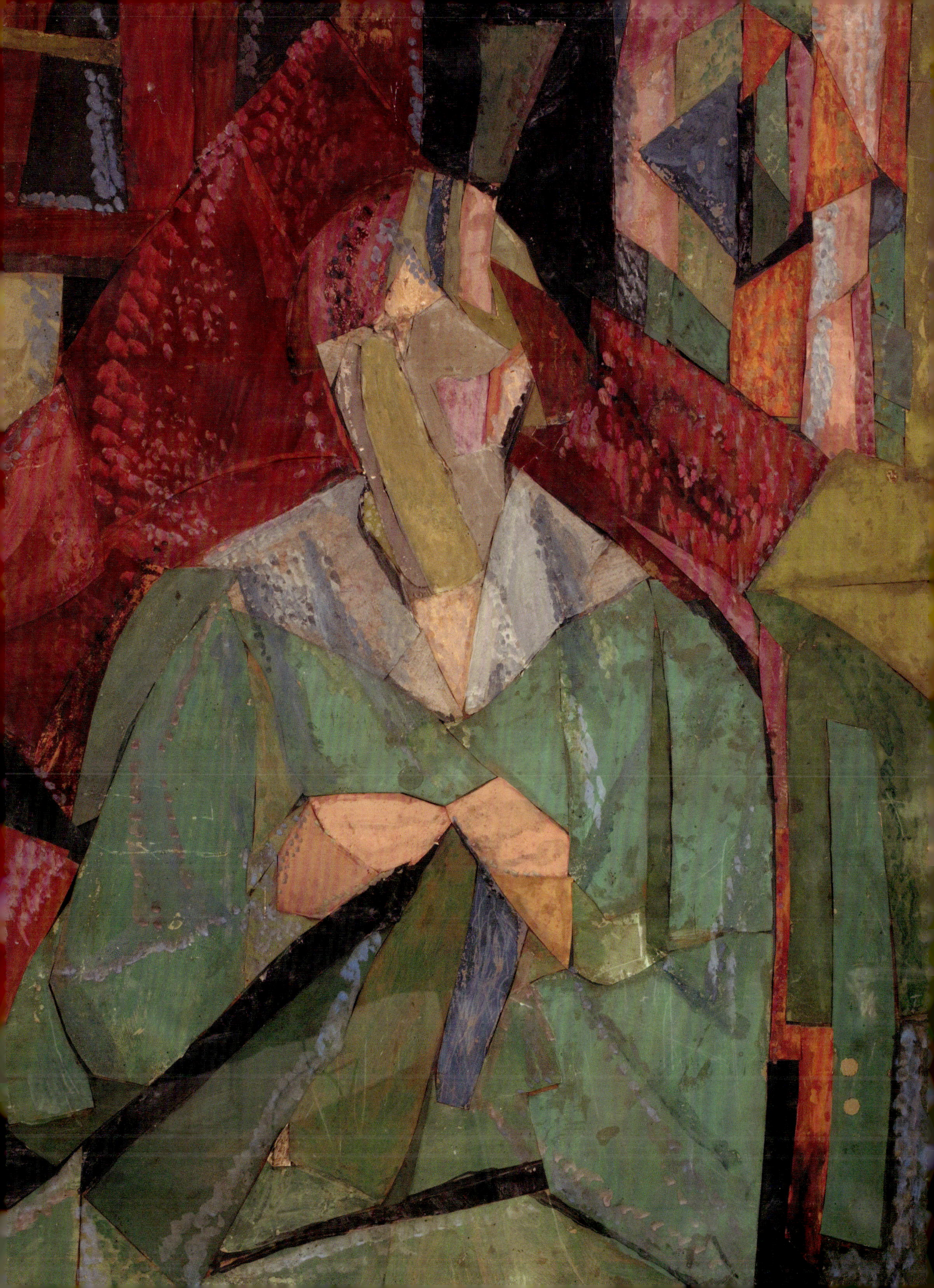

Angel

c.1915 | paint and paper on wood | 92 × 43 cm

Constructed from the end of a church pew with paper and paint, *Angel* follows the support in form, with the wings reaching the top edge of the seat back, the praying hands meeting the arm rest and the head bowed down. The angel's rainbow wings and kneeling form evoke examples from the early Renaissance, for example Fra Angelico's *Annunciation* (1442–43, Basilica di San Marco, Florence) and Giotto's *Virgin and Child Enthroned* (*c.*1300–05, The Uffizi, Florence), which Bell is likely to have seen on her several trips to Florence. In light of the interpretation given to *Still Life (Triple Alliance)* (1914, p. 73) as a pacifist statement, *Angel* has been read in the context of the First World War. '*Angel*'s transgression is to repurpose the materials of life into a peaceful vision of beauty and harmony. Is it possible the angel is praying for Europe in a time of war?'[64] During the Second World War, Bell found herself revisiting the kneeling angel for the *Annunciation* mural commissioned for Berwick Church (p. 144).

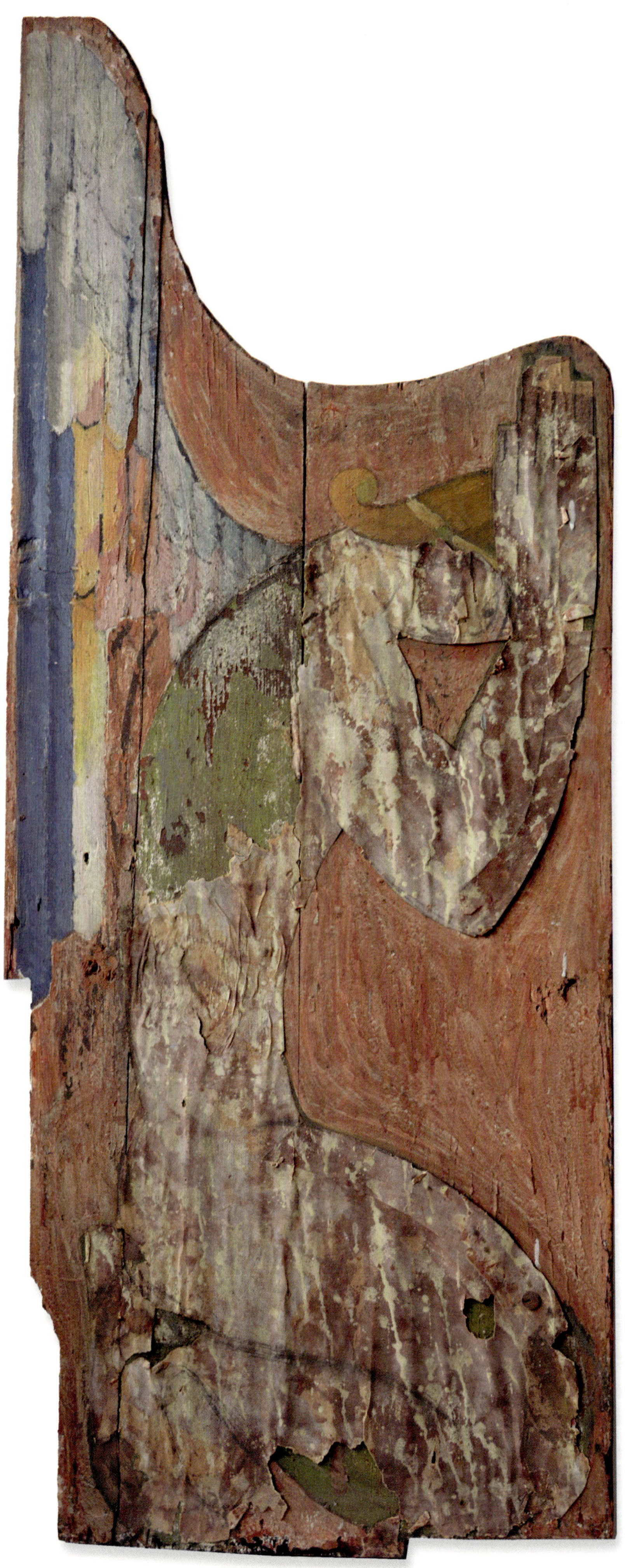

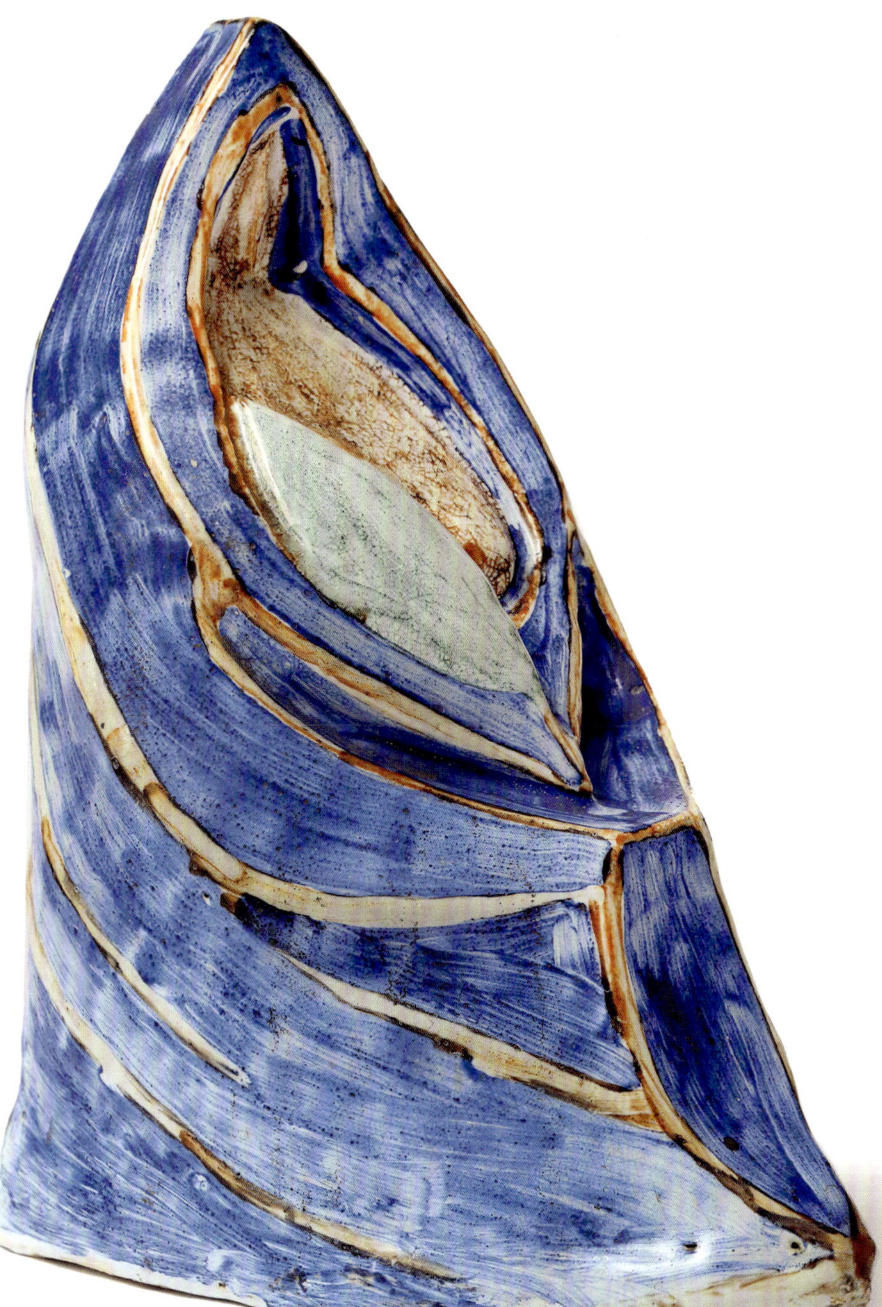

Madonna and Child

*c.*1915 | glazed ceramic |
22.5 × 19 × 11.5 cm

Frustrated with commercially produced ceramics, in 1913 and 1914 Roger Fry set about making his own. Bell writes of visiting a pottery at Mitcham, Surrey, in 1913: 'I have spent hours today trying to model a figure, which of course is most exciting, but I doubt if I'm much good at it.'[65] Again in 1914, both Fry and Bell recount a further trip together: 'Vanessa and I have been potting all day … they'll make quite nice little bowls and pots. It's fearfully exciting when you do get it centred and the stuff begins to come up between your fingers. V. never would make her penises long enough, which I thought very odd. Don't you?'[66] 'We turned out about a dozen small pots, really quite passable…. Of course one couldn't possibly do anything big yet … but the feeling of the clay rising between one's fingers is like the keenest sexual joy!'[67] The sexual associations with which both artists describe working with clay seem at odds with this ostensibly religious-themed sculpture, a radically abstracted Madonna and Child wrapped in a blue cloak. The Madonna and Child as a subject would reappear in Bell's *Nativity* at Berwick Church (p. 145).

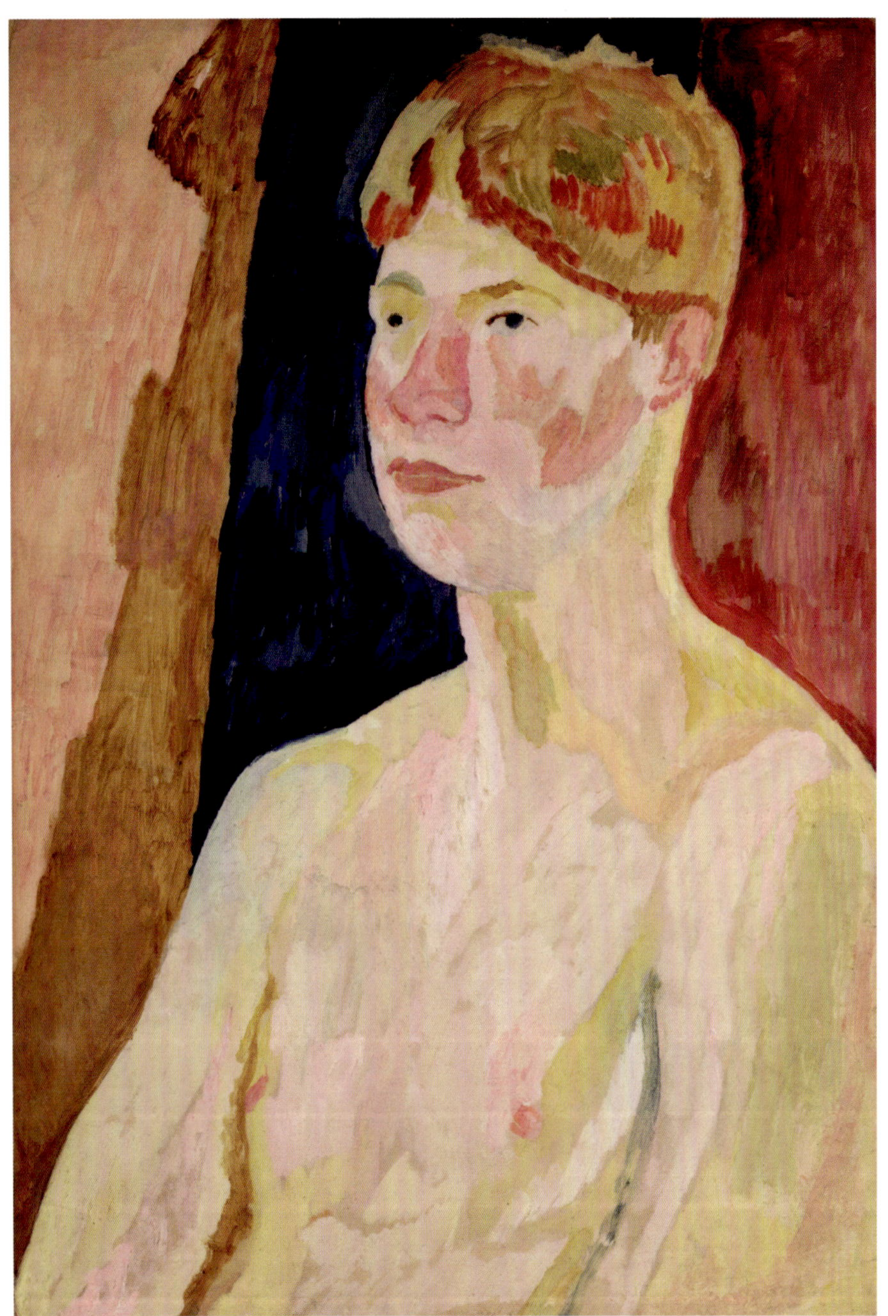

David 'Bunny' Garnett

1915 | oil and gouache on cardboard |
76.4 × 52.6 cm

David Garnett (1892–1981), a
writer and publisher, was given the
nickname 'Bunny' after a rabbit-
skin cloak he had as a child. This
portrait was painted at Eleanor
House, West Wittering, when
Garnett posed for both Duncan
Grant and Bell. At this time Grant,
Garnett and Bell were living
together with Bell's children and
were engaged in anti-conscription
work. Bell's painting is a rare
example, from this period, of a
portrait of an unclothed man by
a female artist. Bell's portrait is
made using patches of colour to
model the skin and face, empha-
sized by the abstract stripes of
colour in the background.

Iris Tree

1915 | oil on canvas | 122 × 91.5 cm

Iris Tree (1897–1968) was a poet,
actress and artist's model. She also
sat for Duncan Grant and Roger
Fry in 1915, when she was 18. Tree
was a 'crop head', one of a group of
young women whose short hair, cut
to just below the ears, suggested
their modernity. Bell's portrait is
a bold study in red and black with
the almost abstract background
perhaps recalling Matisse's *Red
Studio* (1911, Museum of Modern
Art, New York).[68] The chrome
yellow tones in the face and hair
are reflected in the pattern of the
sofa and painted screen behind.
Tree's dress, with its low-cut
V-neck and empire style, may be
of Bell's own design for the Omega
Workshops. Reed has suggested
that Bell portraits of this time
are 'not so much illustrations as
equivalents to Omega rooms in
their effect of giving visual form
to the desire to create environments where life – and especially
women's life – can be lived in a
modern way'.[69]

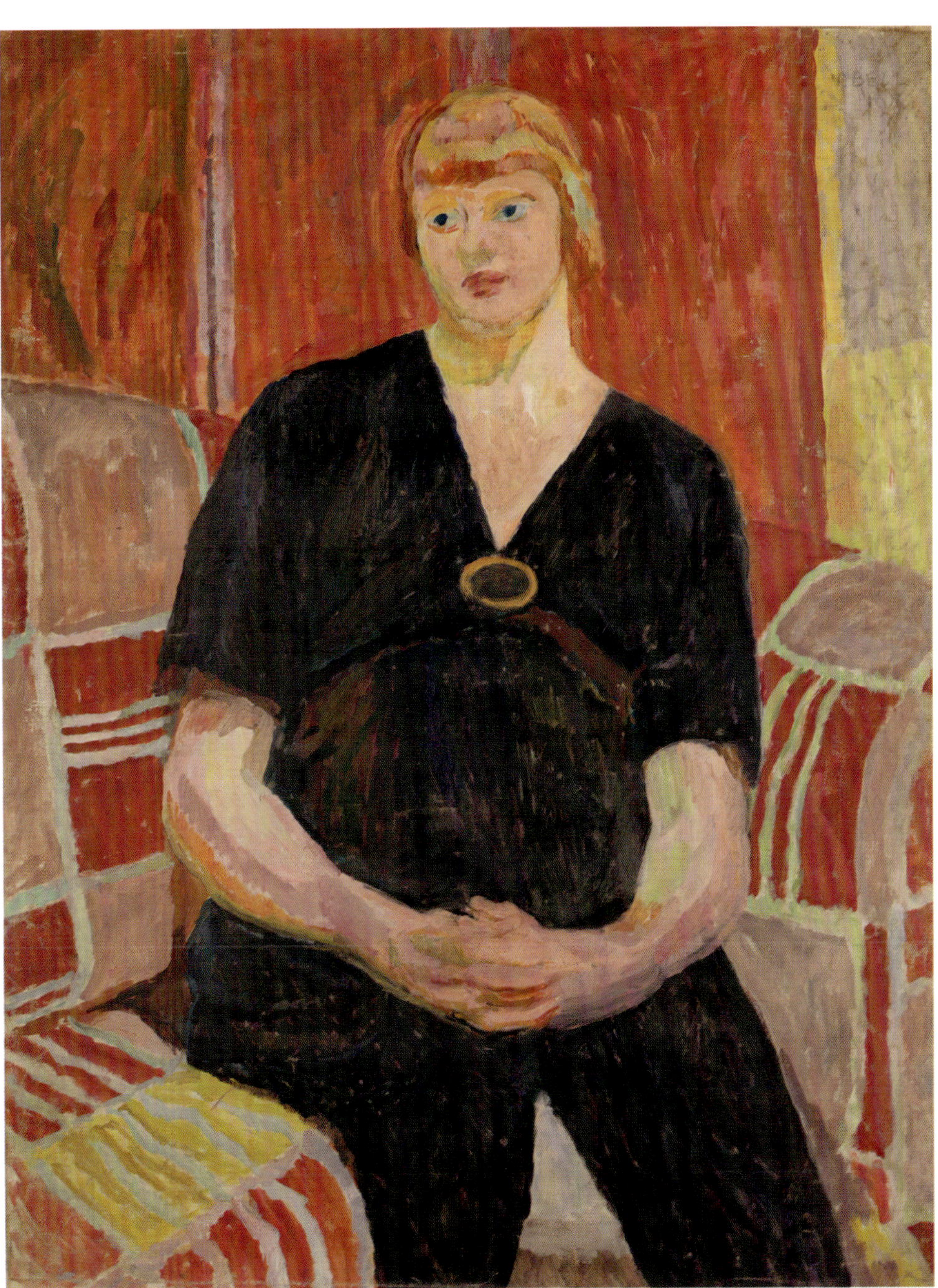

Woman in a Red Hat

1915 | oil on canvas | 76 × 125 cm

There is an unfinished painting by Duncan Grant depicting Bell working on this canvas. This shows her working without a model and indicates the material on the figure's lap may be a partially open fan. *Woman in a Red Hat*'s combination of interior and exterior, with the horizontally banded view through the window, is seen throughout Bell's career, for example *Fredrick and Jessie Etchells Painting* (1912, p. 54). In this painting the head of the model echoes Bell's *Study of a Woman* (*c.* 1917, p. 92). The simplification of the woman's face and her helmet-like red hat contrasts with the very detailed pattern of the material on her lap.

A portrait of Bell by Grant, *Vanessa Bell (The Red Hat)* (*c.* 1917–18, private collection), shows her wearing a similar hat and similarly coloured dress, placed beside a black floral patterned curtain, perhaps suggesting the reuse of clothing and fabric props. *Woman in a Red Hat* was seemingly discarded by Bell, as the reverse of the canvas was used by Grant in the 1920s for a painting of two men on a beach.

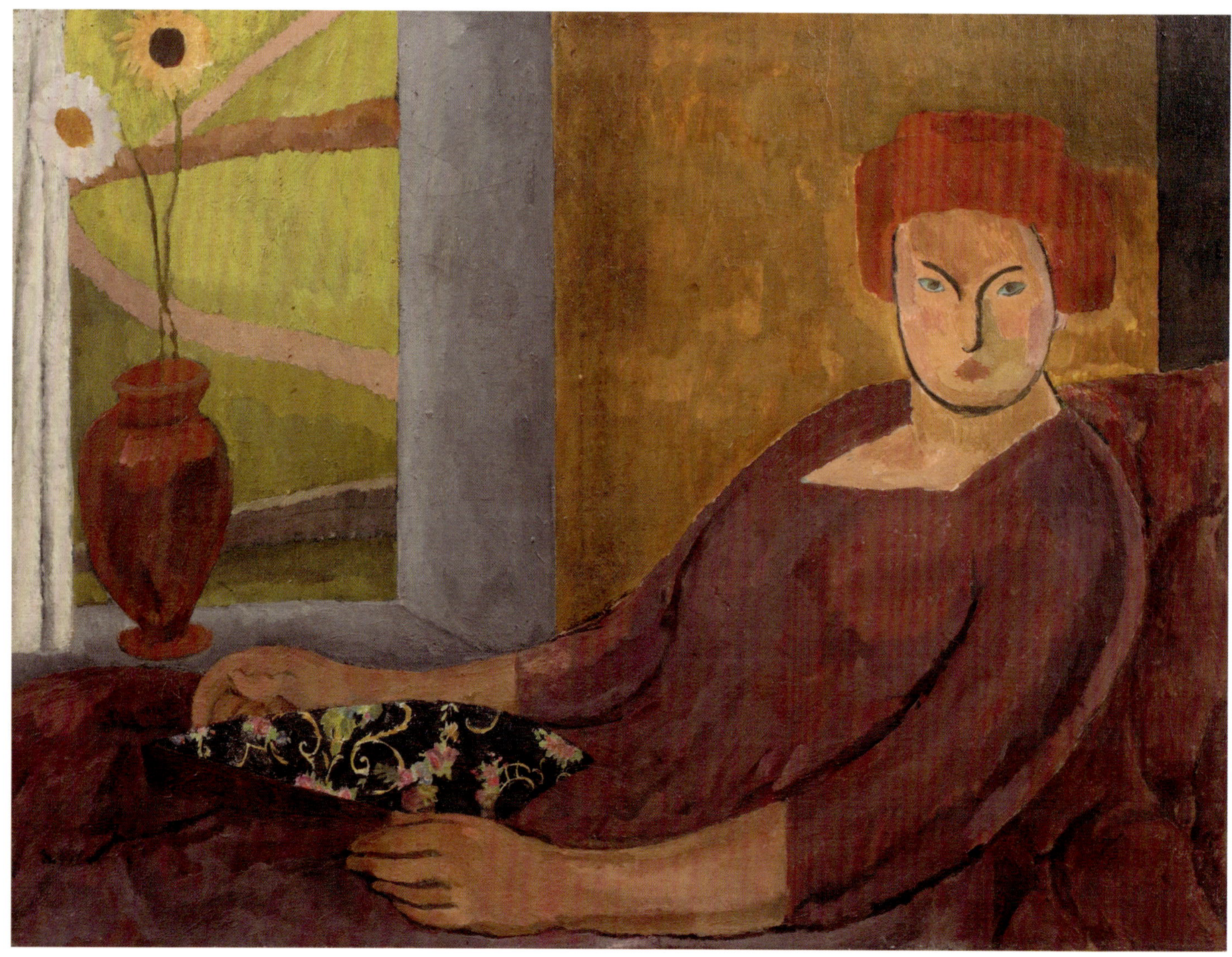

Barns (By the Estuary)

c.1915 | oil on strawboard | 47 × 63.5 cm

Barns (By the Estuary) is a rare example of Bell painting a landscape during the First World War. It also demonstrates the continuing influence of her experimentation in abstraction during 1914. Although depicting farm buildings looking onto the Chichester Estuary, Bell reduces the forms to abstract planes of ochres, purple-greys, yellow and cyan, punctuated by the verticals at either side and the boat mast in the centre.

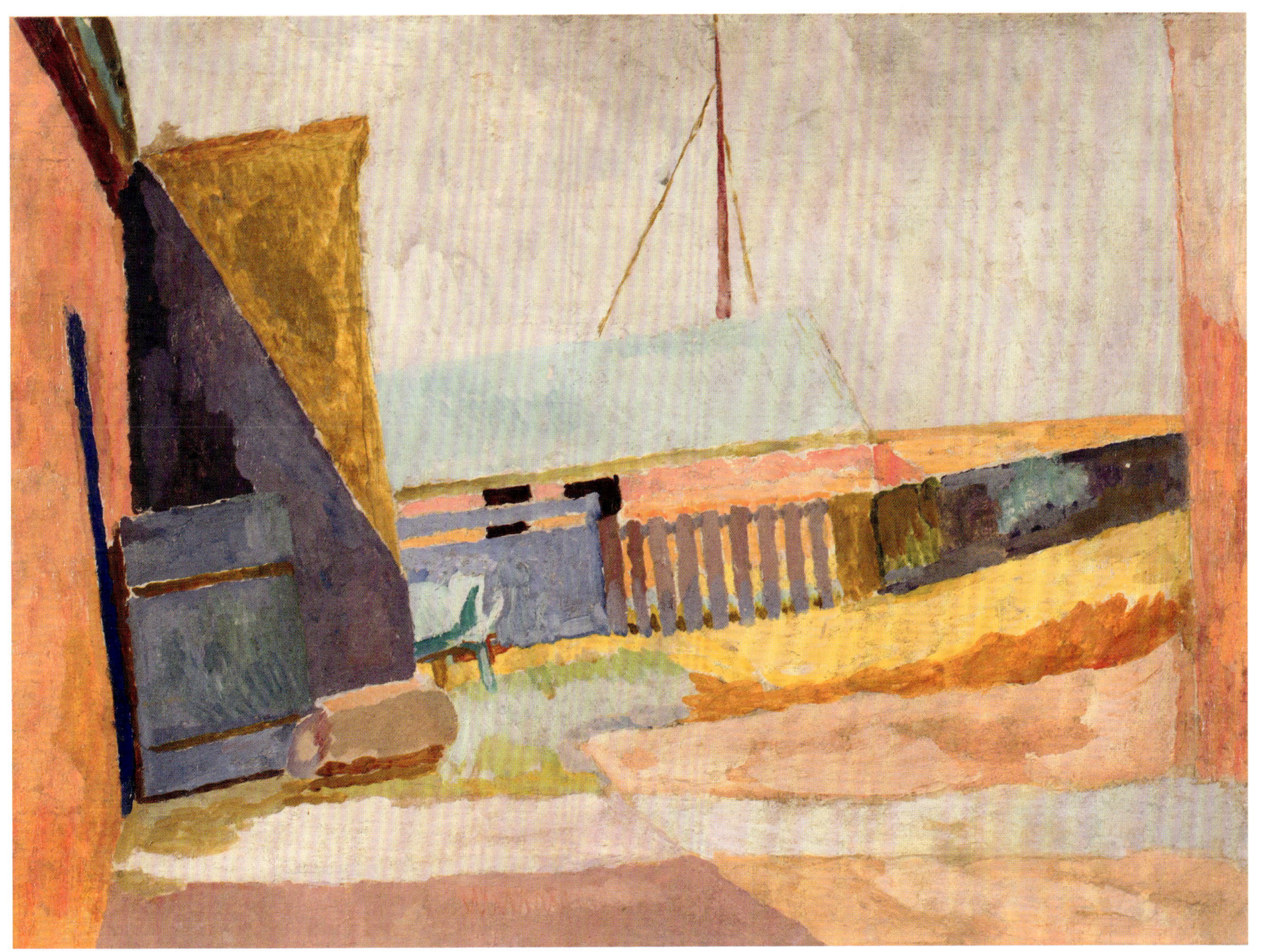

Landscape (verso)

c. 1915 | oil on canvas | 72.8 × 55.7 cm

Landscape uses the colours and shapes of nature to communicate the feeling of being in a landscape, and the land, pond and reflections merge in lines and blocks of colour. It appears as if the fleshy coloured form of a figure midway down the painting is absorbed into this landscape. This painting is on the back of another work, *Window, Still Life* (c. 1915). The canvas of *Landscape* was cut down to fit the size of *Window, Still Life*.

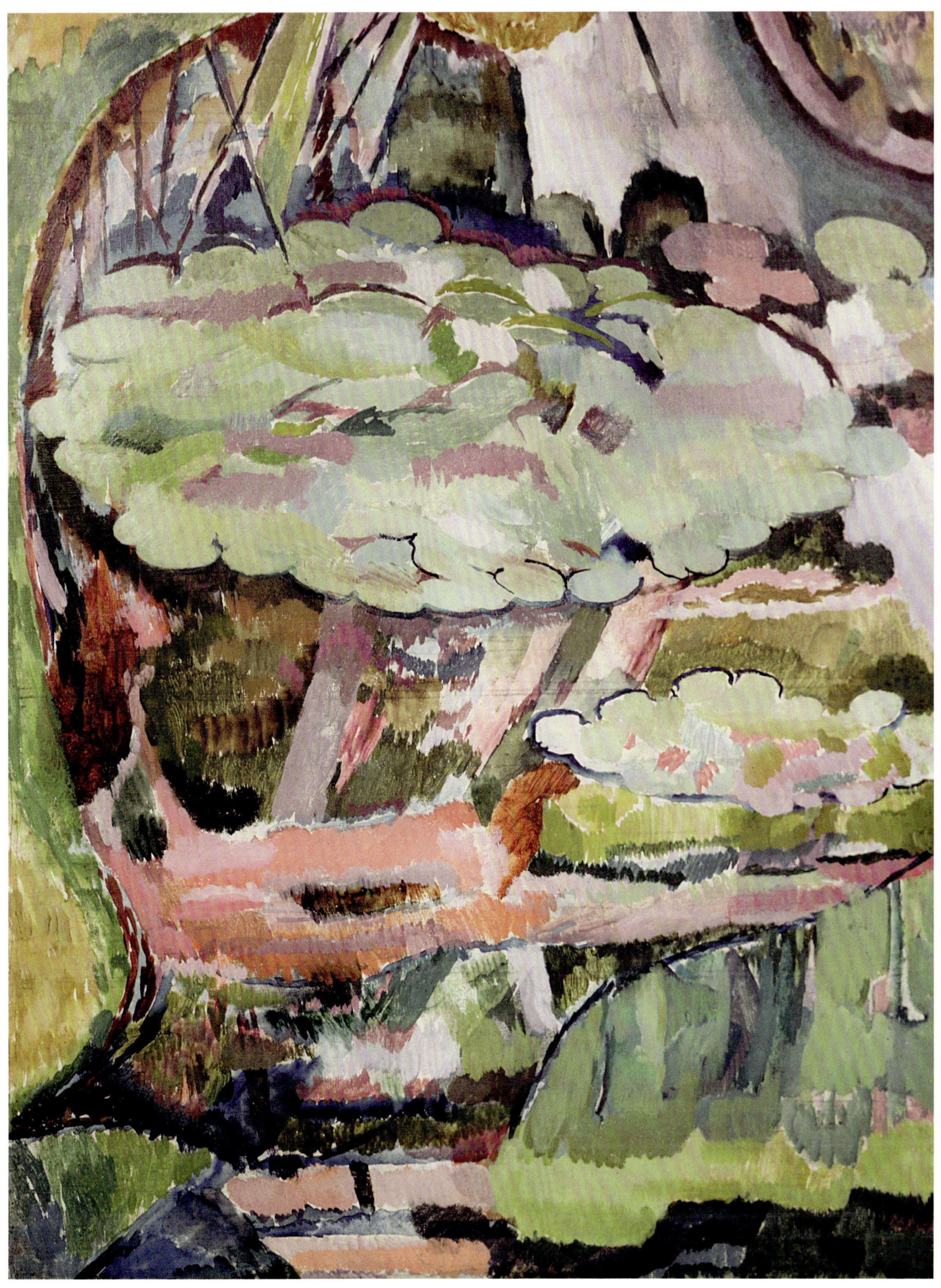

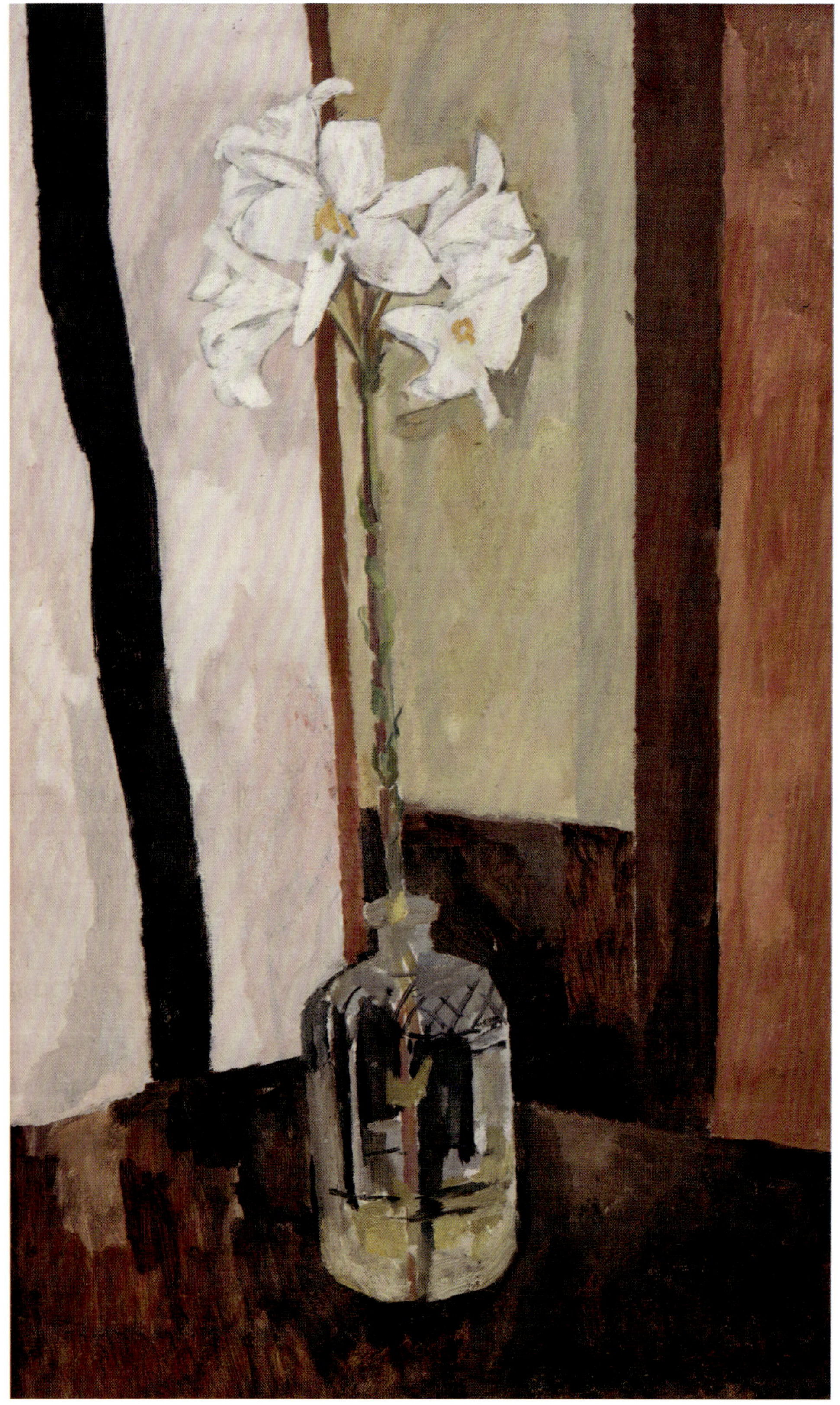

The Madonna Lily

c.1915–17 | oil on canvas | 64 × 39 cm

The Madonna Lily was painted
in March, either 1915 or 1917, at
Roger Fry's house Durbins, in
Guildford.[70] Both artists painted
the same flower, placed in front of
a beaded African arrow case, but,
compared to Fry's painting, Bell
has bunched together her blooms
so they form a compact, round
burst of white. The naturalistic
colours, compared to those of, for
example, *Oranges and Lemons*
(1914, p. 72), show Bell moving
away from abstraction. Much later,
when her son Quentin asked her
why she had made her work more
naturalistic, she replied that 'She
had come to the conclusion that
nature was much richer and more
interesting than anything one
could invent.'[71]

Still Life with Wildflowers

1915 | oil on canvas | 76.2 × 63.5 cm

This still life shows buttercups, a bluebell, a dandelion and other wild flowers arranged in a vase, with what may be books or magazines next to them. The composition is enlivened by the diagonal bands of colour in the background. Writer Richard Shone suggests that the brownish diagonal could be an easel, and there is a similar shape in the background of Bell's portrait of David Garnett (1915, p. 78).[72] This striking composition is produced with an opposing diagonal made by the shadow of the vase (echoed in the lines of the books), together with strong verticals of the large leaf and black shape on the left, all rendered in visible, energetic brushstrokes. Bell gave *Still Life with Wildflowers* to Duncan Grant soon after it was finished, and for many years it hung by his bed at Charleston.

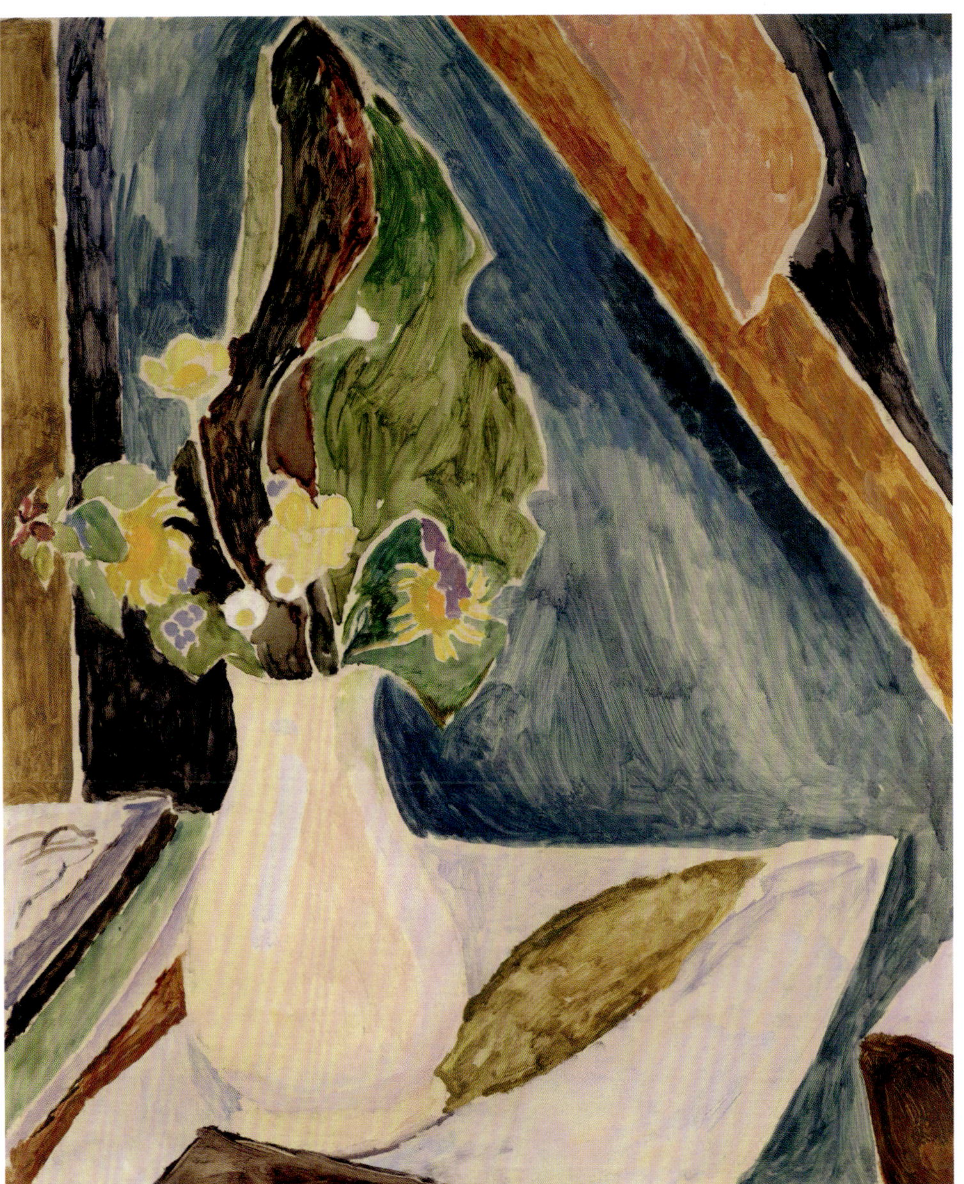

Bottles on a Table

1915-17 | oil on canvas | 81.5 × 62 × 4 cm

Bottles on a Table is a dynamic example of Bell's still-life painting, with the table tipped towards the viewer, and bold colour. Although figurative, the geometric shapes and colours recall works such as *Abstract Painting* (*c.*1914, p. 70) and *Abstract Composition* (1914, p. 71), for example in the vertical of the deep red table legs. The trio of objects on a table is also a repeated motif within Bell's work, seen across very different styles, from *Iceland Poppies* (1908–09, p. 35) to *Still Life (Triple Alliance)* (1914, p. 73).

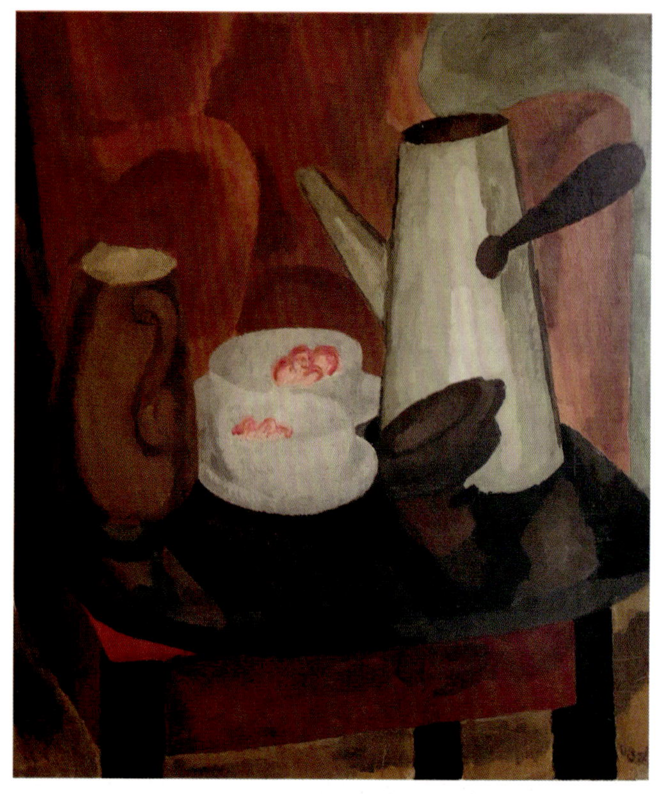

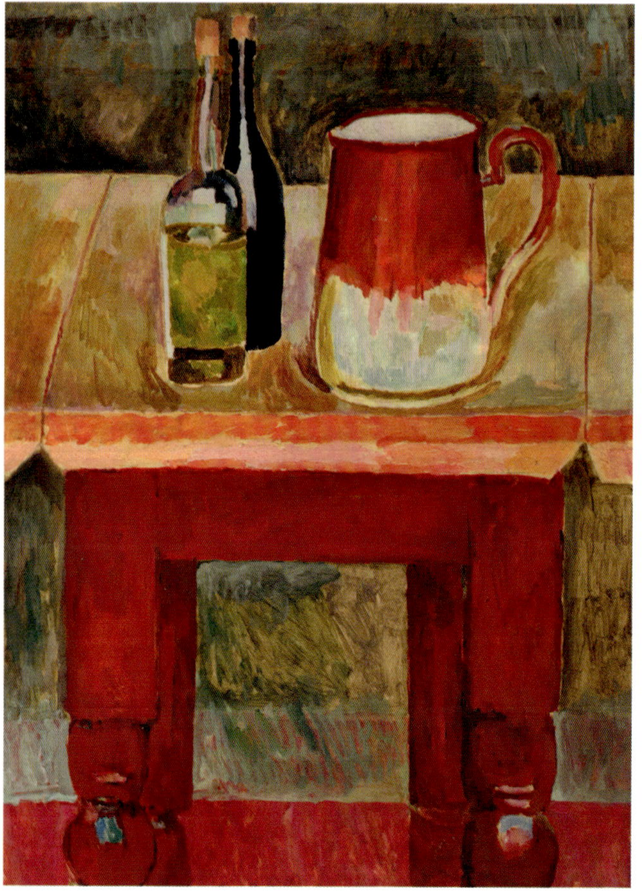

Still Life with Coffee Pot

c.1916-17 | oil on canvas | 54.6 × 45.7 cm

Still Life with Coffee Pot was painted in the dining room at Charleston. A painting featuring the same distinctive pot by Duncan Grant exists from the same period (Metropolitan Museum of Art, New York).

The Blue Room, Wissett Lodge

1916 | oil on canvas | 38.7 × 26.7 cm

In March 1916 Vanessa Bell, Duncan Grant, David Garnett and Bell's children rented Wissett Lodge, near Halesworth in Suffolk. She and Grant distempered the walls a bright blue. *The Blue Room* shows a woman in a white shift with a washstand, pitcher and basin, also in white, contrasted with the black outline of the table and skirting board. The white forms stand against a background of a floral still life, which may be a vase of flowers on a shelf or a wall painting. The effect is to flatten the figure, objects and setting into one plane.

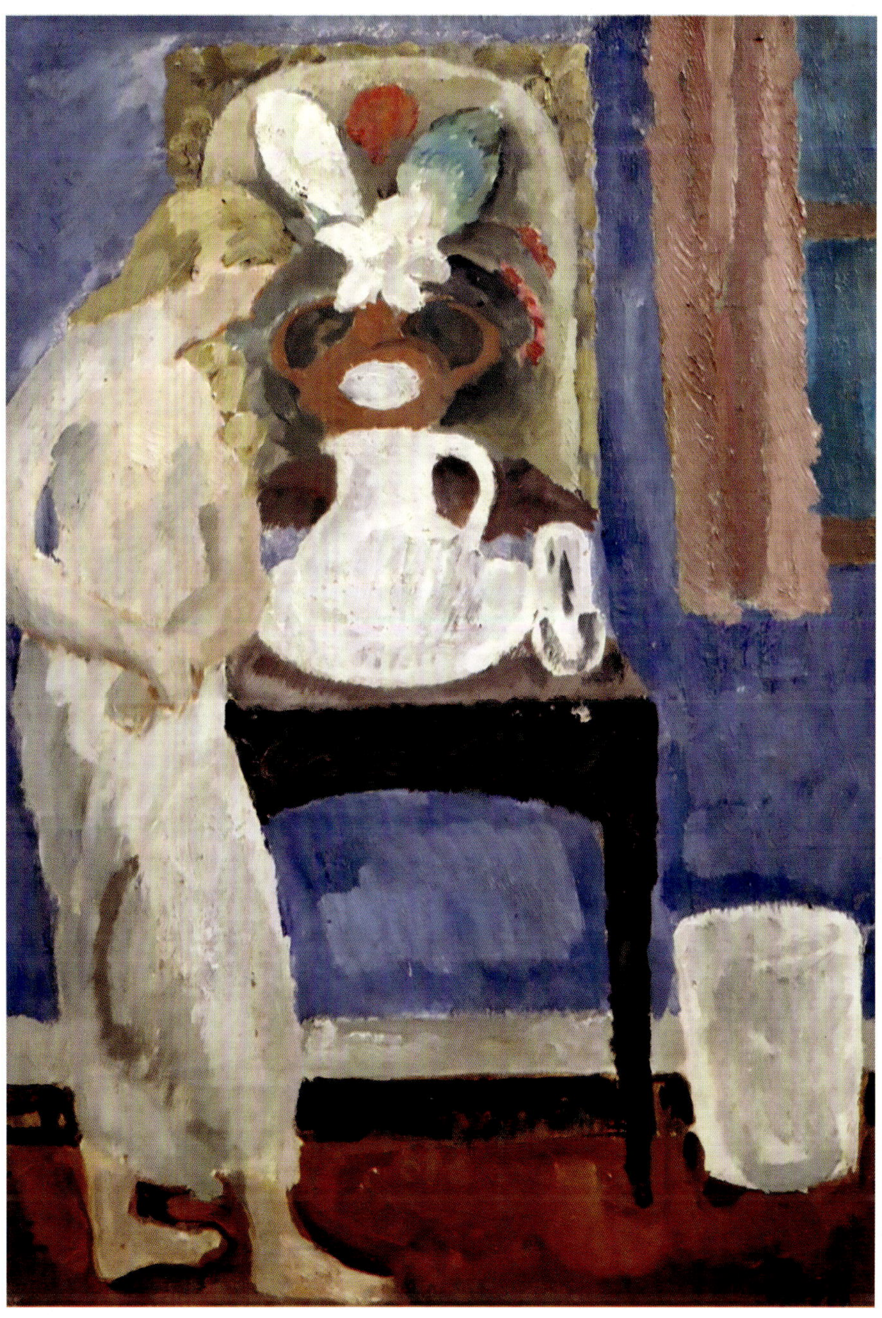

Nude with Poppies

1916 | oil on canvas | 23.4 × 42.4 cm

Bell painted *Nude with Poppies* as a preliminary design for a bed-head that Mary Hutchinson had commissioned. She worried about its reception: 'I hope she won't be horrified to hear there's a nude figure of the most romantic description with poppies…. I don't think it's at all what she wanted.'[73] A further letter offers more description of her theme: 'One side is a woman asleep, rather like *Flaming June* by Lord Leighton with poppies and waves [I think] all very symbolical. On the other is the remains of the dessert she's been eating and down below flowers tied in a true lover's knot of white satin ribbon.'[74]

A few years later, Bell asked Duncan Grant to paint her a headboard and he chose to paint Morpheus, the god of sleep, surrounded by two huge red poppies. Bell painted poppies several times during her life, including *Iceland Poppies* (1908–09, p. 35). The finished commissioned bed appears in a photograph in *Vogue*.[75]

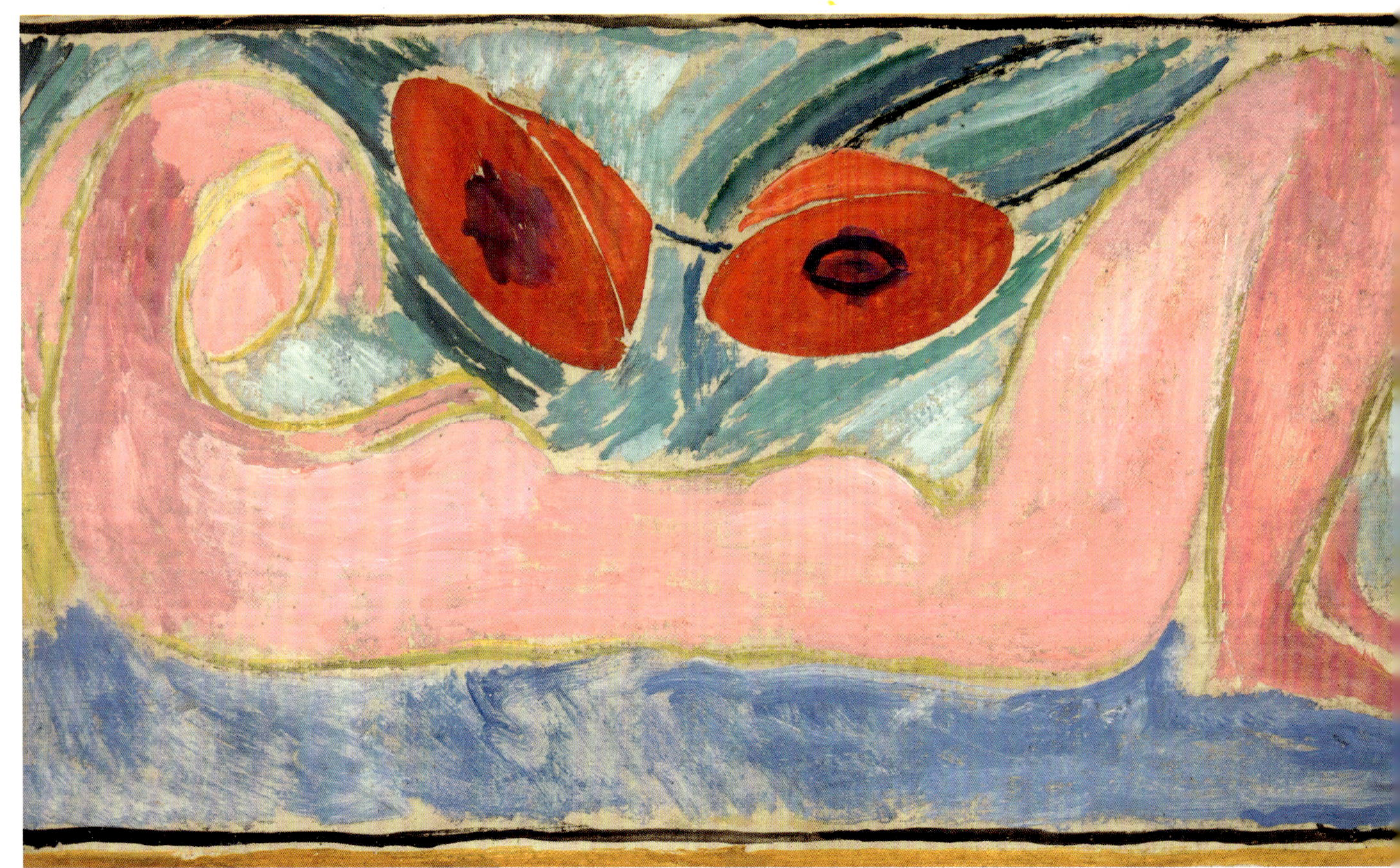

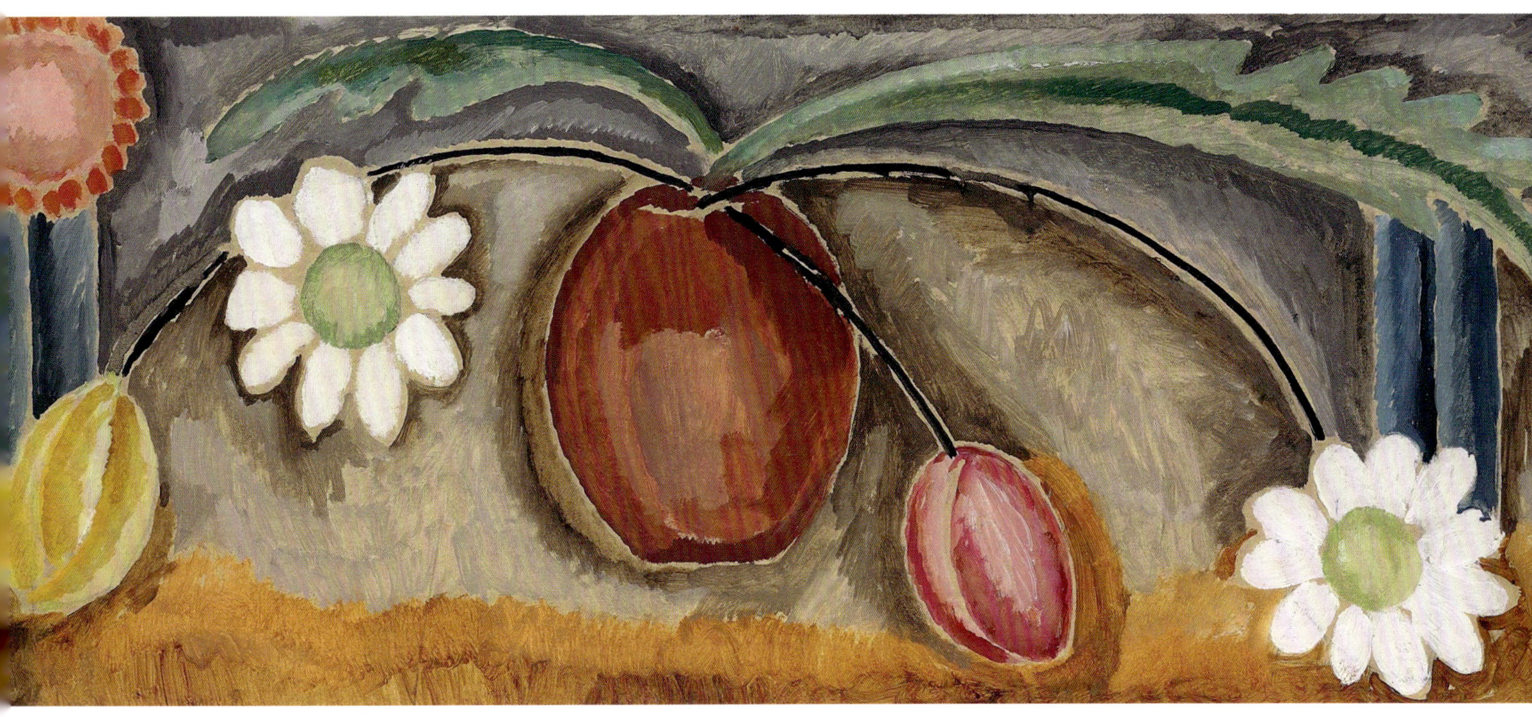

Design for Omega bed-end: Vase of Flowers

1917 | oil and gouache on paper | 38.1 × 94 cm

Several of the artists associated with the Omega Workshops made decorated bed-ends, including Duncan Grant and Roger Fry. A convention emerged within these Omega pieces that the bed-head features a reclining female nude (as seen in *Nude with Poppies*, 1916, p. 88) and the bed-end shows a bowl of fruit or vase of flowers, as seen here. The simplified daisies and tulips on this design are also seen on the doors Bell painted for Grant at Charleston (1918, p. 94). The motif of the brown vase and three main, heavily drooping stems also appear in Bell's painting *The Tub* (1917, Tate, p. vi).

The Pond at Charleston

This painting is thought to be the first Bell made after moving to Charleston, the farmhouse near Firle in Sussex that she rented in October 1916 and retained for the rest of her life. In a letter to Duncan Grant, Bell describes 'A large lake, an orchard, trees all round the back of the house and farm buildings, an old house … a walled garden quite as big or bigger than the Asheham one…. The rooms … are very large and light and numerous.'[76] *The Pond at Charleston* is thought to have been painted in winter, from an upstairs window at the front of the house. It shows the flint-walled pond, a granary building to the right and the curve of the South Downs' Firle Beacon in the background. The pond was a repeated source of inspiration for Bell, who painted it in all seasons.[77] The treatment of the pond here is reminiscent of André Derain's *Window at Vers* (1912, Museum of Modern Art, New York), which was shown in the *Second Post-Impressionist Exhibition* (1912).

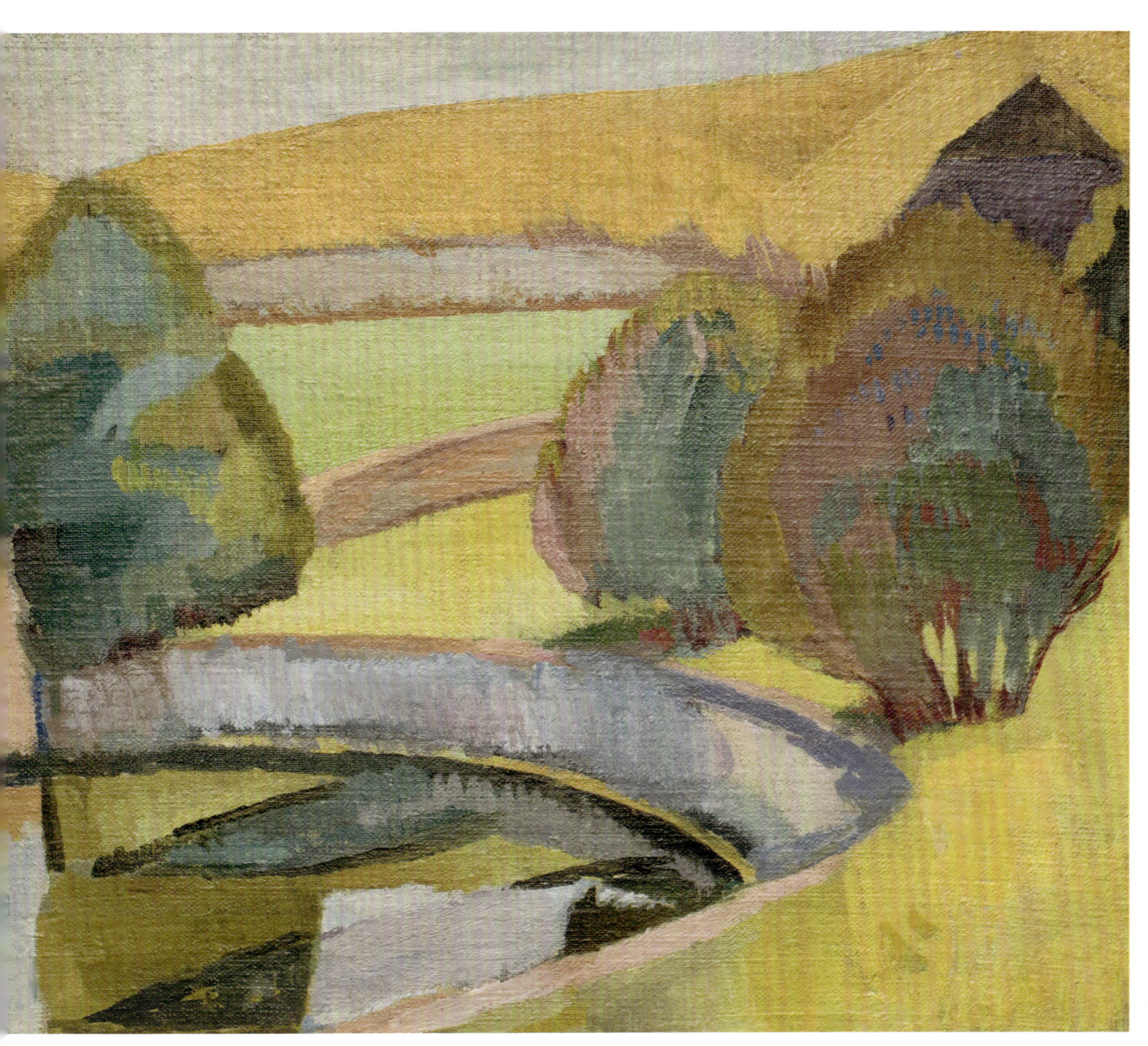

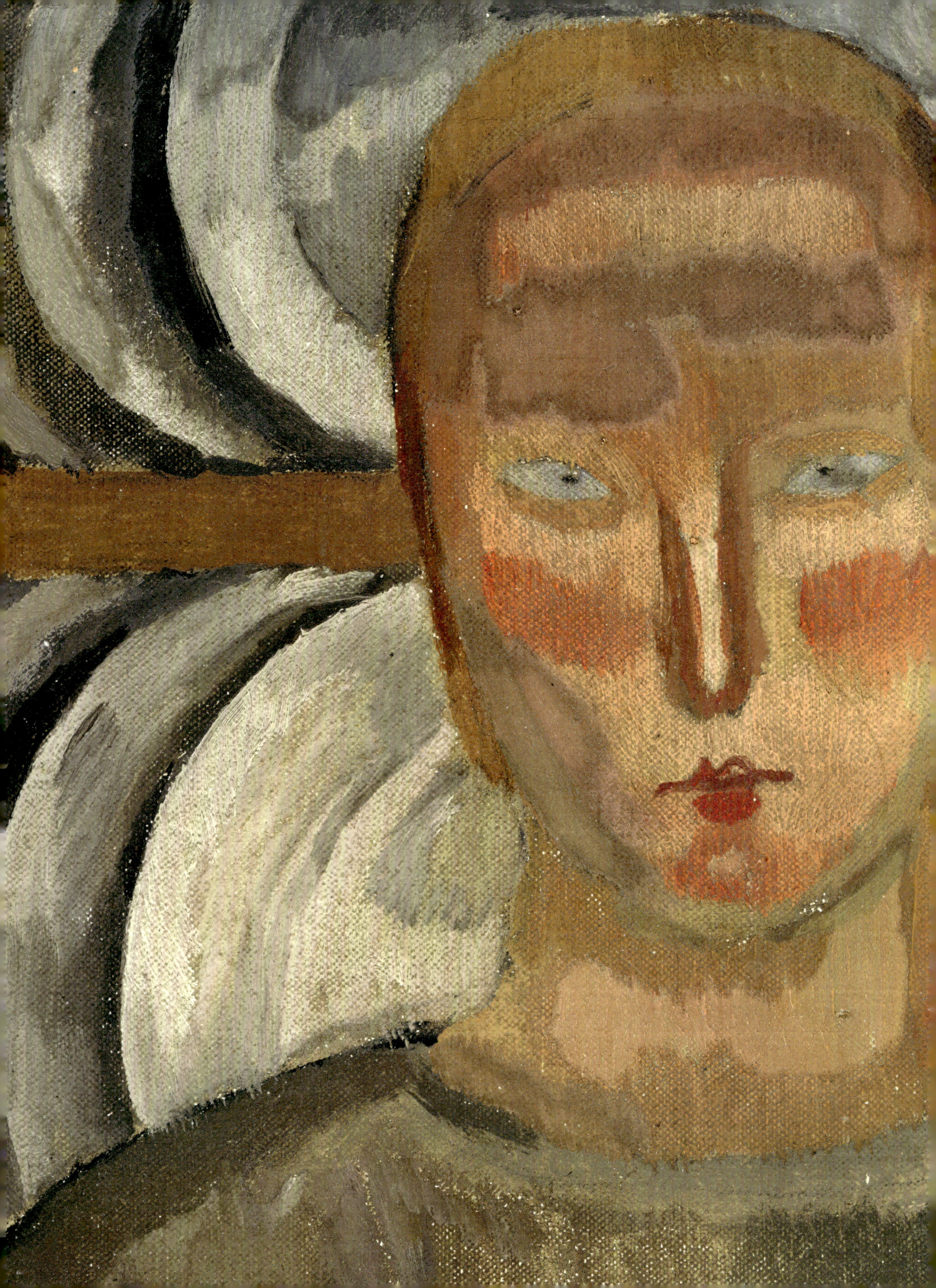

Study of a Woman

c.1917 | oil on canvas | 29.4 × 23 cm

Study of a Woman was originally owned by the writer Mary Hutchinson (1889–1977), and she may also be the model. Hutchinson modelled for Bell on several occasions, including *Mrs St John Hutchinson* (1915, Tate, p. 26). Bell and Hutchinson were friends and often close, but their relationship was complicated by Hutchinson's long-term open affair with Clive Bell between 1914 and 1927. The greyish broad-rimmed plates in the background of this painting bear a strong resemblance to those made by Roger Fry for the Omega Workshops, and this painting places the Omega's work in a modern domestic setting.[78]

Doors of Duncan Grant's bedroom at Charleston

1918 | painted wood | 188 cm × 79 cm

In early 1917 Bell decorated the fireplace in Duncan Grant's bedroom at Charleston, and in 1918 painted the two doors. Bell wrote to Roger Fry: 'They come on either side of the mantelpiece you know which makes it a rather amusing whole but I'm not doing anything very startling – only pots of flowers and marbled circles.'[79] Typical of Bell's decorative style, the liveliness of the freely painted jugs of flowers is contrasted with restrained linear bands and Bell's signature marbled circles.

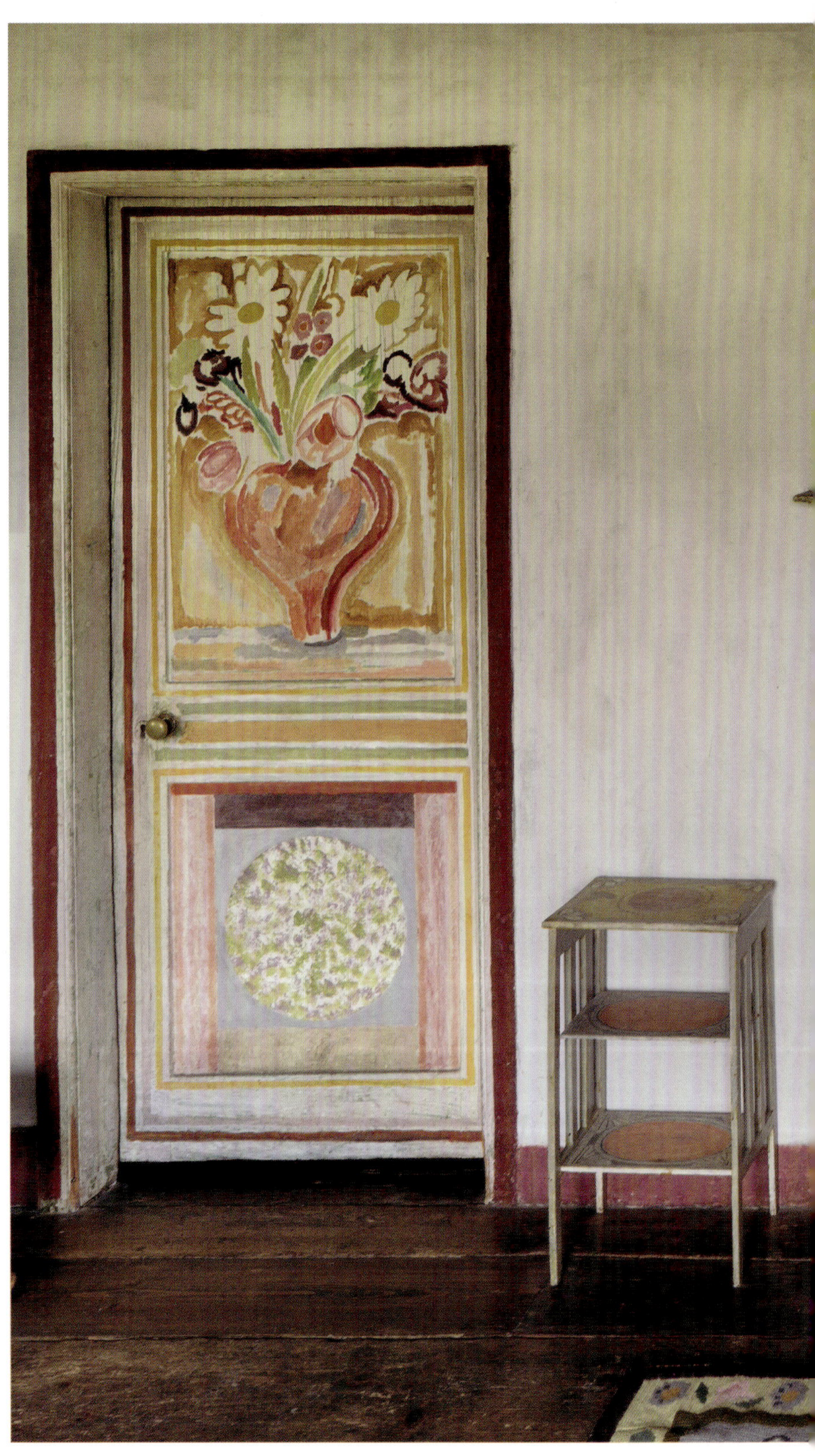

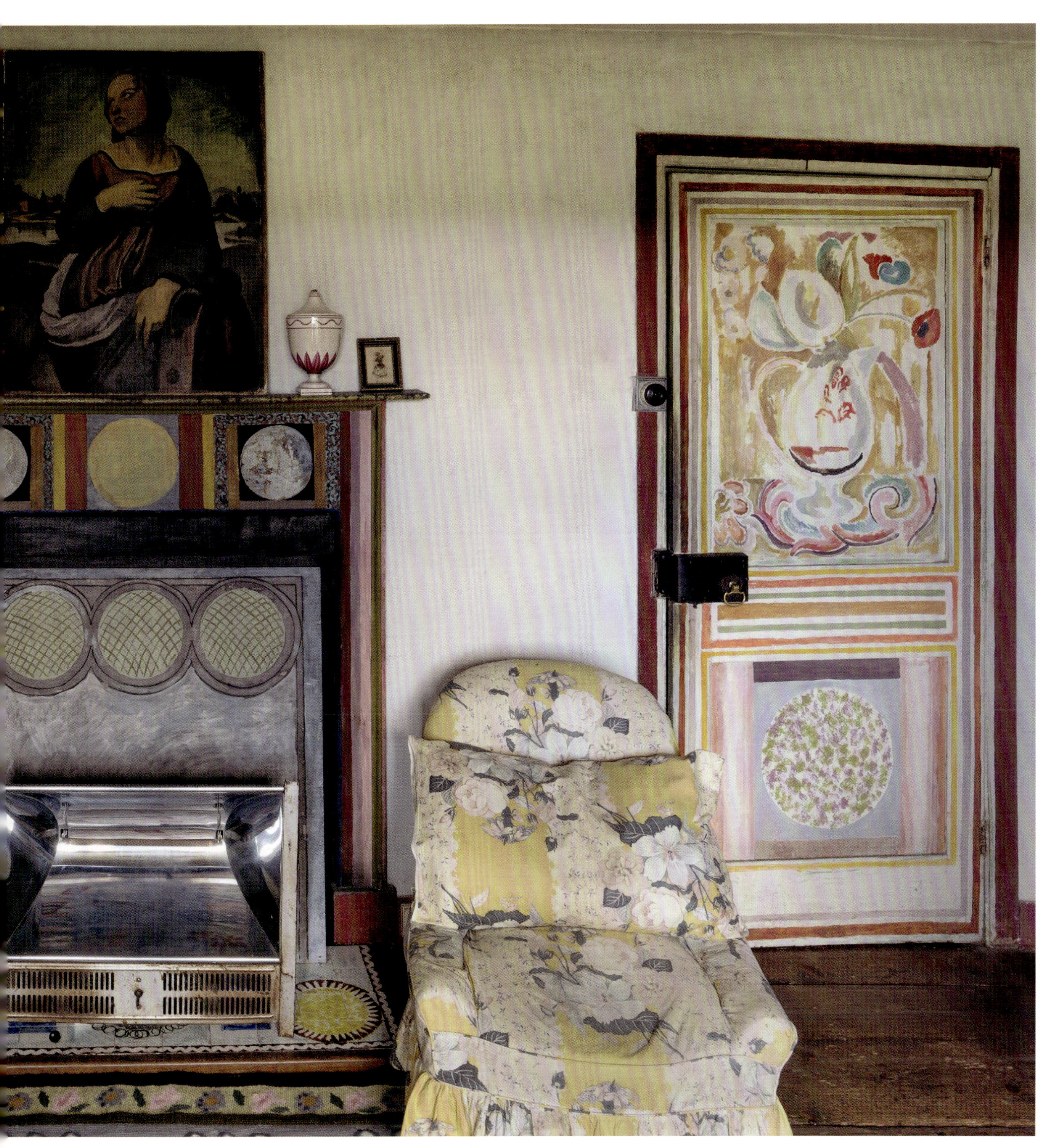

You may have stopped in the garden at Charleston, admiring its lush greenness, anticipating a quaint interior. But once inside it becomes clear your expectations are confounded: you have actually entered something entirely more enigmatic and unexpected.

I went to the farmhouse one afternoon more than twenty years ago with my twin sister and my parents, and it has become framed in my mind ever since as a dream might be. A house full of details, of specific moments. There is something about the place that feels sealed and distant from reality, cut off but intact. It has been taken over, laden with the paintings of Vanessa Bell and her interior design work with Duncan Grant. I remember the lurcher dog Henry painted by Duncan on Vanessa's bedroom wall above a small bed, to watch over and protect her. The numerous intimate, sturdy, robust paintings of babies. Later as you proceed through the house, speaking with enthusiastic tour guides, you hear a story of loss and heartbreak, a house that held the knowledge of an early death of a beloved son in the Spanish Civil War; a sister's recurring mental illness and death by suicide.

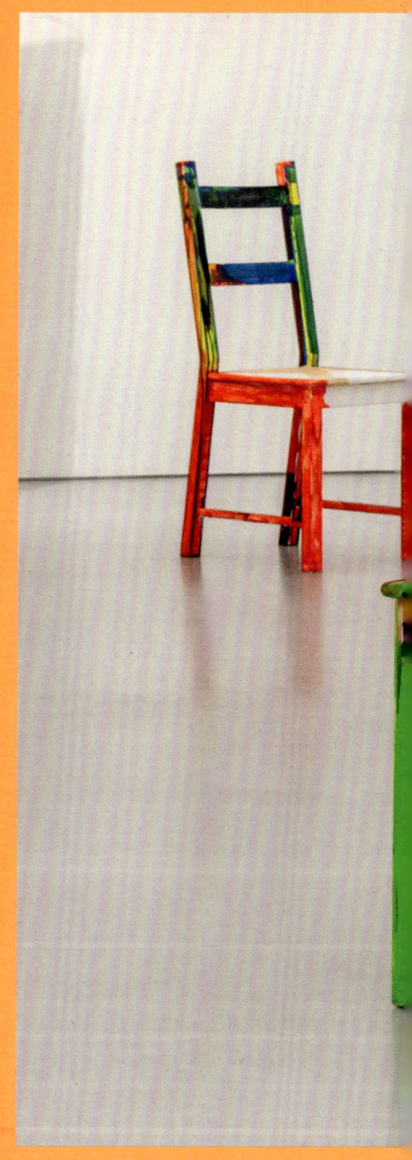

It's as though the place is steeped in tones, always muted, some tired-looking fabric, sunned, all a little bleached in my recollection. When the house was first occupied by the pair they painted it white – to eradicate, to make anew, before beginning a layered work-in-progress. Something of a complete *Gesamtkunstwerk*, a tapestry-like glittering array of painted surface and textile: glowing, dappled, full of light but also dark and cosy, apparently freezing in winter. This must have been the way the house became a living organism, a thing. It appears to almost breathe – it's both alive and utterly dead – but stopped in time. Some of the surfaces look like they were painted yesterday, but then isn't that the mysterious nature of art: to approach something and see it almost fizz with life, all the while knowing its moment of creation is definitely over?

There seems to be a film of otherness across all surfaces, like a fluid painting-over, but also repainting, because this is not a painting-out or an obliteration. Still polite, making enough room for each other, hints of eroticism but not overwhelming, always coherent and surprising at once – a very conscious play. There must be players to embody the space. The painted

fresco-like walls and doorways are not scenes of confessionals –
there is a feeling of entombment nonetheless and of being among
loved, valued and cared-for things.

Vanessa chose this environment, surrounding herself in it, an inner
life made outwards, cross-pollinated across an array of forms – a
sense of spread and roaming. I think the first objects that I really
loved were the lampshades in an upstairs bedroom: misshapen
cloth hung loosely across something that was probably unsafely
wired, a sense of make-do and mend about it all. A good enough
attempt to create a shade. Like a moment inside a Vuillard interior,
all the dots flying and settling, figures masked and blurring into
pillows and tablecloths and walls. Where is the floor? A sense of
a pre-psychedelic all-seeingness and uncertainty. Certainly, where
experimentation would have been valued and allowed.

To live inside a painted interior speaks of permanence. How paint
stays, always outliving the maker. Like a Roman mosaic discovered
centuries later and scrutinized, the house shows us Vanessa's
environment, and from that we try to understand more of her – but
can we ever really know, and do we have a right to? We are seeing
the creativity of a woman who had a long life, who suffered huge
losses but also had enough purpose and drive to keep on living.

I know I have allowed that memory of the visit and lived on it at
different times in my life as an artist. At times, when I've painted a
wooden chair, or a lampshade or a tray, I've known I had permission
to do so in any way I please, and I think that is due in part to a bit
of the magic of that place. Why do I paint things for my own home?
Is it to reflect unconscious parts of myself back, to remind myself
of my other selves, a note to say that I am still here being multi-
dimensional, complicated and faceted. I've certainly painted things
for my own home when no one wanted them – but I wanted to see
them, when I wasn't being asked or paid to make them. I painted for
myself, to spend time, enrich, seek solace, something like that, to get
lost and found again in painting things.

Hayley Tompkins is an artist living in Glasgow, Scotland, who makes
mixed-media installations including painting, objects and film.

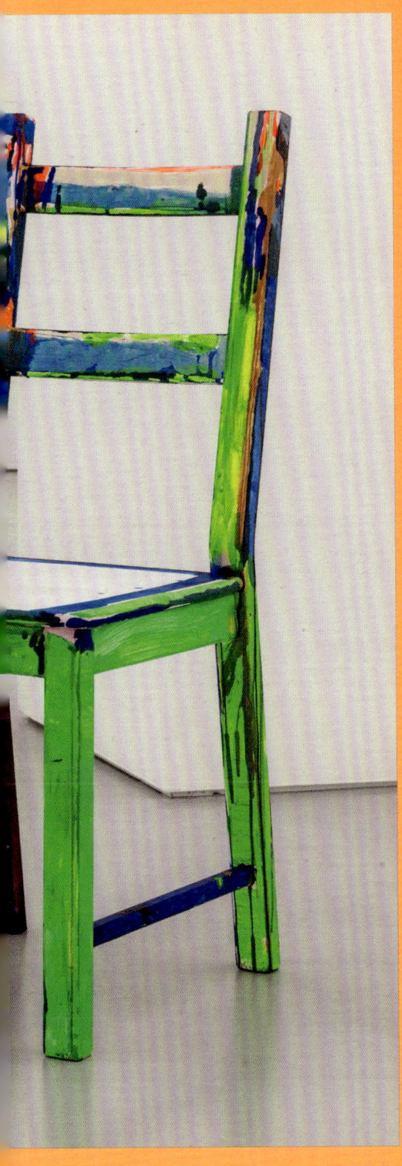

Hayley Tompkins, installation
view, *Life Like Looking*,
Efremidis, Seoul, 2023.

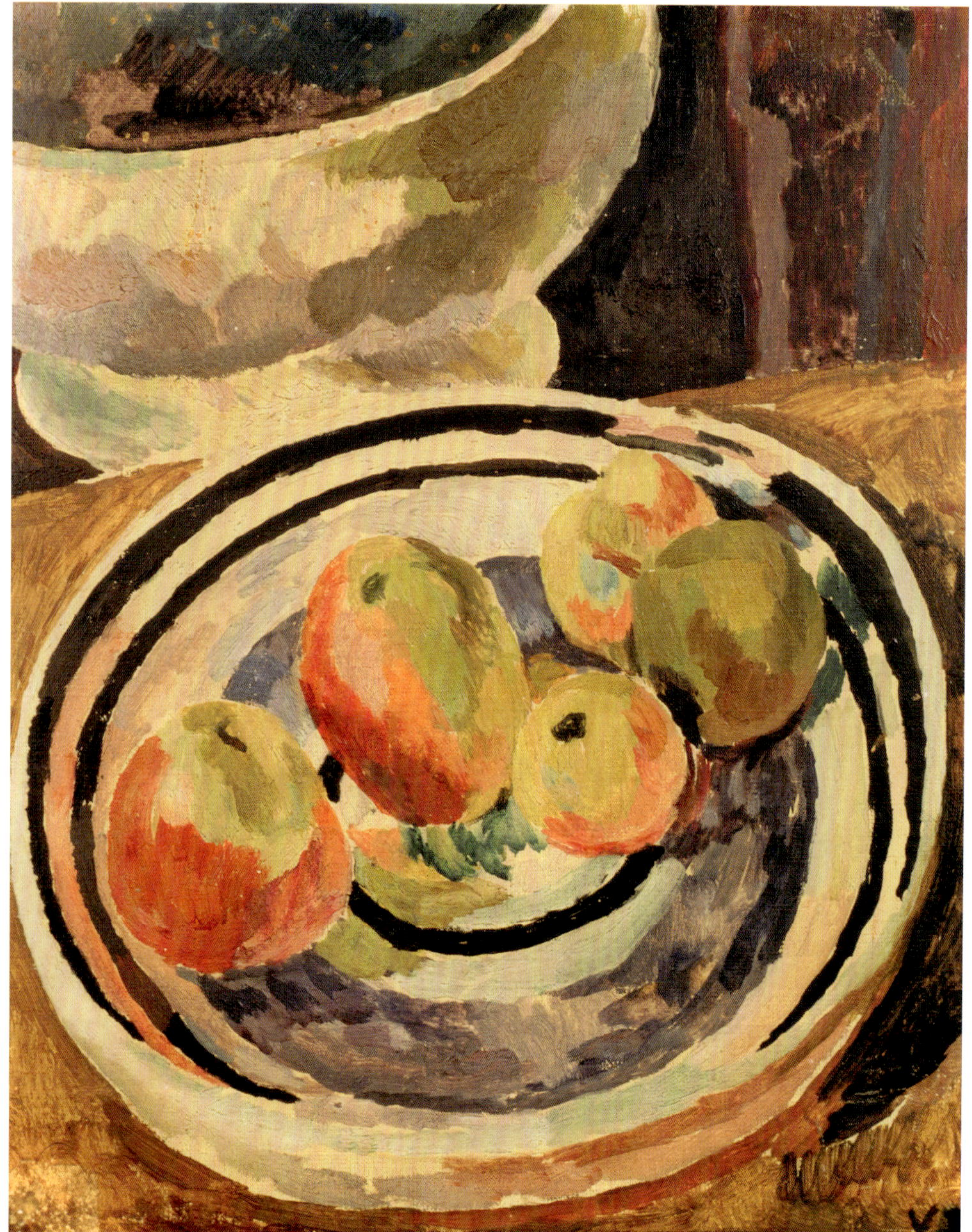

In March 1918 the economist John
Maynard Keynes bought Cézanne's
Still Life with Apples (*c.* 1878, Fitzwilliam Museum) from an auction
in Paris. The painting was brought
back to Charleston, prompting Bell
to write to Roger Fry: 'Maynard
came back suddenly and unexpect-
edly late at night having been
dropped at the bottom of the lane by
Austin Chamberlain in a Government motor and said he had left a
Cézanne by the roadside! Duncan
rushed off to get it and you can
imagine how exciting it all was....
The Cézanne is really amazing and
it's most exciting to have it in the
house. It's so extraordinarily solid
and alive. It's the little one of 7
apples that we liked so much, very
small indeed.'[80] Keynes then took
the painting to his home in Bloomsbury, where Bell and Fry visited
it later that year. Bell had already
taken apples as a still-life subject in
Apples, 46 Gordon Square (*c.* 1909–
10, Charleston) but, unsurprisingly,
after the arrival of the Cézanne
she revisited the subject, with this
painting and *Still Life with Apples
in a Bowl* (*c.* 1919, private collection).
Both paintings show the apples
in the same bowl and both take a
high viewpoint, looking down on
the subject with the same skewed
perspective used by Cézanne.

Portrait of Mrs M.

1919 | oil on canvas | 68.2 × 56.8 cm

This portrait, in Bell's more subdued post-war palette, shows Dr Marie Mathilde Alice Moralt, who came to Charleston when Bell and Duncan Grant's daughter Angelica was gravely ill in January 1919. Moralt took charge and changed the baby's diet, causing immediate improvement. She stayed at Charleston for several weeks and returned in May 1919, when she sat for this portrait and one by Grant. Bell wrote that Moralt was 'Rather a find, as she's certainly sensible and quite easy to say anything to, which is more than most doctors are … she might supply the general want of an ordinarily intelligent, sensible general practitioner.'[81] Moralt and Bell stayed in touch for many years after, as friends and in a profes-sional capacity. When the painting was exhibited at the Independent Gallery, London, in 1922, Roger Fry wrote that: 'These figures are singularly alive and coherent in gesture and expression. The *Portrait of Mrs M.* is perhaps the most brilliant thing in the exhibition.'[82]

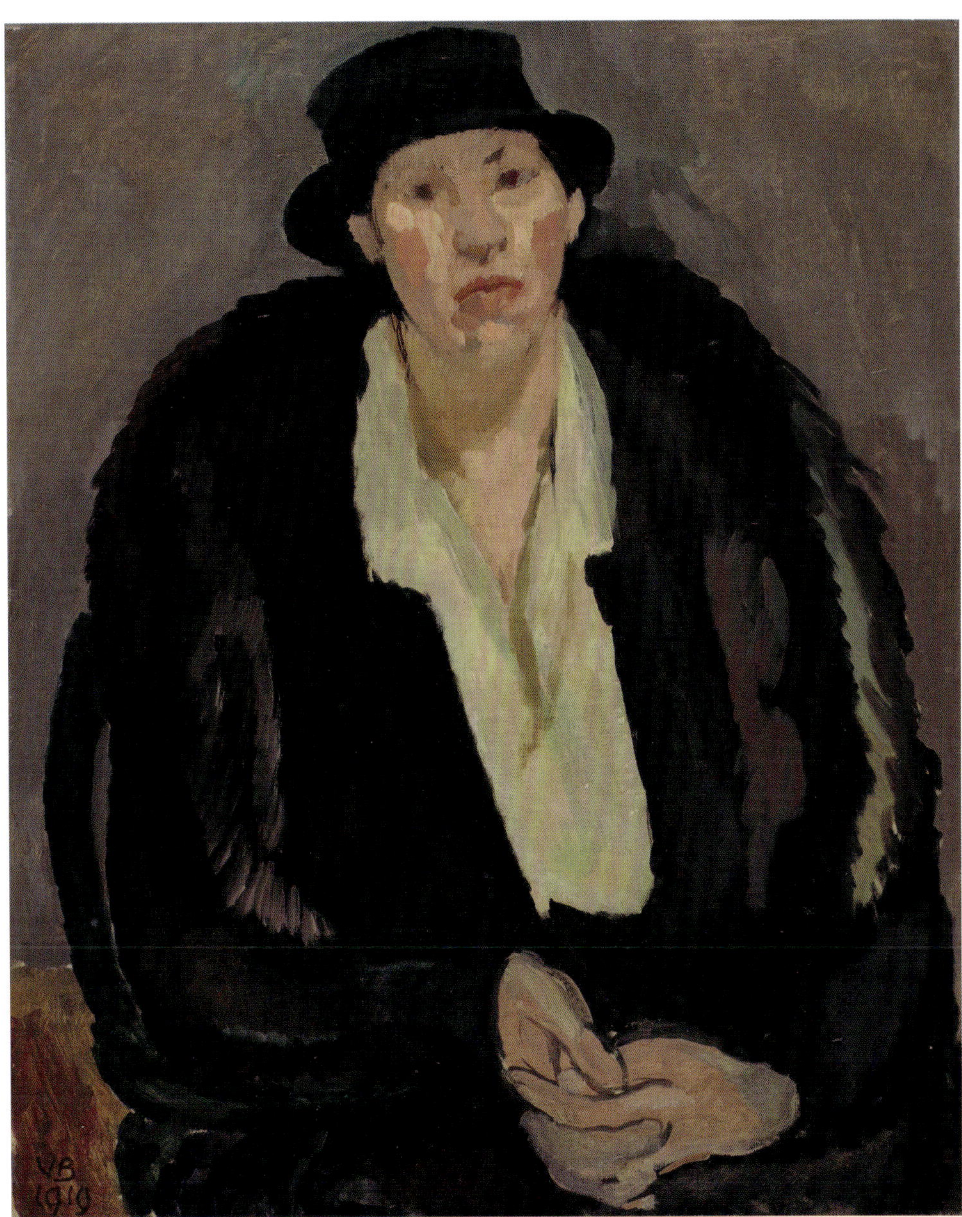

Portrait of Quentin Bell

*c.*1920 | oil on canvas | 71 × 60 cm

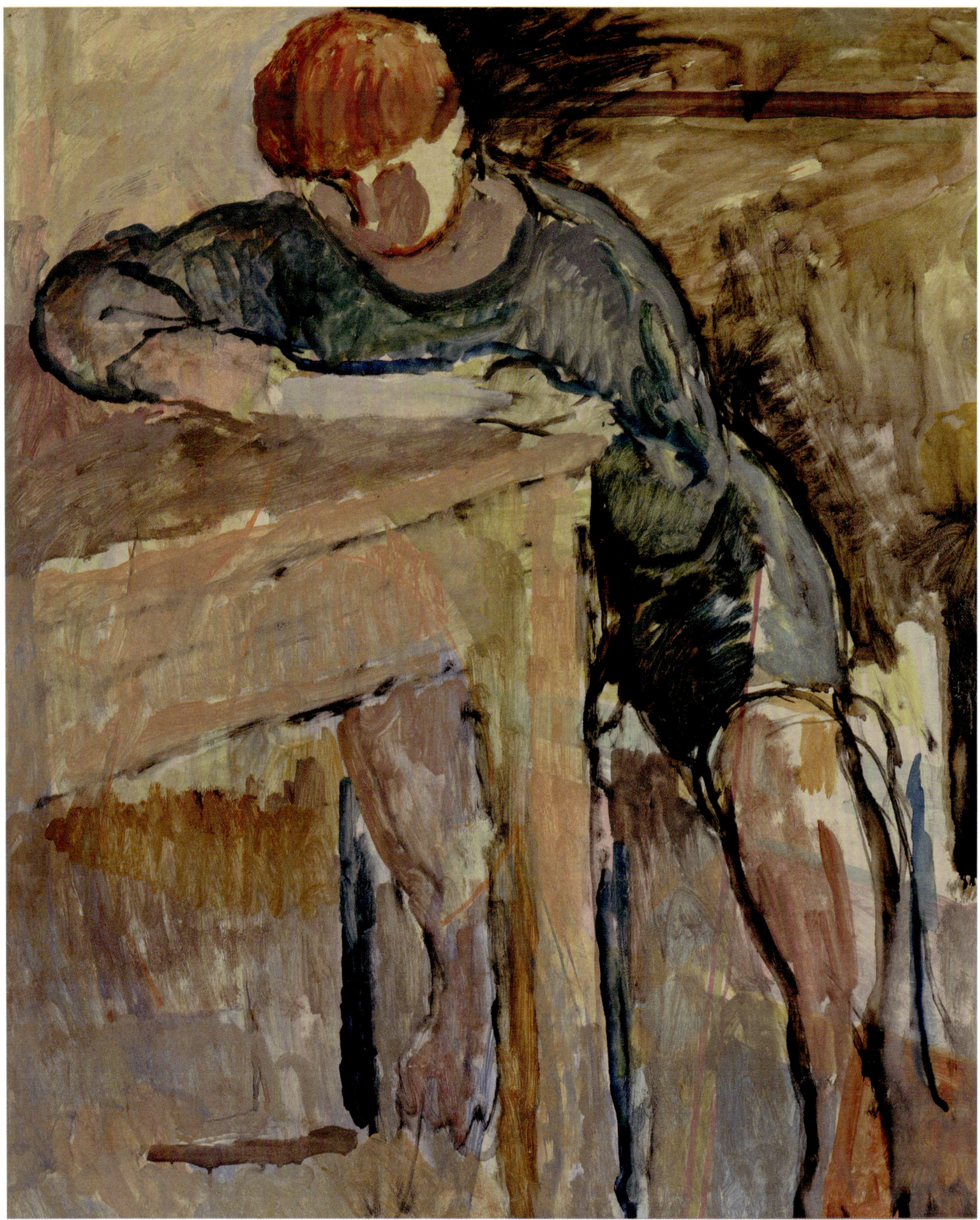

Portrait of Quentin Bell

c.1920 | oil on canvas | 53.3 × 45.6 cm

Bell's most experimental years correspond to her children's youth: 'Bell in her best paintings and her letters, seems to have experienced her children more as creative peers than as dependants.'[83] These are two of a number of studies of Quentin drawing or writing. In the first portrait he is seen, aged around 10, hunched and concentrating on his piece of paper. In the second more highly finished portrait he looks up at his mother with a direct gaze. Virginia Nicholson, Quentin's daughter, writes: 'At Charleston the Bell children grew up in an almost prelapsarian world, a kind of Eden … Julian, Quentin and Angelica grew up barefoot and naked; children of nature, unruly, subject to every danger and subjects in every painting.'[84]

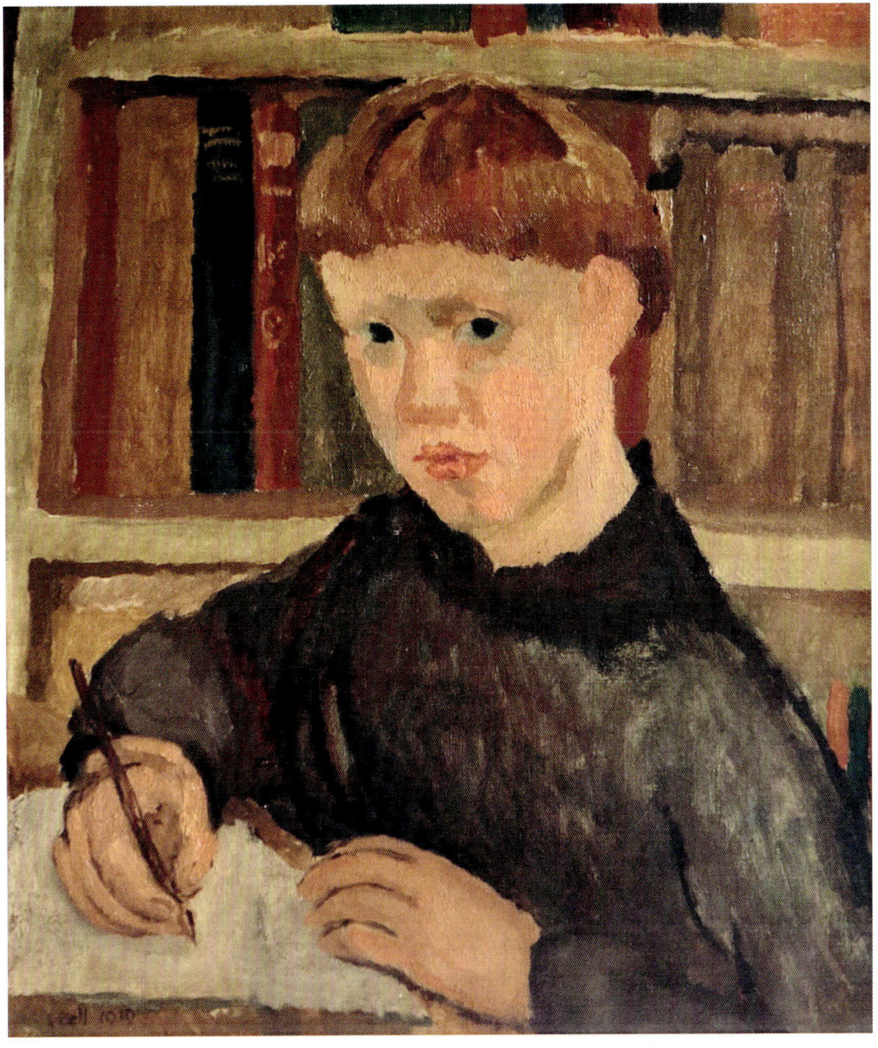

Studies for the Muses of Arts and Sciences

1920 | oil on canvas | each 83.8 × 35.5 cm

In 1920 John Maynard Keynes (1883–1946), then fellow of King's College, Cambridge, commissioned Bell and Duncan Grant to decorate his study at Webb's Court, with related panels on either side of the door and bookcase, as well as curtains and furnishings. While Bell and Grant worked on the decorations, Keynes was living at Charleston writing *The Economic Consequences of the Peace* (1919). The artists, working in an outdoor studio, planned eight figures – four male (by Grant) and four female (by Bell) – representing the muses of the arts and sciences, although 'they are supposed to represent law, science, history, etc. though you mightn't think it – in fact we're always changing their arts and their sciences'.[85] Earlier in 1920, Grant, Bell and Keynes had spent over a month in Italy,

mostly in Rome and Florence. This recent experience of Italian Renaissance fresco painting may have influenced these decorations, although 'they did not recreate any particular precedent' but 'invoked proto-Renaissance art more generally'.[86]

In 1910 Grant had painted a previous mural in Keynes's study which depicted nude and semi-nude male and female figures celebrating a grape harvest. As Reed notes: 'The provocative sensuality of this bacchanal may have grown inappropriate to the economist's new found public stature.' Bell and Grant's new decorative scheme 'supplanted an iconography of uninhibited private sensuality with subjects more in keeping with the discipline[s] of an academic institution'.[87]

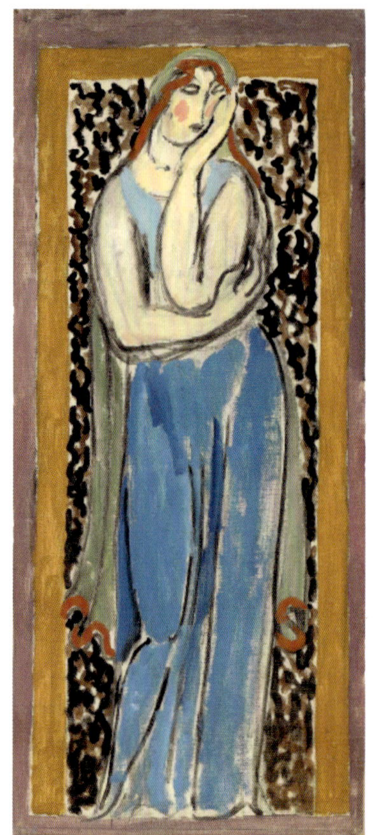

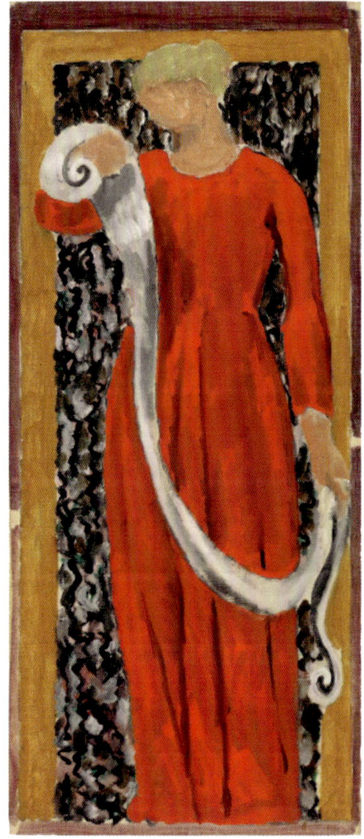

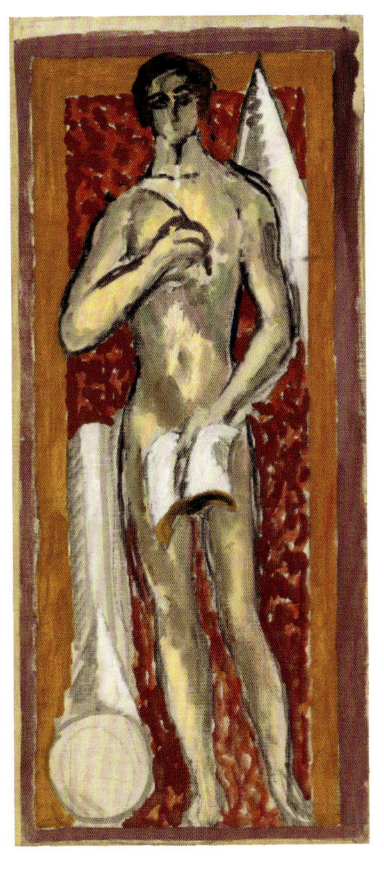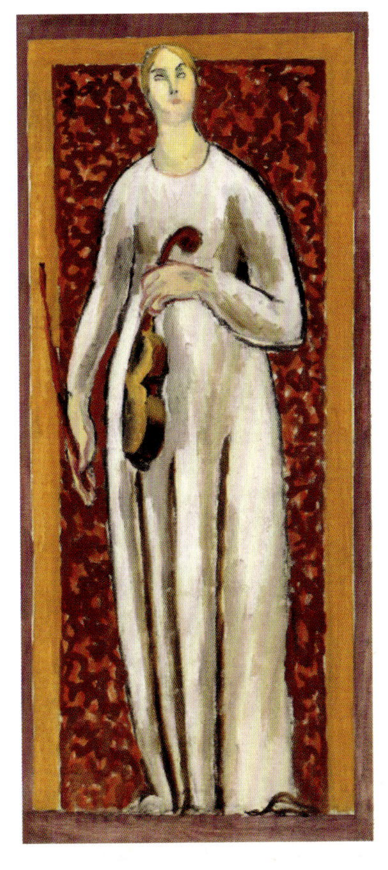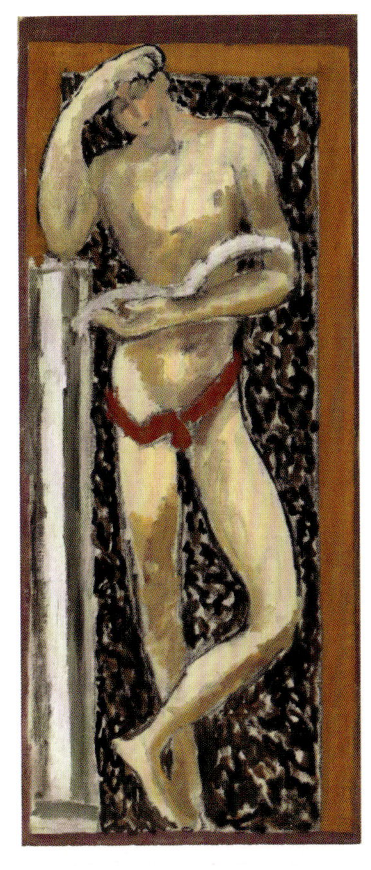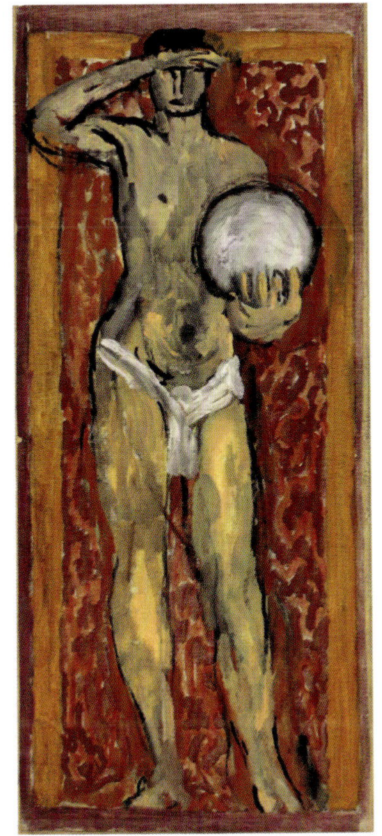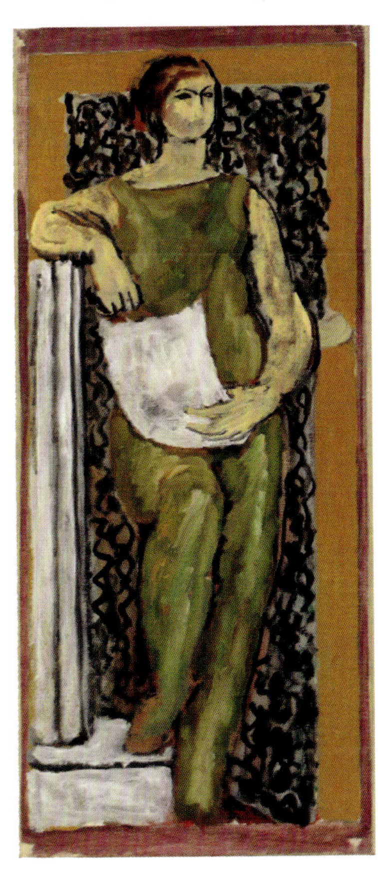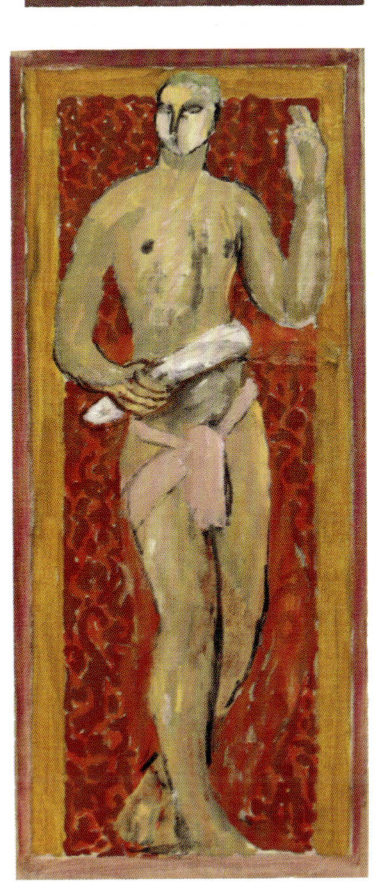

Interior with a Table

1921 | oil on canvas | 54 × 64.1 cm

This picture was painted at La Maison Blanche, a villa outside St Tropez overlooking the bay. As Bell describes it: 'The rooms are large and bright, all brand new and spotless, but very practical, with tiled floors.... Then there are vineyards all round. We are high up and look over the town and across the bay. The sea is very blue and today the weather is perfect.'[88] At this time, Bell was worried her painting was becoming too like Duncan Grant's and had decided they should paint separately and not look at each other's work for a period. Bell often used windows, doorways and bridges to frame her landscapes, and this example contrasts the bright sunlit valley with the silvery tones of the interior. The scene is enlivened by the interplay of curves of the furniture with the verticals of the window and curtains.

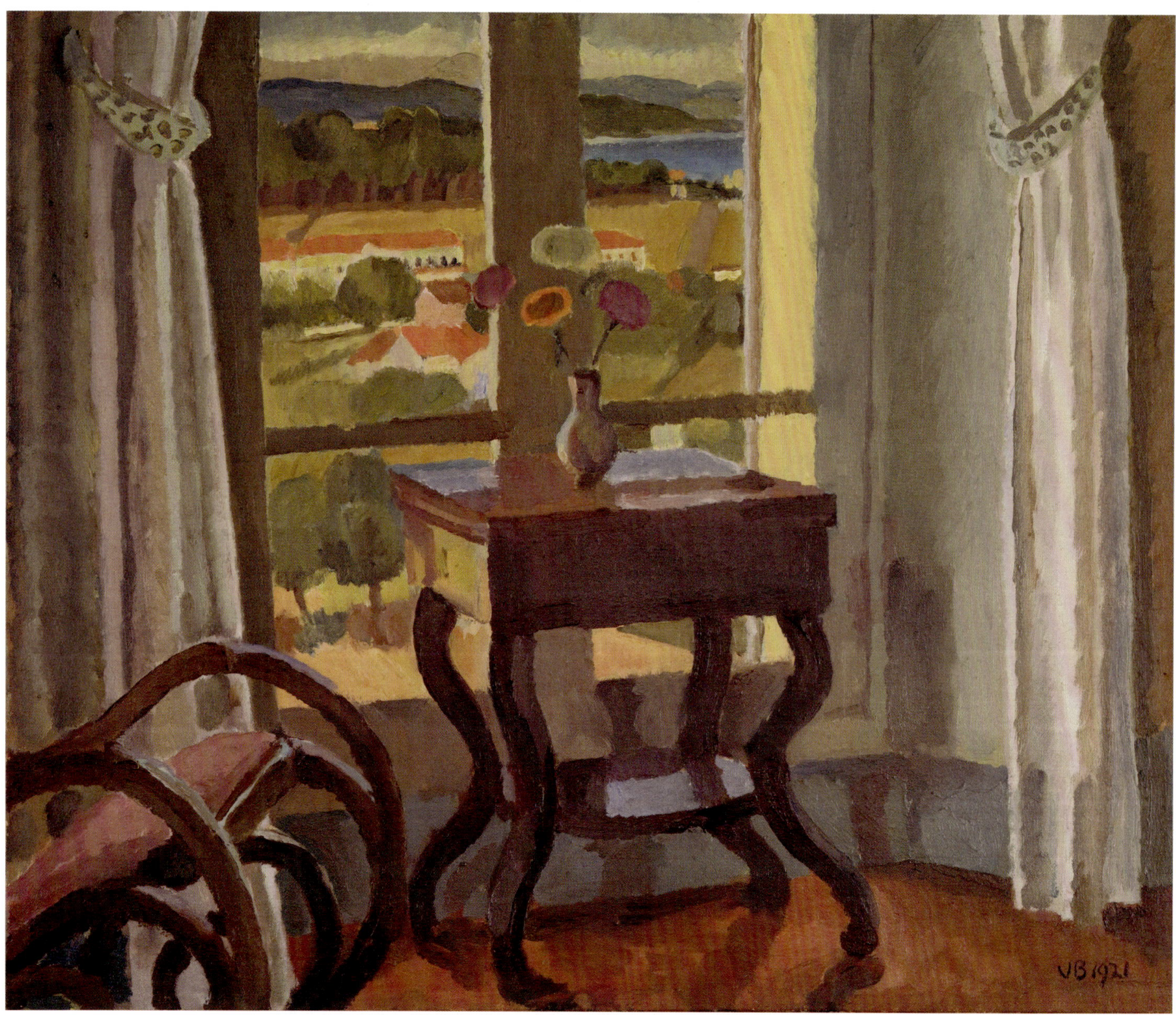

Nude

c. 1922–23 | oil on canvas | 81.3 × 65.4 cm

Bell made this study of a professional model in London, a couple of years after visiting Picasso's studio where she saw 'an astonishing painting of two nudes most elaborately finished and rounded'.[89] Earlier the same year, in Paris, she saw 'a magnificent large nude by Matisse, really splendid'.[90] Curator Sarah Milroy suggests that, in this painting, 'Bell seems to picture the brute force required to be in the world and do the kinds of things that women's bodies have always had to do – carrying, cooking, cleaning, birthing, nursing and holding the world together.'[91]

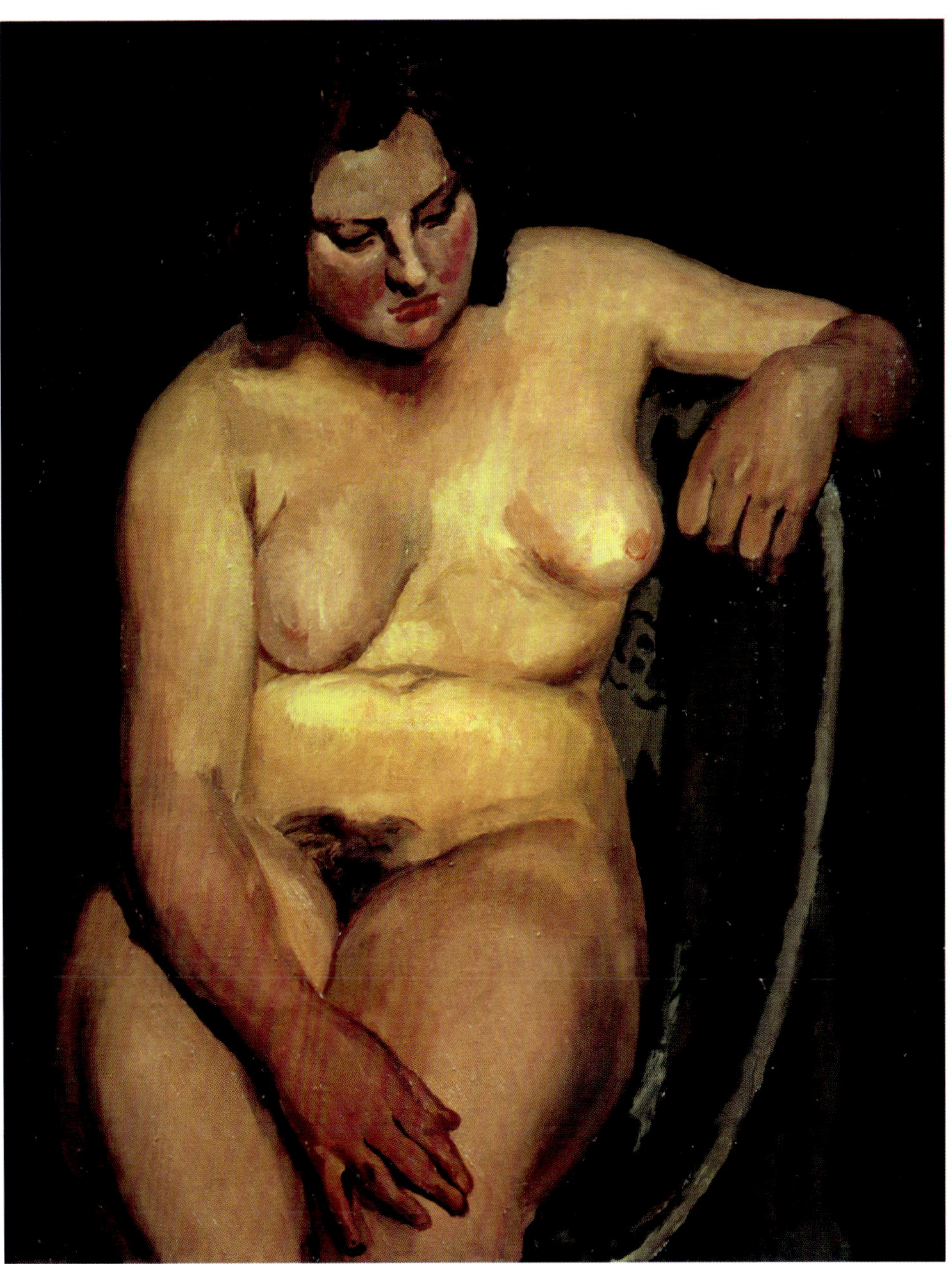

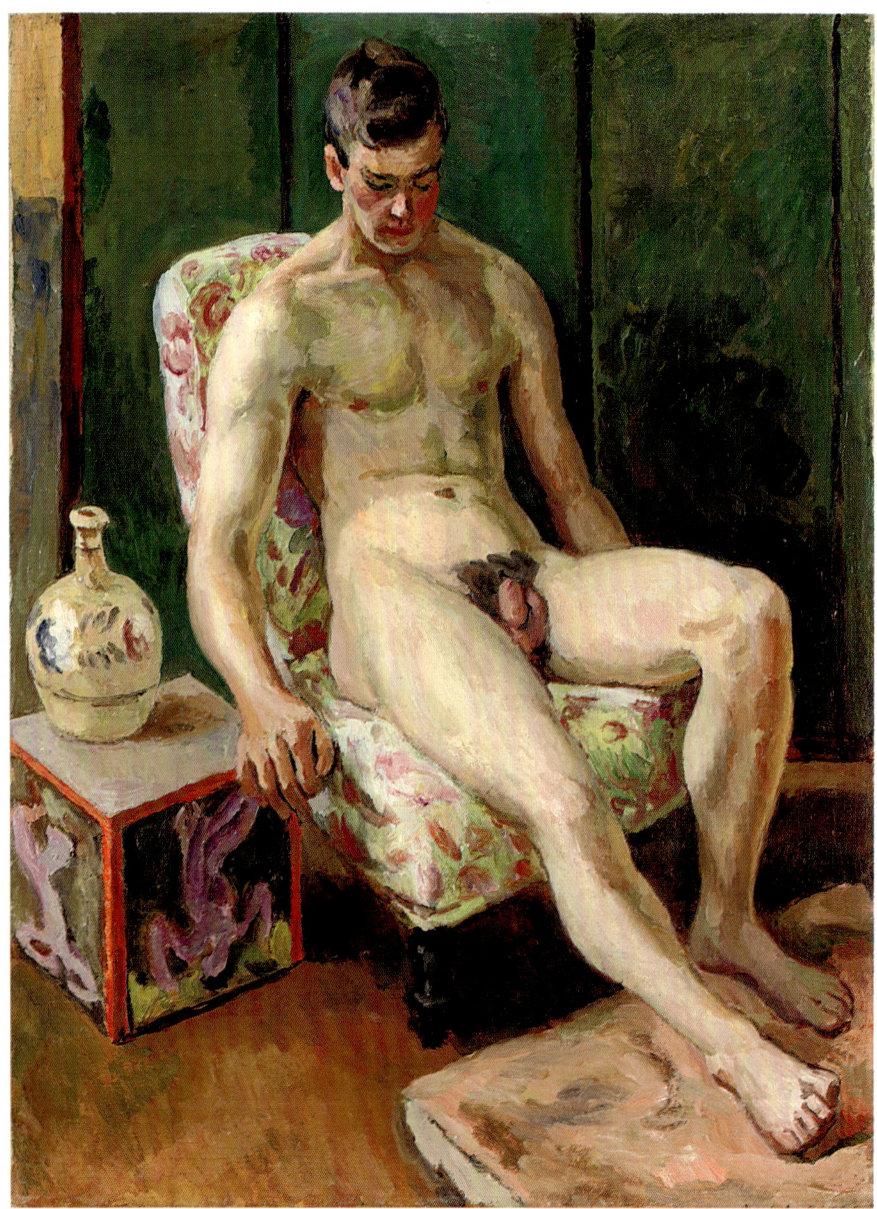

Seated Model at Charleston

c.1922 | oil on canvas | 72.5 × 53.5 cm

These are rare Bell representations of male nudes. During the early 1920s Bell painted a number of male and female nudes (for example, *Nude*, 1922–23, p. 105) which have much more attention to realism and solidity than her earlier figures. Painted at the studio in Charleston, the log box which appears upside down in this painting was decorated by Duncan Grant in 1916–17, and both this and the vase are still at Charleston. The model for this painting may be Angus Davidson, who was a regular visitor to Charleston from 1922, a friend and lover (during 1922) of Grant and secretary of the Hogarth Press 1924–27. An ink drawing by Grant of a nude Davidson sleeping exists from 1922, as well as a photograph of him in shorts taken by Vanessa, in which his physique bears a strong resemblance to the model here.[92]

Seated Male Nude Model

undated | pencil on paper | 25.4 × 36.6 cm

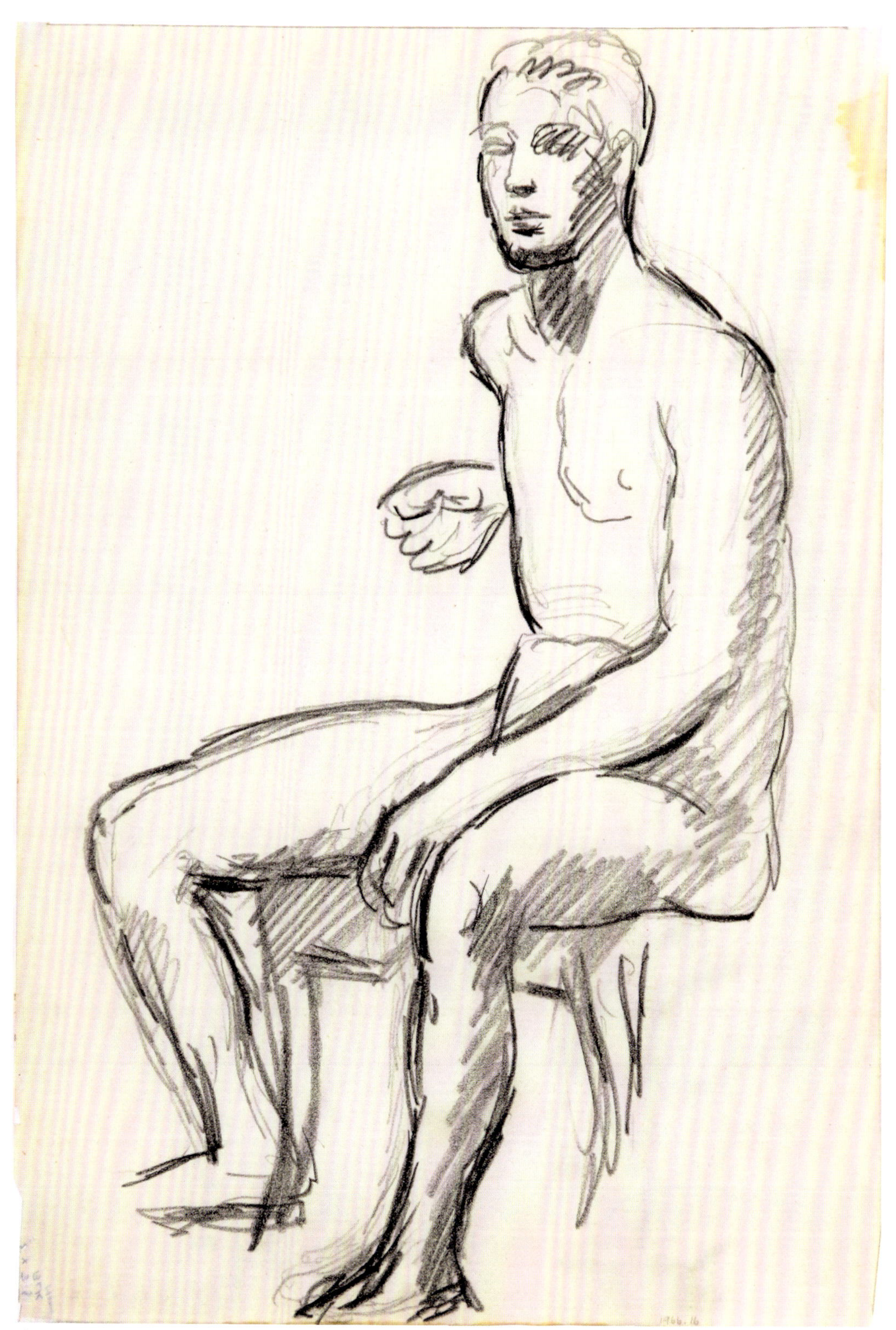

Chair seat

VANESSA BELL AND ETHEL GRANT

1924 | polychrome wools cross-stitched
by Ethel Grant | 41 × 51 cm

Bell produced needlework designs
for the Omega Workshops from its
opening in 1913. After the Omega
closed in 1919, she continued to
design such objects and a number
of friends and professional em-
broiderers carried out the work.
Duncan Grant's mother Ethel
Grant was the most prolific. These
designs for a chair seat or stool
cover and cushion are very characteristic examples of Bell's work,
showing a vase of flowers, framed
by abstract elements created using
pinks and yellows.

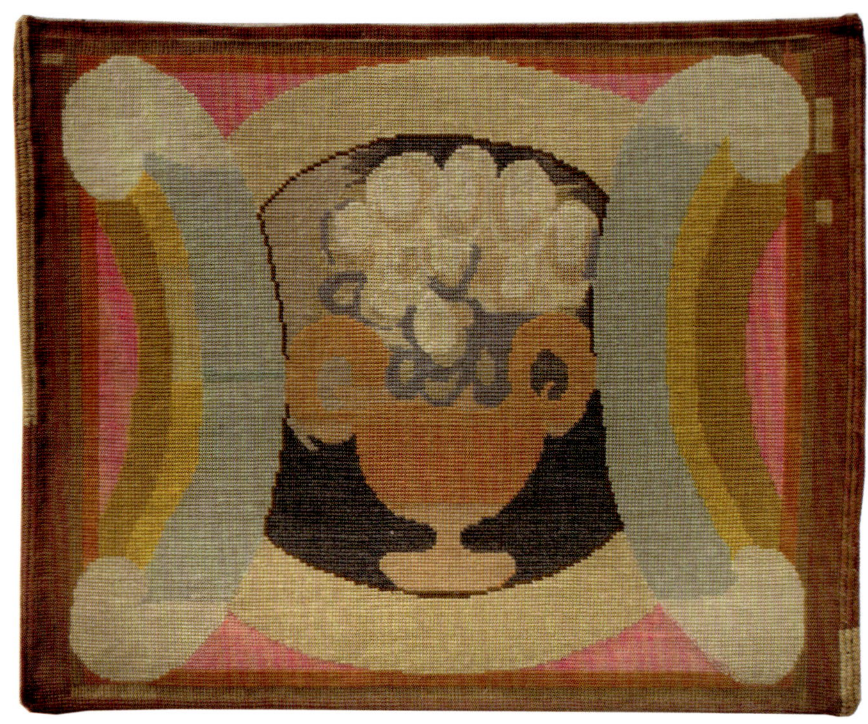

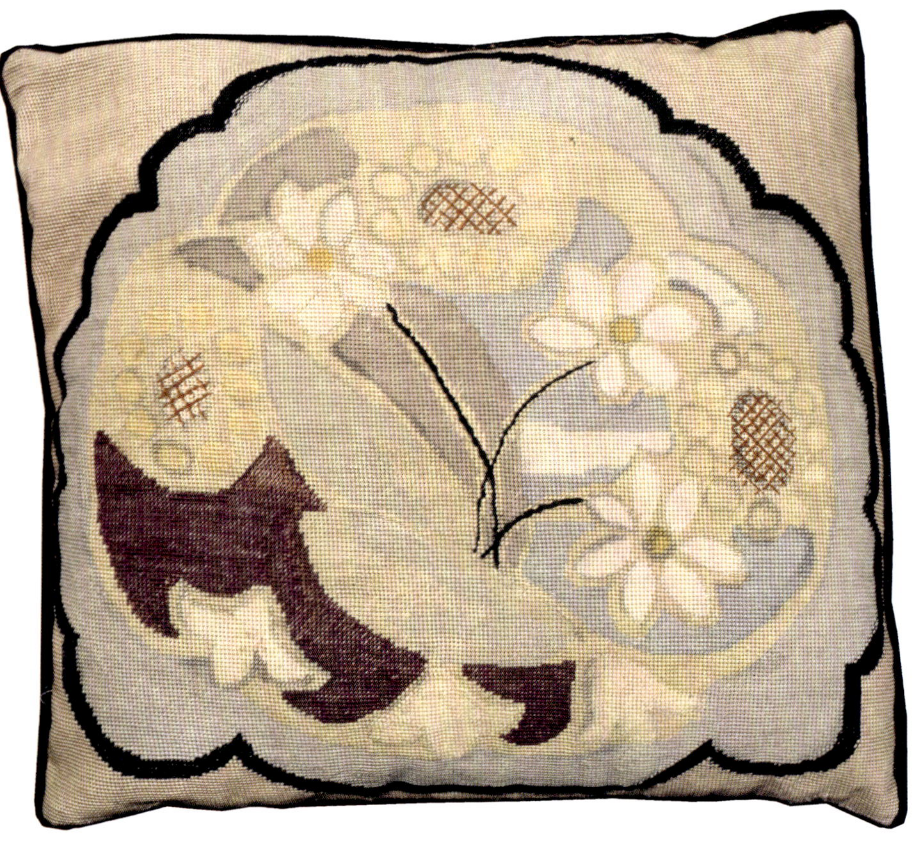

Cushion

VANESSA BELL AND ETHEL GRANT

1925 | canvas, wool | 57 × 49 cm

Long stool

VANESSA BELL AND ETHEL GRANT

1925 | polychrome wools cross-stitched by Ethel Grant | design 34.3 × 86 cm;
stool 66.3 × 113.4 × 40.2 cm

This stool may have been designed for the *Modern Designs in Needlework* exhibition at the Independent Gallery in London (1925). The design of the stool is somewhat at odds with the angular, abstract decoration, but reflects the Bloomsbury attitude of layering new over historic rather than stripping back to the modern.

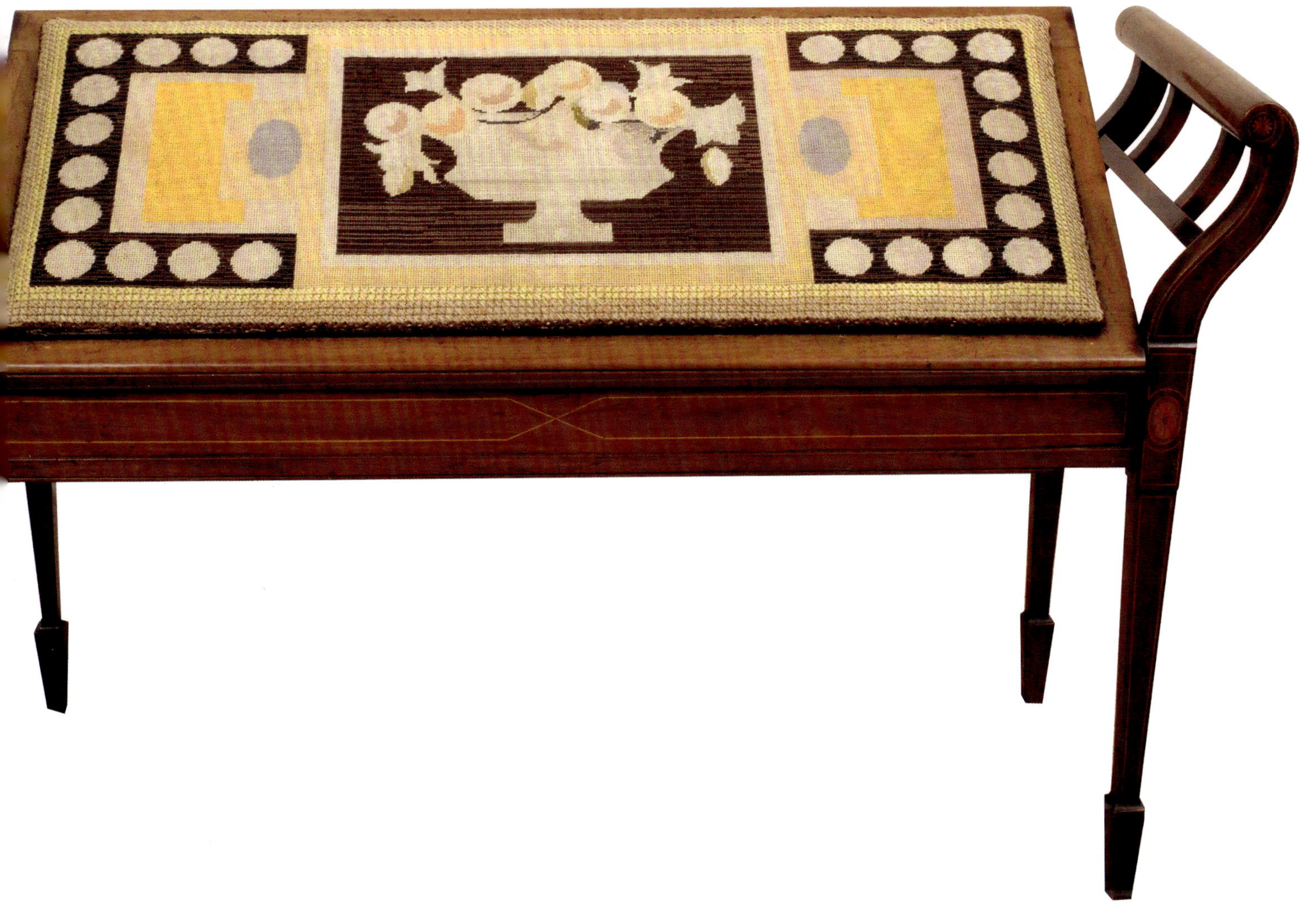

Decorated jar

ROGER FRY AND VANESSA BELL

c.1922 | painted and glazed earthenware |
height 13.8 cm

Following the opening of the
Omega Workshops, Roger Fry was
dissatisfied with the ready-made
ceramic shapes available and set
out to create his own. During the
First World War, Fry worked with
Roger Carter of Poole to make
pieces in quantity, while retain-
ing the personal irregularities of
surface and thickness. After the
closure of the Omega Workshops,
Fry and Bell continued to work
with ceramics: the decoration of
this jar, with its blue and turquoise
seated female nudes and looping
brown decoration at the base and
neck, relates strongly to Bell's 1931
lampstand (p. 126).

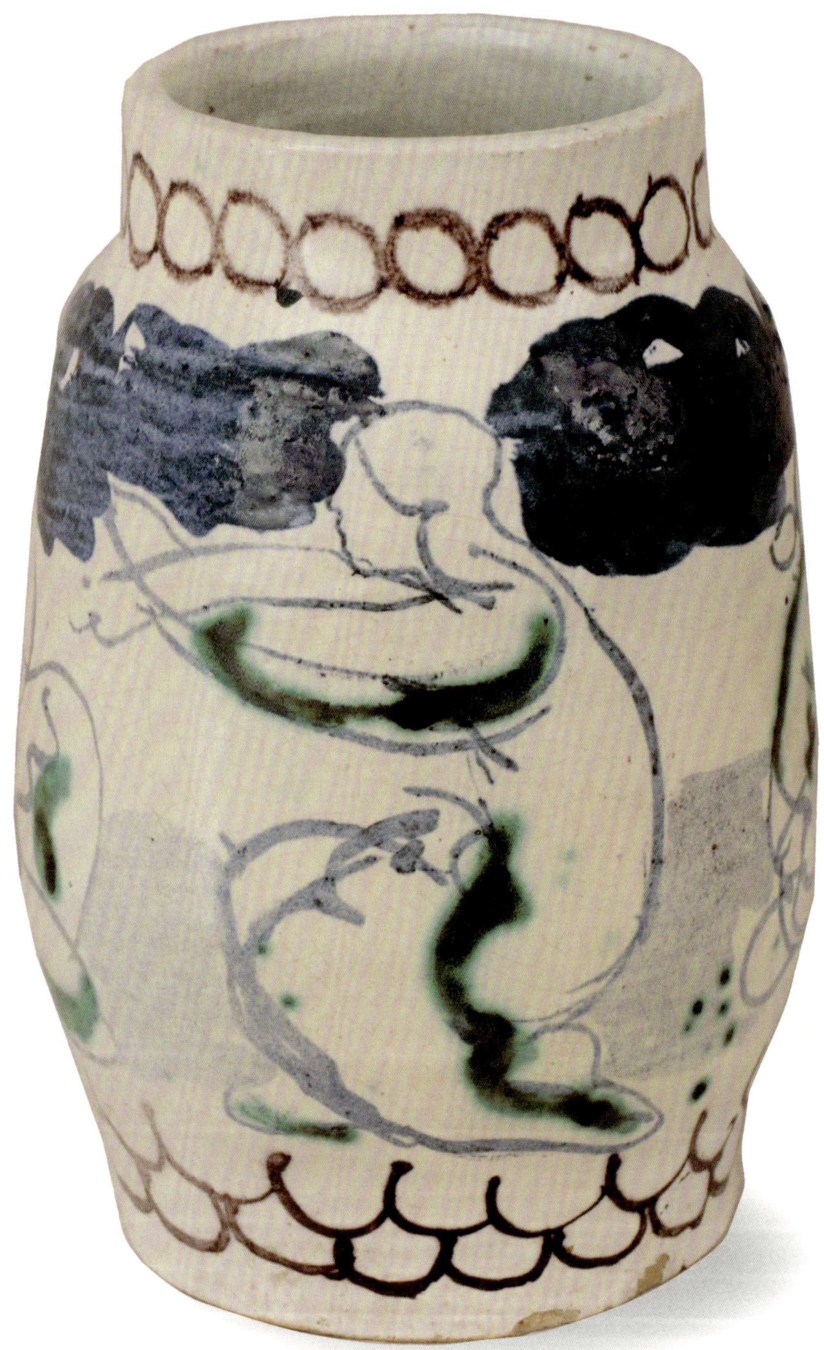

Flower pattern

undated | black biro and ink | 38.5 × 25.5 cm

Decorative motifs

undated | pencil on paper | 26.4 × 17.9 cm

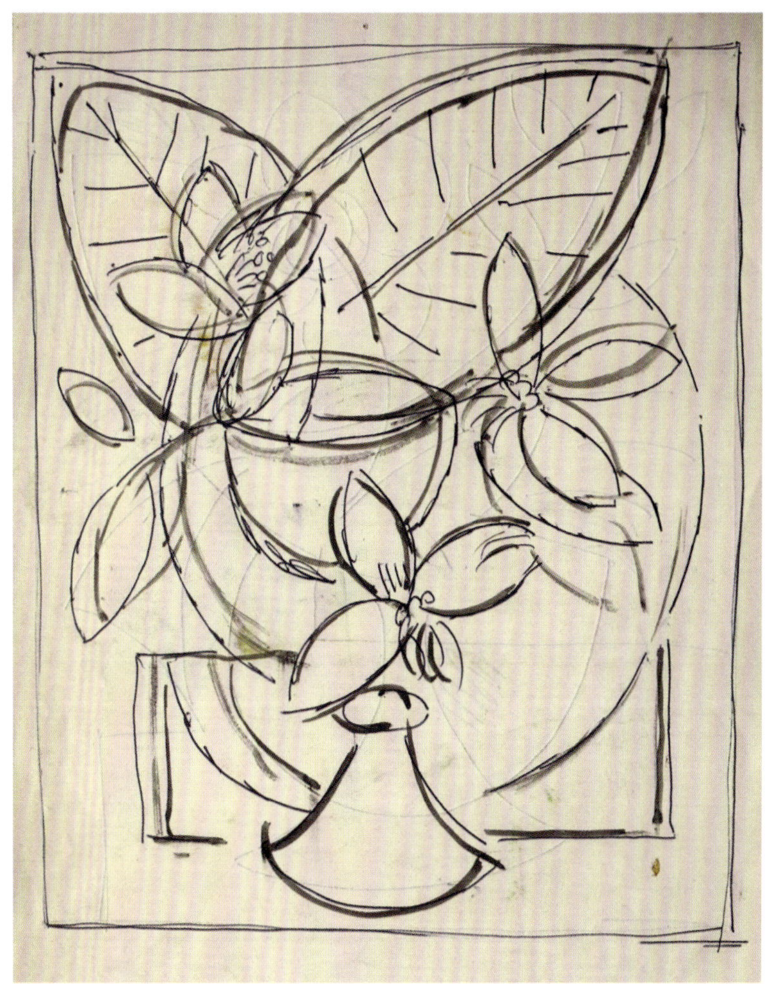

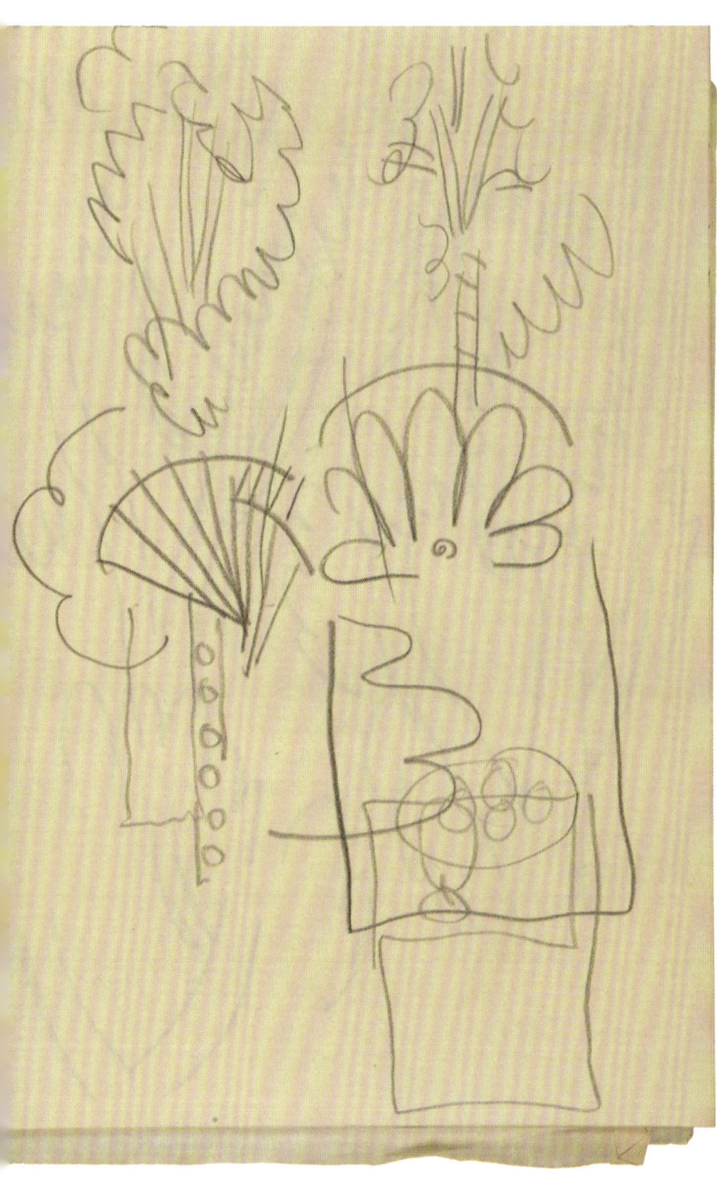

These sketchbook pages may contain designs for embroidery, textiles or ceramic decorations. *Flower pattern* reflects Bell's cushion design (p. 128). *Decorative motifs* is found in a sketchbook which includes various studies of fans and has been read as a sketch 'in which two well-dressed ladies are reduced to the shapes of their fans and feathered hats themselves, standing before a table abstractedly set with a glass of wine and a bowl of fruit for lunch'.[93] Bell also designed a fabric based on fans around 1946.[94]

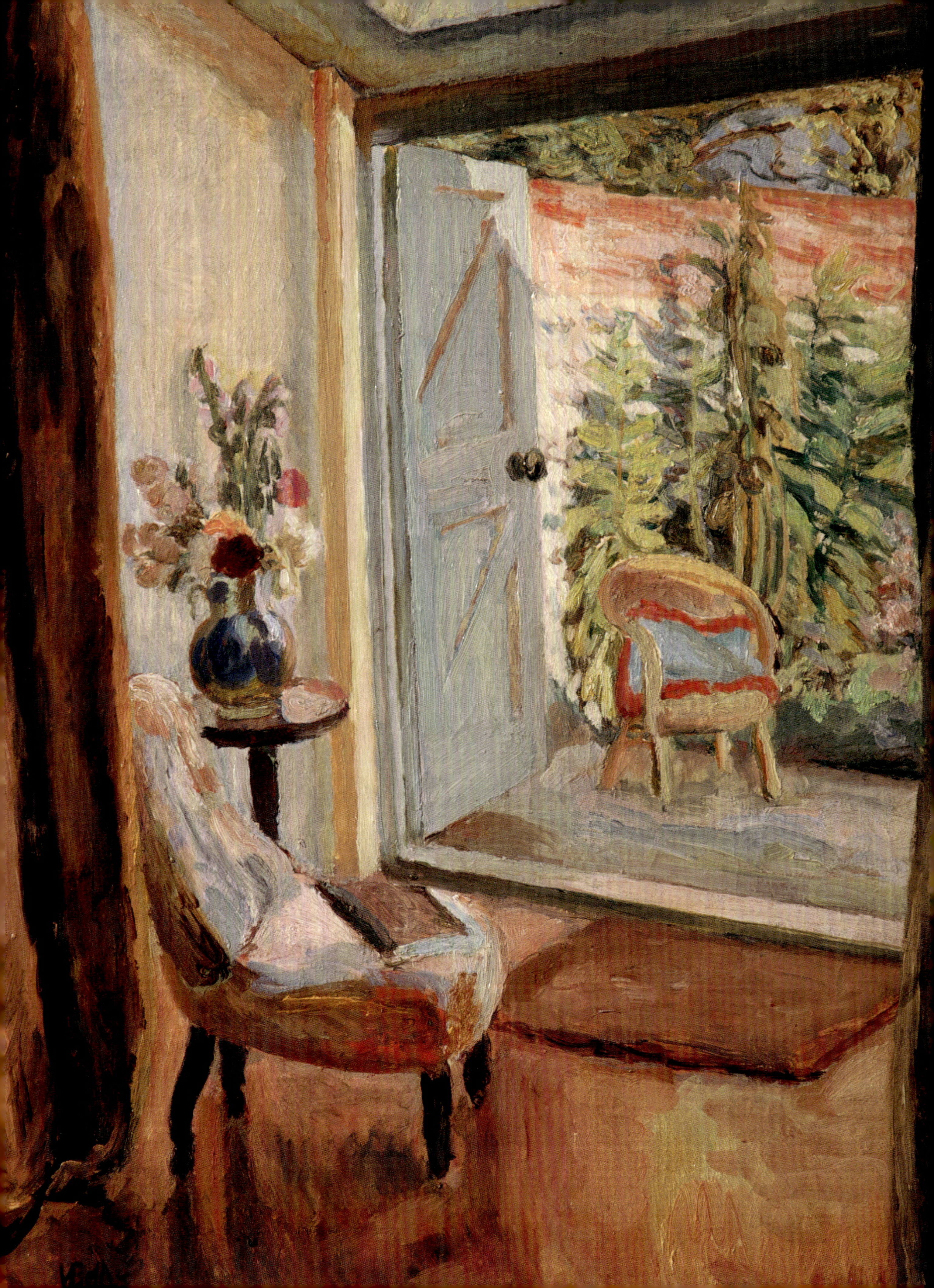

View into a Garden

1926 | oil on board | 70 × 56 cm

View into a Garden is an example of Bell's 'domestic modernism' at Charleston.[95] The viewpoint is from the studio built at Charleston in 1925 to Roger Fry's design. Just over a decade after Bell's experiments with pure abstraction, here the mirrored placement of the chairs and framing of the two spaces with the curtains and door creates a formal harmony. The interior and exterior merge, and the textured garden wall behind flattens the scene, bringing everything back to the picture surface. It is a carefully balanced image with a play of blues and reds across the vase and cushions and repeated rectangular shapes across the book on the chair, mat and paved area outside. The creation with Duncan Grant of Charleston, and the space this allowed for members of Bloomsbury to live and work, is one of Bell's more important legacies. The openness depicted in this work, yet still shielded from the outside world by the garden wall, acts perhaps as a visual metaphor for the environment they created. The motif of the empty chair becomes common in Bell's work from about 1920 onwards (for example, *Interior with a House-maid, c.*1939, p. 141).

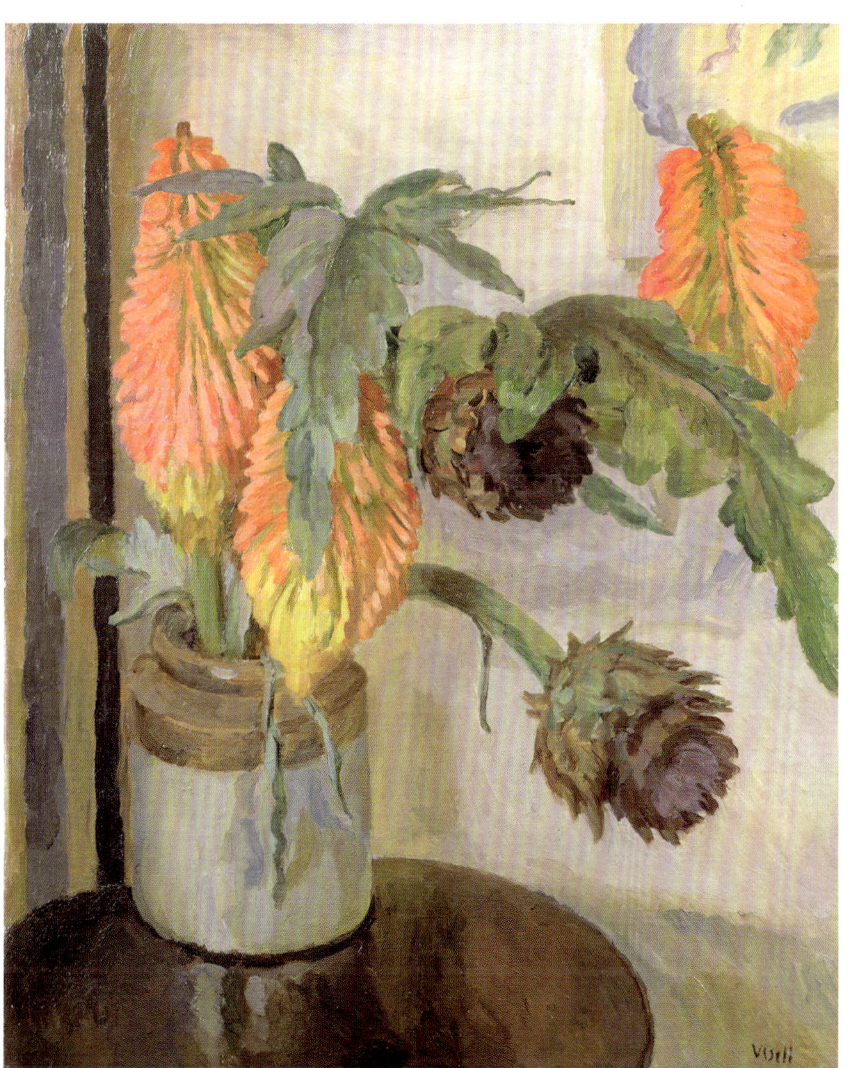

Red Hot Pokers

1926 | oil on canvas | 66 × 53.3 cm

Red hot pokers, together with the artichoke flowers and leaves depicted in this painting, grew in the garden at Charleston, which was redesigned by Roger Fry following the First World War. Both plants were clearly favourites of Bell's, as many paintings exist of them over several decades: *Red-Hot Pokers* (1921, Manchester Art Gallery), *Still Life of Flowers and Thistles* (1937, private collection) and *Red Hot Poker and Fuchsia in a Vase* (1940, private collection). Artichoke flowers also feature prominently in the foreground of *Interior with the Artist's Daughter* (1920, p. 140). Virginia Woolf describes, in 1922: 'Charleston is as usual ... Nessa emerges from a great variegated quilt of asters and artichokes.'[96]

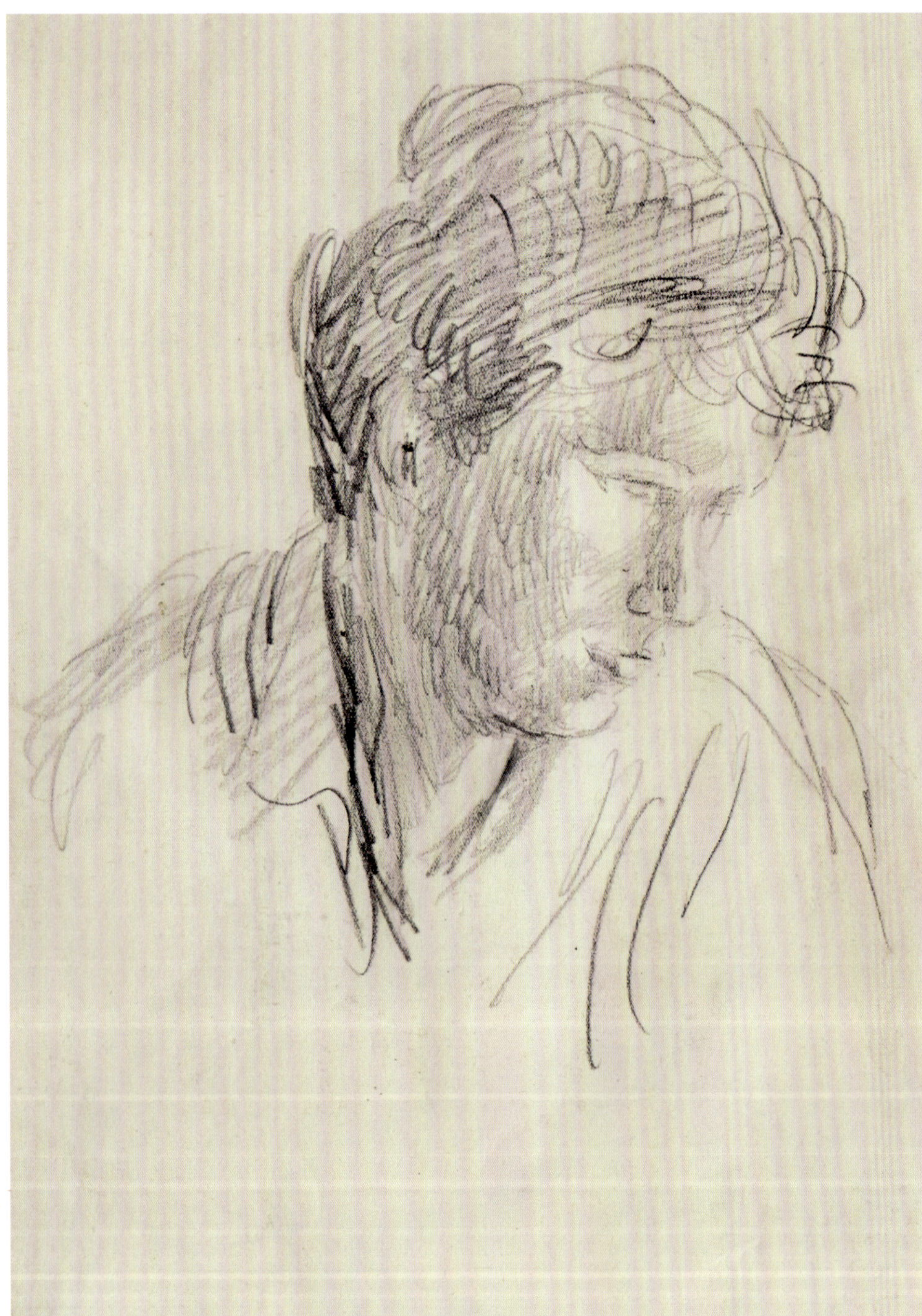

*c.*1928 | pencil on paper | 33 cm × 24 cm

Julian Bell (1908–1937) was Clive and Vanessa Bell's first child. After graduating from King's College, Cambridge, and being an active campaigner for the Labour Party, in 1935 he took a position teaching English at Wuhan University, China. Vanessa missed him greatly and wrote to him from Charleston: 'I think of you so much here, you are essential to this place. It belongs to you and you to it.'[97] At the outbreak of the Spanish Civil War in 1937 Julian felt compelled to take part in the resistance. His pacifist parents tried to dissuade him, but he went as an ambulance driver on the Republican side. After just a month in Spain he was hit by bomb fragments, sustaining a massive lung wound, and later died in a military hospital aged 29. His death devastated Vanessa and she wrote to one of his former girlfriends: 'I am old enough to know a little what he might have done and been if he had lived. I know that his life would have given infinite good and possibilities of good to the world which are now lost.... Fascism wants to destroy intelligence – we must not let it do so. The world depends upon people like Julian to help it out of its troubles later – and their memory will not help as their presence would.'[98]

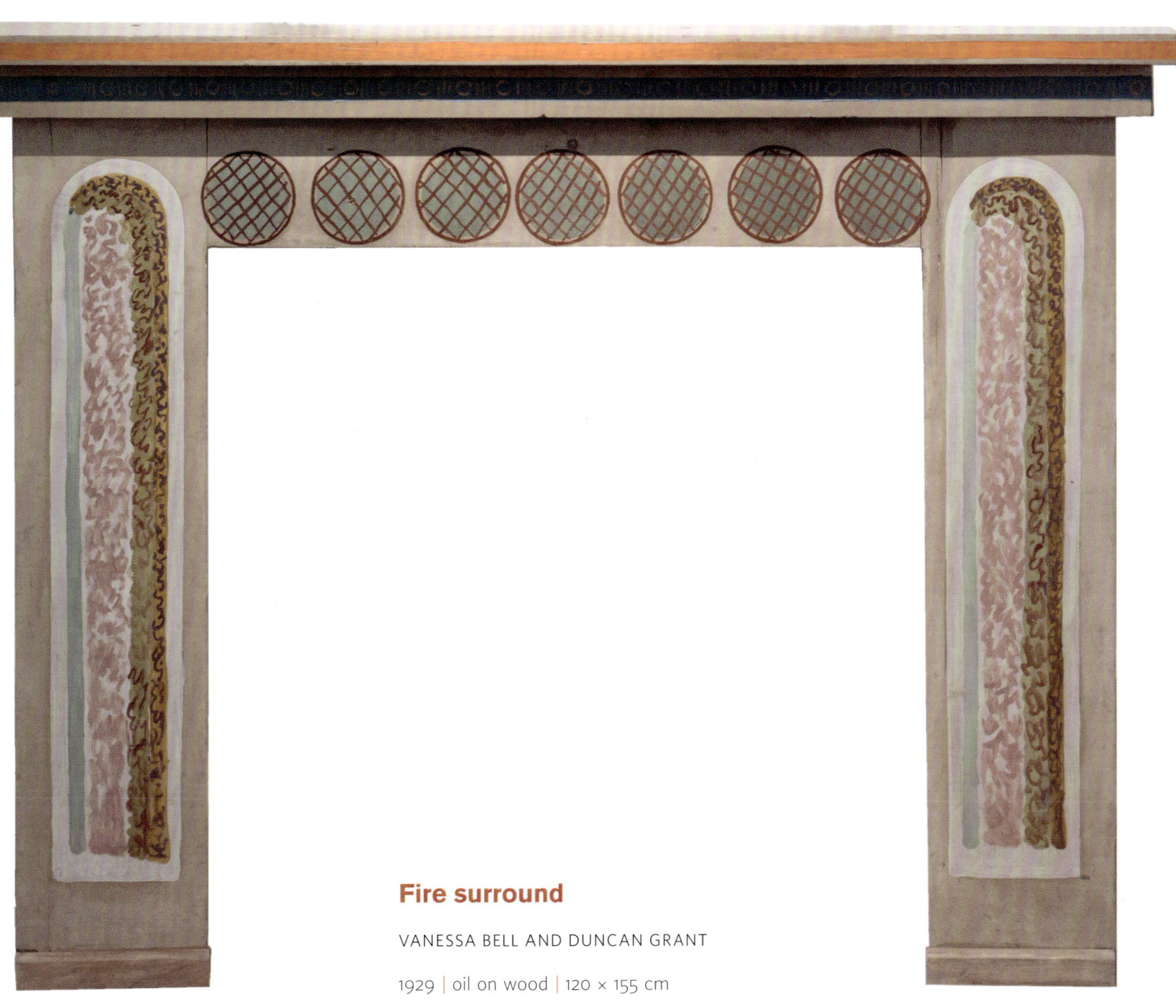

Fire surround

VANESSA BELL AND DUNCAN GRANT

1929 | oil on wood | 120 × 155 cm

In 1929 Bell and Duncan Grant were commissioned by Lady Dorothy Wellesley to decorate her dining room at Penns in the Rocks near Tunbridge Wells. In summer that year, while in France, Bell experimented with techniques and styles for the panels and settled on using a sponge to create a dappled effect, allowing the brown-pink underpaint to show through. Bell and Grant were given free rein with the design. The house had a collection of Italian baroque paintings and their panels reflect this in their Italianate style. The design consisted of five painted panels on green-grey walls with borders of white circles and pastel hatching, an octagonal table with cane-backed chairs, semi-circular tables and a sideboard, a fireplace surround, lights and six small octagonal mirrors, and

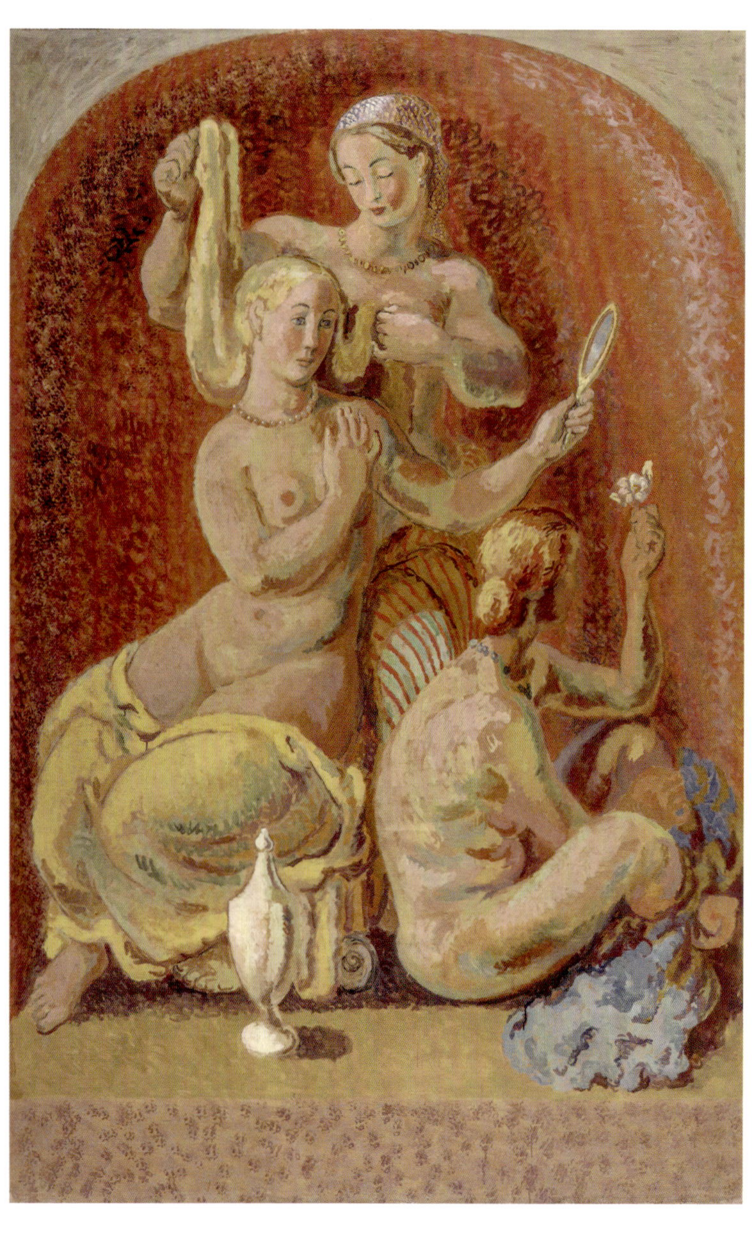

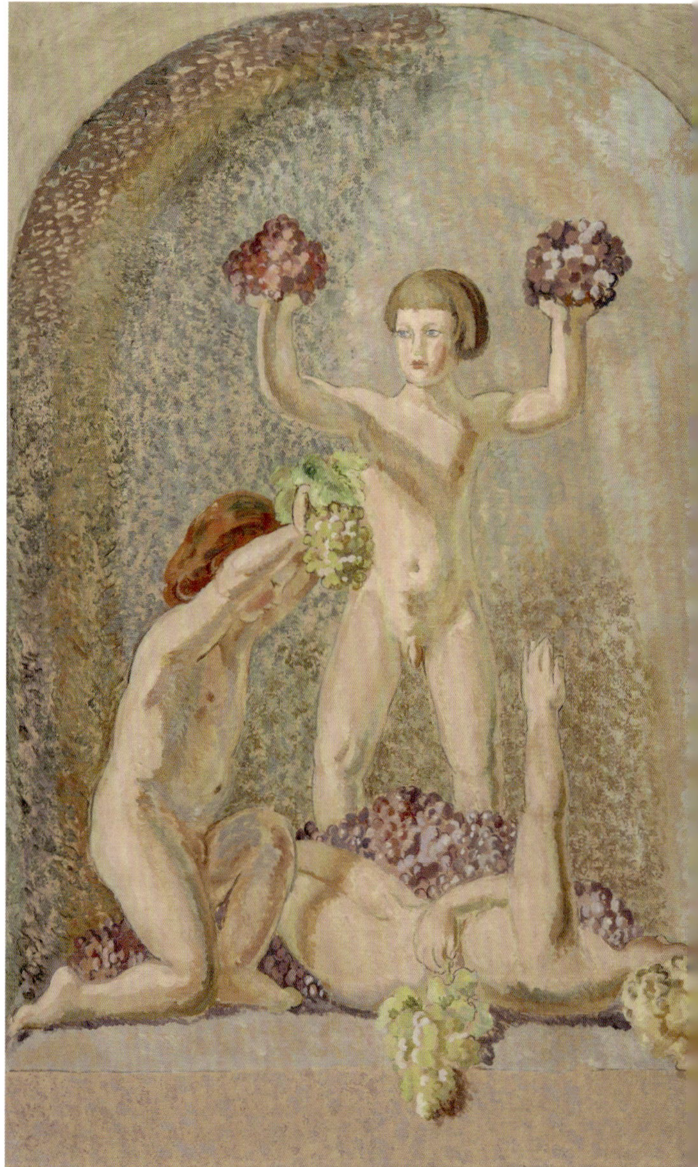

Vase and Flowers

1929 | oil on canvas | 213.4 × 91.6 cm

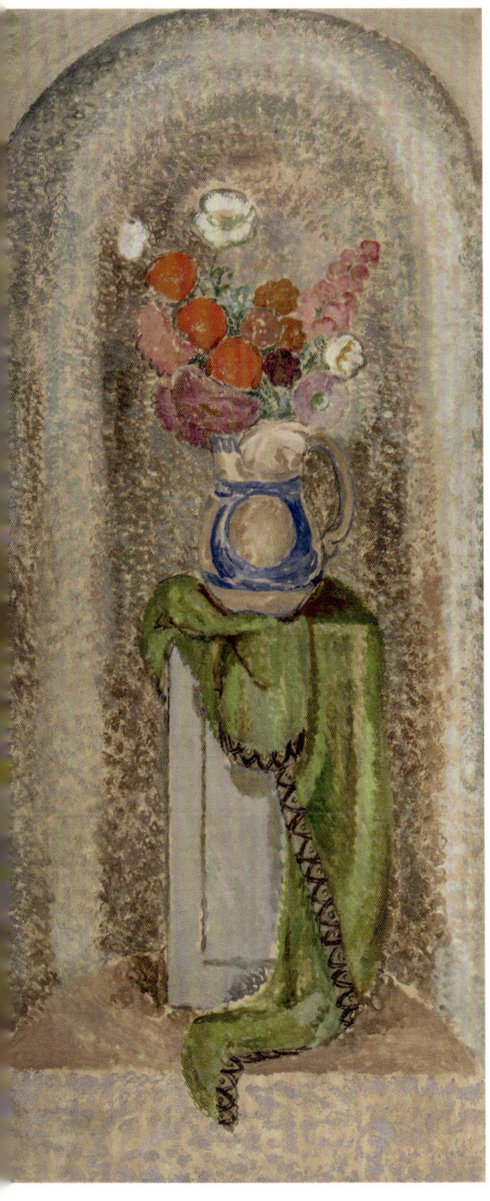

sequinned and appliquéd silk curtains. During this period, Bell and Grant were gaining notoriety for their interiors and were able to command good rates. They were paid a joint fee of £350 (around £20,000 today).[99]

The Studio magazine commented that 'Duncan Grant and Vanessa Bell have evolved a room of outstanding beauty, rich in colour, harmonious in design… The colouring is extraordinarily limpid and clear. Although almost every colour is called into play, the tones are so subtle, the blending so ingenious that the general effect is one of iridescence, rather than of any particular colour scheme.'[100]

The overall effect is an example of 'the celebratory form of artifice known as "camp"'.[101] 'What makes this project modern, in Bloomsbury's terms, is that these elements are not real mouldings, panels, niches, or frames, nor do they make any claims to trompe l'œil or historical accuracy. Instead they foreground their handmade facture as an expression of their makers' individual sensibilities.'[102]

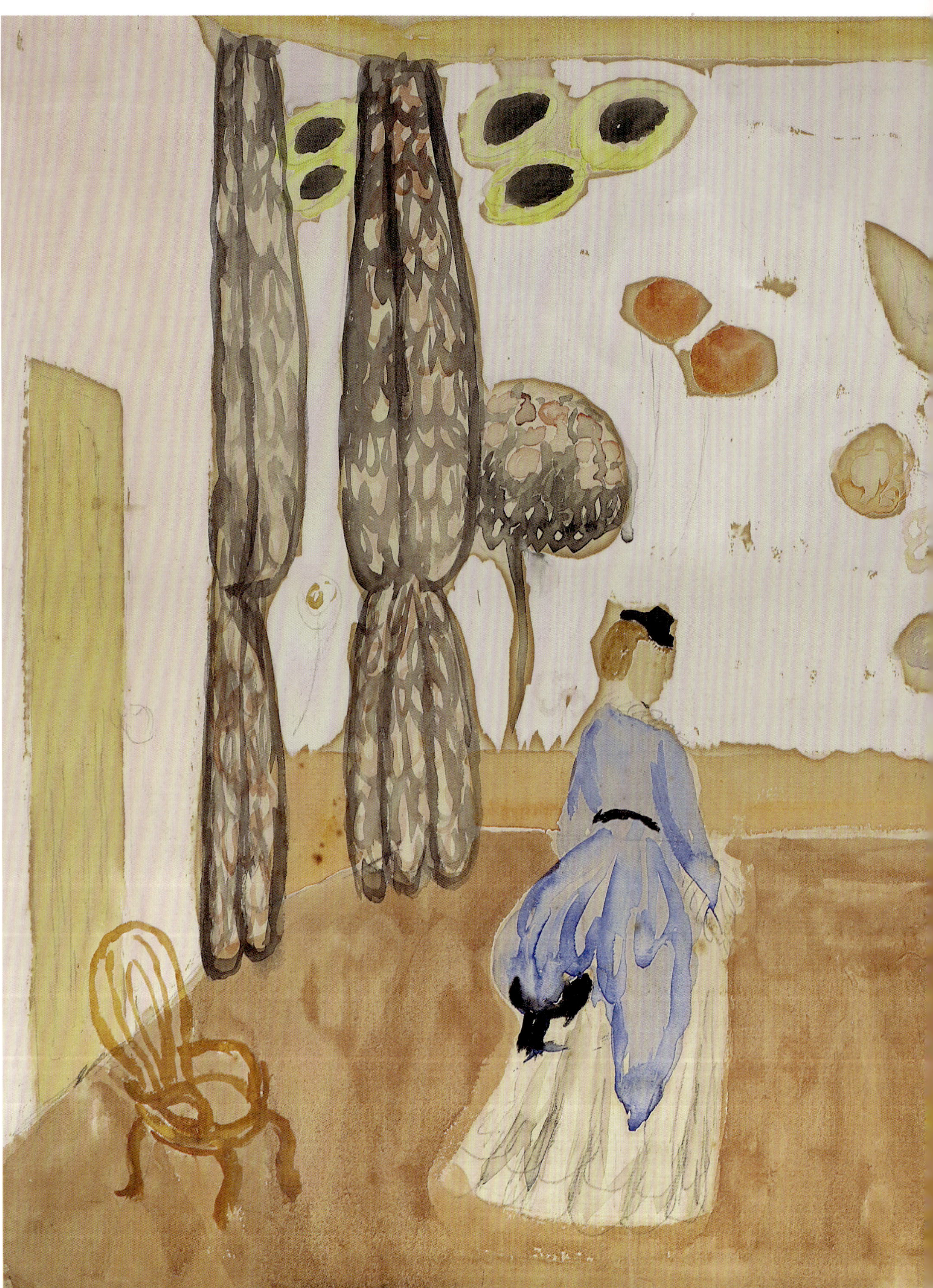

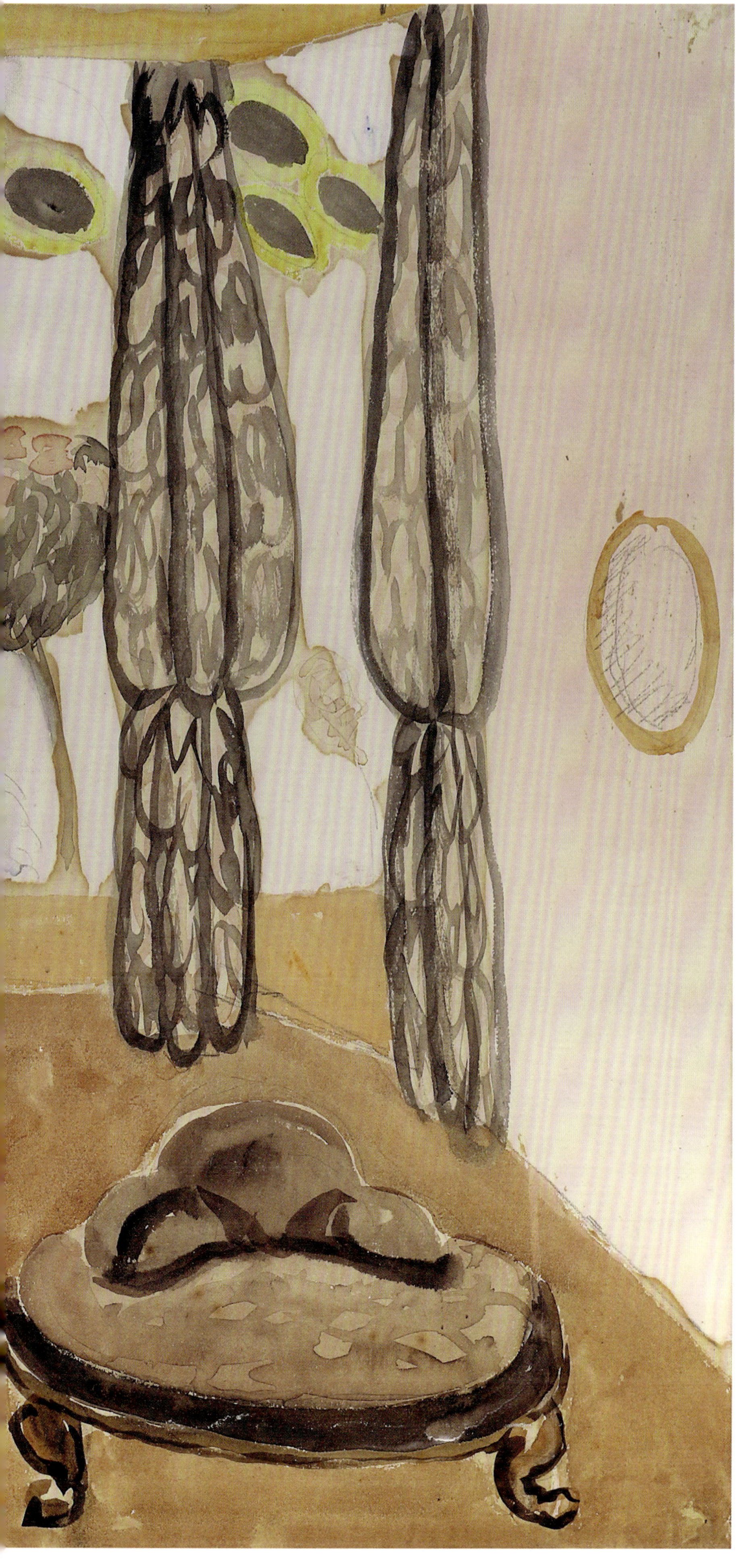

Study for stage set

c. 1925–30 | watercolour | 46 × 61.5 cm

Bell designed several stage sets, for *High Yellow* by the Camargo Ballet in 1932, the Sadler's Wells production of *Pomona* in 1933, and Ethel Smyth's ballet *Fête Galante* in 1934. Virginia Woolf wrote of the sets for *Pomona*, for which Bell also designed the costumes, 'Scenery – all very pale and bright – I mean Fra Angelico against a background of Cassis.'[103]

8 Fitzroy Street

*c.*1930 | oil on canvas | 65 × 47 cm

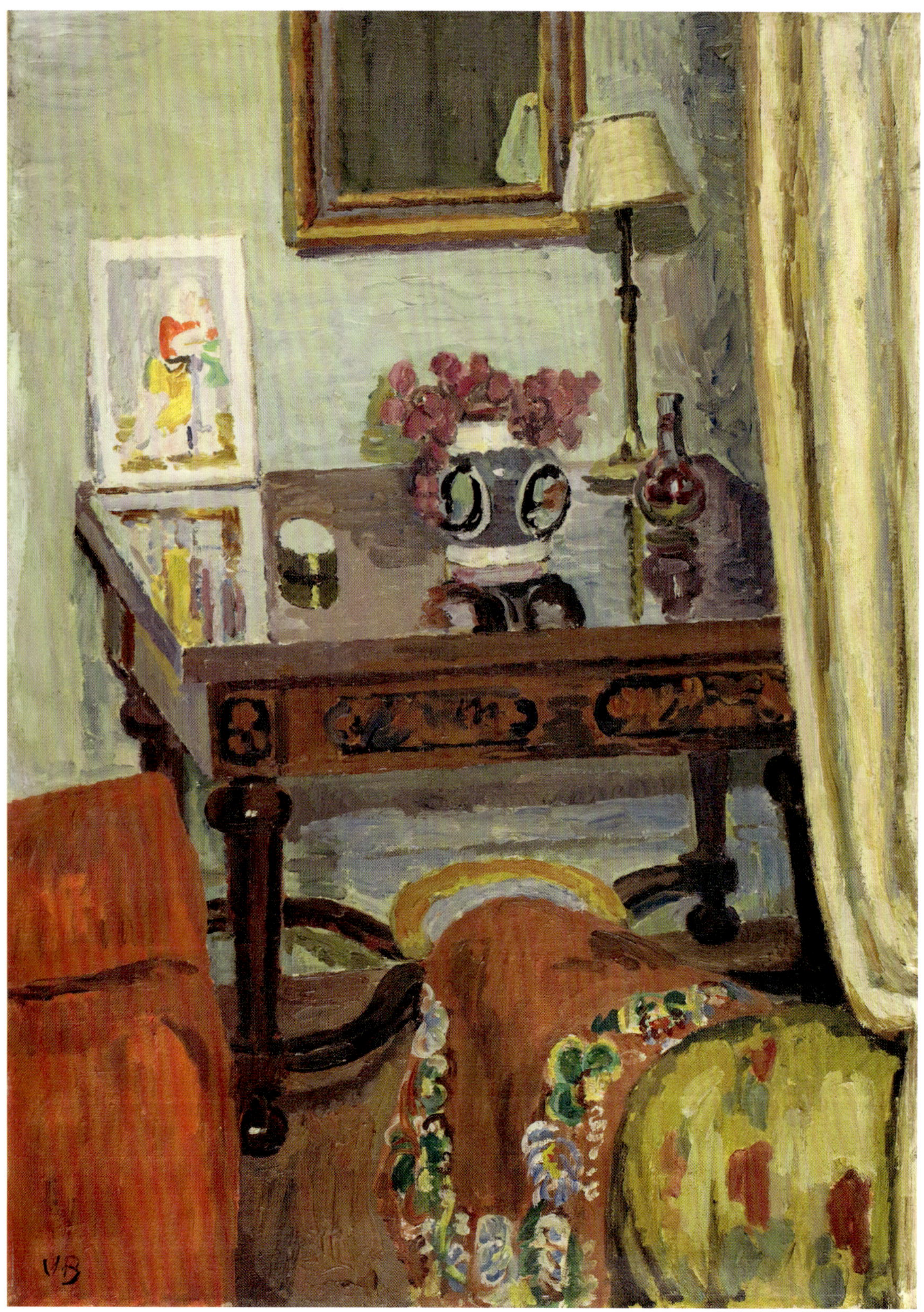

Interior, 8 Fitzroy Street

1935 | oil on canvas | 75 × 62 cm

In 1920 Duncan Grant took a studio at 8 Fitzroy Street, London, and in 1928 the large room backing onto it became Bell's.[104] Her children had left home for boarding school and university and so she had returned, as Virginia Woolf recalled, 'perhaps rather sadly to the life she would have liked best of all once, to be a painter on her own'.[105]

8 Fitzroy Street shows a claustrophobic space with the viewer held back from the table still life by the chairs in front and curtain to the right. There are several items which perhaps held personal significance for Bell: the marquetry table was a wedding present and the small painting of a mother and child was made by Grant.[106] *Interior, 8 Fitzroy Street*, has a floral display at its centre, resting on a decorative textile. In the background is an octagonal table, as well as Duncan Grant's *Painted Omega Screen* (1913, also seen in *Interior with a Housemaid*, *c.*1939, p. 141, after it had been moved to Charleston). In these interiors, Bell and Grant's artworks and designs, including ceramics and textiles, are layered to depict the artistic environments they were creating together. In 1940, 8 Fitzroy Street was destroyed by an incendiary bomb, along with much of Bell's early work.

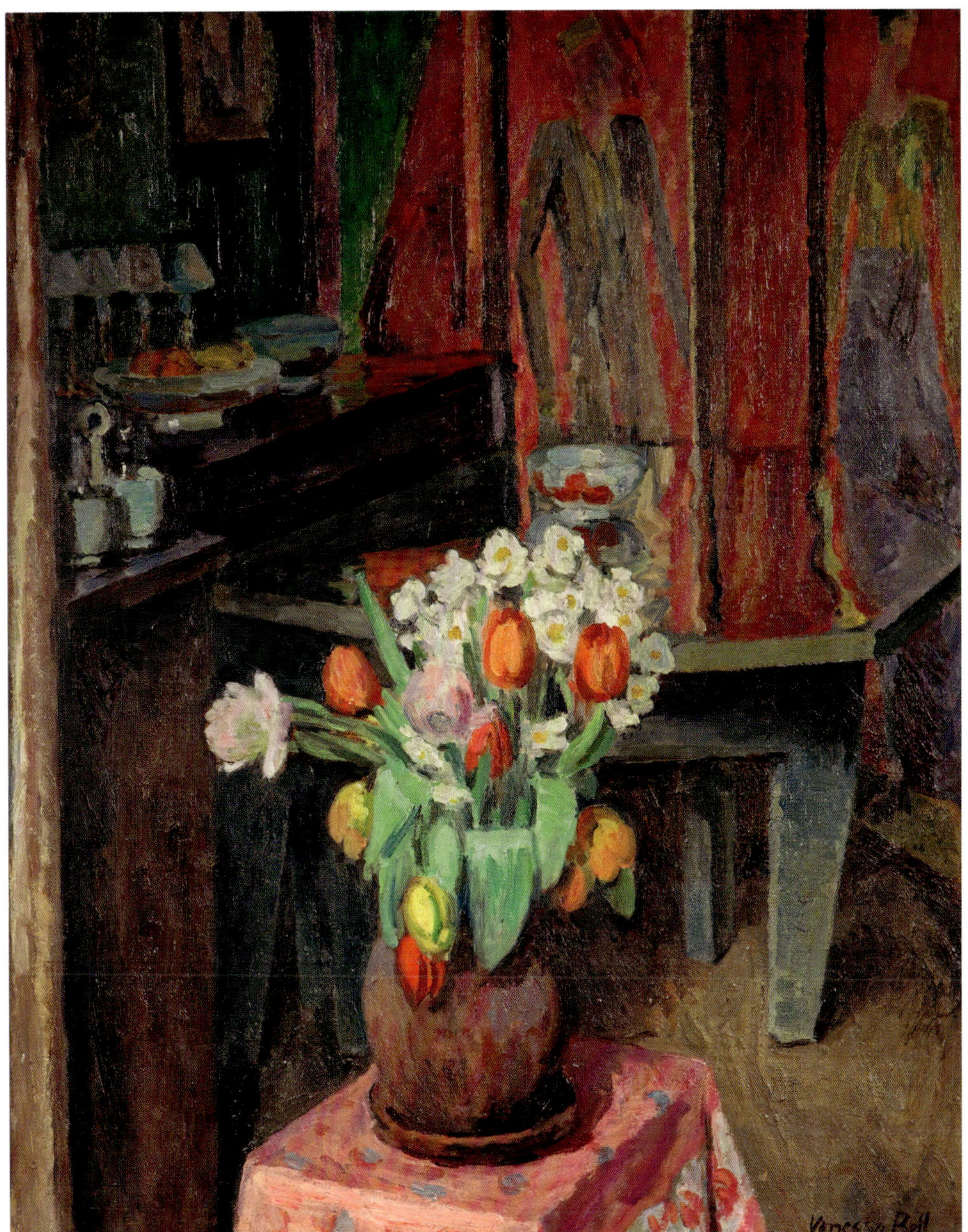

Flowers in a Glass Jar

c.1930 | oil on canvas | 75 × 50.2 cm

Asters and Hydrangeas

c.1930s–40s | oil on canvas | 55 × 46 cm

Bell's later work repeatedly depicts domestic objects: vases of flowers, fruit, fabrics, books and ceramics, usually on a tabletop. In these still lifes Bell experiments with light, form and colour. Throughout her life, her letters remark on 'the positive delights also of flowers and trees and innumerable unexpected sights and sounds keep one perpetually happy.'[107] Around the time these paintings were made she expresses delight in her garden, a 'medley of apples, hollyhocks, plums, zinnias. Dahlias, all mixed up together', 'a mass of flowers and as gay as possible… I often wander about in it at odd moments for the pleasure of the sights and smells.'[108]

As seen in earlier portraits such as *Mrs St John Hutchinson* (1915, Tate, p. 26), the backgrounds in these paintings are made up of geometric abstract blocks of colour. It may be that there was a painting or painted screen behind the still lifes – or potentially Bell was continuing her earlier exploration with invented abstraction (*Abstract Painting*, c.1914, p. 70), now combined with a figurative subject. *Asters and Hydrangeas* includes a painted frame of black lines which recalls her decorative interior schemes of the time. In her one known lecture on art Bell stated: 'Suppose you are drawing a flower. If you are capable of seeing that flower with all its subtleties of form, the way its edges recede or are sharp against the space behind you, you have to try and express your feelings about those things in line. It must be sensitive, everywhere – nowhere must it become mechanical.'[109]

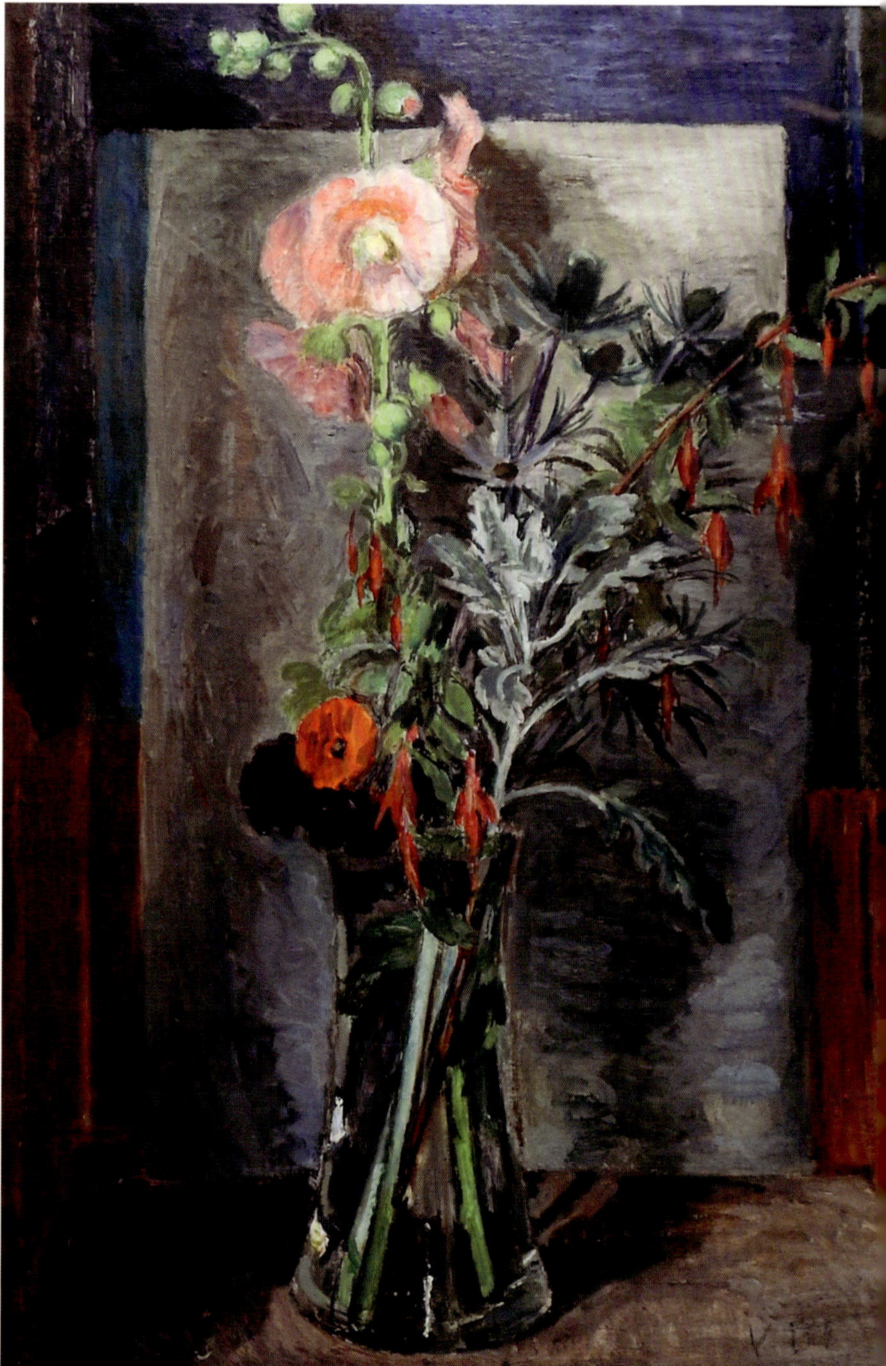

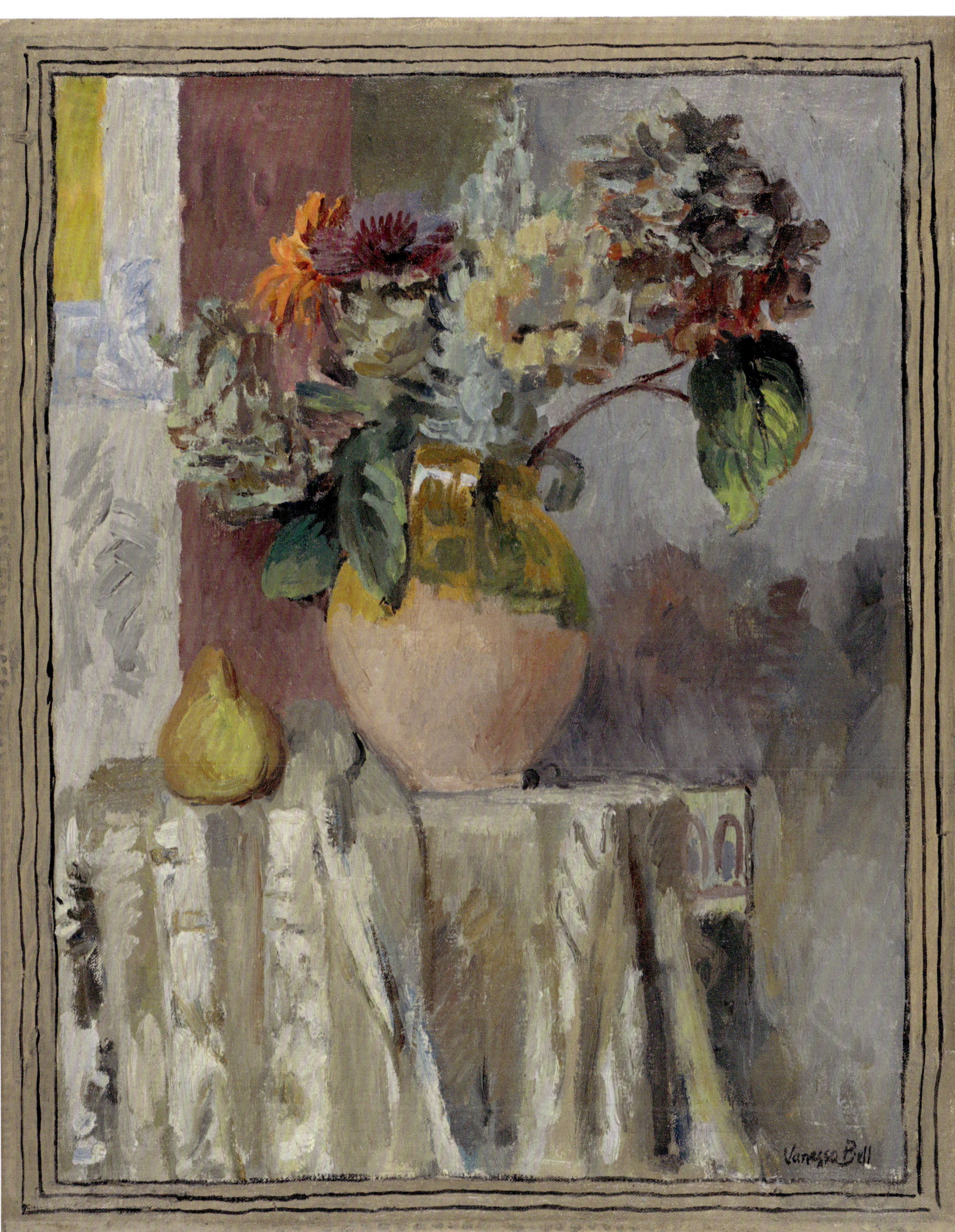

Vanessa Bell

Alfriston

c.1931 | ink on paper | 57.5 × 107 cm

From the 1920s Shell-Mex commissioned artists to design posters with the strapline 'See Britain First – on Shell', to encourage a newly mobile public to explore the British countryside in their cars. In 1929 Bell was commissioned to create a painting which could be reproduced by colour lithography.[110] She chose a view of the village of Alfriston in Sussex, near Charleston, and depicts the church and Cuckmere River in a pointillist style. When the posters were exhibited at the New Burlington Galleries, the art critic R.R. Tatlock disparagingly wrote that Bell's poster 'takes us back to the years when it was believed that the only proper way to paint pictures was to touch them up with little dots and dashes, each one differing from its neighbour in colour.'[111] Clive Bell, however, reported that the posters 'are daily bringing new motives of pleasure and surprise into the streets, and have, I believe, already raised perceptibly public, though not official, taste'.[112]

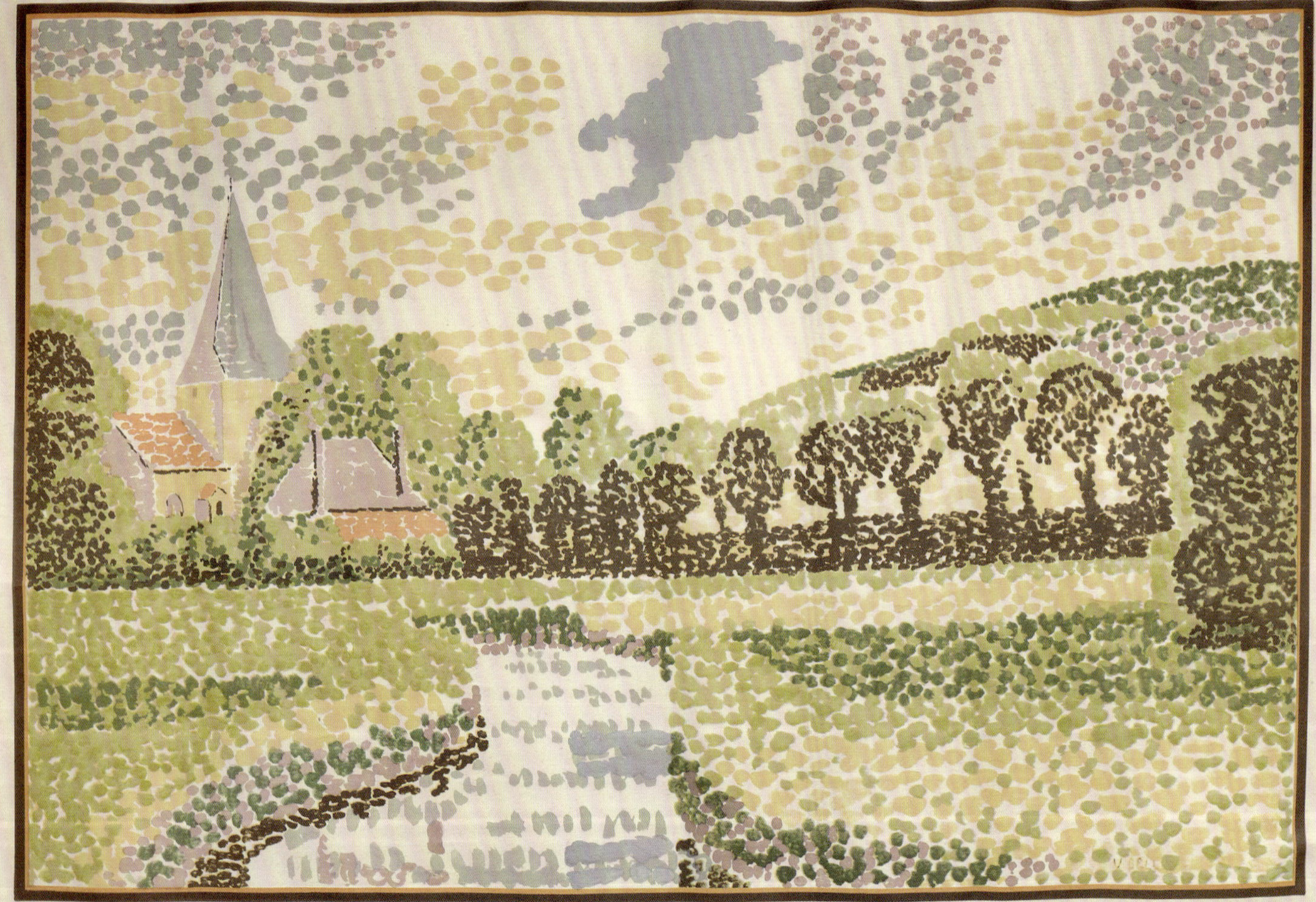

Mother and Child
(design for a tile)

c.1930 | watercolour and pencil on paper |
27.6 × 25.8cm

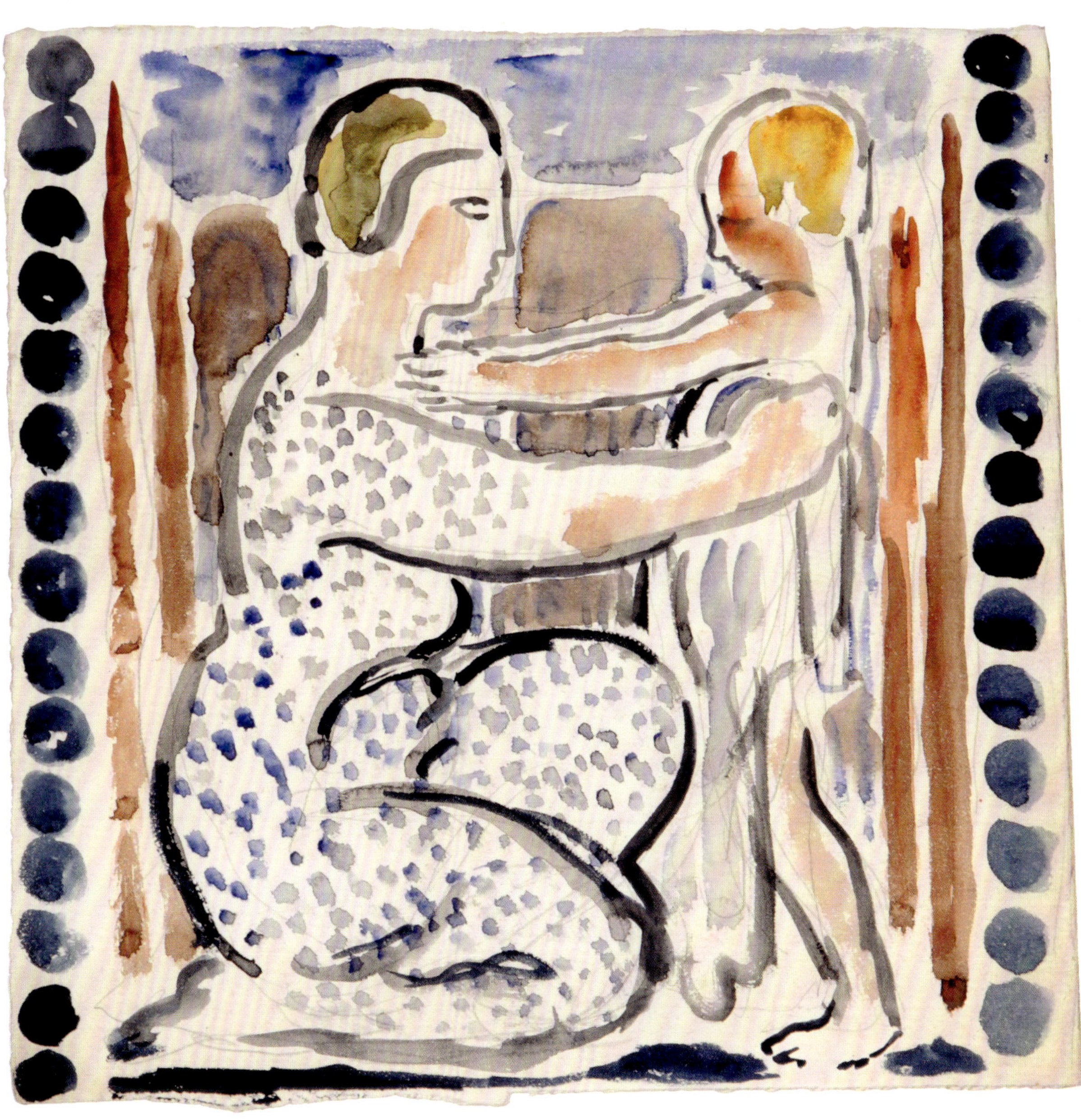

Decorated lamp stand

VANESSA BELL AND PHYLLIS KEYES

c.1931–32 | painted and glazed earthenware, potted by Phyllis Keyes, decorated by Vanessa Bell | 13.5 × 23 cm

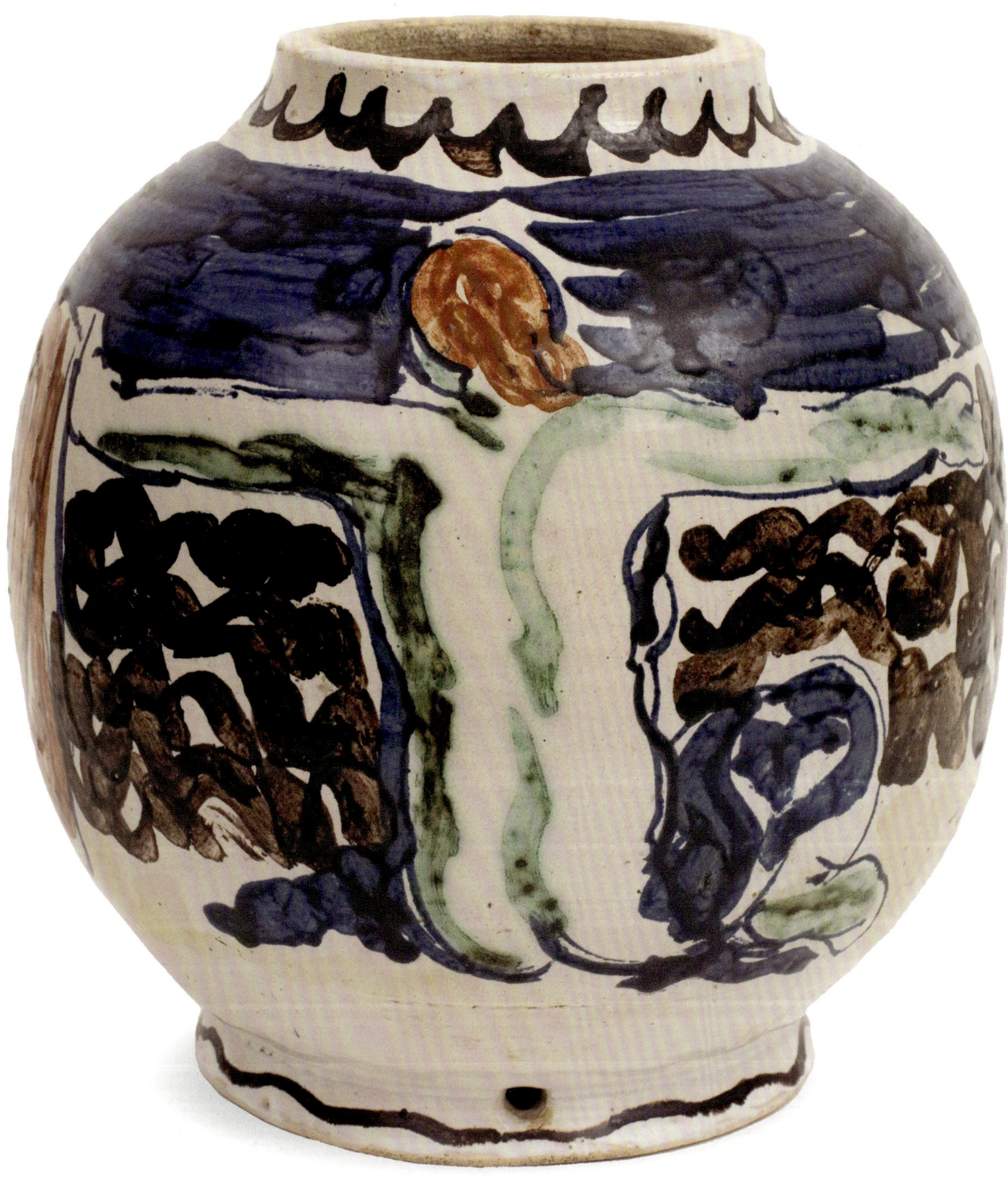

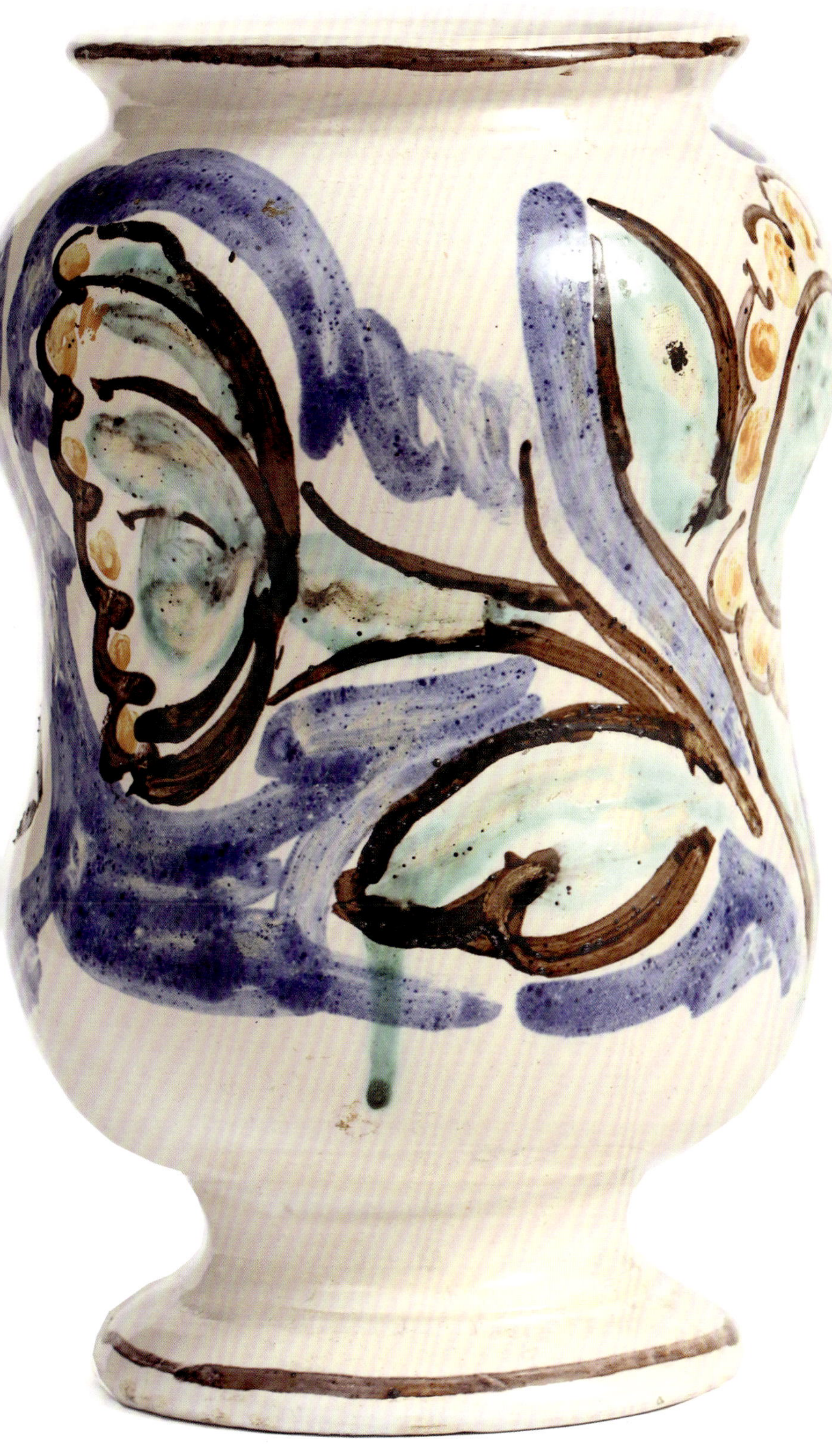

Music Room vase

VANESSA BELL AND PHYLLIS KEYES

c.1932 | ceramic, cast from an Italian or Spanish original | 22 × 13.5 × 13.5 cm

From 1931 Bell and Duncan Grant began collaborating with the potter Phyllis Keyes (1881–1968). Keyes supplied many pots, jugs, tiles and vases for the artists to paint. Bell's tile designs often feature figures in profile and this example (p. 125) also includes the combination of circles and lines seen elsewhere in her decorative work (for example, *Long stool*, 1925, p. 109).[113] The decorated lamp stand shows a seated female nude from the front and back, in one of Bell's most loose and calligraphic decorations. The figure's powerful pose and strong bulky limbs are reminiscent of Bell's earlier work, including *A Conversation* (1913–16, p. 63) and *Iris Tree* (1915, p. 79), but here very rapidly and spontaneously handled. The blue-outlined figure is also reminiscent of a Matisse painted vase (1907, Musée d'Art Moderne de Paris) shown at the *Manet and the Post-Impressionists* exhibition (1910).[114]

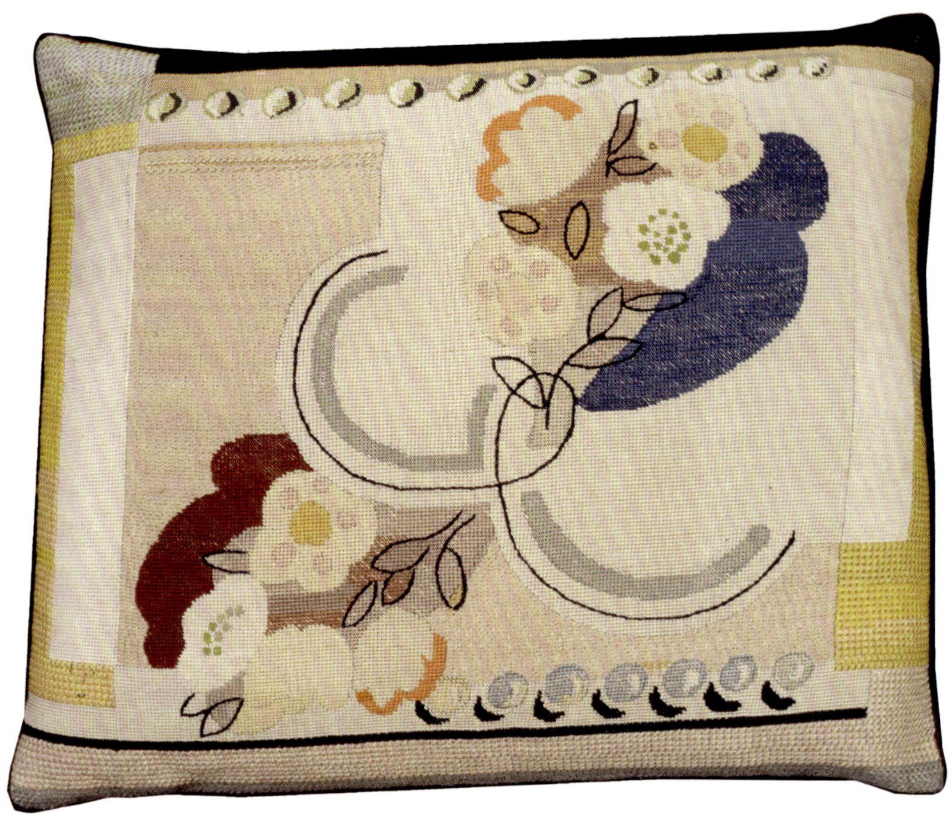

Cushion

VANESSA BELL AND ETHEL GRANT

1932 | canvas, wool | 64 × 53 cm

Bell and Duncan Grant designed a music room for Lefevre Gallery in London in 1932. It was a complete interior aimed at promoting their work as interior designers and advertising the new rugs and upholstery fabrics they had designed for Royal Wilton and Allan Walton.[115] The room included a piano, stool, gramophone cabinet, chairs with embroidered panels, vases, cushions, mirrors, screens, rugs and six painted wall panels supposedly inspired by various composers. However, Bell wrote: 'I can't see that one's more suitable than another. What sort of design would you give to Bach and what to Chopin?'[116] Virginia Woolf subsidized two-thirds of the production costs and launched the project with a glamorous cocktail party: 'It's a purely commercial (don't whisper it) affair, to induce the rich to buy furniture, and so employ a swarm of poor scarecrows who are languishing in Fitzroy Street.'[117] Nevertheless, it was a commercial failure, resulting in no sales. Most of the furniture went to Woolf or to Charleston and it would be Bell and Grant's last domestic interior design. The 'Amusing Style' of interior design was falling out of fashion, as Reed describes: 'The room flaunted its Amusing disdain for the rigors of high modernism with its cheerful pastiche and quotation. The ubiquitous images of swags flouted injunctions to truth to materials.'[118] Reed also notes that Bloomsbury's challenges to 'middle-class norms, of gender, sexuality, self-discipline, and expressiveness … made its domestic aesthetic anathema to the culture of experts, so that, during the 1930s, Bloomsbury was pushed ever further towards the margins of the modern.'[119]

Famous Women Dinner Service

VANESSA BELL AND DUNCAN GRANT

1932–34 | 50 hand-painted Wedgwood ceramic plates |
25.5 cm diameter each

In 1932, the art historian Kenneth Clark and his wife Jane ordered from Bell and Grant '36 large plates, 12 smaller plates, 36 side plates, 12 soup cups and saucers, 1 salad bowl and stand, 2 junket dishes, 6 oval dishes at different sizes, 2 sauce boats and stands, 4 pepper pots, 4 salt pots, 4 mustard pots, 2 sauce tureens and stands and handles, and 3 Liverpool jugs'.[120] Expecting a fine dining set, instead they received this service, including 50 plates painted with portraits of 'famous women', as well as the artists themselves. Bell wrote to Jane Clark that 'our idea is to make it an illustration of women in different capacities – famous queens, actresses and so on – this would give me a great deal of choice. We could have classical figures or modern or anything.... But please say if you or Mr Clark don't like the idea.'[121] In order to produce the set, the artists travelled to Stoke-on-Trent, to the Wedgwood factory, to select 'shapes, glazes and colours'.[122] They chose a fairly chunky shape, similar to those used for Omega ware, for its 'very practical' qualities with a 'cool white' finish.[123]

The 'famous women' they chose to depict came from across the world and from ancient history to the contemporary. Some had appeared in their earlier work; The Queen of Sheba and Empress Theodora appear in Grant's painting *The Queen of Sheba* (1912, Tate) and Bell's *Byzantine Lady* (1912, p. 41).

The *Famous Women Dinner Service* forms part of a wider

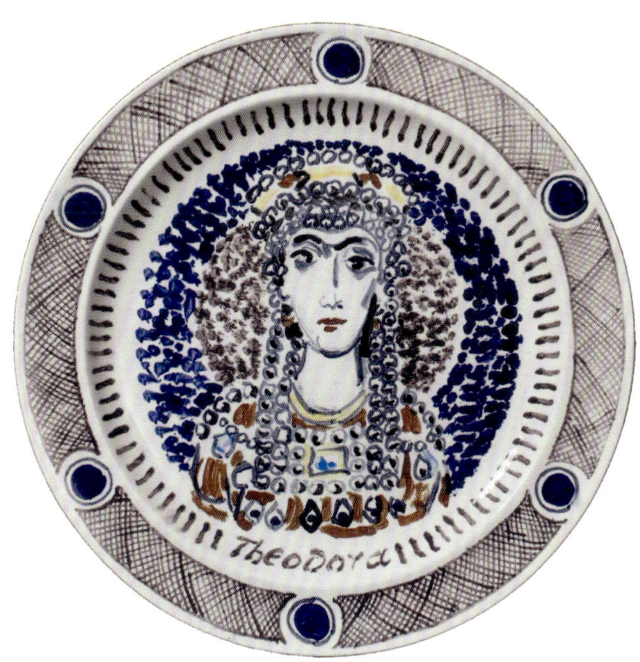

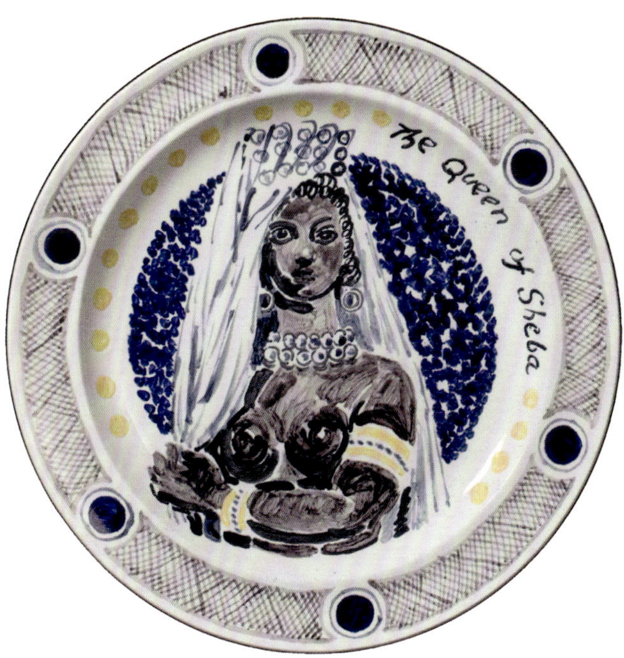

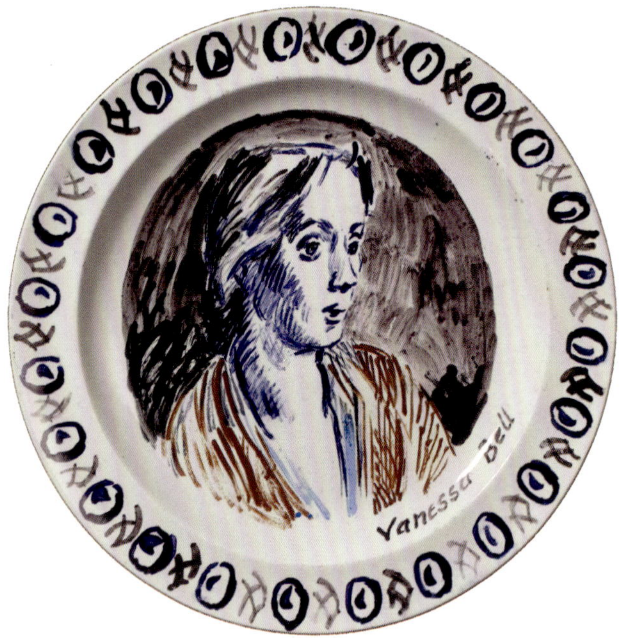 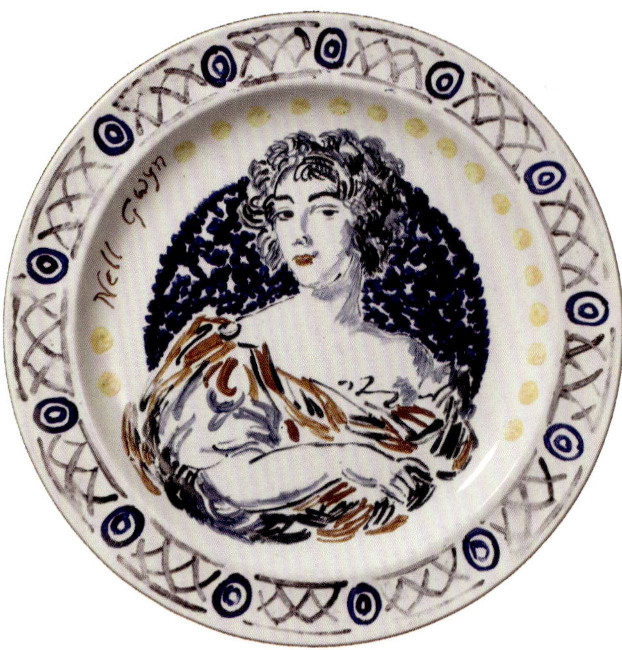

ambition to record women's histories, with Virginia Woolf later writing: 'Very little is known about women. The history of England is the history of the male line, not the female. Of our fathers we know always some fact, some distinction. They were soldiers or they were sailors; they filled that office or made that law. But of our mothers, our grandmothers, our great-grandmothers, what remains?'[124] Art historian Hana Leaper also argues that many of the women depicted 'vigorously crafted identities and statuses at odds with the mores of their historical epochs. Some were professionals; lots were lesbian, bisexual, or had unconventional sexual relationships.... With few exceptions, the lives of

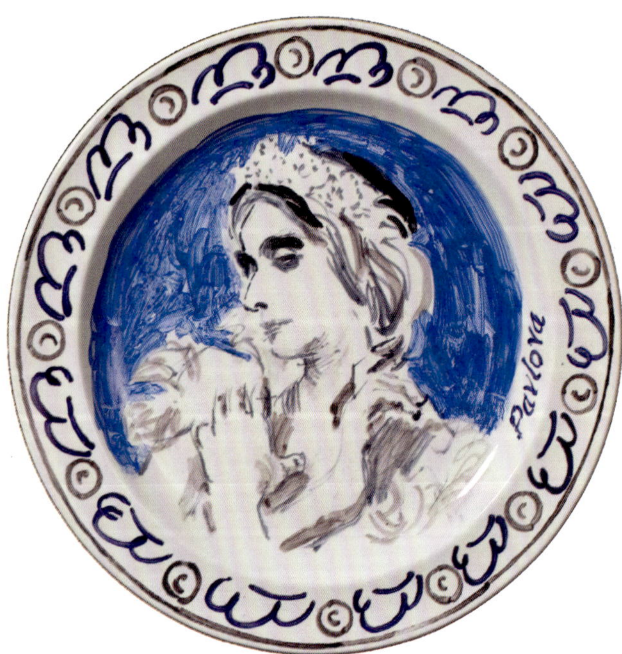 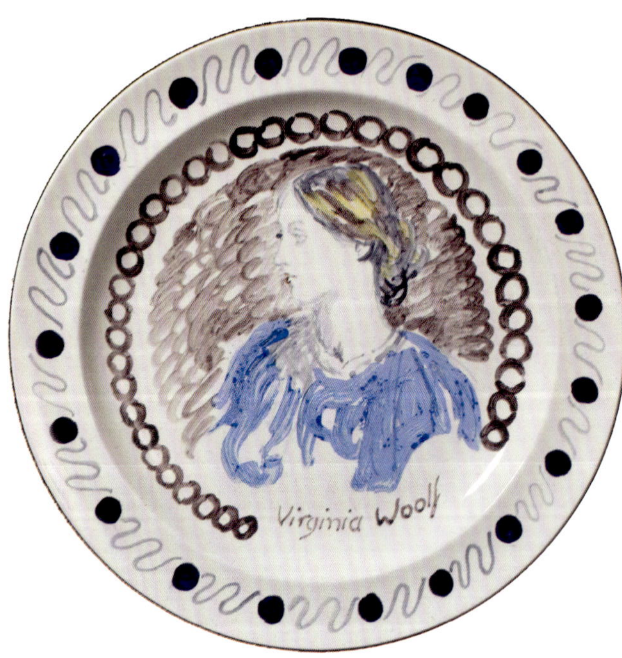

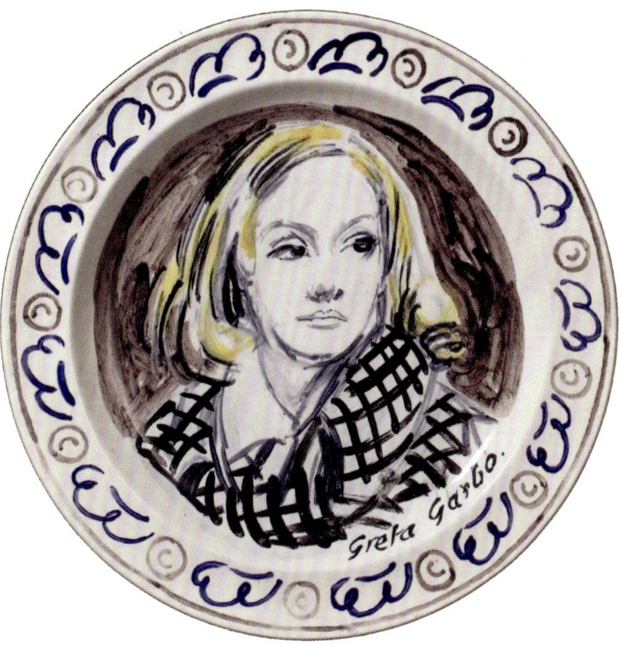

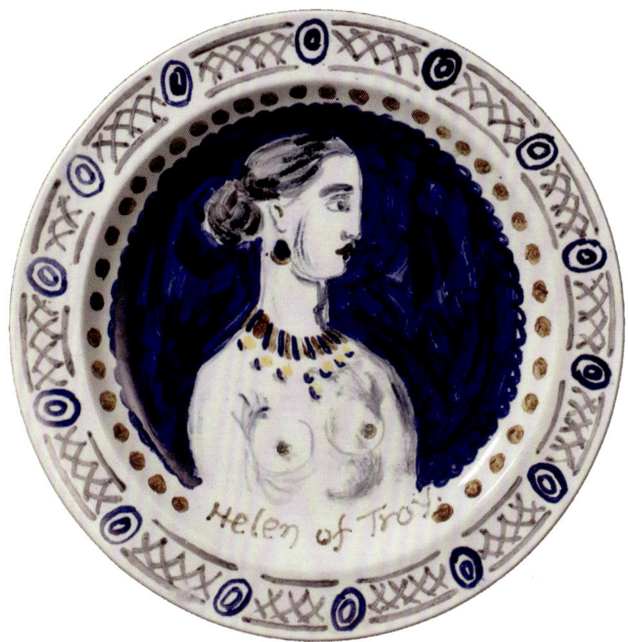

a majority of these women reflect the new sexual politics at the heart of Bloomsbury understanding of humanism.'[125]

As Katy Hessel writes: 'Seen from a twenty-first century perspective, it seems extraordinarily progressive – even more so considering it pre-dated Judy Chicago's *The Dinner Party* by nearly half a century.'[126] Although she was unaware of Bell and Grant's dinner service, three of the women featured also appear in Chicago's work: Empress Theodora, Virginia Woolf and Sappho. Bell described the dinner service in typically modest and tongue-in-cheek fashion, as 'portraits of celebrated females – It ought to please the feminists – of all times.'[127]

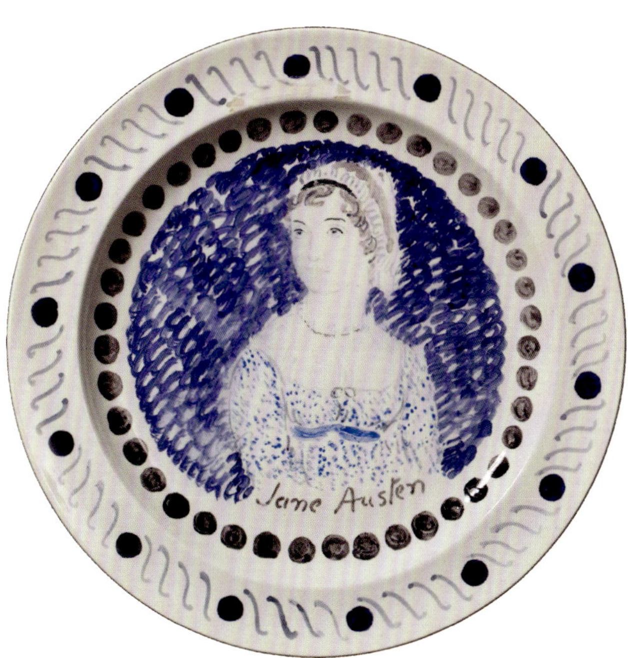

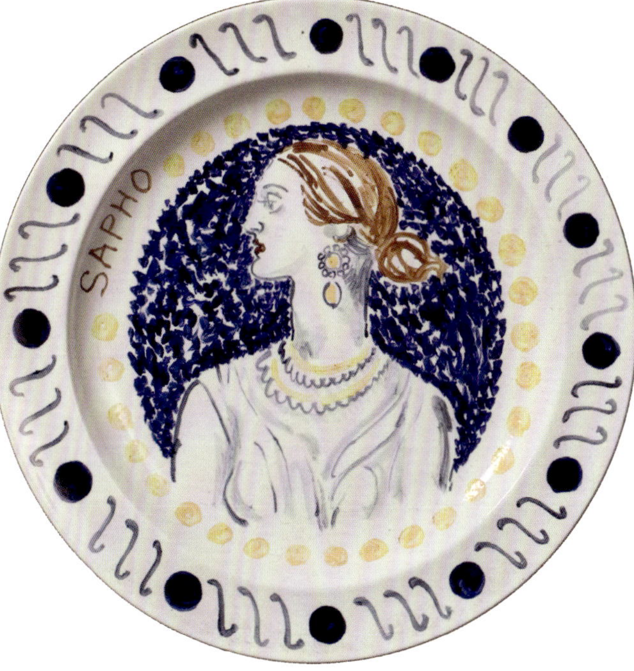

Vanessa Bell's career sits firmly within the history of overlooked women's art. Like too many others to count, she has been overlooked for decades, and what attention has been paid to her has generally focused on a famous relative – in this case, her sister Virginia Woolf. Generally, women's work has been obscured by men close to them: fathers (Artemisia Gentileschi by Orazio), brothers (Caroline Herschel by William), and of course husbands (Frida Kahlo by Diego Rivera). The only unusual aspect of Bell's situation is that it was another woman's fame that hid her own achievements for so many decades.

And, as with so many other women artists, too much of the scarce literature about her focuses on her unusual lifestyle. Although she was married to the art critic Clive Bell, she became increasingly close to Duncan Grant, a homosexual man with whom she shared a domestic and artistic partnership for almost fifty years. She was one of the founding members of the Bloomsbury Group, an early-twentieth-century association of artists, writers, intellectuals and philosophers, whose unconventional attitudes involved a rejection of bourgeois Victorian life in favour of a more informal and private focus on personal relationships and individual pleasure. Historically, when women have been able to achieve it is primarily because of a supportive environment, which this group appears to have provided for Vanessa Bell.

Some time ago, a remarkable and unknown body of art by Bell and Grant came into public view. The *Famous Women Dinner Service* from 1932, originally commissioned by British art historian Kenneth Clark, is a set of fifty painted 9 inch ceramic plates. It was completely unknown to me when I began work on *The Dinner Party* in 1974. However, like my own work, the plates are part of another little-known aspect of women's history: the desire to honour women. This can be dated back as early as *The Book of the City of Ladies*, finished in 1405 by Christine de Pisan, the first woman in Europe to earn her living as an author.

Christine's book arguably marks the beginning of modern feminism, and includes biographies of approximately 500 women, many of whom my research team and I had to discover all over again for *The Dinner Party*. Over the course of many centuries there have been

Judy Chicago, *The Dinner Party*, 1974–79.

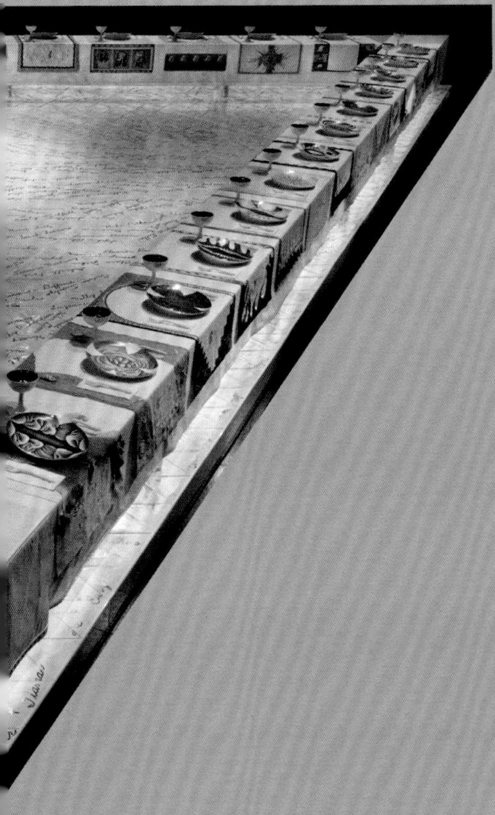

numerous attempts by women to counter the centuries-old ideas about women's inferiority. This reached its apogee at the end of the nineteenth century and the opening of the twentieth, when a number of feminists wrote books about different aspects of women's histories – compendiums of female rulers, artists, writers and other women of achievement. These constituted some of the few materials available to me in the 1970s – sadly, many had not been checked out of the libraries for years.

My own goals with *The Dinner Party* involved teaching women's history to a broad audience through a visually accessible work of art. It ended up travelling around the world to a viewing audience of over a million people; since its 2007 permanent housing at the Brooklyn Museum, the piece has attracted almost 100,000 visitors annually. I mention this not to pat myself on the back but, rather, to wonder why the Bell/Grant undertaking was for a private patron who kept it out of view for such a long time. One would think that everyone involved in this project would have recognized that such work deserved a wider audience, if only to demonstrate how many important women there have been in history.

The other odd thing about Bell's production is that, until recently, most of the focus has been on her paintings, even though – at least to this viewer – her ceramics are just as interesting. But, of course, she lived before the advent of the feminist art movement which challenged the longstanding hierarchy of art and craft – one that often disadvantaged women artists. With hindsight, it becomes clear that Bell's ceramics prefigured such distinguished creators as Beatrice Wood (1893–1998), Viola Frey (1933–2004) and, more recently, Ruby Neri (b. 1970), all of whom have made ceramics their material of choice.

In summary, like too many women artists before and after her, Vanessa Bell – who was exceedingly prolific across multiple media – deserves both greater attention and increased recognition.

Judy Chicago is an American feminist artist, art educator and writer.

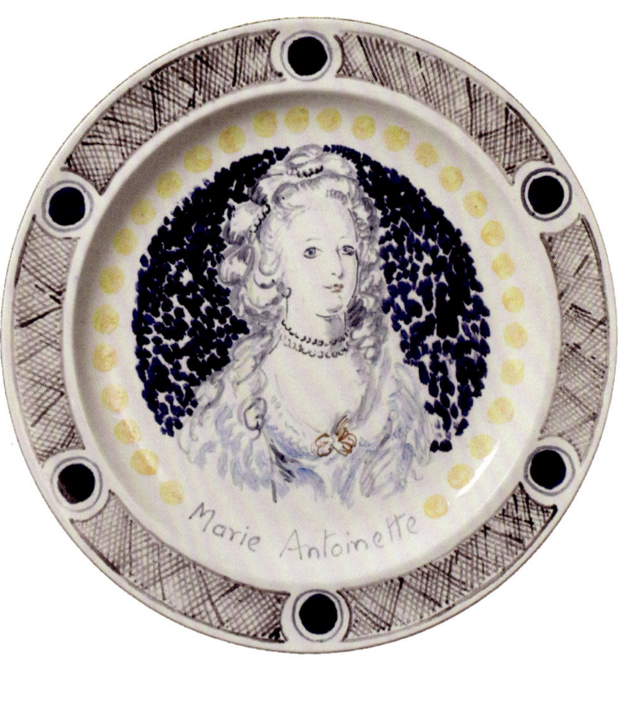

Marie Antoinette

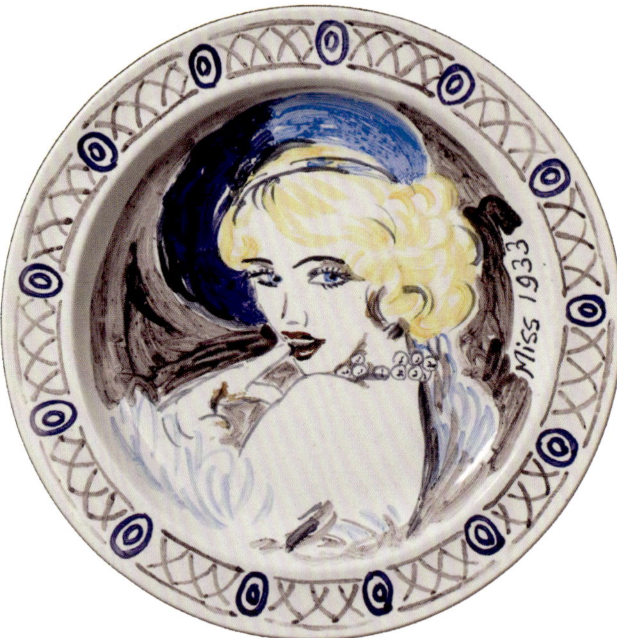

Miss 1933

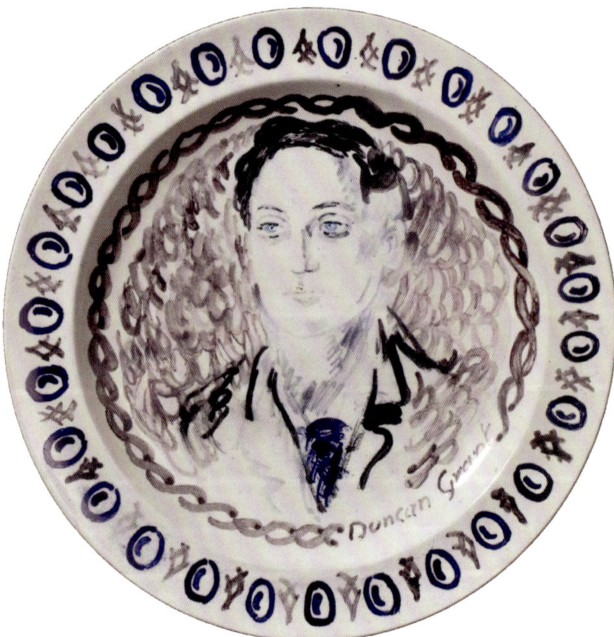

Duncan Grant

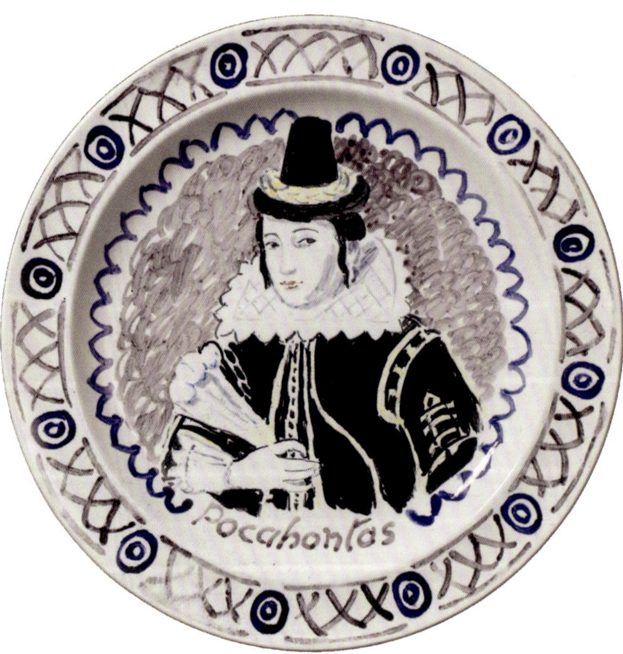

Pocahontas

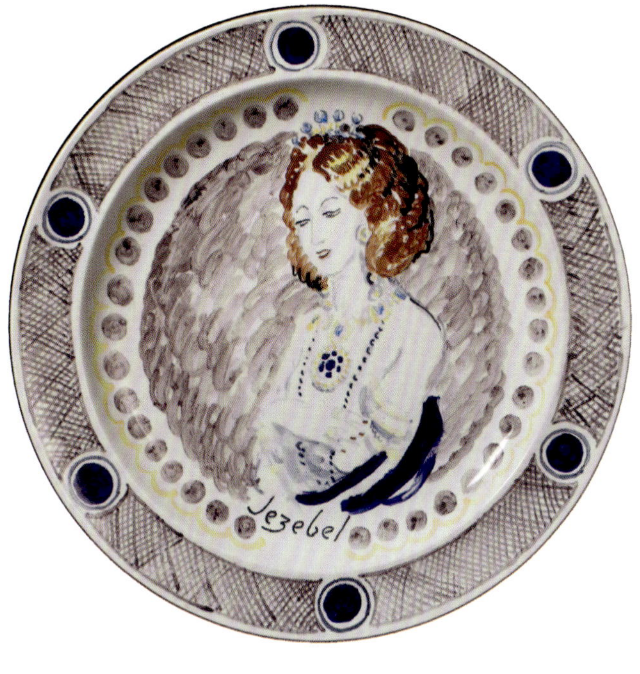
Jezebel

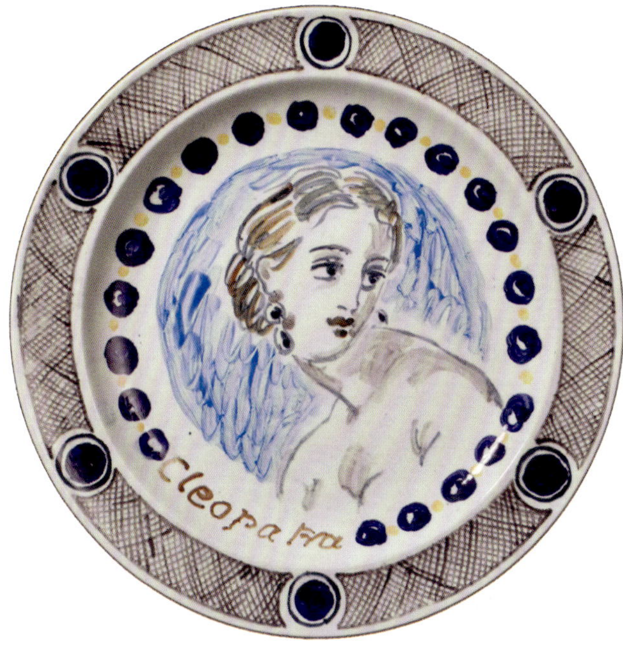
Cleopatra

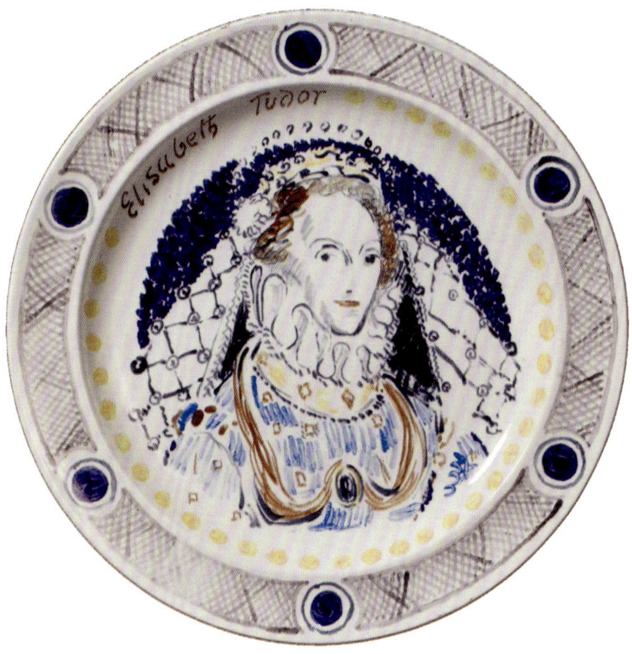
Elisabeth Tudor

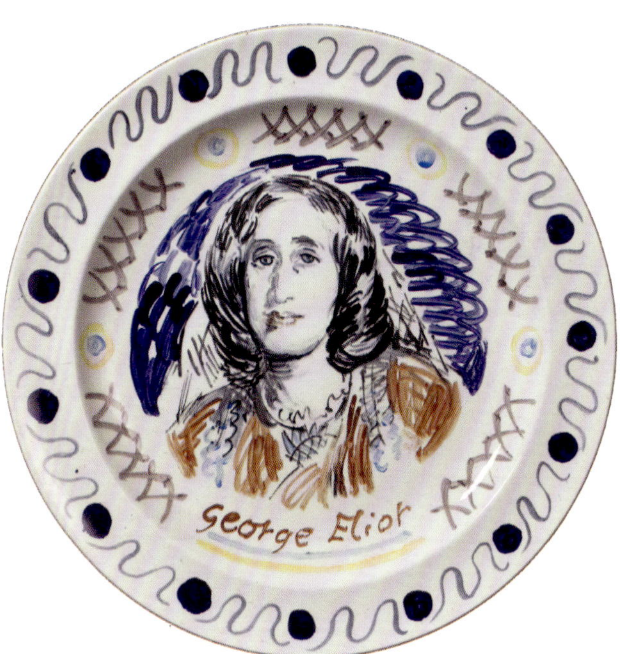
George Eliot

Girl Drawing

c.1932 | oil on canvas | 45.5 × 38 cm

The white column in the background of this painting suggests it is set at La Bergère in Cassis, near Marseille, the house in France which the Bells leased for ten years from 1928.[128] Bell, Grant and various family members and friends spent a portion of each year at the property, a version of Charleston in France.

This painting is one of many of Bell's works in which she closely observes a sitter concentrating on reading, writing, sewing or drawing (*Portrait of Molly MacCarthy*, 1912, p. 52; *Lytton Strachey*, c.1913, p. 59; *Portrait of Quentin Bell*, c.1920, p. 100; *Interior with Duncan Grant*, 1934, p. 139; *Interior with the Artist's Daughter*, c.1935–36, p. 140).

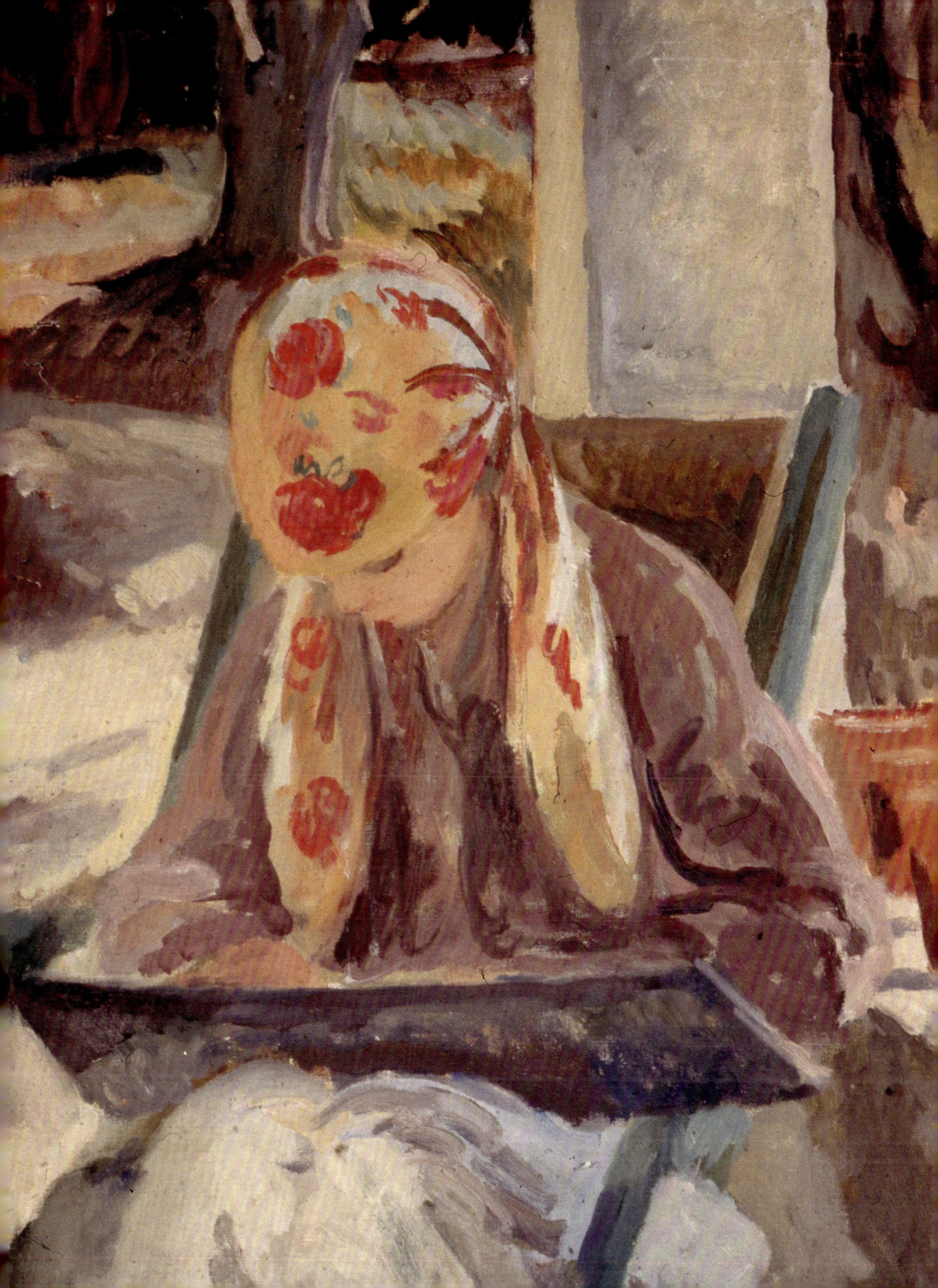

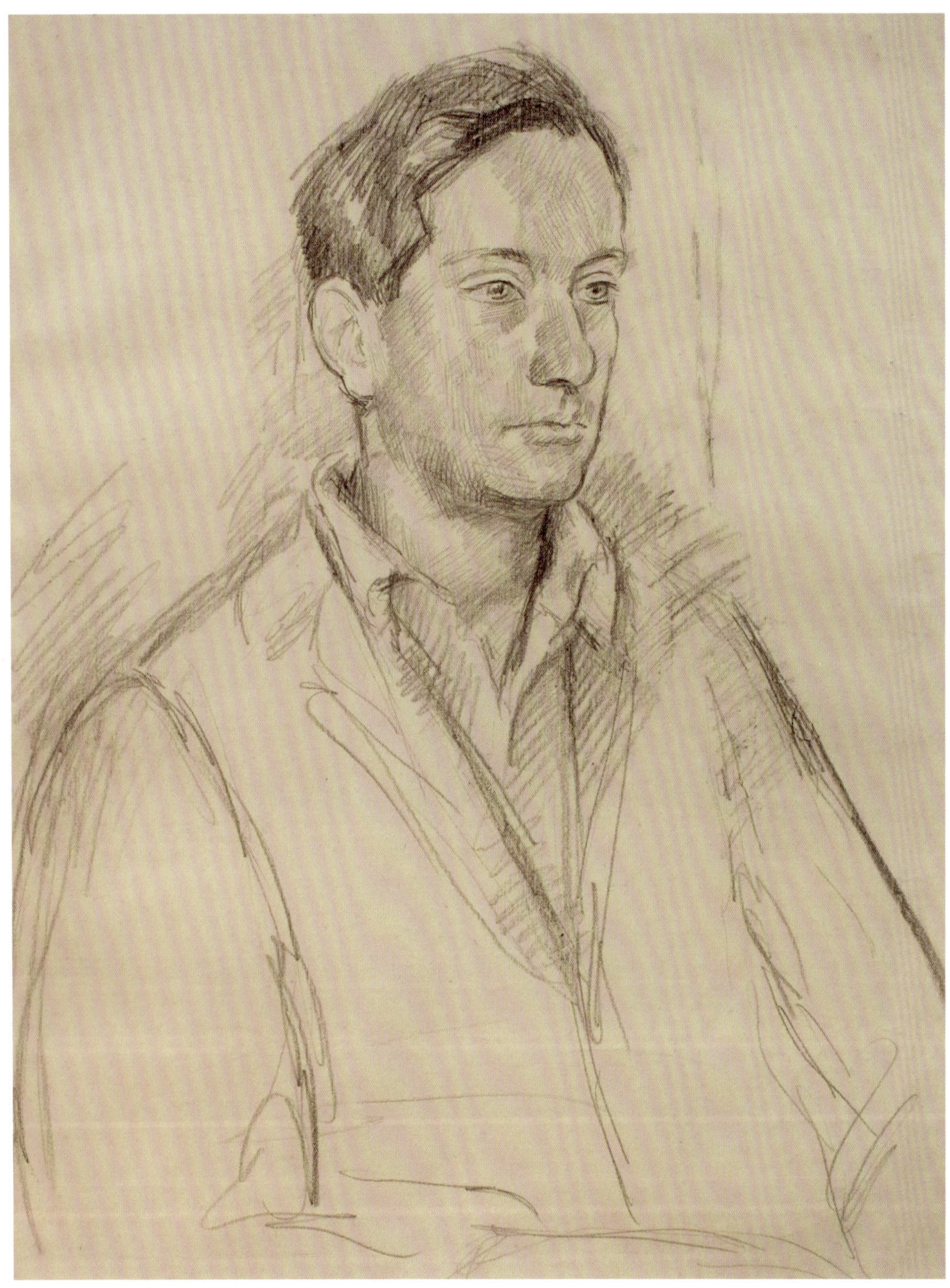

1934 | pencil on paper | 55.9 × 43.2 cm

Duncan Grant (1885–1978) was a Scottish painter and designer of textiles, pottery, theatre sets and costumes. He studied at the Westminster School of Art in London and the Académie de La Palette in Paris. Grant was introduced to Bell (then Stephen) by Pippa Strachey at the Friday Club in the autumn of 1905. Although Grant had always been openly homosexual, a relationship with Bell developed from around 1913 which was both creative and personal. In 1916 Bell and Grant moved to Charleston, Sussex, a home they would share for the next 45 years. In 1918 they had a daughter, Angelica, who was raised as Vanessa and Clive Bell's. In 1930 Virginia Woolf wrote: 'As for Nessa and Duncan, I am persuaded nothing can be now destructive of that easy relationship, because it is based on Bohemianism.'[129] *Interior with Duncan Grant* shows Grant reading surrounded by items of the shared creation of their circle: a painted Omega table, the patterned textile of the chair, decorated ceramics, paintings and on the mantelpiece a cast of the sixth-century figure of Kuan Yin, the Chinese goddess of mercy, the original of which was owned by Roger Fry.[130]

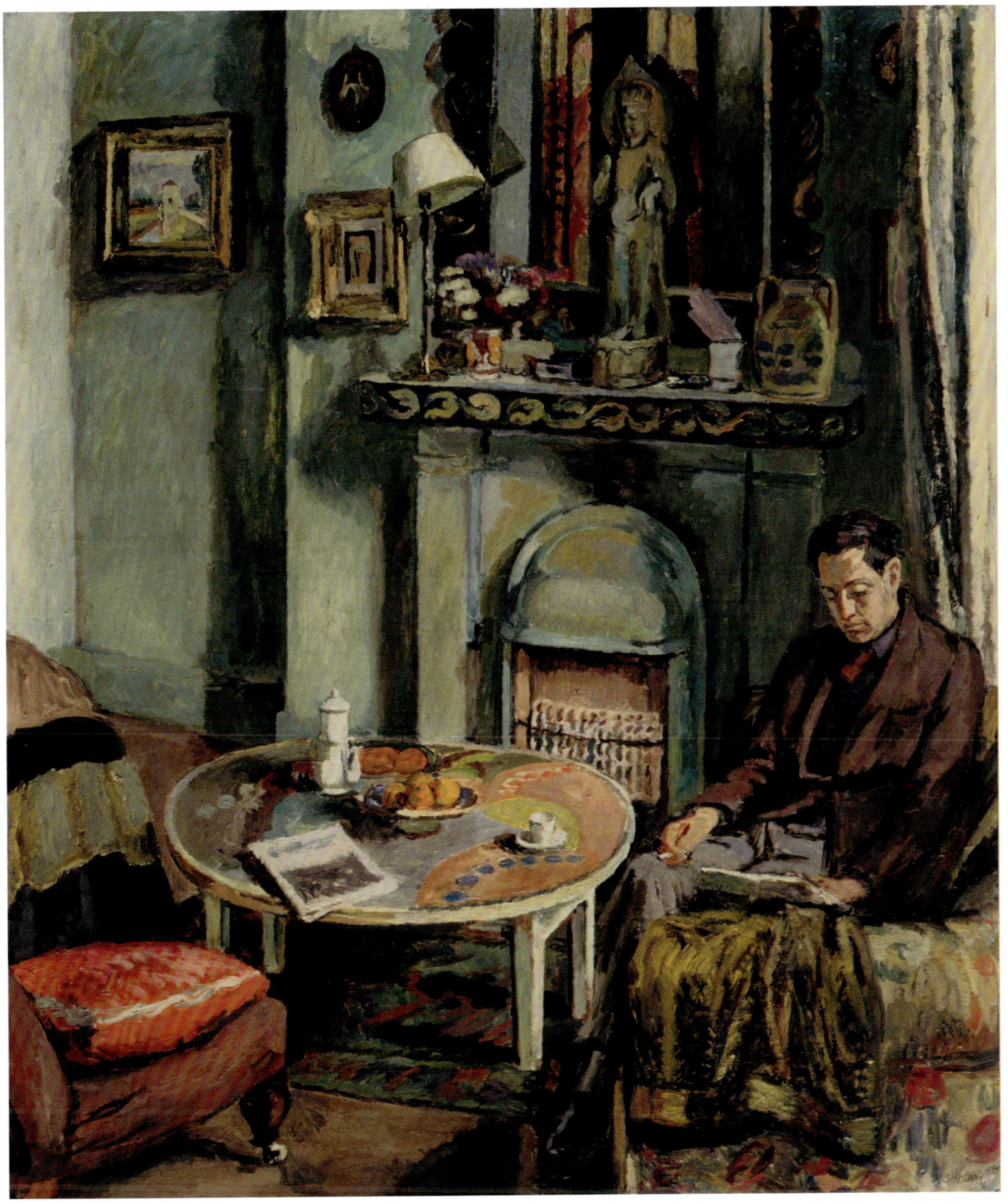

Interior with the Artist's Daughter

c.1935–36 | oil on canvas | 73.7 × 61 cm

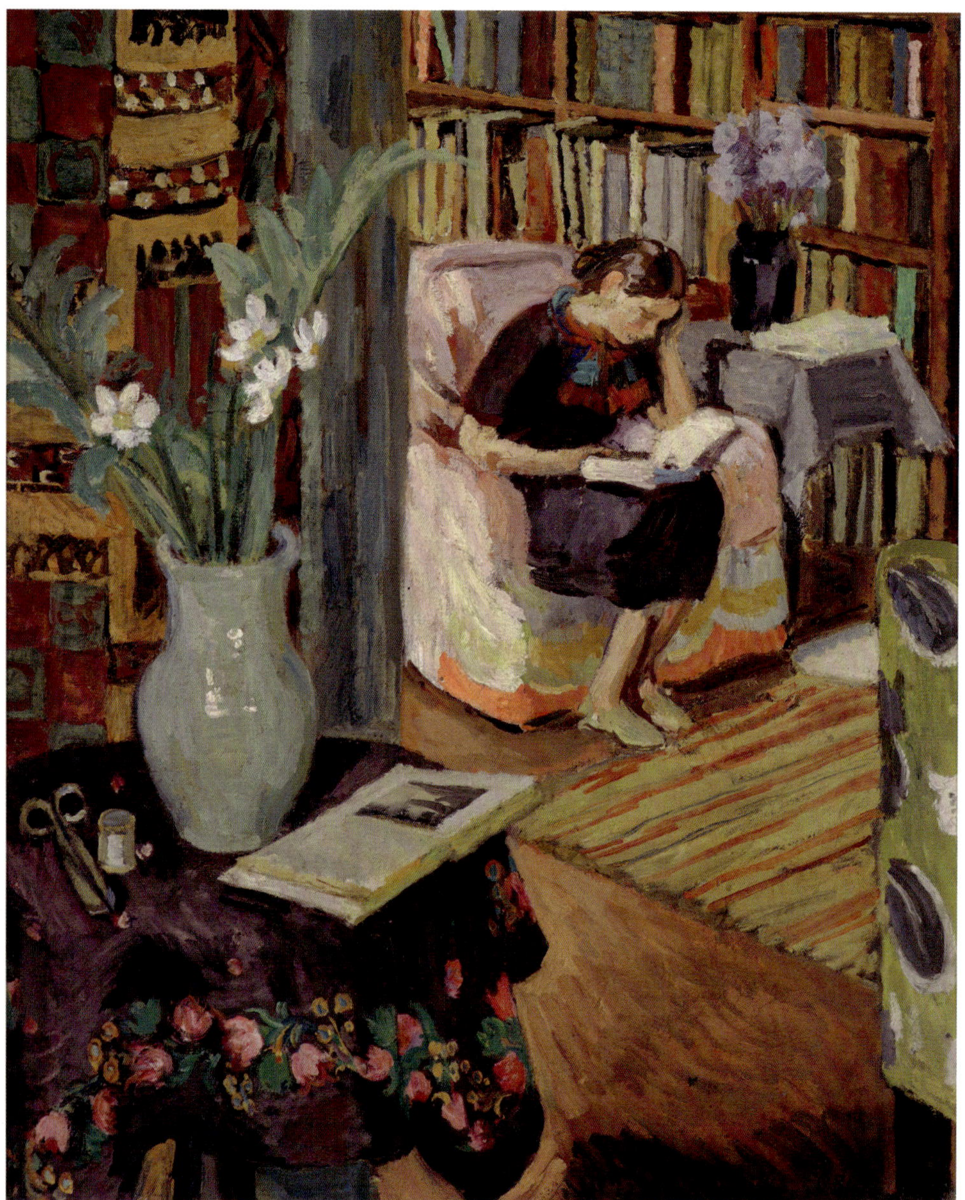

This painting shows Bell and Grant's daughter Angelica reading in the studio at Charleston. Its viewpoint is from the same doorway depicted in *View into a Garden* (1926, p. 112) but from the opposite direction. Angelica later described this room as 'the sanctuary in which I spent the most treasured hours of my life'.[131]

The objects forming a still life in the foreground appear to have been carefully placed, as Reed observes: 'Is the illustrated book in *Interior with the Artist's Daughter* open to a particular page? Do the prominent sewing utensils along with all the depicted textiles assert painting's affiliation with "women's work"? How might that relate to the fact that the upholstery of the chairs is identifiable as Grant's designs (the *Grapes* pattern in yellow on the chair to the right and the whimsical *trompe l'œil* tasselled swags on the chair on the left both come from a display room created at Alex Reid Lefevre Gallery in 1932)?'[132]

Interior with a Housemaid

c.1939 | oil on canvas | 70 × 56 cm

Interior with a Housemaid shows Bell's new bedroom at Charleston viewed from the entrance to the studio on the ground floor, displaying her desk with an empty chair, Duncan Grant's *Painted Omega Screen* (1913, p. 121) and an anonymous housemaid with a broom. In 1939 this room was converted from a pantry and storeroom as part of the preparations to make Charleston, again, a wartime home. The geometric patterns on the rugs and front panel of the screen 'allow for a richly orchestrated arrangement of warm colours – purples, dull reds, ochres and browns, cooled by touches of green and the blue and silver highlights'.[133] The housemaid's presence acknowledges Bell's privileged background, which facilitated her rebellious attitude towards social and artistic conventions.[134]

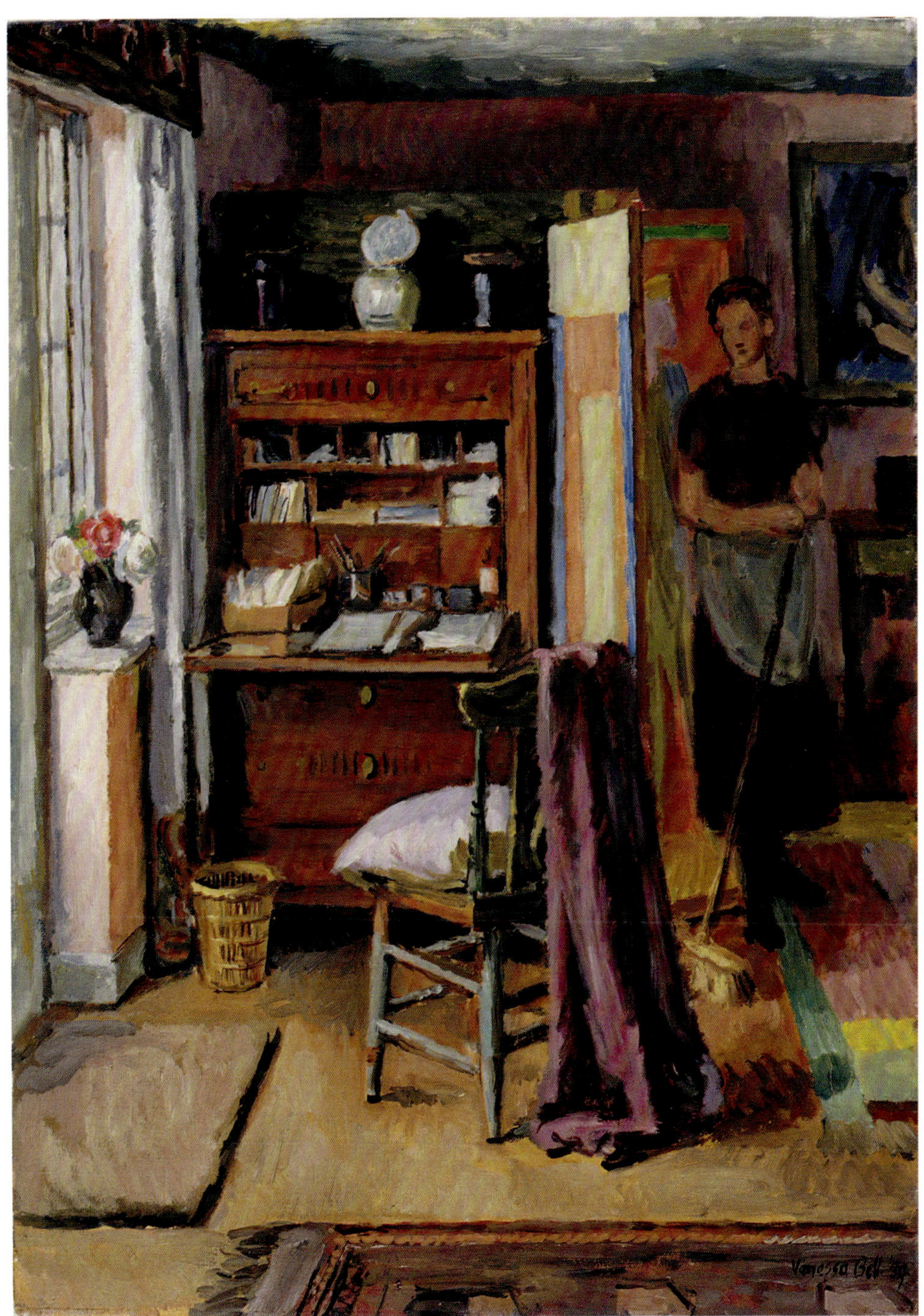

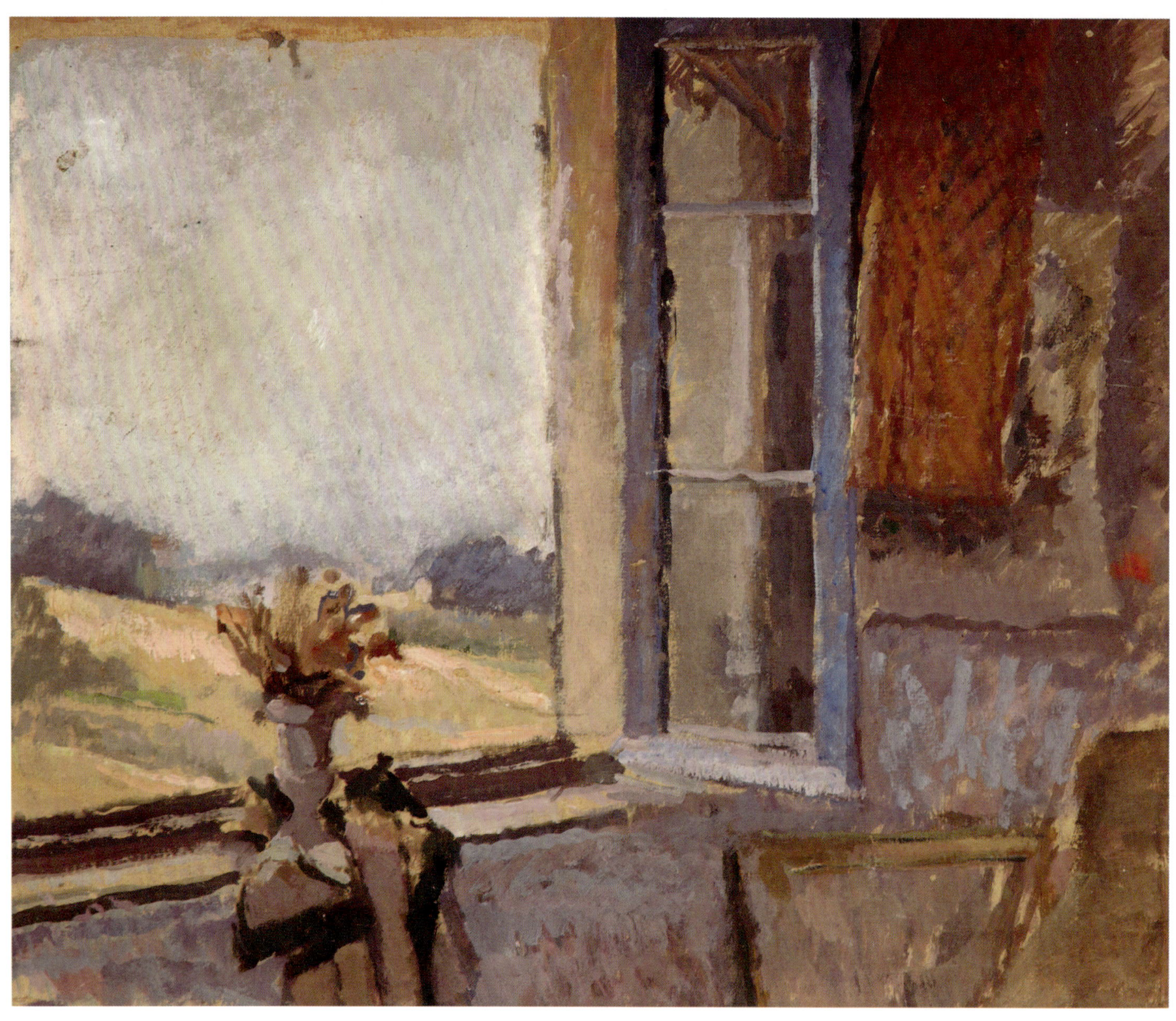

Interior

c. 1940 | gouache on board | 6.5 × 44 cm

In this painting a vase of flowers sits on a windowsill at the border between the house and the garden. A landscape is seen through the open window of a domestic room, a motif which recurs throughout Bell's career – for example, *View of the Pond at Charleston, East Sussex* (*c.* 1919, Sheffield Museums). This composition addresses the modernist concern with the flatness of the picture plane, the window frame forcing the external scene into a firmer relationship with the picture's surface.[135] As Clive Bell had written in 1913: 'A picture is a *surface* covered with lines and colours in a certain order, and it is this arrangement which inspires true aesthetic emotion.'[136]

Translation of Velázquez's
Infanta Margareta (Vienna)

c.1940 | watercolour and gouache on paper | 25.5 × 32 cm

Bell studied and copied the old masters throughout her life, contributing five paintings to Roger Fry's *Copies and Translations of Old Masters* exhibition at the Omega Workshops in 1917. Her copies of Raphael's *Colonna Madonna* (1508, Gemäldegalerie, Berlin) and *Saint Catherine* (1508, National Gallery, London) remain in the collection at Charleston. Bell wrote to Roger Fry that Rembrandt's 'colour is more lovely than one could imagine', and later that revisiting the National Gallery after the Second World War was like visiting 'all one's old friends'.[137] Of Velázquez she noted: 'One never seems to get tired of looking at him. His colour is most surprising. Instead of being all very subdued greys and blacks and browns ... some of the paintings here are almost dazzling, bright blues and all sorts of the gayest colours, almost like Renoir.'[138]

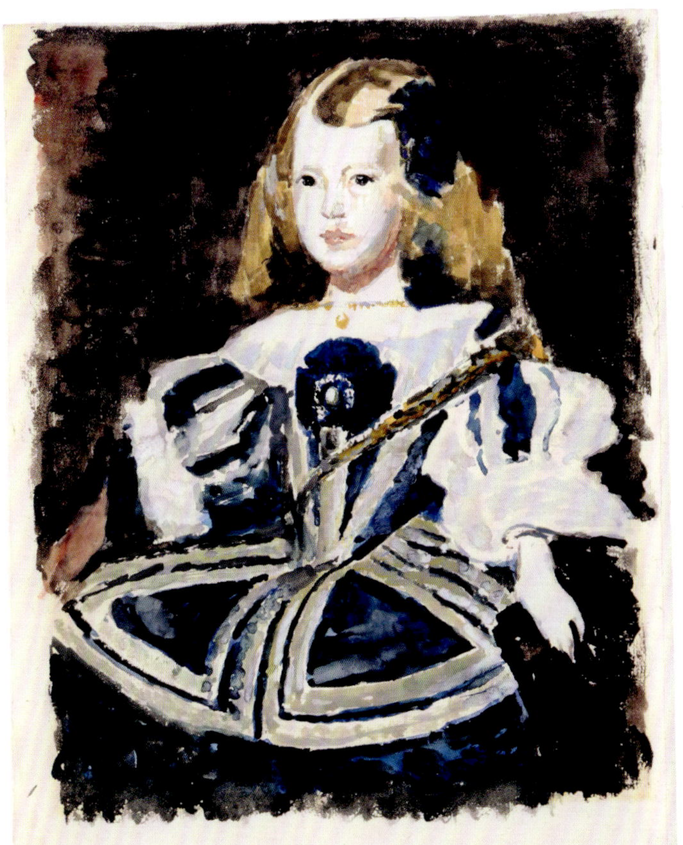

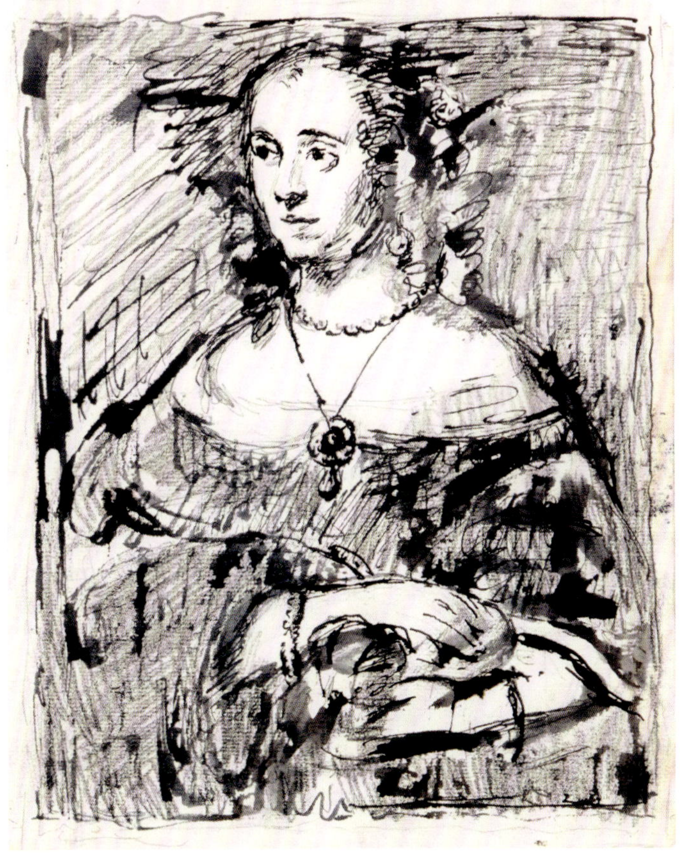

Translation of Rembrandt's
Lady with the Lap Dog (Toronto)

undated | pencil and ink on paper | 3.5 × 31.3 cm

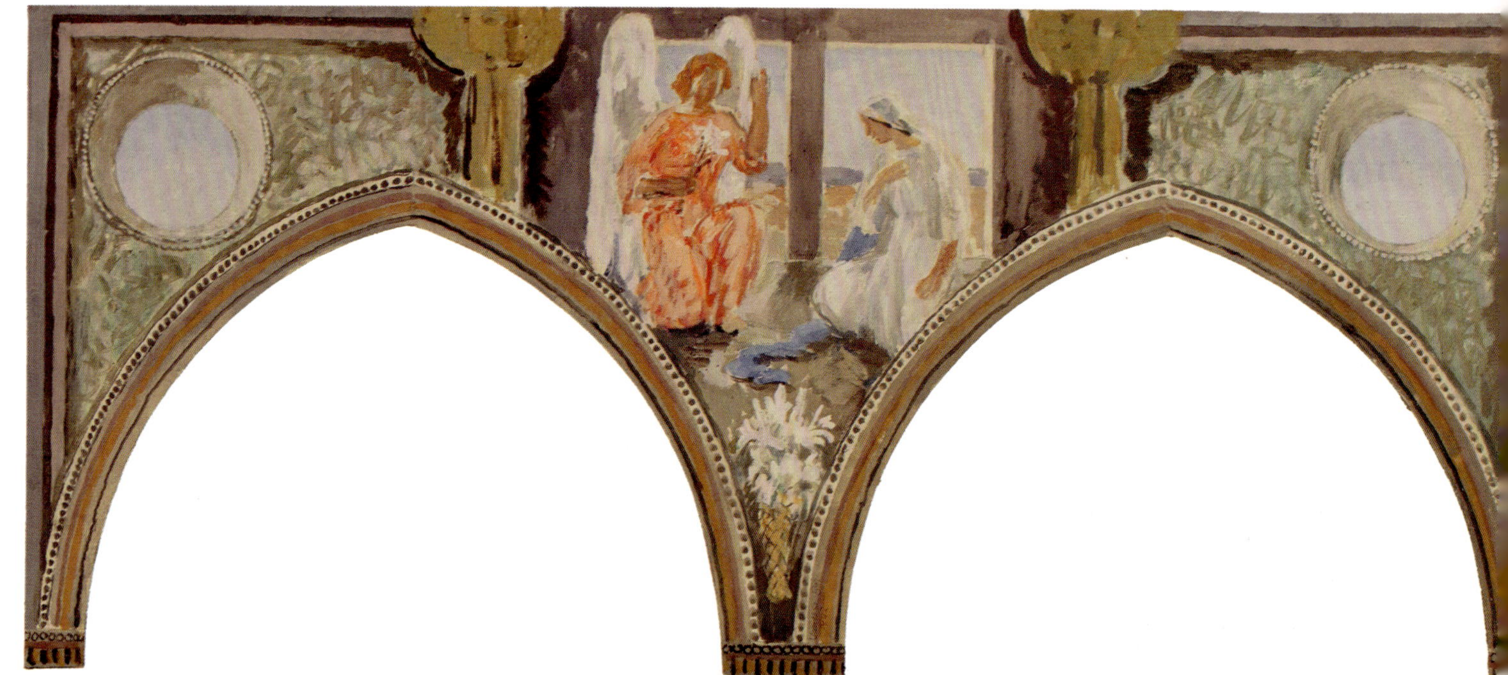

Berwick Church: model showing The Annunciation

1941 | watercolour on cardboard | 67.3 × 83.7 cm

In 1939 Bell and Duncan Grant joined the Society of Mural Painters and in 1940 they were commissioned, together with Quentin Bell, to decorate Berwick Church near their home in Sussex. The commission was instigated by Bishop George Bell (no relation), whose ambition was to provide artists with war work and re-engage the Church's relationship with them.[139] Their motivation was less religious and more concerned with an admiration of Italian murals. Money was raised, and their old friend Frederick Etchells (see p. 54), now an architect, was brought in as an advisor. Vanessa Bell created two decorations for either side of the nave, a *Nativity* and an *Annunciation*. She wrote of the process: 'What a war time occupation! It needed Hitler to bring such things to pass. We have got as far as doing sketches, which have met with approval on the whole though D.s Christ was thought a bit attractive and my Virgin a bit frivolous. Still that's easily changed, and on the whole we accept every suggestion and read our Bibles diligently. How we shall ever manage to paint walls 30 ft. high I can't conceive.'[140] In the end, the decorations were painted on plasterboard, which

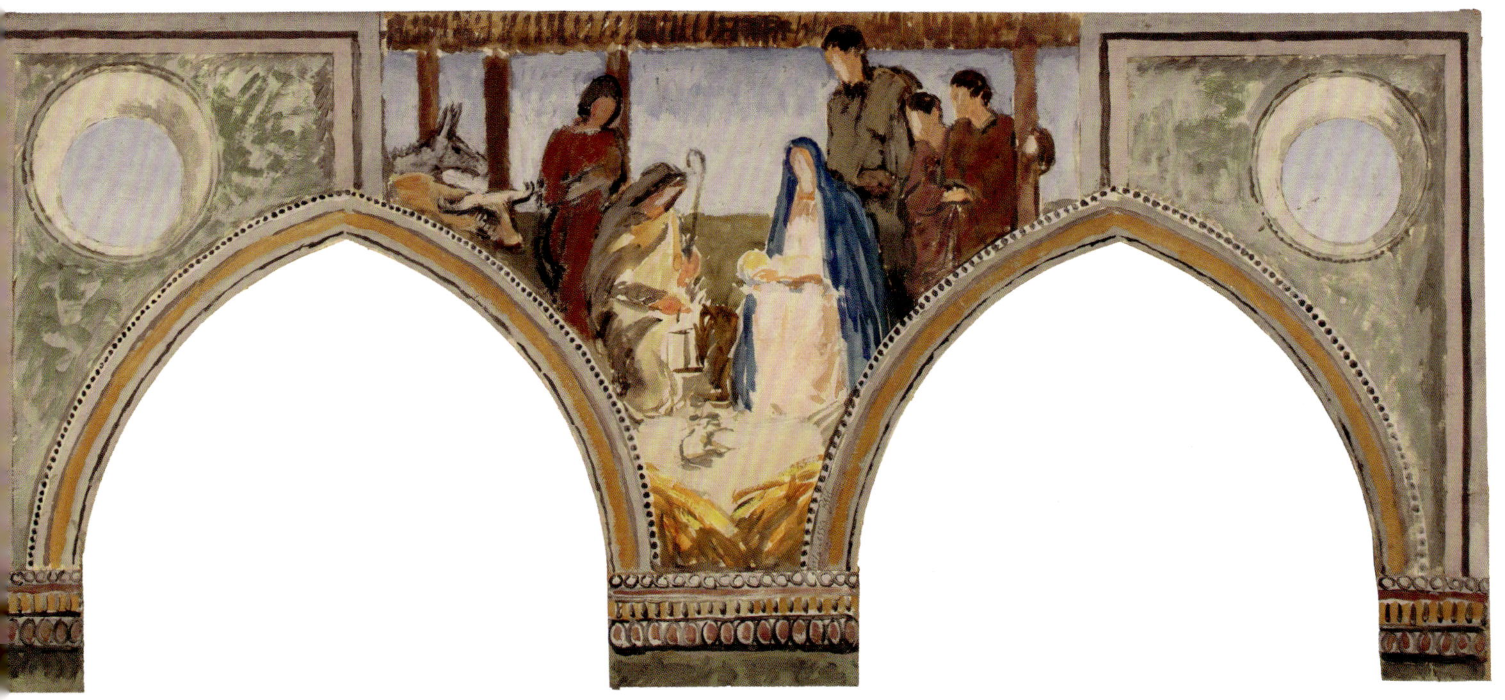

Berwick Church: model showing The Nativity

1941 | watercolour on cardboard | 67.3 × 83.7 cm

was then fixed to the church interior.

The *Annunciation* would have had personal significance for Bell as her mother Julia, while pregnant with Vanessa, was depicted as Mary in Edward Burne-Jones's *Annunciation* (1879, Lady Lever Art Gallery, Wirral). Bell's daughter Angelica modelled for the Virgin Mary, her friend Chattie Salaman for the archangel Gabriel. Between the first and second preparatory paintings the figures have been moved outside, with a view of the South Downs and Cuckmere River in the background and curtains added to frame the scene. In the final painting the background is a walled garden and the curtains have been removed.[141]

All of the models in the *Nativity* were local people. Bell used a local farmhand, Stanley Standon, for one of the shepherds; Peter Durrant, who worked on the Firle Estate, was Joseph; the children of Charleston's gardener and housekeeper posed, and Bell also borrowed some local lambs.[142] Angelica again modelled for Mary. In the finished painting Bell inserts the local landmark of Mount Caburn, which was visible from Virginia Woolf's house at Rodmell.[143]

Angelica Bell kneeling in front of Chattie Salaman, study for The Annunciation

c.1941 | pencil on paper | 56 × 39 cm

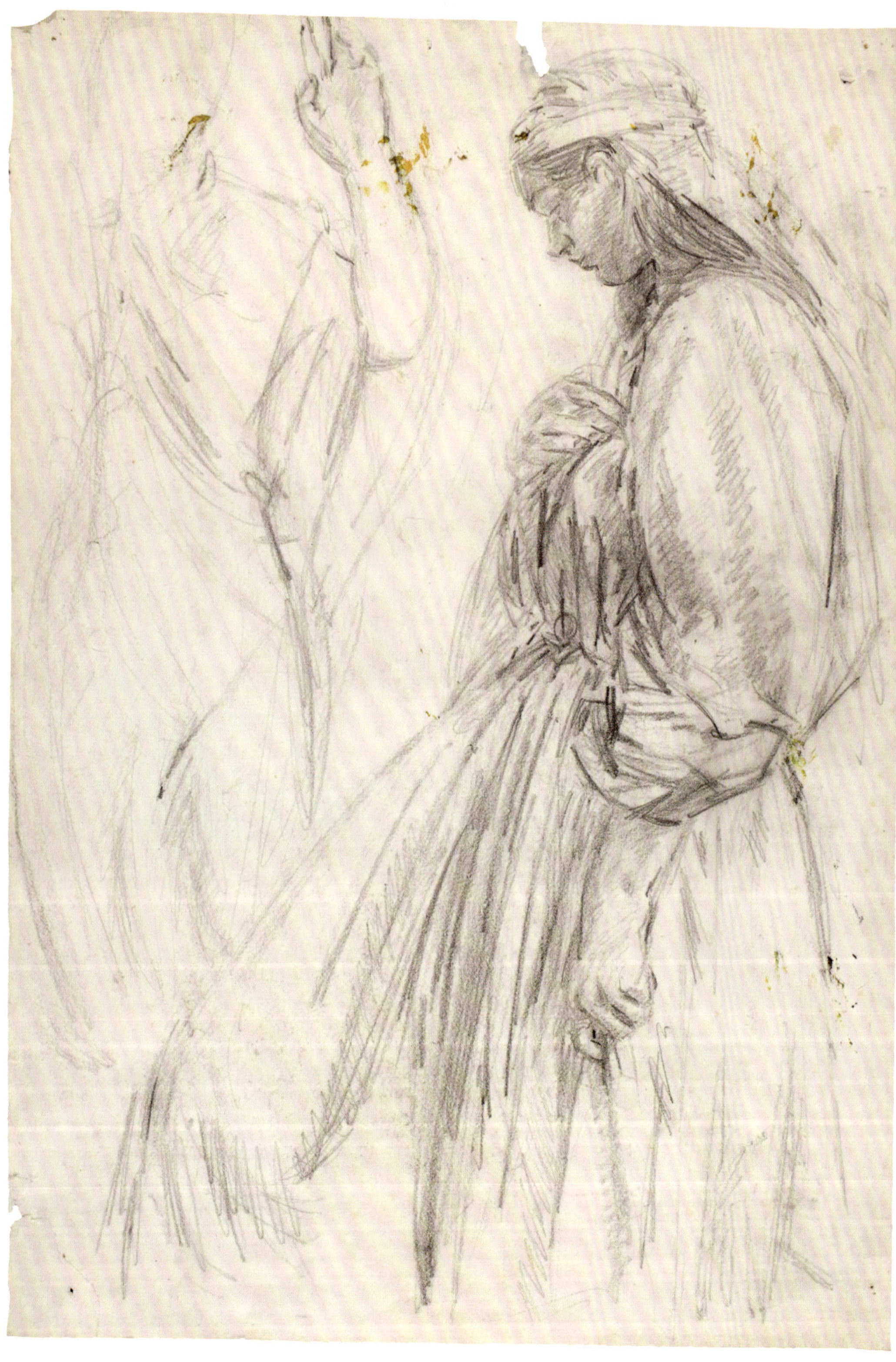

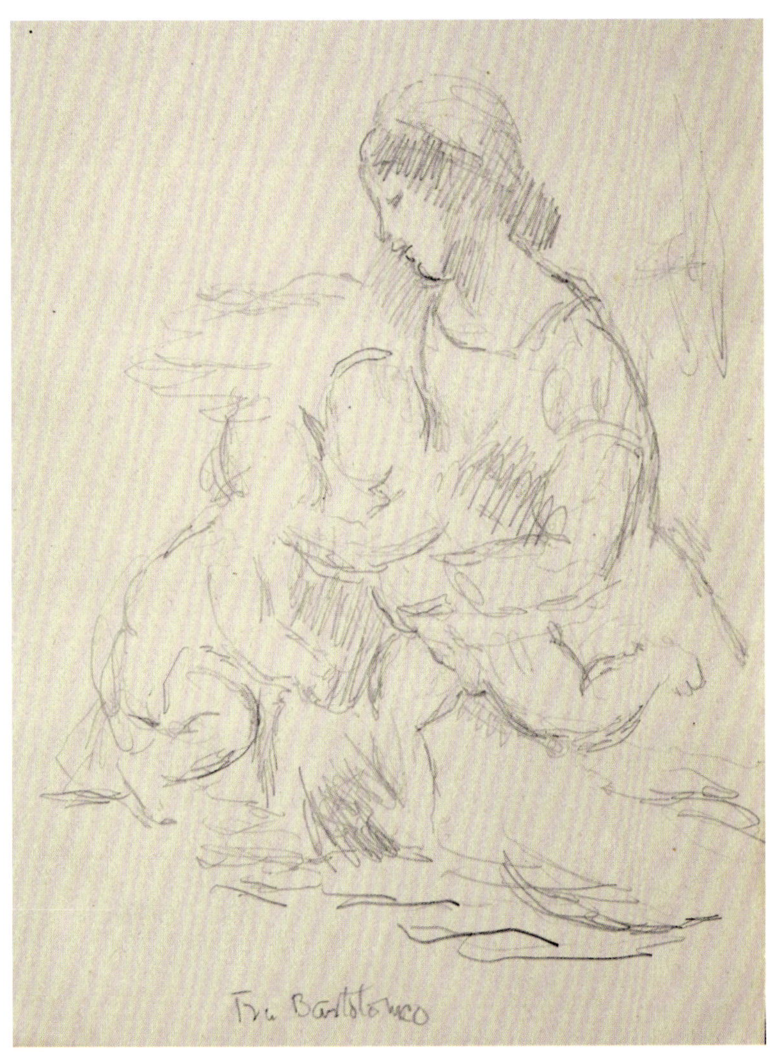

Fra Bartolomeo, *The Madonna and Child with Saint John*, National Gallery

undated | pencil on paper | 25.5 × 18 cm

Study for Berwick Church: The Shepherd

1941 | oil on wood | 121 × 59 cm

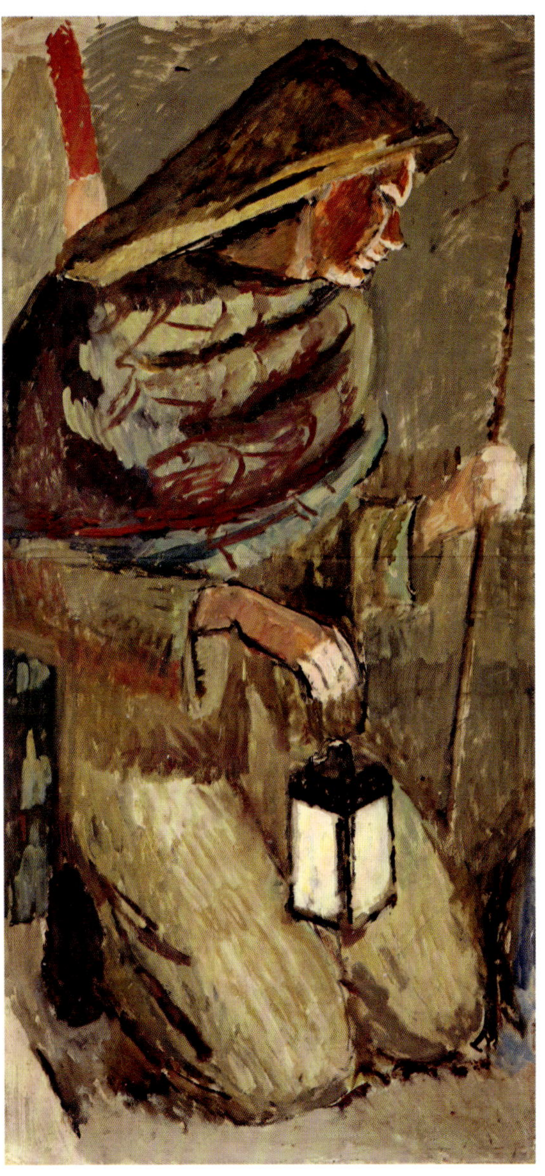

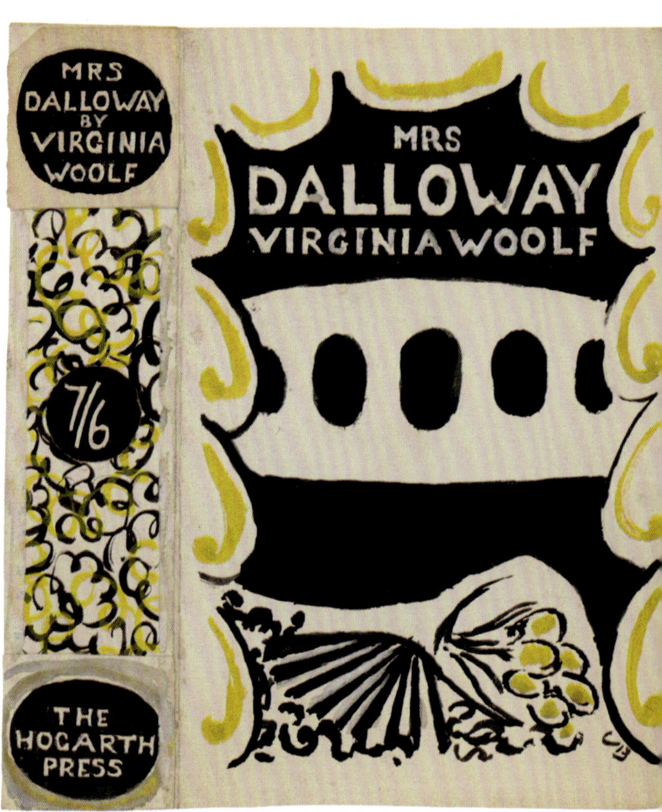

The Hogarth Press was started in 1917 by Virginia and Leonard Woolf after they bought a small hand press. It started as a hobby and a way to publish Virginia's writing autonomously, but quickly became successful, publishing many of the celebrated authors of the day.[144] Bell began by contributing woodcut illustrations for Woolf's *Kew Gardens* (1919) and *Monday or Tuesday* (1921) and started producing dust jackets with *Jacob's Room* (1922). The simplicity of Bell's designs and the lack of obvious reference to the subject of the book was ridiculed by booksellers and reviewers. *The Star* remarked of her design for *The Common Reader* (1925) that 'Only a conscious artist could have done it so badly.'[145] Nevertheless, the Woolfs continued to use Bell to design all of Virginia's book covers as well as those of other authors. Bell's book jackets use many of the decorative motifs from other aspects of her work: flowers, curtains, circles, hatching – 'all images of plenitude and nourishment, merged into almost abstract patterns and often printed in a striking two-colour contrast'.[146]

Original artwork for
Between the Acts
by Virginia Woolf

c.1941 | ink on paper | 22.4 × 19 cm

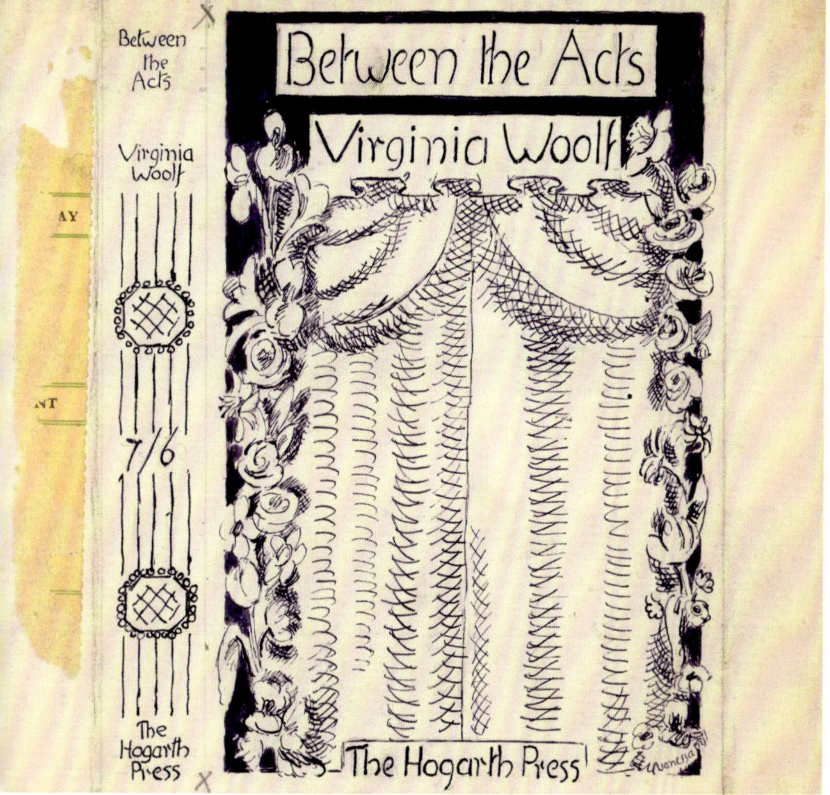

Original artwork
for *A Writer's Diary*
by Virginia Woolf

c.1953 | ink on paper | 26.2 × 20.1 cm

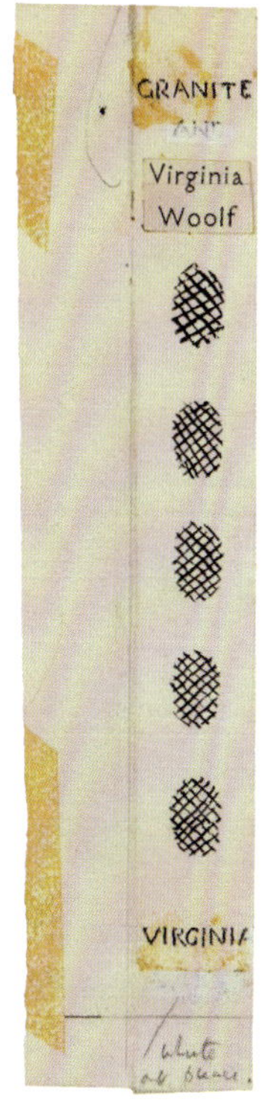

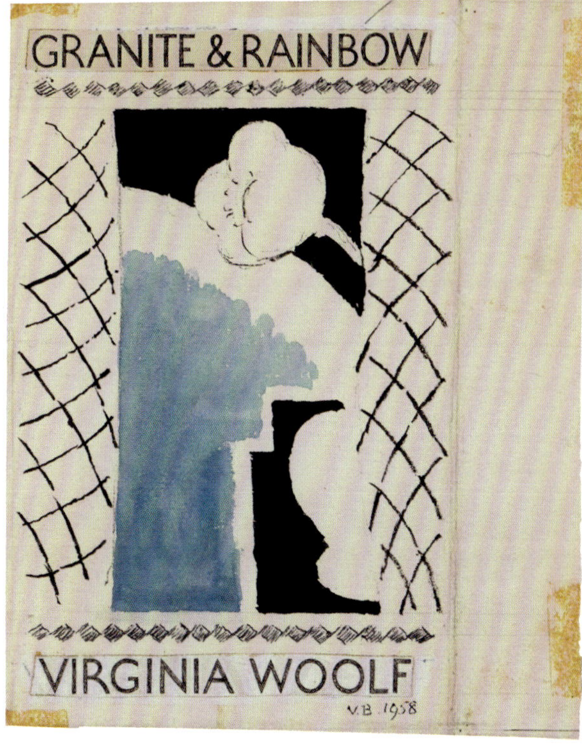

Original artwork for
Granite and Rainbow
by Virginia Woolf

c.1958 | ink on paper | 28.1 × 34.3 cm

**Original design for
*The Funeral March of
a Marionette* by Susan
Buchan**

c.1935 | pencil and pen on paper |
21.8 × 14.2 cm

**Original design for
The Death of the Moth
by Virginia Woolf**

c.1942 | pencil and ink on paper |
15.8 × 25.4 cm

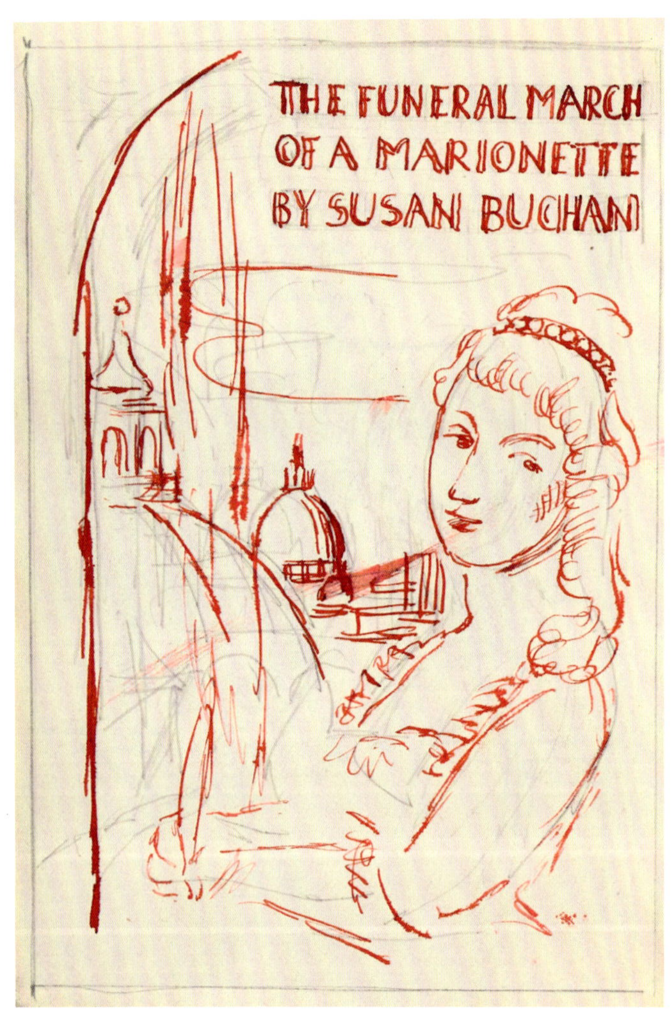

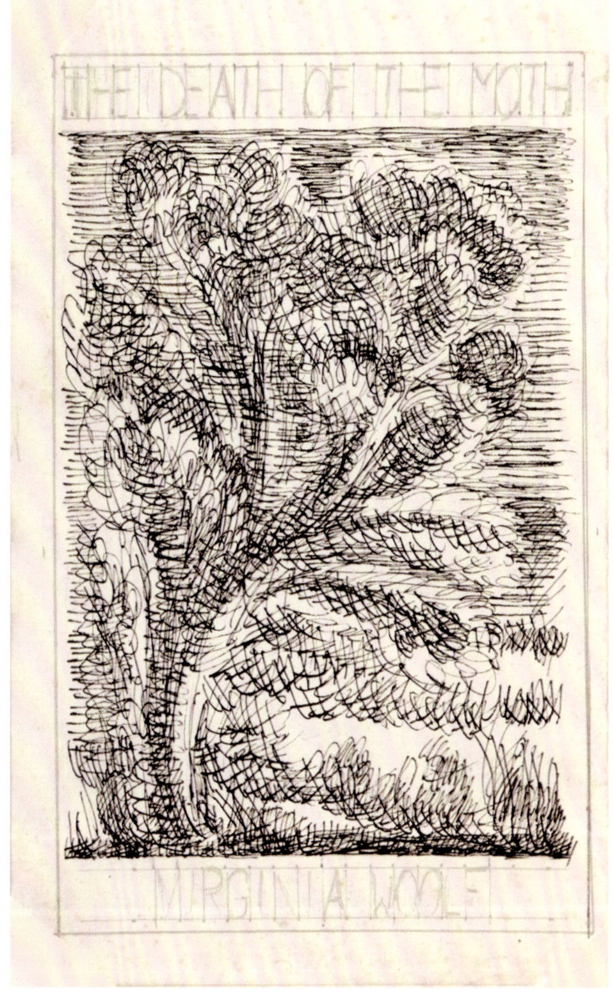

***The Death of the Moth* by
Virginia Woolf**

1942 | book | 21.6 × 13.7 cm

***The Moment and Other
Essays* by Virginia Woolf**

1947 | book | 20.3 × 13.3 cm

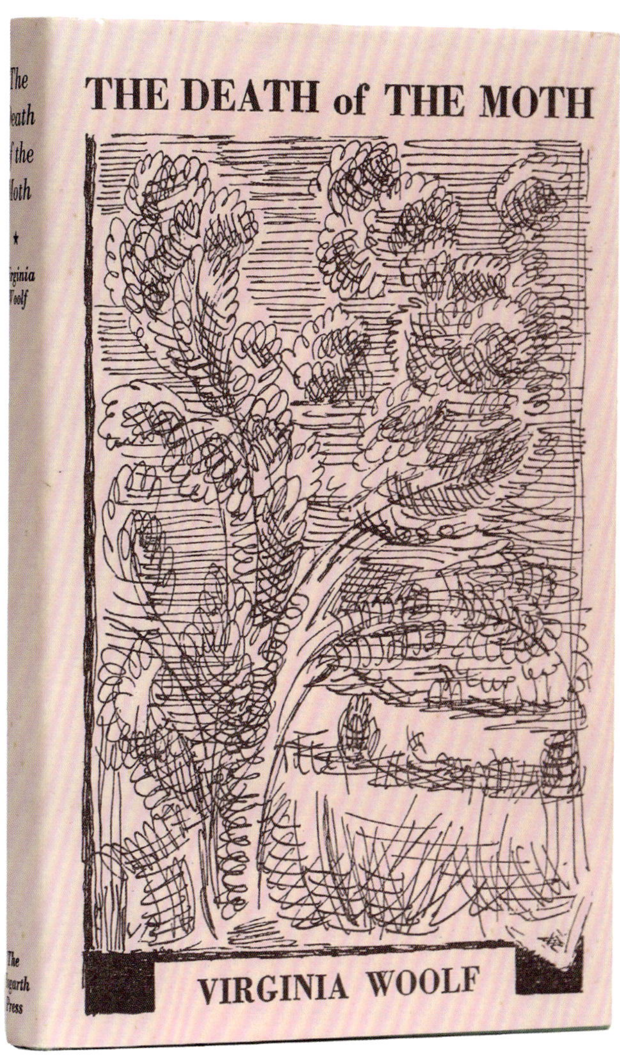
The
Death
of the
Moth

Virginia
Woolf

THE DEATH of THE MOTH

VIRGINIA WOOLF

The
Hogarth
Press

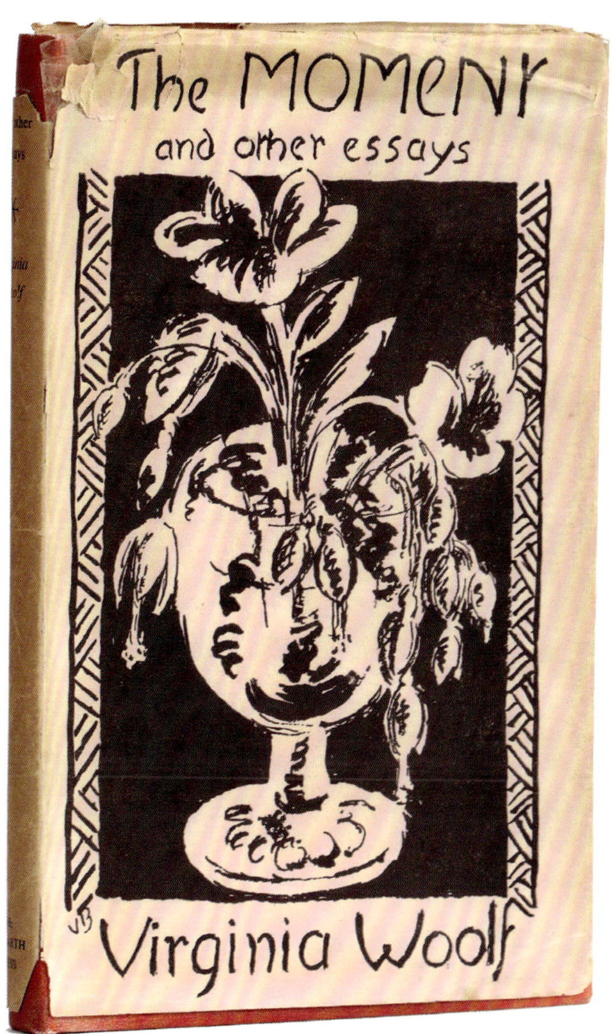
The MOMENT
and other essays

Virginia Woolf

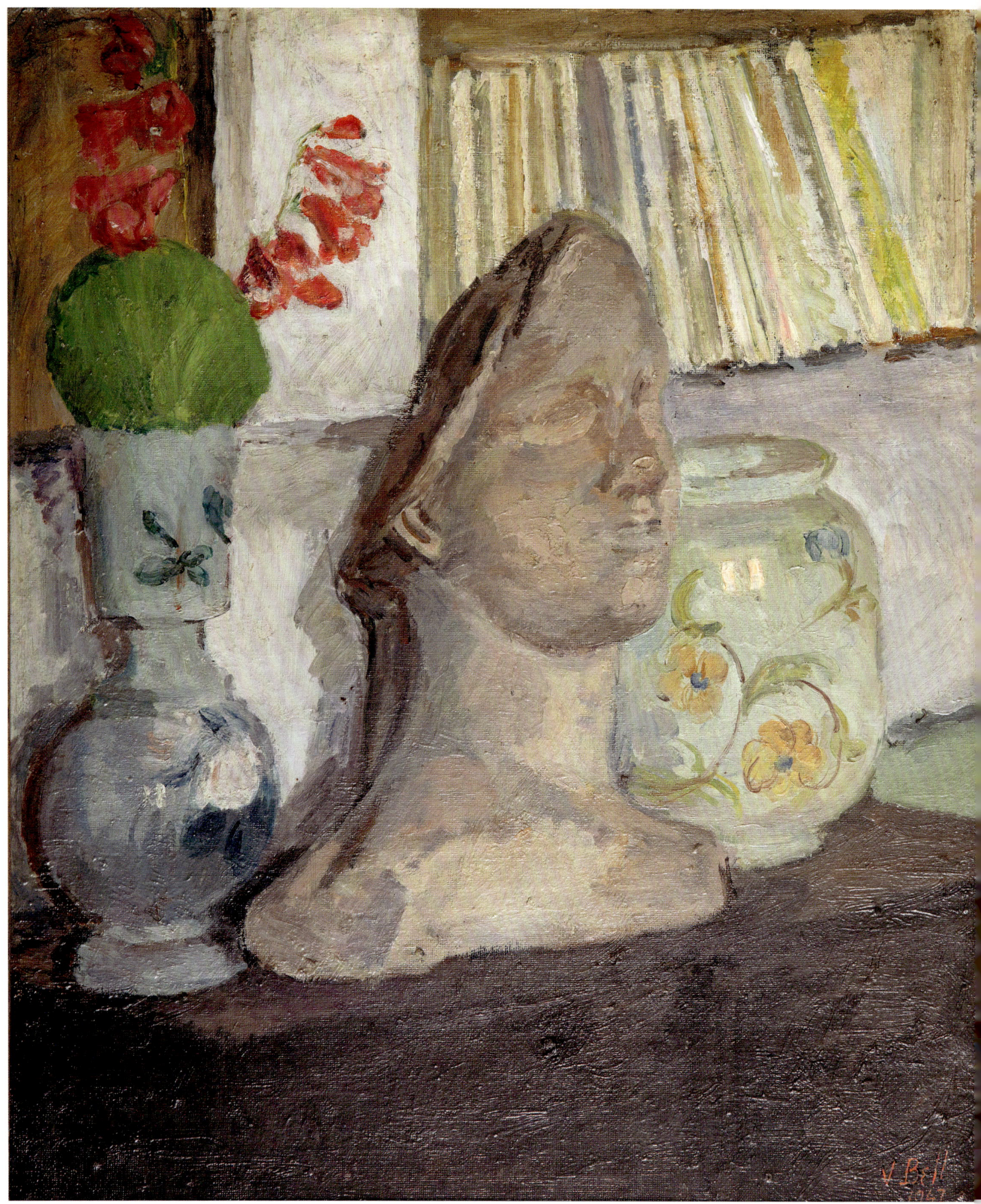

Still Life with a Plaster Head

1947 | oil on board | 53.5 × 44.5 cm

Still Life by the Studio Window

c.1950 | oil on canvas | 68 × 61 cm

Still Life with a Plaster Bust

1949 | oil on canvas | 62.5 × 50.5 cm

These paintings are examples of Bell's late work. They are painted with more highly finished detail, and concentrate on observation of everyday life in and around the studio. She wrote to Roger Fry: 'I don't think I'm nearly as enterprising as you (or Duncan), about painting anything I don't find at my door.'[147] In 1939 Bell had converted an attic room into a studio, which overlooked the garden. There were large collections of ceramics and fabrics at Charleston, often collected by Bell during her travels, and these form the cast of characters in her still lifes. The bust seen in these paintings is a plaster cast from an antique sculpture acquired by Duncan Grant, along with several others, from Lewes Art School. In *Still Life with a Plaster Head*, to the left of the cast is a nineteenth-century 'French opaline glass vase holding two penstemons and … a Bergenia; to the right, an 18th century faience polychrome drugs jar (both vases are still at Charleston)'. In *Still Life by the Studio Window* the bust and a glass holding primulas sit on a piece of black and purple fabric which was used for furnishings in the house.[148]

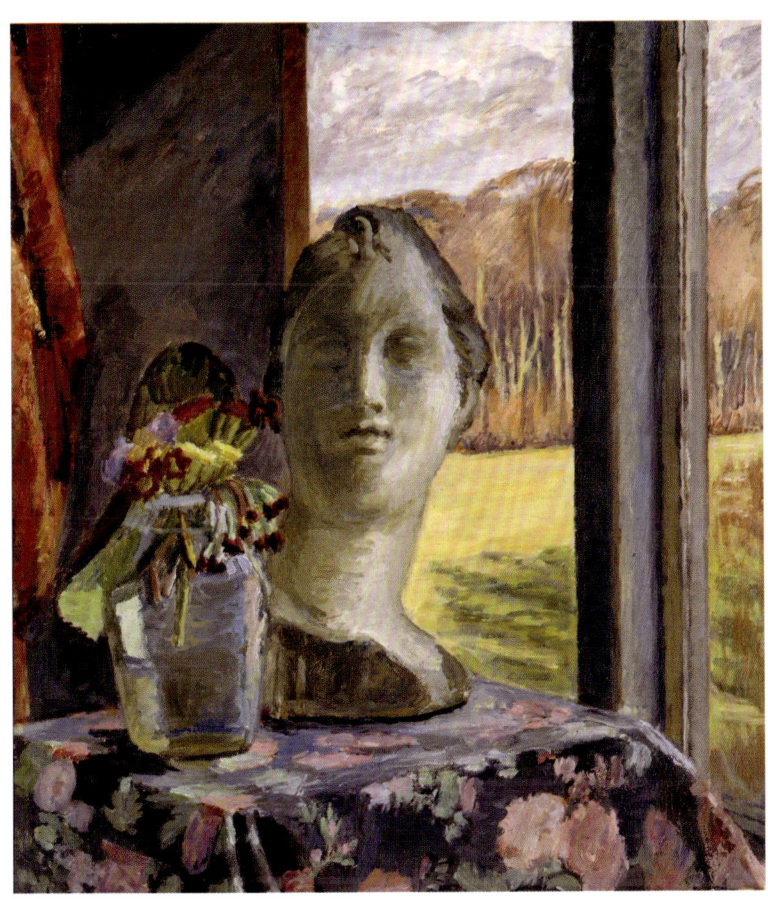

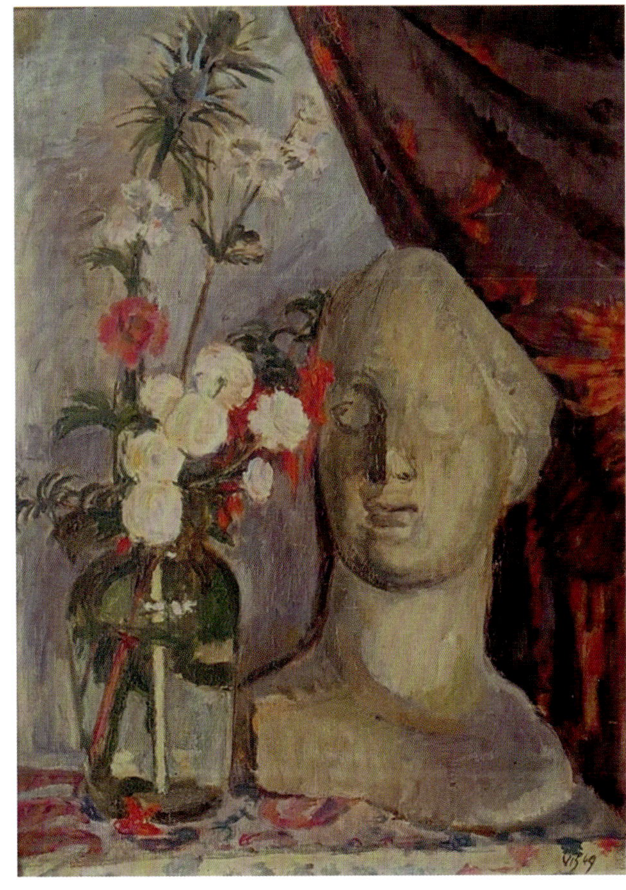

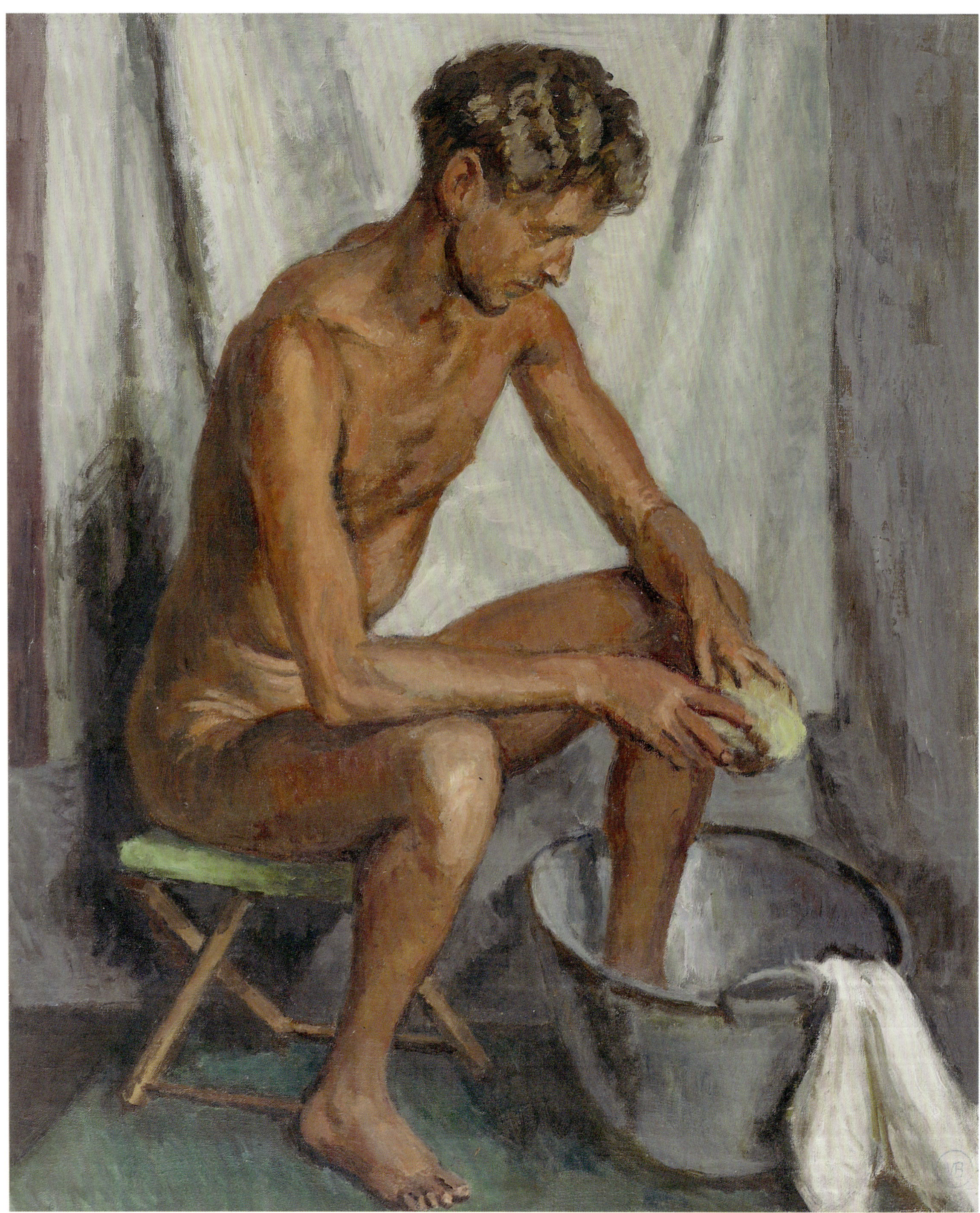

Study of Paul Roche Bathing

c.1948 | oil on canvas | 65 × 53 cm

Paul Roche (1916–2007) was a poet, novelist, professor of English and translator of Greek and Latin classics. He was ordained as a priest in 1943 but left the priesthood in the 1950s.[149] In the mid–1940s Roche met Duncan Grant, 'with whom he quickly developed an intimate, if apparently one-sided, sexual friendship'.[150] Roche and Grant's relationship continued after Bell's death in 1961. Although Roche had married Clarissa Tanner in 1954, he took care of Grant in his last years. Grant eventually died in Roche's home in 1978. Unlike David Garnett (p. 78), Roche did not live at Charleston and he generally met with Grant in London. Given that he was not particularly close to Bell, the intimacy of this study is perhaps surprising. Here the tin bath, which was a central motif in *The Tub* (1917, Tate, p. vi), reappears, with a much more realistic and down-to-earth male figure against a pale fabric backcloth.

Teapot

VANESSA BELL AND QUENTIN BELL

c.1950 | glazed ceramic | 11.5 × 22 × 12 cm

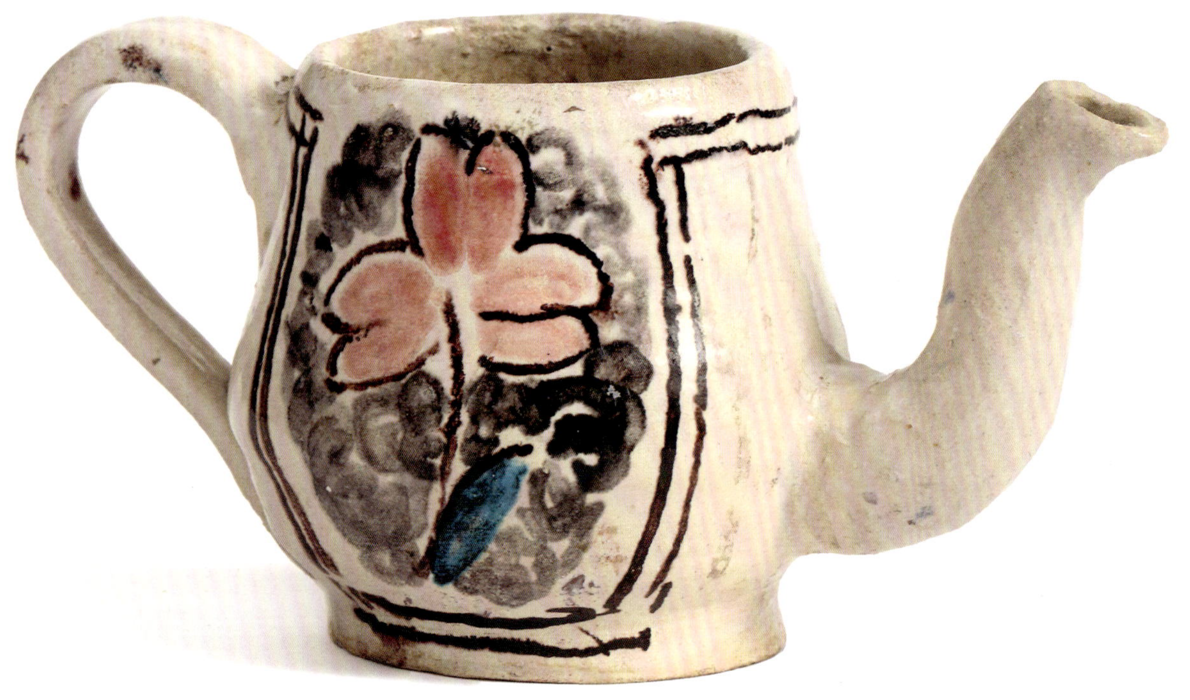

Mug

VANESSA BELL AND QUENTIN BELL

c.1950–70 | glazed ceramic |
10.6 × 15 × 11 cm

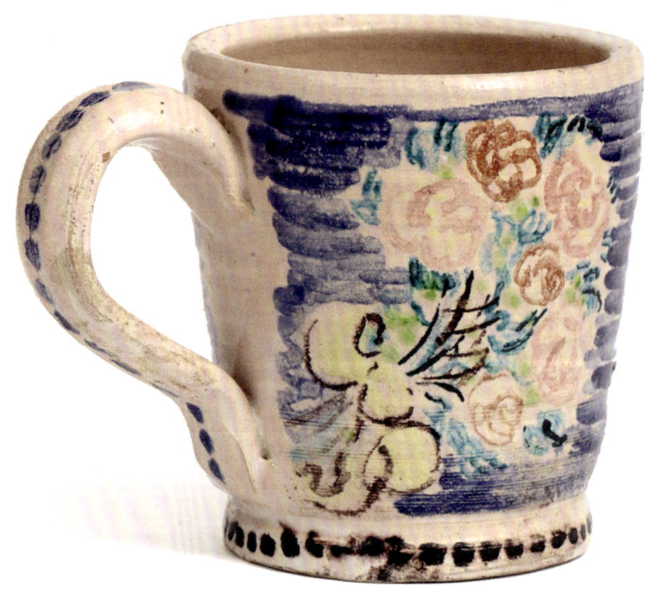

Bowl

VANESSA BELL AND QUENTIN BELL

*c.*1950 | glazed ceramic | 17.8 × 21.3 × 21.3 cm

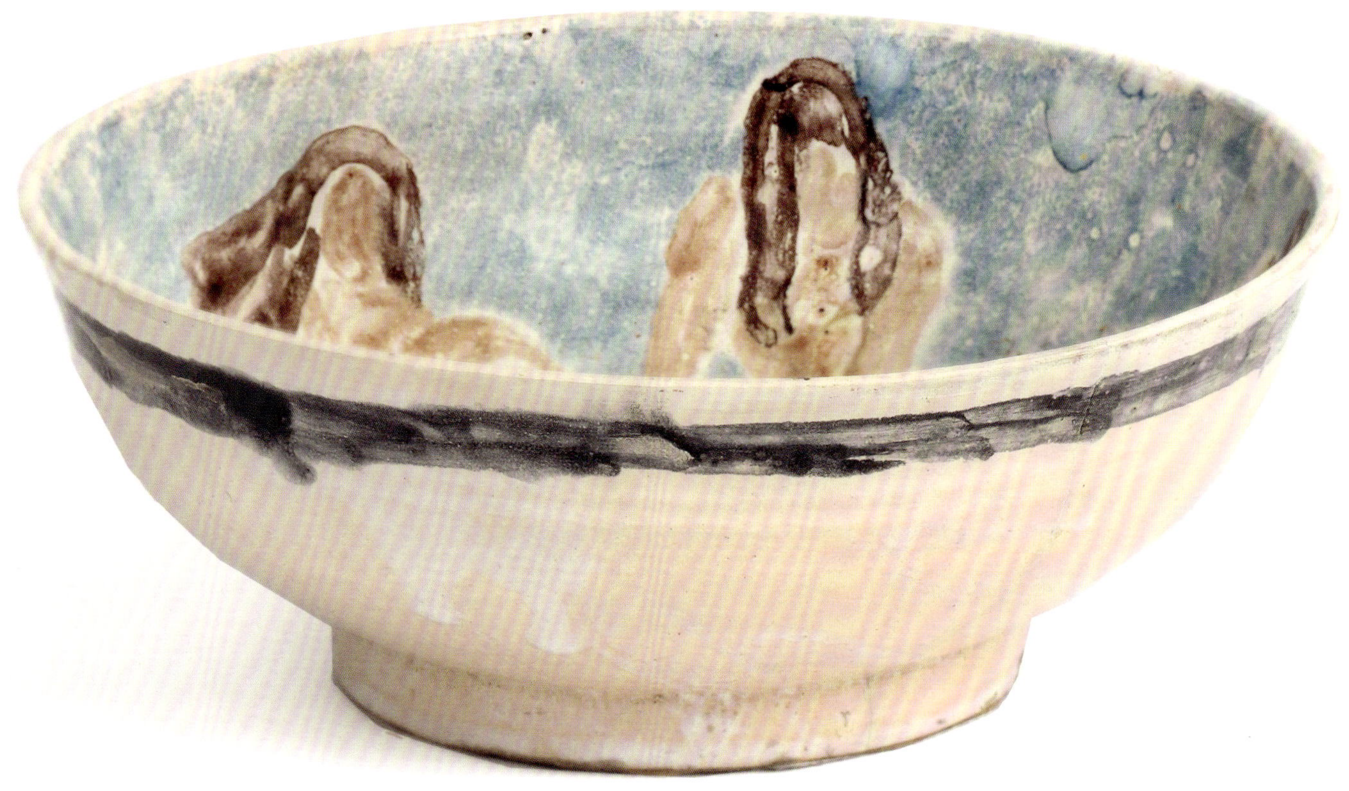

These ceramic pieces were decorated by Vanessa and potted by her younger son Quentin. Bell writes of Quentin's work in ceramics in 1936: 'I must say that I think it's very impressive, and Q. has really done some lovely things.... Altogether I am delighted and I think he must set up a pottery here.'[151] He did set up a pottery at Charleston, outside the ground floor studio, and in 1946 Bell reports: 'Q. goes on experimenting all the time and I think is getting daily technically better. He always has masses of new ideas ... we shall all be able to make a little extra cash by twiddling our brushes about on his pots.'[152] The decoration of these items is typical of Bell's motifs – loosely, spontaneously painted floral designs with black line work and dots. The bowl, with its decoration of three nude figures around blue and yellow central discs, recalls her *Design for fireplace mural* (1912, p. 60).

Table

DECORATED BY VANESSA BELL

*c.*1950 | painted wood | 46.5 × 30.5 × 30.5 cm

Table

DECORATED BY VANESSA BELL

*c.*1950 | painted wood | 63.6 × 33.3 × 25.4 cm

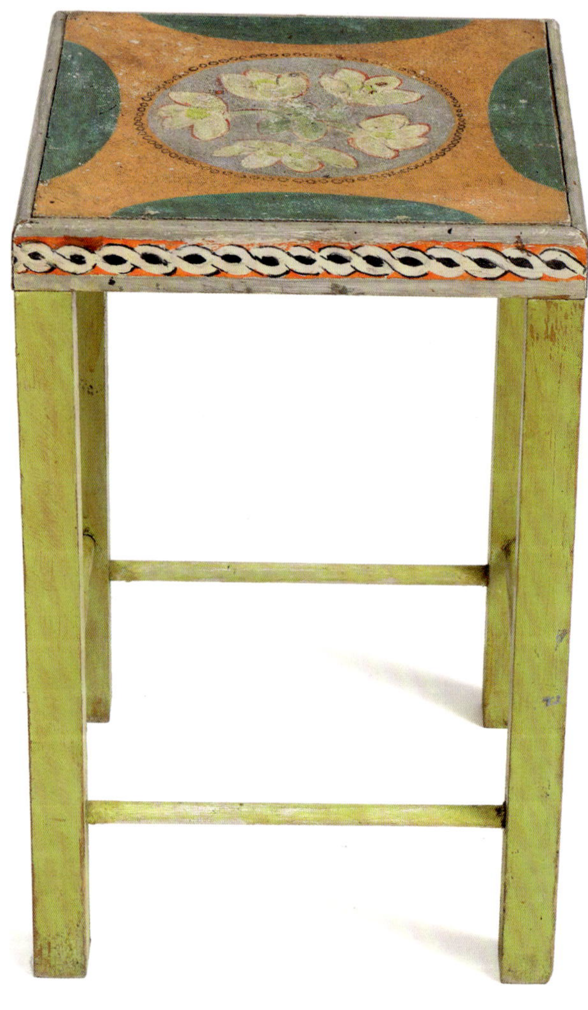

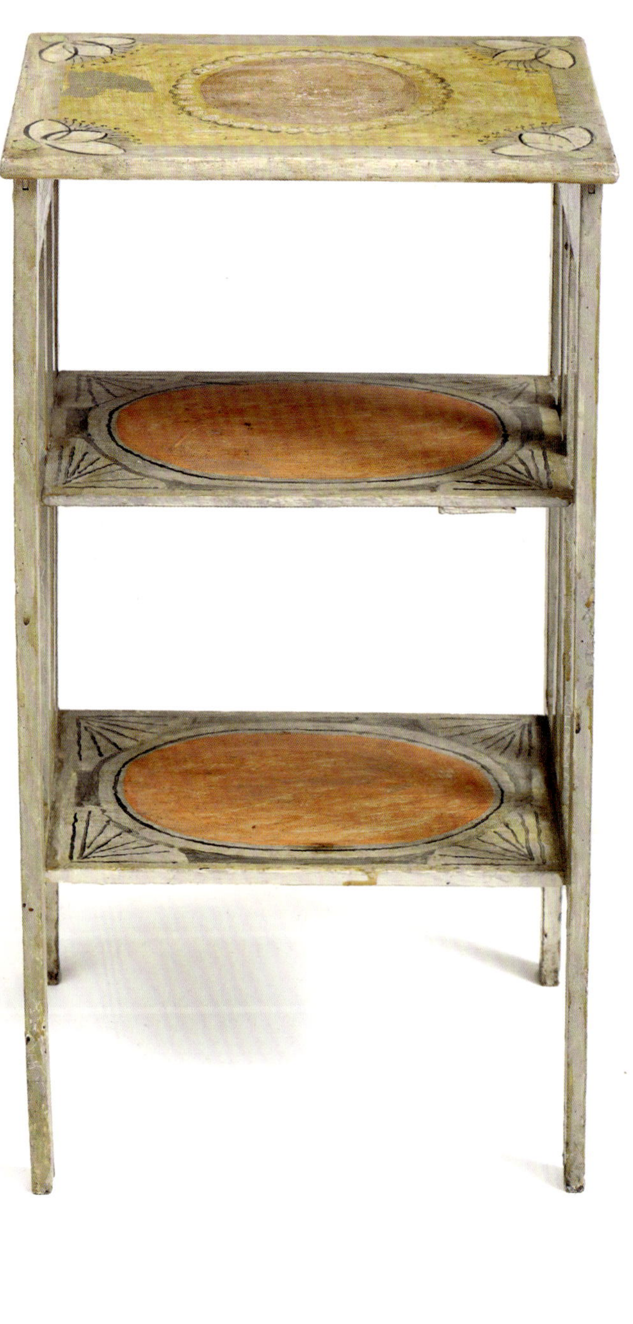

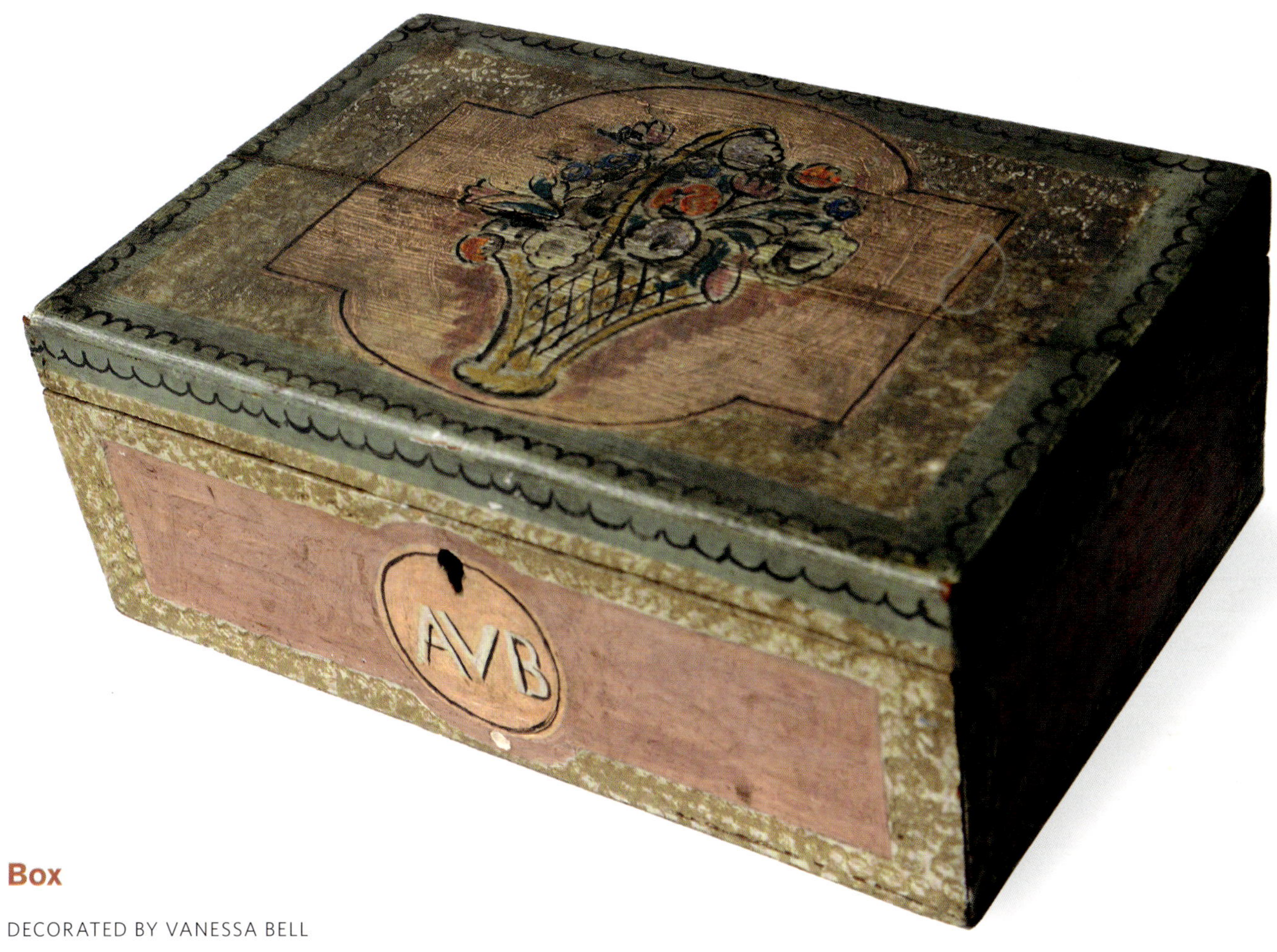

Box

DECORATED BY VANESSA BELL

undated | painted wood | 9 × 25 × 16.2 cm

These decorated wooden furnishings all come from Charleston, the home that Bell and Duncan Grant decorated and redecorated over forty years. Although Charleston creates the impression of being decorated on all surfaces, Bell and Grant actually often used subtle plain wall colourings of white, grey, pale blue, pink and yellow; others were plain black. Against these walls, the colours of all the objects the artists made and collected resonate and chime with clarity.[153] The rhythm of decoration across these painted items, with their abstracted floral motifs in yellows, teals and pinks, and Bell's signature black lines and accents, creates an informal decorative order which makes the house seem alive with colour. Personal touches are frequent in Charleston objects – the box here was decorated for Bell's daughter Angelica, with her initials *AVB* painted on the front.

Charleston was a home and refuge for the artists, but also a complete work of art and their most important collaboration. As Rebecca Birrell describes, Charleston was 'an enormous living canvas … with domestic life and radical aesthetics forever intermingling and bolstering each other…. The artistic traditions in which Charleston was steeped – a camp eclecticism that embraced decorative art, Italian culture and still life – constituted a highly politicized style which made clear their departure from patriarchal society and its values: the taste makers, the authority figures, the cultural heroes and models of well-being were all drawn from a world of women and queer men.'[154] The 'queer arcadia' of Charleston also provided a haven for other creatives including John Maynard Keynes, Lytton Strachey, E.M. Forster and Raymond Mortimer, all of whom stayed at or visited Charleston and found inspiration there.[155]

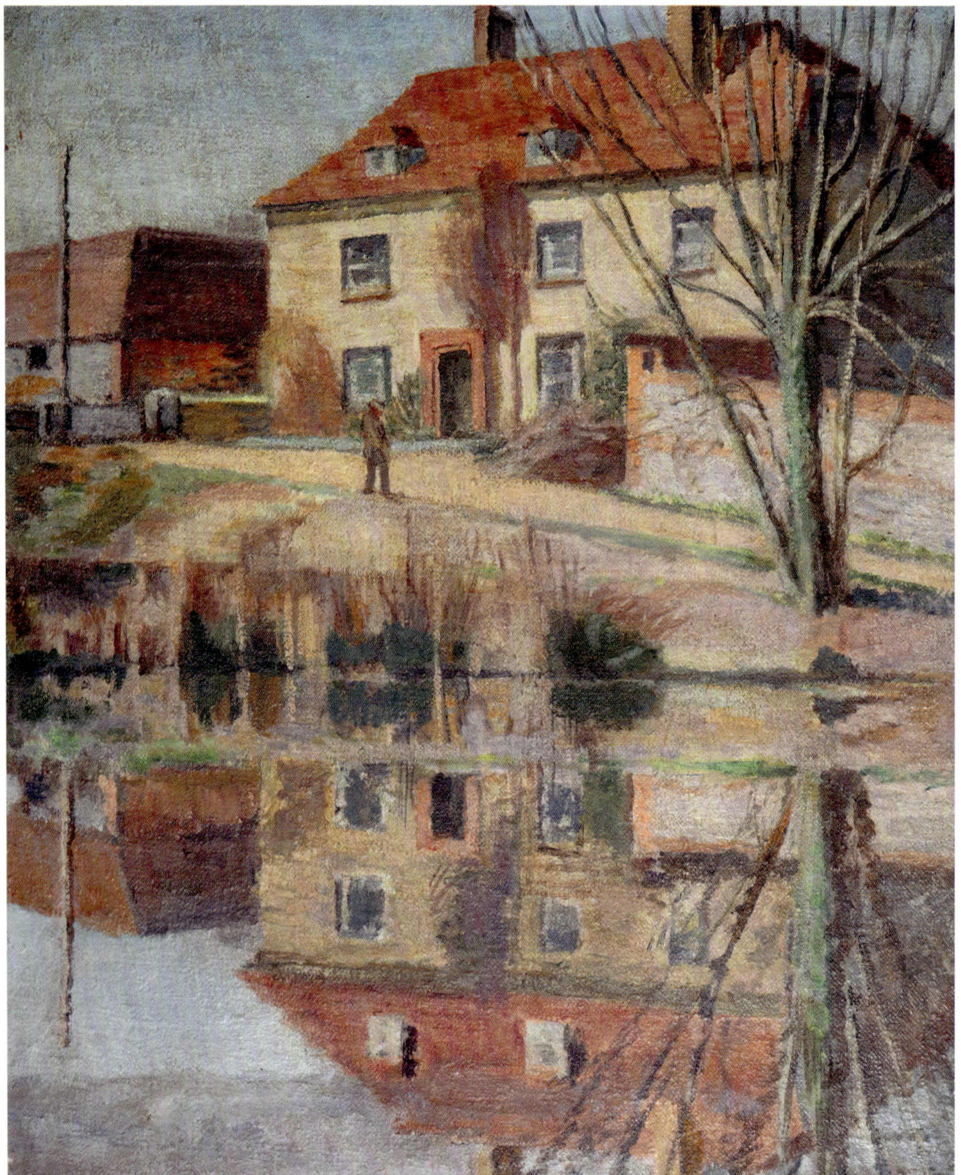

Charleston

1950 | oil on canvas | 59.4 × 49 cm

This painting possibly shows Clive Bell, who based himself at Charleston from 1939 until he died in 1964, walking down the path by the pond.[156] Duncan Grant continued to live at Charleston with Grace Germany (née Higgens), the housekeeper who worked for Vanessa Bell for more than fifty years, until her retirement in 1970.[157]

On first visiting Charleston, Bell wrote: 'It was quite quiet and one is overcome by the extraordinary peace and beauty of the place. The colour is too amazing now, all very warm, most lovely browns and greys and reds with the chalk everywhere giving that odd kind of softness.'[158] 'The pond is most beautiful, with a willow at one side and a stone or flint wall edging it around the garden part, and a little lawn sloping down to it with formal bushes in it.... There's a wall of trees – one single line of elms all round two sides, which shelters us from the west winds.'[159]

The Garden Room at Charleston

c.1950 | paint on paper | 61.5 × 51.4 cm

Bell was commissioned by the Arts Council to produce a painting for the exhibition *Sixty Paintings for '51*, to coincide with the Festival of Britain. The painting she submitted was *The Garden Room* (1951), for which this may be a study. It shows several generations of women in Bell's family, perhaps including her daughter Angelica, granddaughter Amaryllis and Anne Olivier Popham, who married Quentin Bell in 1952. Bell was dissatisfied with the large final painting, which went unsold in the exhibition.[160] Compared to the rather stiff exhibited work, this study is far livelier and freely handled. The figure in the chair turns towards the woman in the doorway, leaning forward like the figure on the left in *A Conversation* (1913–16, p. 63), whereas in the larger painting she looks down at a book on her lap. The placement of figures mirroring each other inside and out is also seen in *View into a Garden* (1926, p. 112). Bell wrote of starting the work: 'Duncan is I hope going to use a very rakish affair he did a long time ago.... Mine is very sober by comparison, simply figures at the drawing room window which is open to the garden with sun outside – all very *terre à terre* but then I'm interested in *terre à terre* subjects and encourage myself by thinking that many good artists have been. Certainly, Velasquez was better when he didn't leave the earth.'[161]

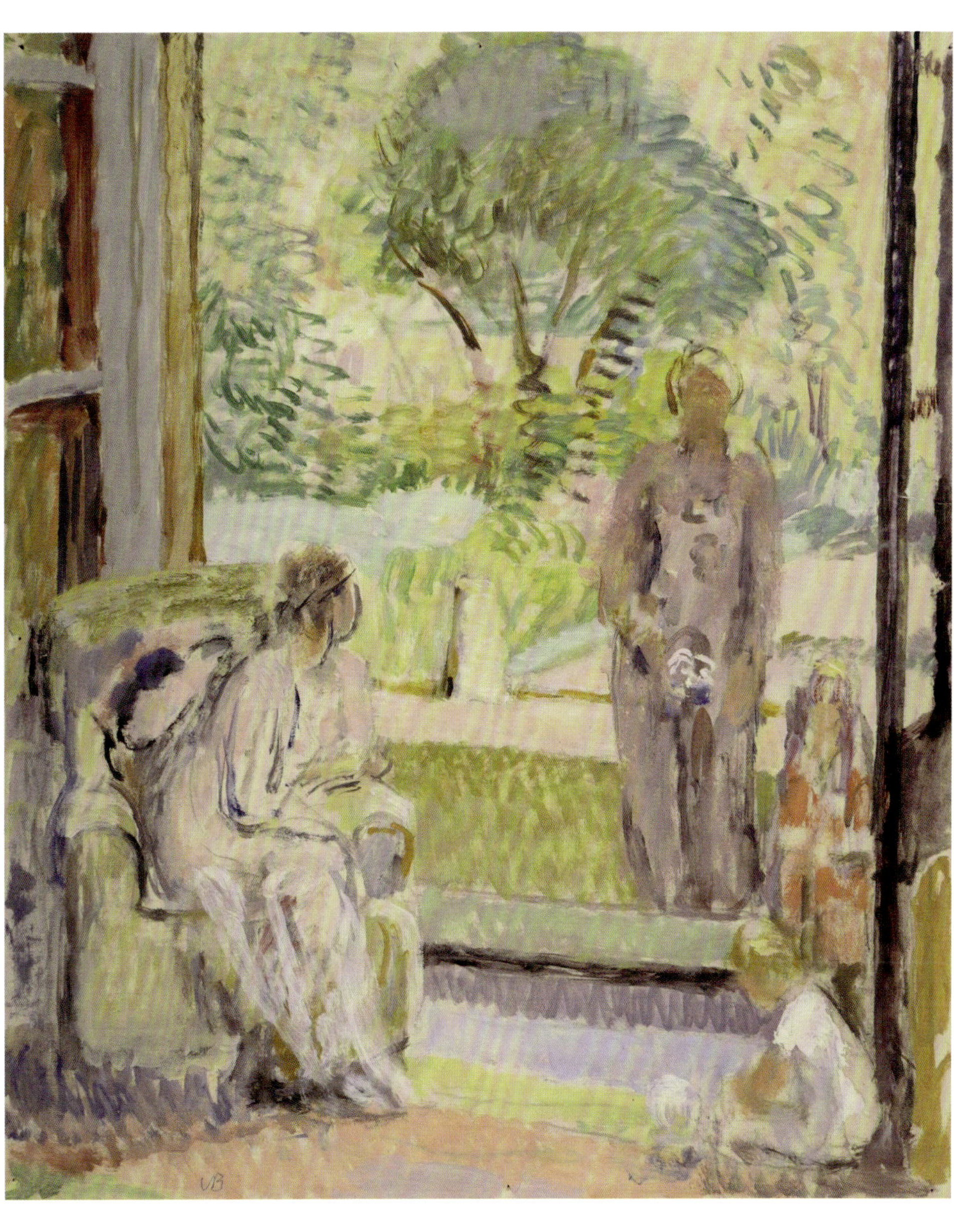

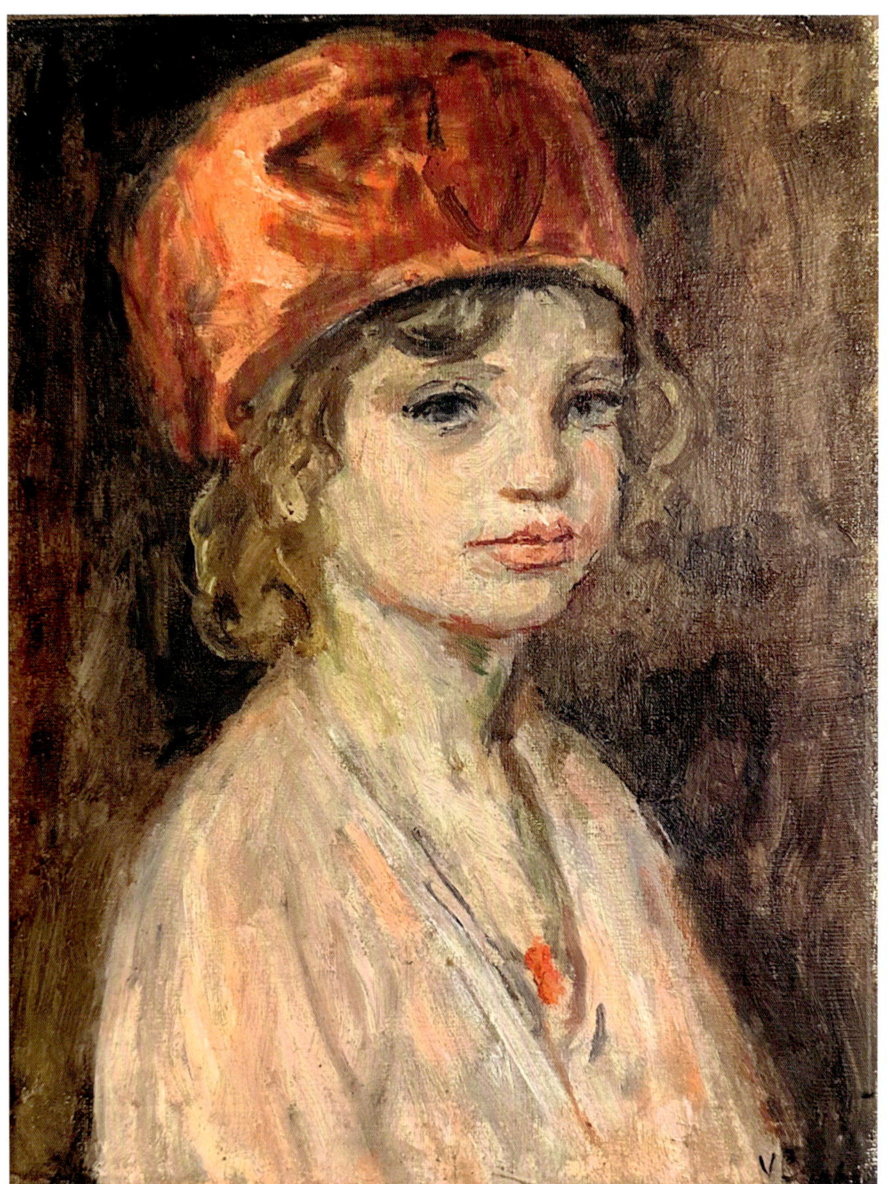

Portrait of Henrietta Garnett

c.1950 | oil on canvas | 49 × 39 cm

Henrietta Garnett (1945–2019) was a writer and Bell's granddaughter. She later described her visits to Charleston: 'Amaryllis and I were always made to sit as models…. We were not altogether willing models and both of us charged our grandparents sixpence for each hour that we endured. We were seldom painted in our ordinary clothes. In her bedroom, next to Duncan's studio, Nessa kept a huge painted cupboard which was filled with a fantastic assortment of coloured silks, discarded dresses and motheaten tapestries in which we were variously draped. I remember there was a vermilion hat, like the head-dress of a Venetian Doge, which was excruciatingly itchy for me to wear. Generally, Nessa sat down to paint … mixing the colours on her palette, glancing first at one and then the portrait, gently stabbing the canvas so that, posing somewhat uneasily and swathed in remnants on the model's throne, one could see the back of her canvas quiver from the impressions she made on it. The glances she sent to one across the room were extraordinarily intimate and reassuring; an observant nod, an amused smile in order to encourage one to keep still.'[162] Bell wrote of her grandchildren: 'What a blessing they exist and what an incredible difference such small creatures make to life. They're so full of it, it seems to spill over all round.'[163]

Still Life with a Bowl of Medlars

1953 | oil on canvas | 33 × 45.7 cm

In Bell's later paintings, still lifes form the majority of her subjects. The printed square of cloth shown here belonged to a group of textiles which Bell kept for backgrounds, its abstract purple circles echoing those of the fruits. When travelling in Turkey with Roger Fry in 1911, Bell met a Turkish weaver and shopped for textiles, perhaps finding in her collections of Middle Eastern and Mediterranean textiles an antidote to 'London greyness'.[164]

At the Omega Workshops, Omega products were sold alongside 'Asian and North African textiles and ceramics … reproductions of Byzantine mosaics at Ravenna and contemporary Italian folk art' and these objects make frequent appearances in Bell's still lifes.[165] *Still Life with a Bowl of Medlars* was almost certainly painted at her home Charleston, East Sussex, where medlar trees were (and are) a feature of the garden.

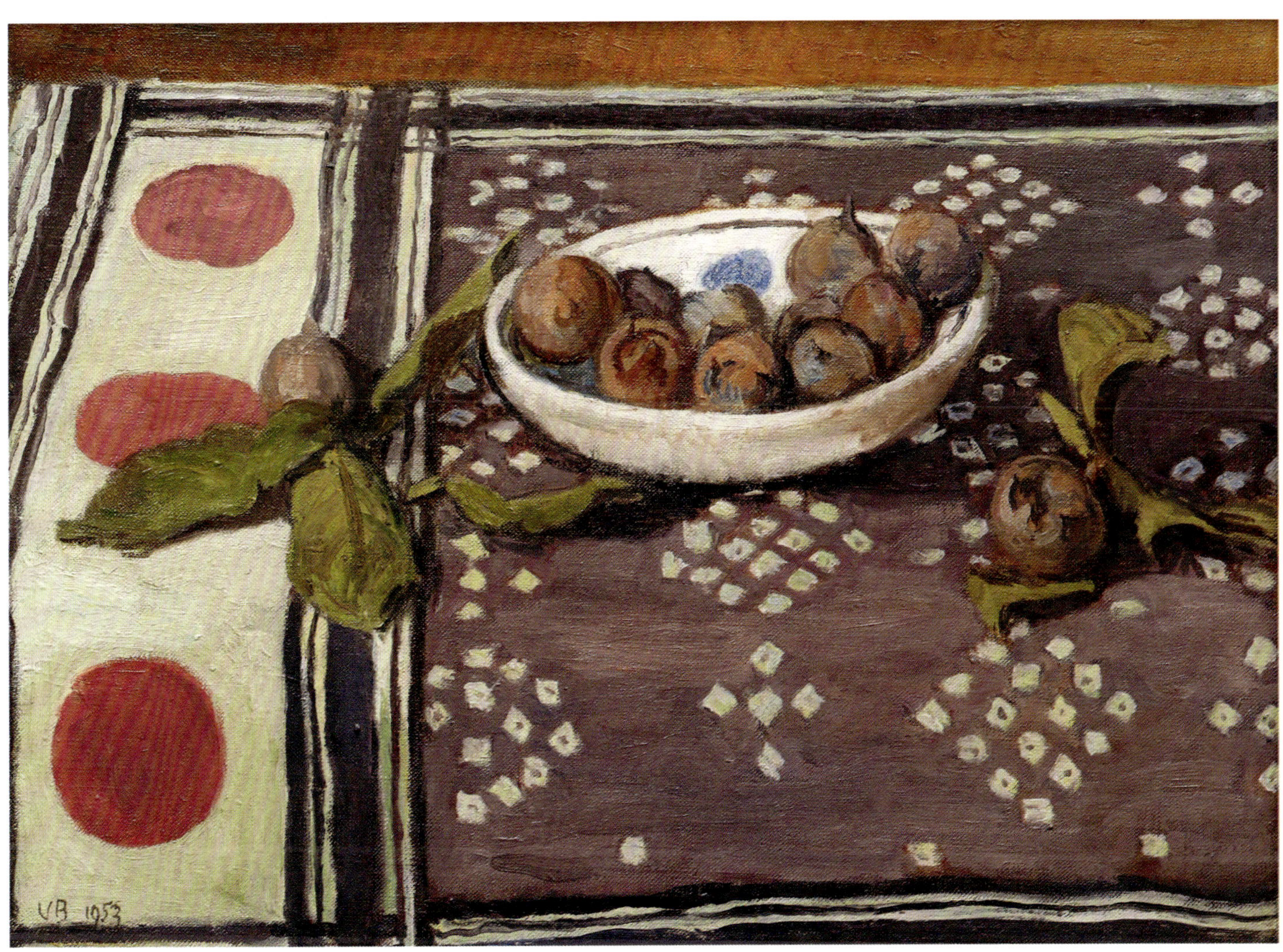

In 2008 we completed a commissioned artwork titled *Arts Matters: The Pool of Life*, celebrating Liverpool's year as European Capital of Culture. Currently on long-term display at the Museum of Liverpool, the commission incorporated a detail from Vanessa Bell's *The Tub* (p. vi). What prompted us to reference Bell's work was its association with a time in our lives as young art students that influenced our decision to become professional artists and shaped our artistic aims.

It was while studying art at university that we first came across Vanessa Bell. She was one of several artists whose work our art tutors insisted we study, rather than the Indian miniature painting tradition we'd chosen to explore as a visual language through which to express our British Asian identity and personal observations of the modern world. Instead of being taken as a valid form of self-expression (something that was drummed in to us as being the be-all and end-all of modern art), tutors dismissed our work as 'backward', 'outdated' and 'having no place in contemporary art'. We were told to look to Western artists such as Bell, Matisse, Gauguin, Picasso and Van Gogh, who were radical innovators in the use of colour, form and abstraction – or so we were taught. The irony of the situation, as we saw it, was that what made them so innovative was the influence they drew (directly and indirectly) from non-European traditional art forms, including African sculpture, Japanese woodcuts and Persian miniatures, for example. In view of this, we chose to uphold our modern development of Indian miniatures and justified our stance by presenting final dissertations that showed how key artists and movements

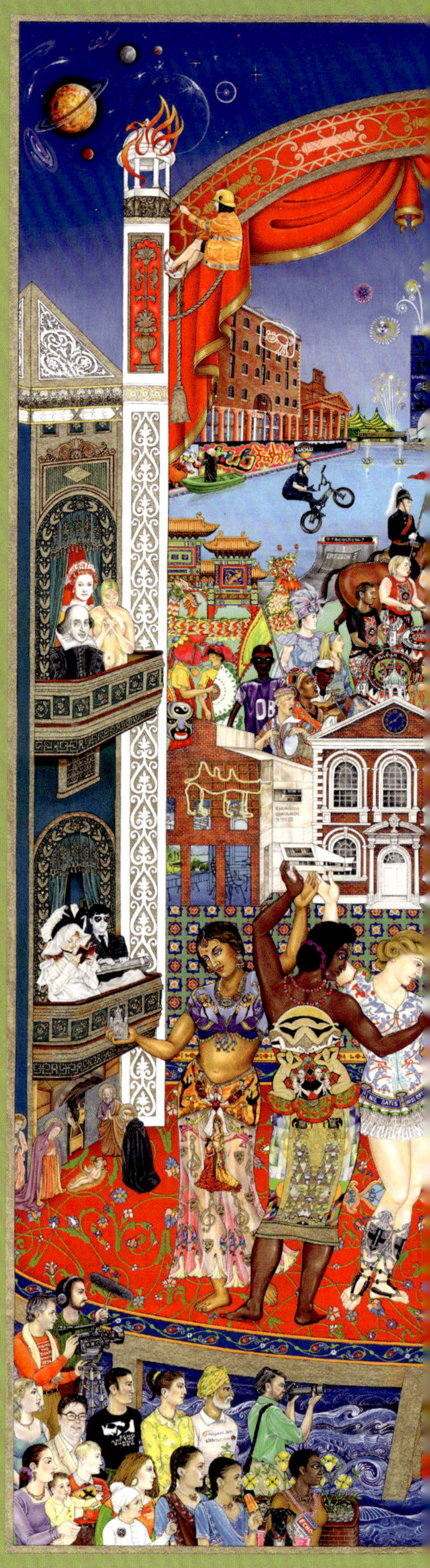

The Singh Twins, *Arts Matters: The Pool of Life*, 2008 (including figure from *The Tub* on upper left balcony)

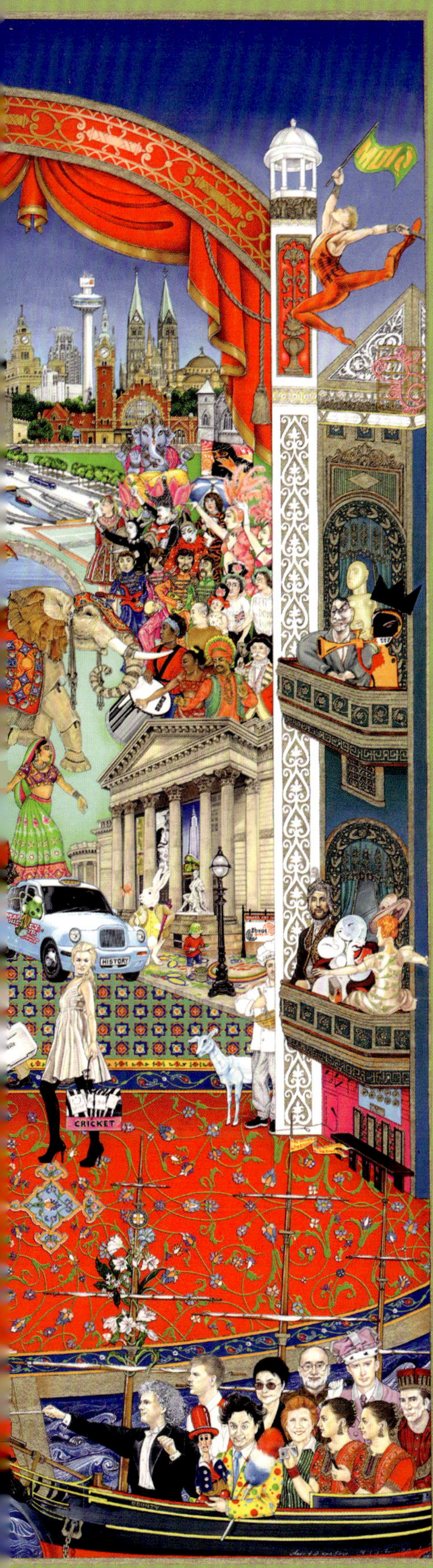

in Western modern art would not have evolved as they did without the influence of non-Western traditions. The external examiner described both dissertations as 'undoubtedly scholarly' and 'PhD level' – but refused to mark them. His decision cost us our degrees. During a subsequent appeal procedure, we were told that the examiner simply hadn't liked what we'd written. We believed that his inability to acknowledge the impact of non-European artistic traditions on Western art, and the value judgements that art tutors made on our work, exposed the existence of a deep-seated institutional prejudice rooted in colonial attitudes of Western superiority.

Our core aim as artists ever since has been to challenge the hypocrisy of a Western contemporary art world and society that claim to support freedom of self-expression yet still dictate how art and culture are evaluated and defined. We question why modernity is equated with the West, and why non-European aesthetic traditions, which are often described by Western art criticism as backward, naive and primitive, are only considered cutting-edge once the West has refashioned them. Within this context, Vanessa Bell's work holds significance for us, not because of how art history views her as a radical contributor to modern art, but because of the important discussions regarding decolonization, cultural ownership and originality that pieces like *The Tub* provoke.

The Singh Twins are award-winning contemporary British artists, writers and film-makers.

AMRIT KD KAUR SINGH, MBE, DFA, DART, LITT.D
& RABINDRA KD KAUR SINGH, MBE, DFA, DART, LITT.D

undated (purchased 1959) | oil on board |
57.5 × 38.5 cm

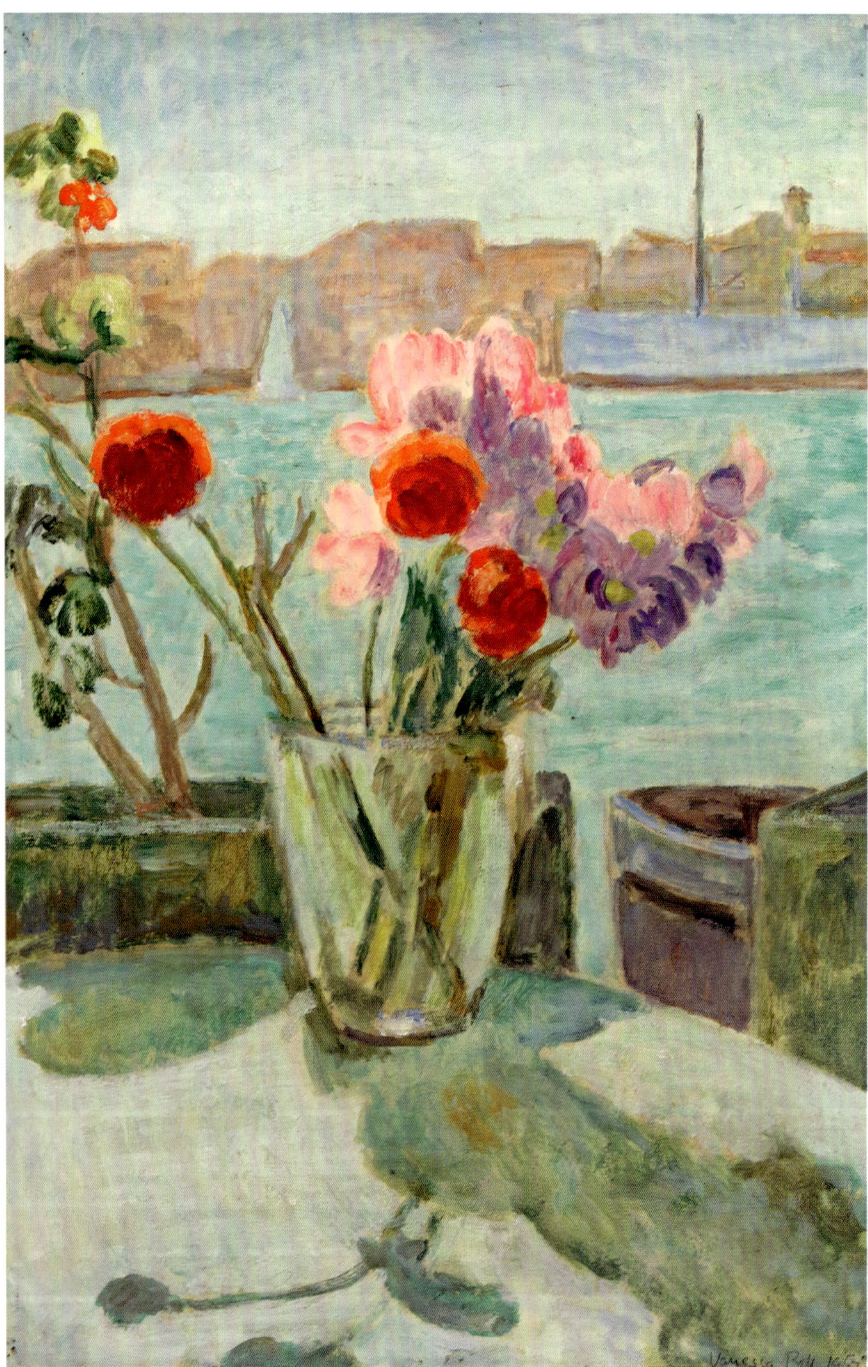

Bell painted many still lifes of
flowers throughout her career,
including the early *Iceland Poppies*
(1908–09, p. 35). In this example,
possibly painted during one of
Bell's trips to Europe, the flowers
combine with a landscape. Bell
uses colour to merge the balcony
table with the water behind and
sky above, unifying the composition and creating a flatness on
which the circles of the red flowers
and rectangles of the buildings sit
like abstract forms. Movement is
also created in the dynamic shape
of the shadow of the vase and the
diagonals of the stems on the left.

West Pier, Brighton, East Sussex

c.1955 | oil on canvas | 49.5 × 37 cm

Bell's previous paintings of the beach, such as *Bathers* (1911, private collection) and *Studland Beach* (*c.*1912, Tate, see p. 23), focused on the relationships between figures, with the beach and sea used as flat patches of colour and compositional devices to provide diagonals. Later in life her attention turned to the architectural structures they housed, for example *Newhaven Lighthouse* (1938, Charleston), and this painting, showing the now ruined West Pier at Brighton. Its shadow on the water and the boat mast provide the strong vertical and horizontal elements characteristic of Bell's painting. Two seated figures are almost hidden to the left of the boat.

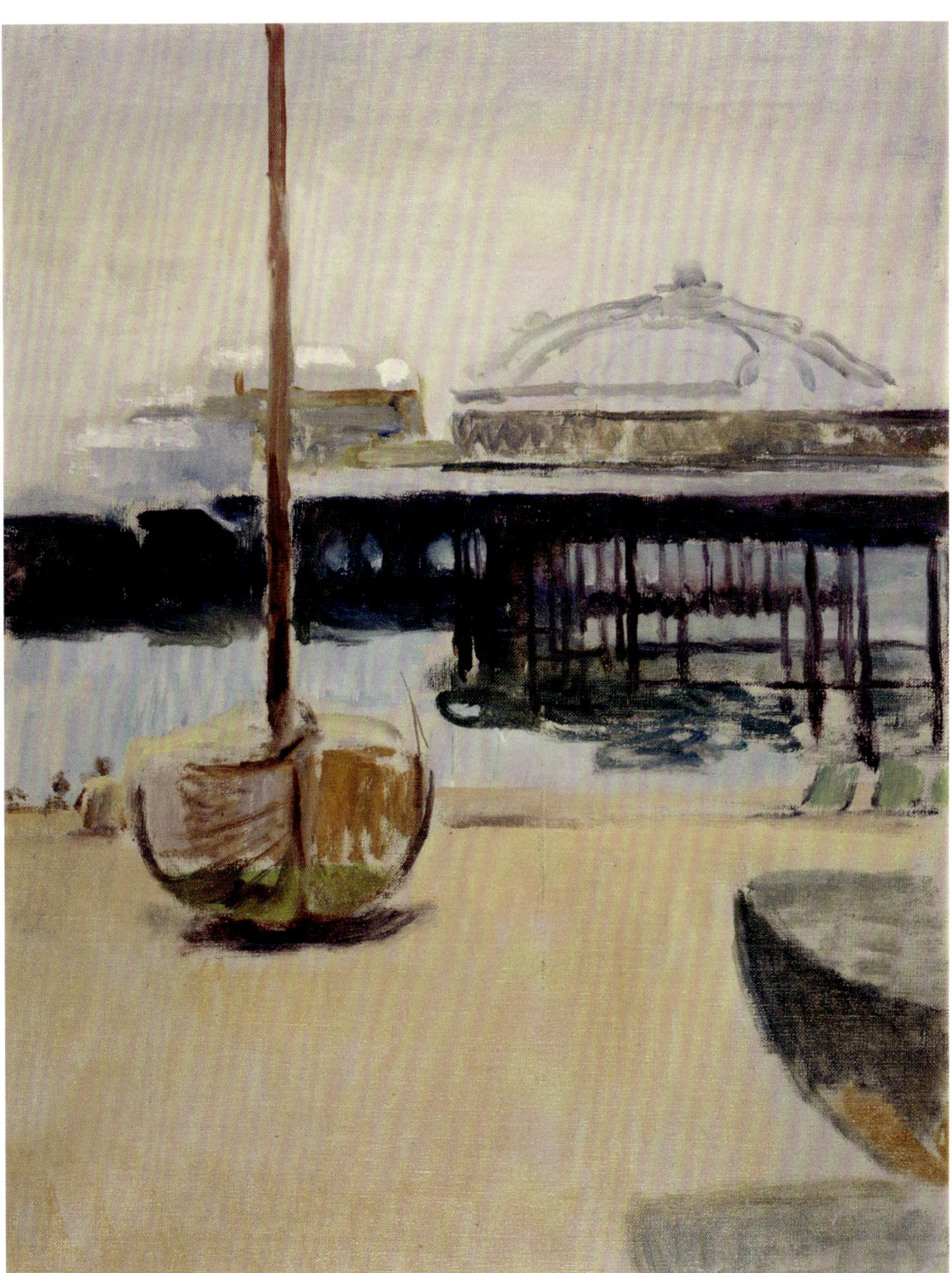

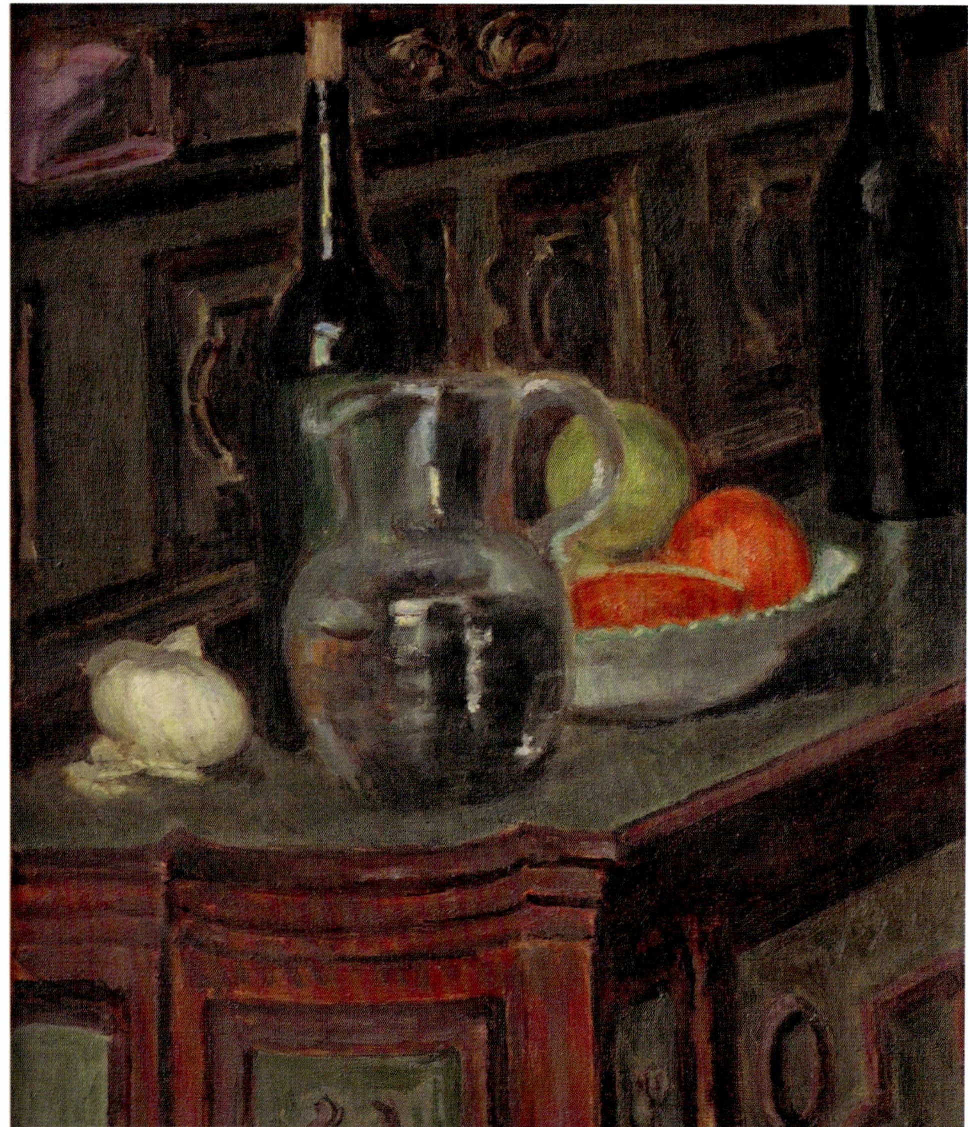

Still Life, Asolo, Italy

1955 | oil on canvas | 45.7 × 38.1 cm

In spring 1955 Bell and Duncan Grant drove through France to Asolo in Italy, where they rented a house called La Mura. Built partly into the ancient town walls, it had a room with windows on three sides at the top of the building, which lent itself to being used as a studio. Bell wrote to her daughter Angelica, remarking: 'Of course the light is so amazing, every-thing is colour and definite and exciting.'[166] Painted just six years before the artist's death in 1961, this still life exemplifies some of Bell's lifelong interests, with fruits becoming almost abstract forms and areas of carefully balanced high colour.

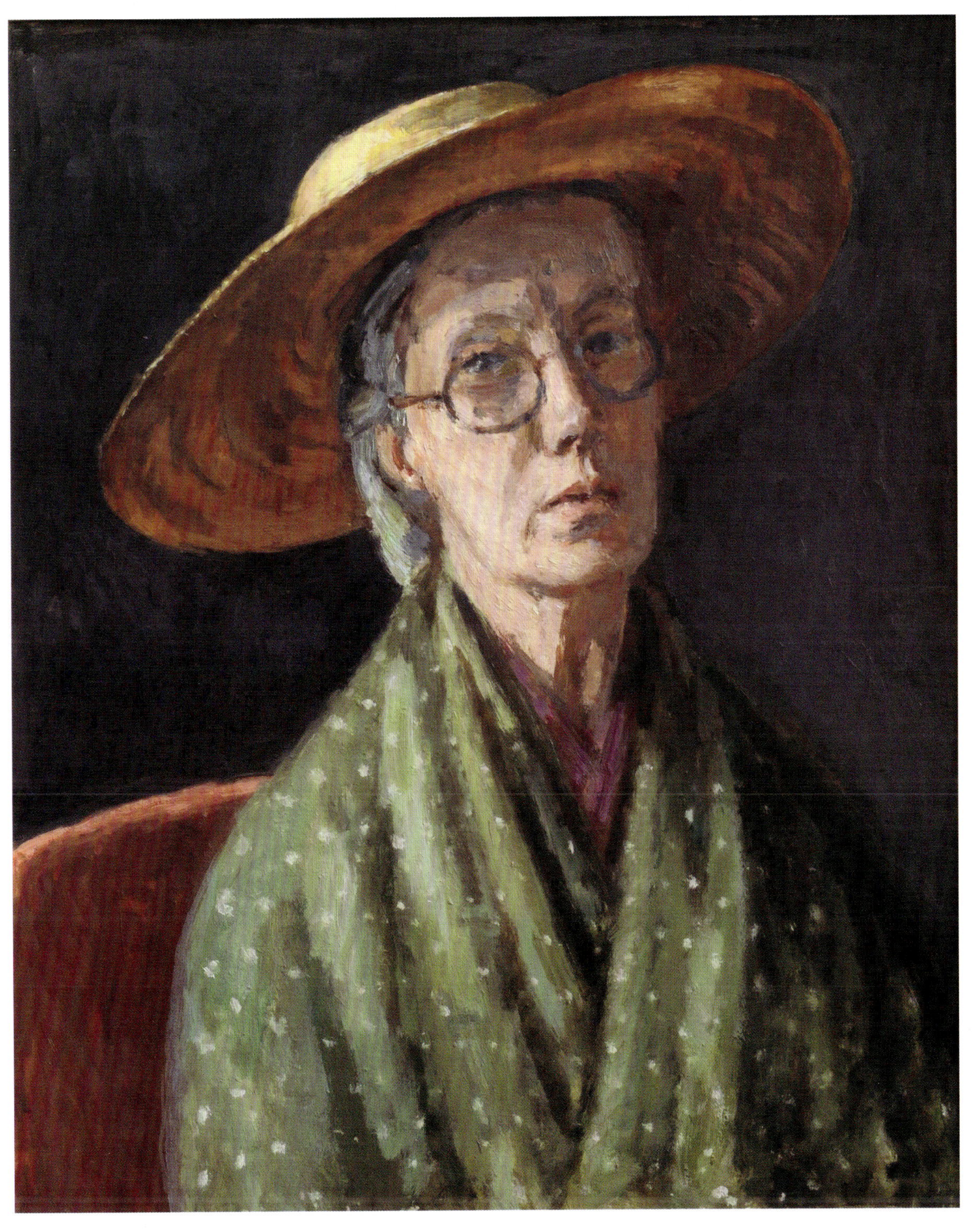

Self-Portrait

*c.*1952 | oil on canvas | *42 × 31 cm*

The *c.*1952 self-portrait shows Bell in her attic studio at her home in Charleston. Bell depicts herself as an artist and creator, surrounding herself with paintbrushes, a plate for a palette, one of her paintings, probably an Italian townscape, leaning against shelving behind her. Even the chair she is sitting in is covered in the fabric Bell had designed for Alan Walton's company in the early 1930s. In this ambiguous self-portrait, Bell's facial features are only barely indicated, in a way that harks intriguingly back to her portraits of Virginia Woolf four decades earlier (1912, National Portrait Gallery).

In the 1958 self-portrait, Bell removes the accessories of painting and looks directly at the viewer, framed by her sun hat and sloping shoulders wrapped in her green shawl. Painted two years before her death, it has been interpreted as 'A token of farewell … steeped in emotion deep but contained and pervaded by a moving sense of resignation'.[167] As her son Quentin recalled: 'To the end of her life, she painted pictures replete with psychological interest, while at the same time firmly denying that the story of a picture had any importance whatsoever.'[168]

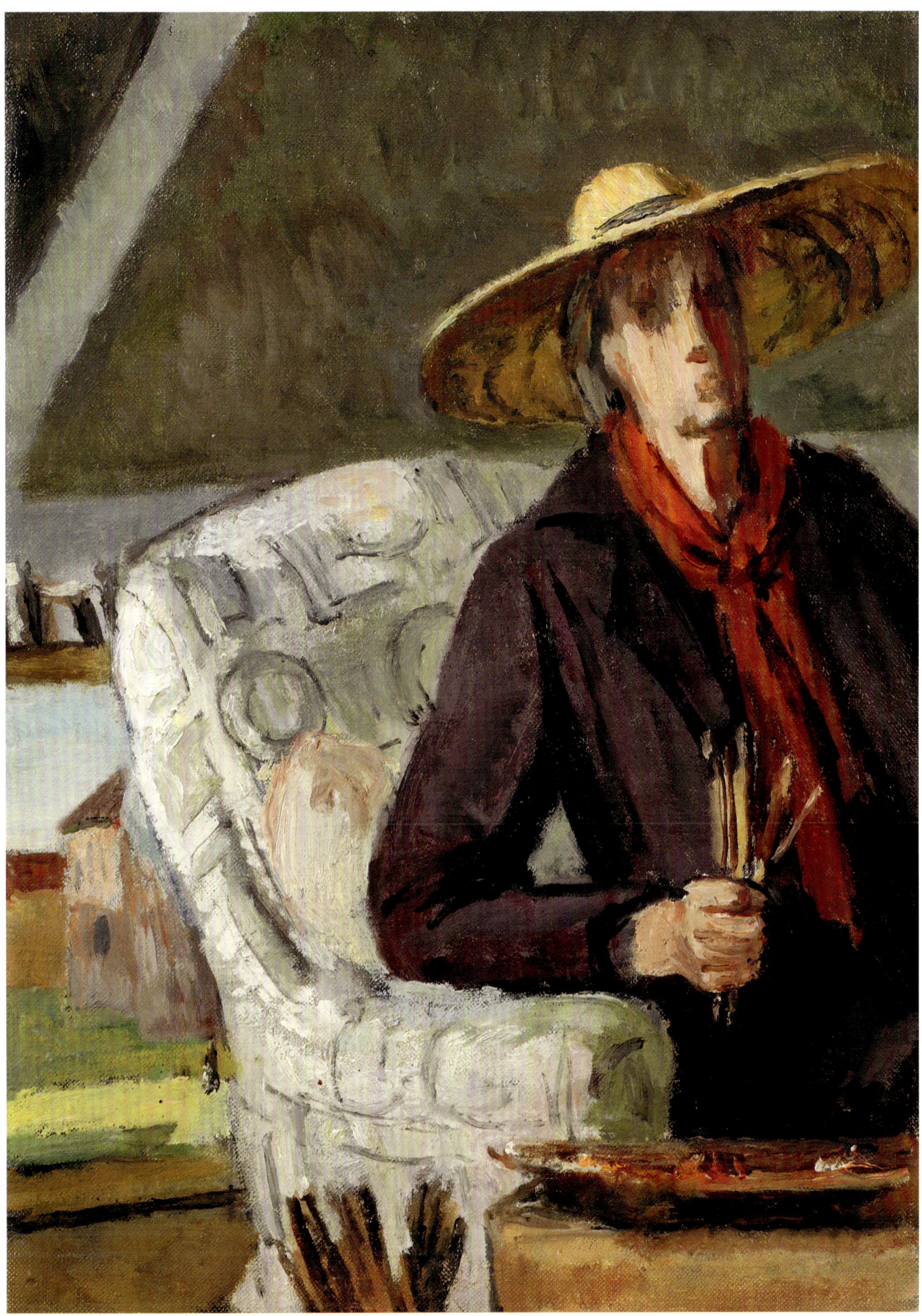

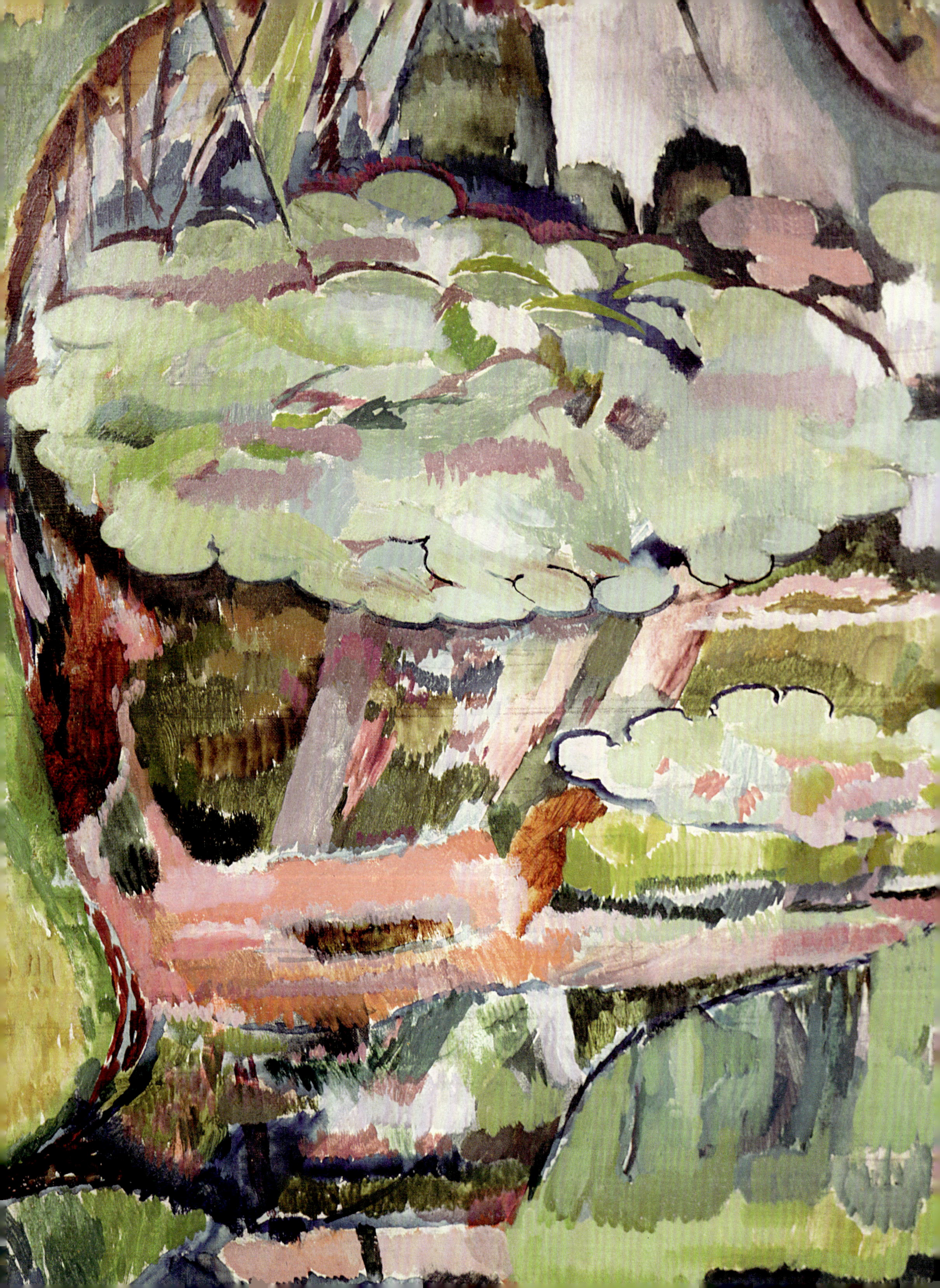

NOTES

INTRODUCTION

1. Vanessa Bell 1998, p. 118.
2. Quoted in Shone 1976, p. 22.
3. Woolf, *Moments of Being*, pp. 162–3.
4. Woolf, *Letters*, vol. 1, p. 201, quoted in Spalding 1983, p. 56.
5. Vanessa Bell 1998, p. 126.
6. Vanessa Bell to Roger Fry 21? July 1912, in Marler 1993, p. 121.
7. Preface to the catalogue of *Second Post-Impressionist Exhibition*, Grafton Galleries, 1912, quoted in Fry 1920, p. 157.
8. Vanessa Bell to Leonard Woolf, 22 January 1913, in Marler 1993, pp. 133–4.
9. Vanessa Bell 1998, p. 112.
10. Vanessa Bell to Madge Vaughan, 16 March 1920, in Marler 1993, p. 237.

CHRONOLOGY

1. Shone 1976, p. 20.
2. Leslie Stephen to Julia Duckworth, 18 July 1877, quoted in Spalding 1983, p. 18.
3. Shone 1999, p. 278.
4. Marler 1993, p. xxii.
5. Vanessa Bell 1998, pp. 73–4.
6. Vanessa Bell, quoted in Spalding 1983, p. 38.
7. Vanessa Stephen to Margery Snowden, October–November, 1903, in Marler 1993, p. 11.
8. Vanessa Bell 1998, p. 118.
9. Quoted in Shone 1976, p. 22.
10. Shone 1976, p. 23.
11. Vanessa Bell 1998, pp. 98–9.
12. Vanessa Bell 1998, p. 98.
13. Woolf, *Moments of Being*, pp. 162–3.
14. Hitchmough 2020, p. 134.
15. Woolf, *Letters*, vol. 1, p. 201, quoted in Spalding 1983, p. 56.
16. Vanessa Stephen to Margery Snowden, 13 August 1905, in Marler 1993, p. 34.
17. Vanessa Stephen to Clive Bell, 30 July 1906, in Marler 1993, p. 41.
18. Vanessa Stephen to Clive Bell, 15 April 1906, quoted in Spalding 1983, p. 59.
19. Duncan Grant to Lytton Strachey, 7 April 1907, quoted in Shone 1976, p. 48.
20. Clive Bell to Virginia Stephen, 30 December 1908, University of Sussex Library.
21. Marler 1993, p. 84.
22. Marler 1993, p. xxxi.
23. Vanessa Bell 1998, pp. 128–30.
24. 'Mr Bennett and Mrs Brown', in Woolf, *Collected Essays*, vol. 1, p. 320.
25. Spalding 1983, p. 113.
26. *Observer*, 27 October 1912, quoted in Spalding 1983, p. 114.
27. Hitchmough 2020, p. 135.
28. Marler 1993, p. 139.
29. L.G.S., 24 January 1914, p. 5.
30. Quoted in Shone 1976, p. 135.
31. Vanessa Bell, 1998, p. 111.
32. Duncan Grant to Ottoline Morrell, autumn 1915, quoted in Reed 2004, p. 162.
33. Quoted in Shone 1976, p. 151.
34. Hitchmough 2020, p. 101.
35. Vanessa Bell to Virginia Woolf, 22 August 1915, in Marler 1993, p. 186.
36. Vanessa Bell to Roger Fry, spring 1915, quoted in Shone 1976, p. 135.
37. Vanessa Bell 1998, p. 112.
38. Reed 2004, p. 183.
39. Shone 1976, p. 172.

40. £685 today. Roger Fry to Vanessa Bell, 11 June 1917, quoted in Reed 2004, p. 205.
41. Vanessa Bell to Duncan Grant, 22 September 1918, quoted in Birrell 2021, pp. 218–19.
42. Vanessa Bell 1998, p. 133.
43. Vanessa Bell to Roger Fry, 17 May 1920, in Marler 1993, p. 244.
44. Garnett in Vanessa Bell 1998, p. 4.
45. Quoted in Shone 1976, p. 218.
46. Fry 1922, pp. 237–8.
47. *Burlington Magazine*, November 1923, p. 250, quoted in Brockington 2017, p. 90.
48. Spalding 1983, p. 202.
49. *Vogue*, February 1926, quoted in Spalding 1983, p. 235.
50. Vanessa Bell to Roger Fry, 21 July 1927, in Marler 1993, p. 320.
51. Spalding 1983, p. 217.
52. Vanessa Bell to Duncan Grant, 7 February 1930, in Marler 1993, p. 351.
53. 'Mrs Vanessa Bell's Work', *Daily Telegraph*, 10 February 1930, p. 3.
54. Lewis 1930, p. 132.
55. 2 September 1931, p. 7.
56. 16 September 1931, p. 7,
57. Vanessa Bell to Quentin Bell, 3 March 1934, in Marler 1993, p. 376.
58. 9 May 1934, p. 11.
59. Raymond Mortimer, quoted in Reed 2004, p. 266.
60. Foster 2018, p. 283.
61. Foster 2018, p. 283.
62. Vanessa Bell to Julian Bell, 10 October 1936, in Marler 1993, p. 423.
63. *Daily Herald*, 23 June 1937, p. 6.
64. Shone 1976, pp. 256–7.
65. Garnett 1995, p. 151.
66. Vanessa Bell to David Garnett, 19 April 1942, in Marler 1993, p. 480.
67. Garnett 1995, p. 160.
68. Morphet 1999, p. 36, foreword to catalogue of memorial exhibition, Adams Gallery, London, October 1961.

CATALOGUE OF WORKS

1. Spalding 1983, p. 34.
2. map.mappingwomenssuffrage.org.uk/items/show/300.
3. Vanessa Bell to Virginia Stephen, 15 April 1906, in Marler 1993, p. 38.
4. Birrell 2021, p. 201.
5. Avery 2018, p. 21.
6. Shone 1999, p. 59.
7. www.charleston.org.uk/stories/before-post-impressionism-vanessa-bells-iceland-poppies.
8. Clive Bell 1949, p. 45.
9. Vanessa Bell to Virginia Woolf, 29 December 1932, in Marler 1993, p. 374.
10. Vanessa Bell to Clive Bell, 23 June 1910, in Marler 1993, p. 93.
11. Clive Bell to Vanessa Bell, 20 June 1928, quoted in Shone 1976, p. 223.
12. Vanessa Bell to Virginia Stephen, 3 August 1907, in Marler 1993, p. 54.
13. Vanessa Bell to Virginia Woolf, 10 August 1908, quoted in Milroy 2017, p. 32.
14. Vanessa Bell to Julian Bell, 1 November 1935, in Marler 1993, p. 401.
15. Vanessa Bell 1998, pp. 133–4.
16. Vanessa Bell to Julian Bell, 29 August 1936, in Marler 1993, p. 419.
17. Roger Fry, introduction to *Second Post-Impressionist Exhibition* catalogue, reprinted in Fry, 1920, p. 157.
18. Vanessa Bell to Clive Bell, January 1912, quoted in Shone 1976, p. 87.
19. Spalding 2017, p. 69.
20. Virginia Woolf to Vanessa Bell, in Woolf, *Letters*, vol. 3, p. 390.
21. Vanessa Bell to Roger Fry, 17 May 1920, in Marler 1993, p. 244.
22. Vanessa Bell to Angelica Garnett, 5 October 1949, in Marler 1993, p. 522.
23. Roger Fry to Vanessa Bell, 17 May 1930, quoted in Shone 1999, p. 84.
24. Spalding 1983, p. 105.
25. www.bonhams.com/auction/30121/lot October vanessa-bell-british-1879–1961–portrait-of-henri-doucet-418-x-345-cm-16-12-x-13-58-in-painted-in-1912.
26. Reed 2004, p. 126.
27. See Shone 1999, pp. 84–5.
28. Brockington 2013, pp. 140–41, quoting Leonard Woolf, *Sowing*, 1964, p. 160.
29. Vanessa Bell to Roger Fry, 5 June 1912, in Marler 1993, p. 119.
30. Vanessa Bell to Roger Fry, 5 June 1912, quoted in Spalding 1983, p. 105.
31. Vanessa Bell to Virginia Stephen, 19 October 1911, in Marler 1993, p. 109.
32. artuk.org/discover/artworks/landscape-with-buildings-73746.
33. www.charleston.org.uk/object/pots-et-citron-copy-of-pablo-picasso.
34. Shone 1999, p. 100.
35. Quoted in Shone 1999, p. 100.
36. Vanessa Bell 1998, p. 106.
37. John Maynard Keynes to Duncan Grant, 2 August 1910, quoted in Quentin Bell 1972, p. 124.
38. The other is in the Yale Centre for British Art, New Haven, collections. britishart.yale.edu/catalog/tms:1373.
39. Leaper 2017, p. 46.
40. Reed 2004, p. 138.
41. Vanessa Bell to Virginia Woolf, 3 May 1913, in Marler 1993, p. 139.

42. Elkin 2018, p. 115.

43. Spalding 1983, pp. 154–5.

44. Woolf, *Letters*, vol. 2, pp. 498–9.

45. Woolf, *A Room of One's Own*, 1929, p. 82.

46. Elkin 2018, p. 117.

47. Brockington 2017, p. 89.

48. Brockington, 'The Painting', n.p.

49. Brockington 2017, p. 90.

50. Brockington, 'The Painting', n.p.

51. Quoted in Tobin 2017.

52. Spalding 1983, p. 125.

53. Watney 1980, p. 100.

54. Affron 2012, p. 183.

55. Vanessa Bell to Duncan Grant, 25 March 1914, in Marler 1993, p. 160; redated by Marler to 29 January 1914 in Marler 2017, p. 113.

56. Leaper 2017, p. 47.

57. Marler 2017, p. 112.

58. Brockington 2013, p. 147.

59. Brockington 2013, p. 145.

60. Brockington 2013, p. 146.

61. It attracted the following review: 'What it represents I don't know (and I question if the artist does) but it is mainly made up of newspaper gummed on to areas of the canvas with a paint brush wiped across them occasionally… But it makes a pretty colour scheme nonetheless. Here Mr Fry's theories are carried out loyally.' Watson Smith 2017.

62. Brockington 2010, pp. 78–81; Risdon 2018, pp. 114–16.

63. Vanessa Bell to Duncan Grant, 25 March 1914, in Marler 1993, p. 160.

64. Ashley Foster 2018, p. 282.

65. Vanessa Bell to Roger Fry, late October 1913, in Marler 1993, p. 151.

66. Roger Fry to Duncan Grant, January 1914, quoted in Shone 1976, p. 121.

67. Vanessa Bell to Duncan Grant, 25 March 1914, in Marler 1993, p. 162.

68. Milroy 2017, p. 29.

69. Reed 2004, p. 152.

70. Spalding 1983, p. 163, and www.tate.org.uk/art/archive/items/tga-20078-1-44-62/letter-from-vanessa-bell-to-duncan-grant/1.

71. Spalding 1983, p. 163.

72. Shone 2018, p. 50.

73. Vanessa Bell to St John Hutchinson, 24 August 1916, quoted in Shone 1999, p. 164.

74. Vanessa Bell to Roger Fry, summer 1916, quoted in Spalding 1983, p. 154.

75. *Vogue*, early February 1919 p. 41. Shone 1999, p. 164.

76. Letter from Vanessa Bell to Duncan Grant c.1916, www.tate.org.uk/art/archive/items/tga-20078-1-44-53/letter-from-vanessa-bell-to-duncan-grant.

77. artuk.org/discover/artworks/view-of-the-pond-at-charleston-east-sussex-72269.

78. Clarke 2019.

79. Vanessa Bell to Roger Fry, 22 February 1918, quoted in Shone 1976, p. 165.

80. Vanessa Bell to Roger Fry, March 1918, quoted in Shone 1976, p. 182; 3 April 1918, in Marler 1993, p. 213.

81. Vanessa Bell to Roger Fry, 6 February 1919, in Marler 1993, p. 230.

82. Fry 1922, pp. 237–8.

83. Milroy 2017, p. 29.

84. Nicholson 2003, p. 72.

85. Vanessa Bell to Roger Fry, 15 August 1920, quoted in Reed 2004, p. 220.

86. Reed 2004, p. 220.

87. Reed 2004, p. 220.

88. Vanessa Bell to Clive Bell, 12 October 1921, in Marler 1993, p. 256.

89. Vanessa Bell to Roger Fry, 17 May 1920, in Marler 1993, p. 243.

90. Vanessa Bell to Roger Fry, 24 March 1920, in Marler 1993, p. 238.

91. Milroy 2017, p. 36.

92. www.christies.com/en/lot/lot-2106696 'Black and white negative of Angus Davidson wearing a wide brimmed sun hat outdoors at Charleston, Firle, Sussex', Vanessa Bell, [c1928]', Vanessa Bell, [c1928] – Tate Archive | Tate.

93. thecharlestonattic.wordpress.com/2016/02/17/the-process-of-abstraction.

94. www.artnet.com/artists/vanessa-bell/design-for-fabric-LYZsk8o_YcAcjsw S9HA4FA2.

95. Reed 2004, p. 4.

96. Naylor 1990, p. 152.

97. Vanessa Bell to Julian Bell, 29 March 1936, in Marler 1993, p. 411.

98. Vanessa Bell to Y (one of Julian's girlfriends), 24 August 1937, quoted in Spalding 1983, p. 300.

99. www.bankofengland.co.uk/monetary-policy/inflation/inflation-calculator.

100. *The Studio: An Illustrated Magazine of Fine and Applied Art*, August 1930 quoted https://itstartedwithajug.blogspot.com/2011/04/dorothy-wellesleys-dining-room-1930.html.

101. Reed 2004, p. 241.

102. Reed 2004, p. 257.

103. Woolf, *Diary*, vol. 4, p. 144.

104. Artists Henry Lamb, Augustus John, James McNeill Whistler and Walter Sickert had also previously had studios there: Shone 1976, p. 34.

105. Woolf, *Diary*, vol. 3, p. 255, quoted in Spalding 1983, p. 232.

106. Reed 2017, p. 133.

107. Vanessa Bell to Lytton Strachey, 27 April 1916, in Marler 1993, p. 195.
108. Vanessa Bell to Roger Fry, 15 August 1930, and Vanessa Bell to Julian Bell, 15 August 1936, quoted in Clarke 2021, p.18.
109. Vanessa Bell 1998, p. 161.
110. Duncan Grant was also commissioned and chose as his subject St Ives, Huntington.
111. Tatlock 1931.
112. Clive Bell 1938, p. 75.
113. https://lissllewellyn.com/product/portrait-of-a-girl-in-profile-with-a-decorated-background.
114. Reed 2004, p. 62.
115. Hitchmough 2020, p. 149.
116. Vanessa Bell to Roger Fry, 9 September 1933, quoted in Reed 2004, p. 271.
117. Reed 2004, p. 269. Virginia Woolf to Ottoline Morrell, 25 November 1932, in Woolf, *Letters*, vol. 5, p. 130.
118. Reed 2004, p. 271.
119. Reed 2004, p. 272.
120. Leaper 2018, p. 103.
121. Vanessa Bell to Jane Clark, 21 September 1932?, quoted in Leaper 2018, p. 104.
122. Vanessa Bell to Jane Clark, 3 June 1933, quoted in Leaper 2018, p. 109
123. Vanessa Bell to Jane Clark, 3 June 1933, quoted in Leaper 2018, p. 109.
124. Virginia Woolf, 'Women and Fiction', first published in *The Forum* 1929 and reprinted in the 1958 collection *Granite and Rainbow*; in Woolf, *Women and Writing*, 1979, p. 44.
125. Leaper 2018, p. 116.
126. Hessel 2022, pp. 140–41.
127. Vanessa Bell to Roger Fry, 2 October 1932, quoted in Reed 2004, p. 265.
128. www.tate.org.uk/art/archive/items/tga-9020-11-22/black-and-white-negative-of-angelica-bell-seated-behind-a-large-pot-at-la-bergere-in.
129. Virginia Woolf diary entry, 30 September 1930, quoted in Shone 1976, p. 208.
130. Clarke 2021, p. 20.
131. Garnett 1995, p. 97; Shone 1999, p. 224.
132. Reed 2017, p. 133.
133. Spalding 1983, p. 312.
134. Birrell 2021, p. 203.
135. Spalding 1983, p. 153.
136. Clive Bell 1913, pp. 1060–61.
137. Vanessa Bell to Roger Fry, 16 May 1921, in Marler 1993, p. 248. Vanessa Bell to Angelica Garnett, 18 May 1945, in Marler 1993, p. 498.
138. Vanessa Bell to Margery Snowden, 24 May 1923, in Marler 1993, p. 271.
139. Blee 2023, p. 18.
140. Vanessa Bell to Jane Bussy, 13 January 1941, in Marler 1993, p. 472.
141. Blee 2023, pp. 68–9.
142. Spalding 1983, p. 319; Blee 2023, p. 78.
143. Blee 2023, p. 84.
144. Beechey 1999, pp. 14–15.
145. Beechey 1999, p. 16.
146. Beechey 1999, p. 17.
147. Shone 1976, p. 17.
148. Shone 1999, pp. 233–5.
149. www.theguardian.com/news/2007/nov/24/guardianobituaries.booksobituaries.
150. Avery 2018, p. 27.
151. Vanessa Bell to Julian Bell, 5 July 1936, in Marler 1993, p. 418.
152. Vanessa Bell to Jane Bussy, 20 December 1946, in Marler 1993, pp. 510–11.
153. Nicholson 2003, p. 118.
154. Birrell 2021, pp. 224–5.
155. Birrell 2021, pp. 227–8.
156. Hendra and Smith, 2021, p. 124.
157. McKay 2013.
158. Vanessa Bell to Duncan Grant, 18 September 1916, quoted in Spalding 1983, p. 155.
159. Vanessa Bell to Roger Fry, 16 October 1916, in Marler 1993, p. 200.
160. Spalding 1983, p. 345.
161. Vanessa Bell to Angelica Garnett, 26 March 1950, quoted in Spalding 1983, p.344.
162. Henrietta Couper, 'Visits to Charleston: Portrait of Vanessa Bell', unpublished memoir, quoted in Spalding 1983, p.343.
163. Vanessa Bell to Angelica Garnett, 5 May 1948, quoted in Spalding 1983, p.341.
164. Tobin 2017, unpaginated.
165. Reed 2004, p. 125.
166. Quoted www.jerwoodcollection.online/acquisitions/bell-still-life.
167. Dunoyer de Segonzac wrote of her last self-portrait, quoted in Shone 1999, p. 236.
168. Quentin Bell 1968, p. 8.

BIBLIOGRAPHY

Affron, Matthew, 'Decoration and Abstraction in Bloomsbury', in *Inventing Abstraction 1910–1925: How a Radical Idea Changed Modern Art,* ed. Leah Dickerman, Museum of Modern Art, New York, 2012.

Ashley Foster, J., 'Bloomsbury and War', in *The Handbook to the Bloomsbury Group*, ed. Derek Ryan and Stephen Ross, Bloomsbury, London, 2018.

Avery, Todd, 'Bloomsbury and Sexuality', in *The Handbook to the Bloomsbury Group*, ed. Derek Ryan and Stephen Ross, Bloomsbury, London, 2018.

Beechey, James, 'Introduction', in Tony Bradshaw, *The Bloomsbury Artists: Prints and Book Design*, Scolar Press, Aldershot, 1999.

Bell, Clive, 'Post Impressionism Again', *Nation,* 29 March 1913.

Bell, Clive, 'Posters', *New Statesman and Nation,* 9 July 1938.

Bell, Clive, *Art*, Chatto & Windus, London, 1949.

Bell, Quentin, *Bloomsbury*, Weidenfeld & Nicholson, London, 1968.

Bell, Quentin, *Virginia Woolf : A Biography,* Penguin, London, 1972.

Bell, Vanessa, *Sketches in Pen and Ink*, ed. Lia Giachero, Pimlico, London, 1998.

Birrell, Rebecca, *This Dark Country: Women Artists, Still Life and Intimacy in the Early Twentieth Century*, Bloomsbury, London, 2021.

Blee, Peter, *Berwick Church and the Bloomsbury Group*, St Michael & All Angels, Berwick, 2023.

Brockington, Grace, *Above the Battlefield: British Modernism and the Peace Movement 1900–1918*, Yale University Press, New Haven CT and London, 2010.

Brockington, Grace, 'A "Lavender Talent" or "The Most Important Woman Painter in Europe"? Reassessing Vanessa Bell', *Art History*, vol. 36, no. 1, ed. Lucy Bradnock, Oxford University Press, Oxford, 2013.

Brockington, Grace, 'A Moment in Abstraction', in *Vanessa Bell,* ed. Sarah Milroy and Ian A.C. Dejardin, Philip Wilson Publishers, London, 2017.

Brockington, Grace, 'The Painting', in *Abstract Painting c. 1914 by Vanessa Bell*, Tate Research Publication, 2017, www.tate.org.uk/research/in-focus/abstract-painting-vanessa-bell, accessed 5 March 2024.

Clarke, Darren, ed., *Post-Impressionist Living: The Omega Workshops*, Charleston Press, Sussex, 2019.

Clarke, Darren, 'Charleston as Muse', in *Charleston the Bloomsbury Muse*, ed. Lawrence Hendra and Ellie Smith, Philip Mould , London, 2021.

Elkin, Lauren, 'Bloomsbury and Feminism', in *The Handbook to the Bloomsbury Group*, ed. Derek Ryan and Stephen Ross, Bloomsbury, London, 2018.

Fry, Roger, *Vision and Design*, Chatto & Windus, London, 1920.

Fry, Roger, 'Independent Gallery: Vanessa Bell and Othon Friesz', *New Statesman*, 3 June 1922.

Garnett, Angelica, *Deceived with Kindness*, Pimlico, London, 1995.

Garnett, Angelica, 'Prologue', in Vanessa Bell, *Sketches in Pen and Ink*, ed. Lia Giachero, Pimlico, London, 1998.

Hendra, Lawrence and Ellie Smith, 'Catalogue', in *Charleston the Bloomsbury Muse*, ed. Lawrence Hendra and Ellie Smith, Philip Mould, London, 2021.

Hessel, Katy, *The Story of Art Without Men,* Hutchinson Heinemann, London, 2022.

Hitchmough, Wendy, *The Bloomsbury Look*, Yale University Press, New Haven CT, 2020.

Leaper, Hana, 'Between London and Paris', in *Vanessa Bell,* ed. Sarah Milroy and Ian A.C. Dejardin, Philip Wilson Publishers, London, 2017.

Leaper, Hana, 'Talk of the Table: Vanessa Bell and Duncan Grant's Famous Women Dinner Service', in *From Omega to Charleston: The Art of Vanessa Bell and Duncan Grant 1910-1934*, ed. Matthew Travers, Piano Nobile, London, 2018.

'Letters', *Daily Herald,* 23 June 1937.

Lewis, Wyndham, *Apes of God*, Arthur Press, London, 1930.

L.G.S., 'London Letter', *American Art News*, 24 January 1914.

Marler, Regina, ed., *Selected Letters of Vanessa Bell*, Bloomsbury, London, 1993.

Marler, Regina, 'Love, Actually', in *Vanessa Bell,* ed. Sarah Milroy and Ian A.C. Dejardin, Philip Wilson Publishers, London, 2017.

Mayfayre, Marianne, 'Farmhouse Homes', *Daily Telegraph,* 2 September 1931.

McKay, Stewart. *The Angel of Charleston: Grace Higgens*, British Library Publishing, London, 2013.

Milroy, Sarah, 'Some Rough Eloquence', in *Vanessa Bell,* ed. Sarah Milroy and Ian A.C. Dejardin, Philip Wilson Publishers, London, 2017.

Morphet, Richard, 'Image and Theme in Bloomsbury Art', in Richard Shone, *The Art of Bloomsbury*, Tate, London, 1999.

'Mrs Vanessa Bell's Work', *The Daily Telegraph,* 10 February 1930.

Naylor, Gillian, ed., *Bloomsbury: Its Artists, Authors and Designers*, Bulfinch, New York, 1990.

Nicholson, Virginia, *Among the Bohemians: Experiments in Living 1900–1939*, Penguin, London, 2003.

'Painters of Today – Vanessa Bell', *Daily Mirror*, 9 May 1934.

Reed, Christopher, *Bloomsbury Rooms: Modernism, Subculture and Domesticity*, Yale University Press, New Haven CT, 2004.

Reed, Christopher, 'Domestic Modernism', in *Vanessa Bell,* ed. Sarah Milroy and Ian A.C. Dejardin, Philip Wilson Publishers, London, 2017.

Risdon, Peter, 'Still-Life (Triple Alliance) by Vanessa Bell (1879–1961): A Problematic Title.' *The British Art Journal*, vol. 19, no. 3, 2018, www.jstor.org/stable/48584559; accessed 24 April 2024.

Shone, Richard, *Bloomsbury Portraits: Vanessa Bell, Duncan Grant and Their Circle*, Phaidon Press, London, 1976.

Shone, Richard, *The Art of Bloomsbury*, Tate, London, 1999.

Shone, Richard, 'Works', in *From Omega to Charleston: The Art of Vanessa Bell and Duncan Grant 1910–1934*, ed. Matthew Travers, Piano Nobile, London, 2018.

Spalding, Frances, *Vanessa Bell*, Ticknor & Fields, Boston MA, 1983.

Spalding, Frances, 'Vanessa, Virginia and the Modern Portrait', in *Vanessa Bell,* ed. Sarah Milroy and Ian A.C. Dejardin, Philip Wilson Publishers, London, 2017.

Tatlock, R.R., 'The London Group', *Burlington Magazine for Connoisseurs*, vol 43, no, 248, November 1923.

Tatlock, R.R., 'Art and Advertising', *Daily Telegraph*, 17 June 1931.

Tobin, Claudia, 'Decoration, Abstraction and the Influence of Middle Eastern Textiles',
    in *Abstract Painting c. 1914 by Vanessa Bell*, Tate Research Publication, 2017, www.
    tate.org.uk/research/in-focus/abstract-painting-vanessa-bell; accessed 5 March
    2024.
Tobin, Claudia, 'Test for Chrome Yellow: The Eloquence of Colour', in *Abstract Painting
    c. 1914 by Vanessa Bell*, Tate Research Publication, 2017, www.tate.org.uk/research/
    in-focus/abstract-painting-vanessa-bell/test-for-chrome-yellow; accessed 8 May
    2024.
Watney, Simon, *English Post-Impressionism*, Littlehampton, London, 1980.
Watson Smith, H., 'The New Art Movement', *Birmingham Daily Post,* 30 July 1917.
Woolf, Virginia, *A Room of One's Own*, Hogarth Press, London, 1929.
Woolf, Virginia, *Recent Paintings by Vanessa Bell with a Foreword by Virginia Woolf*,
    London Artist's Association, London, 1930.
Woolf, Virginia, *Catalogue of Recent Paintings of Vanessa Bell with a Foreword by Virginia
    Woolf*, Alex, Reid & Lefevre, London, 1934.
Woolf, Virginia, 'Mr Bennett and Mrs Brown', in *Collected Essays*, vol. 1, ed. Leonard
    Woolf, Hogarth Press, London, 1966.
Woolf, Virginia, *The Letters of Virginia Woolf*, vol. 1, ed. Nigel Nicholson and Joanne
    Trautmann, Harcourt Brace Jovanovich, New York, 1975.
Woolf, Virginia, *Moments of Being: Unpublished Autobiographical Writings*, Harcourt
    Brace Jovanovich, New York, 1976.
Woolf, Virginia, *The Letters of Virginia Woolf*, vol. 2, ed. Nigel Nicholson and Joanne
    Trautmann, Harcourt Brace Jovanovich, New York, 1978.
Woolf, Virginia, *The Letters of Virginia Woolf*, vol. 3, ed. Nigel Nicholson and Joanne
    Trautmann, Harcourt Brace Jovanovich, New York, 1978.
Woolf, Virginia, *The Letters of Virginia Woolf*, vol. 5, ed. Nigel Nicholson and Joanne
    Trautmann, Harcourt Brace Jovanovich, New York, 1979.
Woolf, Virginia, *Women and Writing*, ed. Michèle Barrett, Harcourt Brace Jovanovich,
    New York, 1979.
Woolf, Virginia, *The Diary of Virginia Woolf*, vol. 3: *1925–1930*, ed. Anne Olivier Bell and
    Andrew McNeillie, Harcourt Brace, San Diego CA, 1980.
Woolf, Virginia, *The Diary of Virginia Woolf*, vol. 4: *1931–1935*, ed. Anne Olivier Bell and
    Andrew McNeillie, Harcourt Brace, San Diego CA, 1982.

IMAGE CREDITS

ii see p. 71.

iv see p. 91.

vi *The Tub*, 1917, Oil paint and gouache on canvas, 180.4 × 166.6 cm, T02010, Tate, Purchased 1975. Photograph © Tate.

2 *Venetian Boatyard*, Undated, Oil on canvas, 56 x 66 cm, Cherie Blair. Photograph © Sotheby's.

3 *Tea Things*, 1919, Oil on panel, 37.5 x 94 cm, private collection. Photograph © 2012 Christie's Images Limited.

4 *Decorative Panel with Flowers and Goldfish*, Undated, Oil on board, 48 x 135 cm, private collection.

6 see p. 171.

8 Photo by George C. Beresford/Beresford/Hulton Archive/Getty Images.

9 Photo by Hulton Archive/Getty Images.

10 Charleston. Photograph © Charleston Trust

11 Photo by Mondadori via Getty Images.

12 Photo by Frances Partridge/Getty Images.

13 Photo by Topical Press Agency/Getty Images.

14 Charleston. Photograph © Charleston Trust.

15 Charleston. Photograph © Charleston Trust.

16 Photo by Gisele Freund/Photo Researchers History/Getty Images.

18 see p. 70.

23 *Studland Beach*, 1912, Oil on canvas, 76.2 × 101.6 cm, T02080, Tate, Purchased 1976. Photograph © Tate.

26 *Mrs St John Hutchinson*, 1915, Oil paint on board, 73.7 × 57.8 cm, T01768, Tate, Purchased 1973. Photograph © Tate.

27 *Self-portrait*, c. 1915, Oil on canvas laid on panel, 63.8 x 45.9 cm, 5050-B1982.16.2, Yale Centre for British Art, Paul Mellon Fund.

29 see p. 141.

30 see p. 61.

32 CHA/P/245, Charleston. Photograph © The Charleston Trust.

33 (top) Private collection, courtesy Piano Nobile. Photograph © Piano Nobile.

33 (bottom) Private collection.

34 CHA/P/6, Charleston. Photograph © The Charleston Trust.

35 CHA/P/468, Charleston. Photograph © The Charleston Trust.

36 CHA/P/423, Charleston. Photograph © The Charleston Trust.

37 (top) CHA/P/621, Charleston. Photograph © The Charleston Trust.

37 (bottom) CHA/P/1919, Charleston. Photograph © The Charleston Trust.

38 Private collection.

39 Private collection, London.

40 CHA/P/4380, Charleston. Photograph © The Charleston Trust.

41 GAC: 13349, UK Government Art Collection.

42 NPG 6684 Lent by the National Portrait Gallery, London. Photograph © National Portrait Gallery, London.

45 NT 768417, National Trust Monk's House, Rodmell, East Sussex. Photograph © National Trust Images.

47 Photograph Luis Gomez. Courtesy of Miami Design District.

48 Private collection.

49 LL/CHA/P/5, Charleston. Photograph © The Charleston Trust.

50 Photograph © Piano Nobile.

51 Private collection, courtesy of Philip Mould & Co. Photograph © Philip Mould & Co.

52 Private collection, UK. Photograph © 2004 Christie's Images Limited.

53 Private collection. Photograph © Bonhams.

54 T01277, Tate, Purchased 1971. Photograph © Tate.

55 57, University of Hull Art Collection. Photograph © University of Hull Art Collection.

56 Private collection. Photograph © 2006 Christie's Images Limited.

57 CHA/P/244, Charleston. Photograph © The Charleston Trust.

58 Private collection, Courtesy John Swarbrooke. Photograph © John Swarbrooke.

59 Private collection.

60 Private collection. Photograph © Bonhams.

61 D.1958.PD.85, The Courtauld, London (Samuel Courtauld Trust). Photo © The Courtauld/Bridgeman Images.

63 P.1935.RF.24, The Courtauld, London (Samuel Courtauld Trust). Photo © The Courtauld/Bridgeman Images.

64 Private collection. Photograph © Colin Mills.

66 D.1958.PD.86, The Courtauld, London (Samuel Courtauld Trust). Photo © The Courtauld/Bridgeman Images.

67 D.1958.PD.7, The Courtauld, London (Samuel Courtauld Trust). Photo © The Courtauld/Bridgeman Images.

68 D.1958.PD.89, The Courtauld, London (Samuel Courtauld Trust). Photo © The Courtauld/Bridgeman Images.

69 Private collection, London.

70 T01935, Tate: Purchased 1974. © Tate.

71 Private collection. Photograph © Justin Piperger.

72 Private collection. Photograph © Matthew Hollow.

73 LEEUA 1923.001, University of Leeds Art Collection. Photograph © University of Leeds Art Collection.

75 Private collection. Photograph © 2006 Christie's Images Limited.

76 CHA/P/466, Charleston. Photograph © The Charleston Trust.

77 CHA/C/142, Charleston. Photograph © The Charleston Trust.

78 NPG 6046, Lent by the National Portrait Gallery, London. Photograph © National

Portrait Gallery, London.

79 L02306, Tate, Lent from a private collection 2000. Photograph © Tate.

80 Courtesy of Piano Nobile. Photograph © Piano Nobile, London.

81 Private collection. Photograph © Max Browne.

83 1989.102, The Cheltenham Trust and Cheltenham Borough Council. Image courtesy of The Wilson and Cheltenham Borough Council.

84 Private collection. Photograph © Peter J. Stone Photography.

85 CHA/P/1241, Charleston. Photograph © The Charleston Trust.

86 (top) Private collection. Photograph © Browse and Derby, London.

86 (bottom) NT 768420, National Trust Monk's House, Rodmell, East Sussex. Photograph © National Trust Images.

87 Private collection. Photograph © Mark Heathcote.

88 SWIMG:1973.294, On Loan from Museum & Art Swindon. Photograph courtesy of Museum & Art Swindon.

89 Private collection, London.

91 CHA/P/78, Charleston. Photograph © The Charleston Trust.

92 CHA/P/5218, Charleston. Photograph © The Charleston Trust.

94 CHA/DEC/14a, CHA/DEC/14b, Charleston. Photograph © The Charleston Trust.

96 Courtesy of The Artist and The Modern Institute/Toby Webster Ltd, Glasgow.

98 NT 768421, National Trust Monk's House, Rodmell, East Sussex. Photograph © National Trust Images.

99 2376, The Syndics of the Fitzwilliam Museum, University of Cambridge. Photograph © Fitzwilliam Museum, University of Cambridge.

100 Private collection. Photograph © Mark Heathcote.

101 Private collection.

102 Philip Mould & Company, London. Photograph © Philip Mould & Company.

104 N05078, Tate, Bequeathed by Frank Hindley Smith 1940. Photograph © Tate.

105 N05077, Tate, Bequeathed by Frank Hindley Smith 1940. Photograph © Tate.

106 Private collection. Photograph © 2006 Christie's Images Limited.

107 LEEUA 1966.016, University of Leeds Art Collection. Photograph © University of Leeds Art Collection.

108 (top) Julia and Michael Pruskin.

108 (bottom) CHA/T/17, Charleston. Photograph © The Charleston Trust.

109 Private collection, courtesy of Piano Nobile. Photograph © Piano Nobile, London.

110 Private collection, courtesy of Piano Nobile. Photograph © Piano Nobile, London.

111 (top) CHA/P/4350, Charleston. Photograph © The Charleston Trust.

111 (bottom) CHA/P/606/42, Charleston. Photograph © The Charleston Trust.

112 BOLMG:1940.4.1, On loan from Bolton Library & Museum Services. Reproduced courtesy of Bolton Library & Museum Services.

113 Private collection. Photograph Bridgeman Images.

114 CHA/P/306, Charleston. Photograph © The Charleston Trust.

115 SOTAG: 1995/1, Southampton City Art Gallery. Photograph © Southampton City Art Gallery and Paul Carter.

116 SOTAG: 1972/10, SOTAG: 1972/11, SOTAG: 1972/13, Southampton City Art Gallery. Photograph © Southampton City Art Gallery and Paul Carter.

118 CHA/P/249, Charleston. Photograph © The Charleston Trust.

120 89, Royal West of England Academy. Photograph © Royal West of England Academy.

121 EASTG 1190, on loan from Towner Eastbourne. Photograph © Towner Eastbourne.

122 1949.9, Tullie House Museum and Art Gallery Trust, Carlisle. Image © Tullie House Museum and Art Gallery Trust.

123 GAC: 5793, UK Government Art Collection.

124 CHA/P/318, Charleston. Photograph © The Charleston Trust.

125 LEEUA 1966.001, University of Leeds Art Collection. Photograph © University of Leeds Art Collection.

126 Private collection, courtesy of Piano Nobile. Photograph © Piano Nobile, London.

127 CHA/C/326, Charleston. Photograph © The Charleston Trust.

128 CHA/T/18, Charleston. Photograph © The Charleston Trust.

129 130–31, 134–5 CHA/C/684-735, Charleston. Photograph © The Charleston Trust.

132 Brooklyn Museum, Gift of the Elizabeth A. Sackler Foundation, 2002.10. © Judy Chicago/Artist Rights Society (ARS) New York; Photo © Donald Woodman/ARS NY.

137 CHA/P/246, Charleston. Photograph © The Charleston Trust.

138 Private collection, courtesy of Piano Nobile. Photograph © Piano Nobile.

139 BIKGM:2332, Williamson Art Gallery and Museum, Birkenhead (Wirral Museums Service). Photograph © Williamson Art Gallery and Museum.

140 CHA/P/475, Charleston. Photograph © The Charleston Trust.

141 BIKGM:2676, Williamson Art Gallery and Museum, Birkenhead (Wirral Museums Service). Photograph © Williamson Art Gallery and Museum.

142 1273, Touchstones Rochdale. Photograph © Touchstones Rochdale.

143 (left and centre) LEEUA 1966.004, LEEUA 1966.021, University of Leeds Art Collection. Photograph © University of Leeds Art Collection.

143 (right) CHA/P/610, Charleston. Photograph © The Charleston Trust.

144 145 EASTG 602.1, EASTG 602.2, on loan from Towner Eastbourne. Photograph © Towner Eastbourne.

146 EASTG 1572.18, on loan from Towner Eastbourne. Photograph © Towner Eastbourne.

147 400, Royal West of England Academy. Photograph © Royal West of England Academy.

148 CW AW/W/34, CW AW/W/27, University of Reading, Special Collections, Random House Archives. Photograph courtesy University of Reading, Special Collections.

149 CW AW/W/33, CW/AW/W/25, CW/AW/W/29, University of Reading, Special Collections, Random House Archives. Photograph courtesy University of Reading, Special Collections.

150 (left) CHA/P/615, Charleston. Photograph © The Charleston Trust.

150 (right) LEEUA 1966.027, University of Leeds Art Collection. Photograph © University of Leeds Art Collection.

151 CHA/BKS/30, CHA/BKS/29, Charleston. Photograph © The Charleston Trust.

152 CHA/P/212, Charleston. Photograph © The Charleston Trust.

153 (left) ABDAG008478, Aberdeen City Council (Aberdeen Archives, Gallery & Museums collections). Purchased in 1990 with assistance from the National Fund for Acquisitions. Photograph © Aberdeen City Council (Archives, Gallery & Museums Collection).

153 (right) Private collection.

154 CHA/P/481, Charleston. Photograph © The Charleston Trust.

156 157 CHA/C/406, CHA/C/83, CHA/C/269, Charleston. Photograph © The Charleston Trust.

158 159 CHA/F/83, CHA/F/136, CHA/F/159, Charleston. Photograph © The Charleston Trust.

160 CHA/P/225, Charleston. Photograph © The Charleston Trust.

161 CHA/P/1567 Recto, Charleston. Photograph © The Charleston Trust.

162 Private collection.

163 Private collection, courtesy Philip Mould & Company. Photograph © Philip Mould & Company.

164 © The Singh Twins: Commissioned by Liverpool City Council.

166 185, Royal West of England Academy. Photograph © Royal West of England Academy.

167 CHA/P/160, Charleston. Photograph © The Charleston Trust.

168 JC281, Jerwood Collection. Photograph © Jerwood Collection.

169 CHA/P/64, Charleston. Photograph © The Charleston Trust.

171 Private collection courtesy of Piano Nobile, London. Photograph © Piano Nobile.

172 see p. 83.

FRONT COVER Vanessa Bell, *A Conversation* (1913–16), oil on canvas, 86.6 × 81 cm, P.1935. RF.24, The Courtauld, London (Samuel Courtauld Trust). Photograph © The Courtauld/Bridgeman Images.

BACK COVER Vanessa Bell, *Oranges and Lemons* (1914), oil on cardboard, 73 × 51.5 cm, private collection. Photograph © Matthew Hollow/ Bridgeman Images.

INDEX OF WORKS

ACKNOWLEDGEMENTS

This publication accompanies the exhibition
Vanessa Bell: A World of Form and Colour
at MK Gallery, Milton Keynes, from 19 October 2024 to 23 February 2025
and at Charleston, Lewes, from 26 March to 7 September 2025

The exhibition is curated for MK Gallery by Fay Blanchard and Anthony Spira, with assistance from Madeleine Jordan,
and for Charleston by Dr Darren Clarke, with assistance from Polly Jones, Miriam Phelan and Emily Hill.
Catalogue entries by Fay Blanchard with assistance from Dr Darren Clarke.

This catalogue was made possible by the generous support of the Jerwood Foundation and the Vanessa Bell Estate.

Thanks to the Vanessa Bell Circle of Friends, chaired by Matthew Travers at Piano Nobile.

GOLD Calliope Arts Foundation SILVER Margie MacKinnon and Wayne McArdle and those who wish to remain anonymous.

We are grateful to the Anson Charitable Trust, Cherie Blair and Rob Gifford for their enthusiasm and support of this project.

This exhibition has been made possible by the provision of insurance through the Government Indemnity
Scheme. MK Gallery would like to thank HM Government for providing Government Indemnity and the
Department of Culture, Media and Sport and Arts Council England for arranging the indemnity.

We are also grateful for the assistance of James Beechey, Cressida Bell, Julian Bell, Tony Bradshaw, Maren Bramsen
at Nivaagaards Malerisamling, Robin Cawdron-Stewart at Offer Waterman, Laura Edmundson at Philip Mould
& Company, James Elliott at Anthony d'Offay Ltd, Jane Findlay and Jennifer Scott at Dulwich Picture Gallery,
Deborah Gage, Susie Gault, Tamsin Golding Yee at Sotheby's, David Herbert, Wendy Hitchmough, Kim Jones,
Sarah Milroy at the McMichael Canadian Art Collection, Anthony Mould, Alice Murray at Christie's, Virginia
Nicholson, Sophie Partridge, Polly Pentreath at Piano Nobile, Jane Quinn, Ingram Reid at Bonhams, Richard
Shone, Rachel Sloan, Ashleigh Toll and Barnaby Wright at the Courtauld Gallery and John Swarbrooke.

MK GALLERY

900 Midsummer Boulevard, Milton Keynes MK9 3QA
www.mkgallery.org

MK Gallery brings world-class exhibitions and events together with pioneering
learning and community programmes to Milton Keynes. MK Gallery gratefully
acknowledges regular support from Arts Council England and Milton Keynes Council.

CHAIR Liz Gifford   TRUSTEES Sas Amoah, Cllr Robin Bradburn, Sue Carbert,
Natalie Drought, Cllr David Hopkins, David King, Cllr Shanika Mahendran, Roz
Mascarenhas, Ranjit Singh, Neil Smith, Sarah Westacott, Sunita Yeomans

DIRECTOR Anthony Spira

Jamie Aylard, Sophie Bennett, Fay Blanchard, Benjamin Charter, Cherelle Cunningham, Efe Emenuwe, Hannah
Firth, Madeleine Jordan, Judy Kendrick-Simonsen, Samantha Lennon, Monika Lorincova, Rosie May, Ben
Montgomery, Francis Nielsen, Angus Norton, Andrew Papworth, Patrick Phillips, Julia Roach, Sonia Tsesarsky,
Diana Volokha, Xander Webster, Joshua Yon and with thanks to our dedicated team of volunteers

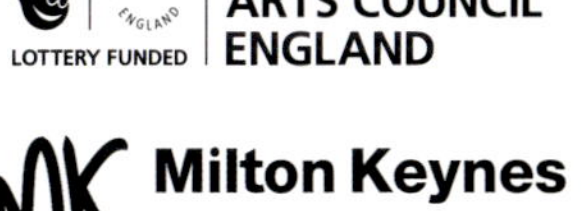

CHARLESTON

Charleston in Firle, East Sussex, BN8 6LL
Charleston in Lewes, Southover Road, Lewes, BN7 1FB
www.charleston.org.uk

Charleston is the modernist home and studio of painters Vanessa Bell and Duncan Grant,
and a place that brings people together to engage with art and ideas.

DIRECTOR Nathaniel Hepburn

COLLECTION AND EXHIBITIONS TEAMS Dr Darren Clarke, Miriam Phelan, Emily Hill, Polly Jones, Shannon Smith

Philip Wilson Publishers
Bloomsbury Publishing Plc
50 Bedford Square, London, WC1B 3DP, UK
29 Earlsfort Terrace, Dublin 2, Ireland

Bloomsbury, Philip Wilson Publishers
and the Philip Wilson logo are trademarks of
Bloomsbury Publishing Plc

Published on the occasion of the exhibition

Vanessa Bell: A World of Form and Colour

MK Gallery, 19 October 2024–23 February 2025
Charleston, Lewes, 26 March–7 September 2025

First published in Great Britain in 2024

A catalogue record for this book is available from the British Library
Library of Congress Cataloging-in-Publication data has been applied for

ISBN 978 1 78130 133 3

10 9 8 7 6 5 4 3 2

Designed and typeset in Walbaum by illuminati, Grosmont
Printed and bound in Turkey by Elma Basim

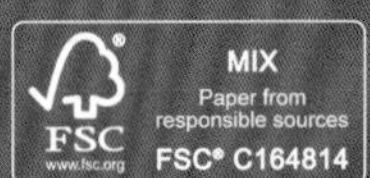

To find out more about our authors and books visit
www.bloomsbury.com and sign up for our newsletters